STRUCK DOWN BUT NOT DESTROYED
The Story of Rudolph Heupel
A German Russian Immigrant

Dr. Ron Baesler

ISBN: 9781795793353

2

ACKNOWLEDGEMENTS

All biblical quotations are from the New Revised Standard Version Bible, copyright ©1989 the Division of Christian Education of the National Council of Churches of Christ in the United States of America. Used by permission. All rights reserved.

Special thanks to the following:

--Sergey Yelizarov our guide and interpreter during our time in the Ukraine.

--The staff at Hephata Diakonie in Treysa, especially Martina Bender, for the hospitality and help in learning more about Rudolph's forty-seven year relationship with that fine institution.

--Judy Iverson, my sister, who is the family archivist, for saving and sharing pictures and documents relating to Rudolph's life.

--Herman Heupel, youngest and only surviving son of Rudolph, for sharing stories and anecdotes of his father and the entire Heupel family, and for encouraging me to use my imagination and to write this book.

COVER PHOTO

Rudolf Heupel, age 20

AUTHOR'S NOTE

This book is based on the life of my grandfather, Rudolph Heupel, who died when I was ten years old. The basic outline of this story is true. He lived, studied, and worked in the all of the places described here. Rudolph, Ida and all of their family members are real people with their names as they appear in this book. All other characters are fictional with fictional names. Many of the dates mentioned here have been gleaned from letters, ship's logs, census records, and personal documents. Many of the stories here are based on actual events in Rudolph's life as remembered by family members, or recorded in documents.

This book also contains dialogue, stories and events that arose out of my imagination. I imagined how my grandfather dealt with life in South Russia, how he coped with the deprivations during WWI, and how he came to know Ida. After his arrival in North Dakota, I was able to more exactly trace the trajectory of his life, since it was lived out in the places where I grew up. Nevertheless, here too I created stories around known events and dared to inhabit Rudolph's soul and see the world through his eyes.

The writing of this book has deepened my appreciation for my own German Russian heritage, and my recognition of how much of my own life and character is indebted to this extraordinary man.

PREFACE

2 Corinthians 4.7-11
But we have this treasure in clay jars, so that it may be made clear that this
extraordinary power belongs to God and does not come from us.
We are afflicted in every way, but not crushed;
perplexed, but not driven to despair;
persecuted, but not forsaken;
struck down, but not destroyed;
always carrying in the body the death of Jesus,
so that the life of Jesus may also be made visible in our bodies.
For while we live, we are always being given up to death for Jesus' sake,
so that the life of Jesus may be made visible in our mortal flesh

8

PART ONE-FREIDORF

MAY 23, 1893, FREIDORF, ODESSA KHERSON GOVERNORATE, RUSSIA

The sweat sheens on Elizabeth's forehead in the morning light. The curtains made of decorated flour sacks and washed almost to transparency, flutter in the spring breeze. The wiry hand of Hannah the midwife grips the weary laboring mother's shoulder.

"Ja, ja, almost you are done. You have worked so hard all night. Just a few more pushes."

Elizabeth has already birthed six children. She has been favored--four of them are still alive. She had hoped that after half dozen births, this one would be less dramatic, and less traumatic.

But all night as she pushed, this babe seemed to shove back. Now, as she enters her tenth hour of exhausting effort, now as the contractions finally come with more urgency, she wonders if this little German baby has stubbornly decided to cling to the dark safety of the womb because it knows it is being delivered into troubled times in a troubled Russian land.

She is spent and throws her head back on the sweat soaked pillow in exhaustion. But the wise old midwife will have none of this. Hannah lifts her off the pillow, so she can give all the energy left in her forty-year-old body to this business of birthing. "Nein, nein. Do not give up now. You are so close Lisbeth."

Elizabeth's eyes swim. Far away as if in a dream she feels the deep pang of muscles contracting. The wind tickles the curtains and she catches glimpses of the greening wheat fields across the road. For an instant, she is standing in the green forests of Germany, a land she's never seen but of which her grandmother so longingly and vividly spoke. For a second, she feels a shaft of sunlight bathing her eyes and pine needles tickling her toes. Then the center of her being clenches, and she is back in the cramped bedroom, on the sweat sodden mattress. She clutches Hannah's hand as though it were a lifeline to keep her from sinking.

"Now! push, push, push!" Hannah shouts, Lisabeth groans, and then…with a gush of watery blood, the baby wails.

In the tidy town of Freidorf, on the plains north of Odessa, Rudolf, son of George and Elizabeth Heupel, is born.

May 23, 1894, FREIDORF

"Strong face, just like his daddy." Tanta [Aunt] Pauline tickled the birthday boy under his chin. One-year-old Rudy scrutinized his aunt, his eyes round, gray, and serious. "Come on, give me a smile!" Pauline playfully tweaked his chubby cheek. The tiniest of grins slipped across his face, almost as though he were teasing her.

"Ha, good luck getting that one to laugh for you. Oh, he laughs alright, but only when his little self chooses to." Elizabeth lovingly eyed her youngest sitting in his high chair. "You should see the kids, doing all sorts of silly things to get him to laugh. Even George Jr. tries it, gets down on his knees and barks like a dog. Rudy just stares and you'd swear he's ready to giggle but all he gives is that tiny little grin."

Rudy stretched up his arms, Elizabeth lifted him out of his chair and wrapped him in a hug. "You are just a rascal, aren't you?" His sweet breath tickled her cheek and she marveled at how solid his one-year old body felt in her arms. She looked around at her family and friends sitting on the emerald grass of the town's little park, talking and digesting the meat and potatoes she'd served for lunch.

First birthdays were momentous occasions in this village and in every village out here on these plains. Disease and death stalked the babies and the elders, especially during the bitter winter months. Elizabeth clasped her precious son to her and remembered that March day three years ago, felt again the wet snow flakes hitting her face, joining her tears. They had buried her little six-month-old Lydia, who had such a sweet smile and had just gotten her first tooth. Her heart ached at the dark memory and she squeezed Rudy tighter. He squirmed to get down.

She set him down on the grass and watched him wobble forward. He learned to walk only two weeks ago and already he was trotting. His stocky legs plowed ahead. His grey eyes gleamed. He was enchanted by the world around him. She wondered how far he would go.

JULY 1898, FREIDORF

"Always exploring, that little one!" George leaned on his hoe and chuckled at the sight of his five-year-old son Rudy squatting down at the edge of the potato field.

"So, what do you guess, Jacob? What's caught his eye—a bug, a worm, a rock?"

2

Fifteen-year-old Jacob paused in his methodical chopping. He wiped the sweat from his forehead, gazed at his little brother and grinned, "Who knows? He's such an imp."

Rudy was on all fours now, scratching excitedly at something in the dirt. The sunshine gleamed on his light brown hair as his head bobbed up and down in time with his digging.

"Remember when you were five?" the lean father asked his son. "You came out to our sunflower field with Junior and me and kept grabbing our hoes. You wanted to work!"

Jacob laughed, "I do remember the little hoe you made for me. I was so excited." The cloud of a question swept across his face. "That must have been the last year we had…."

George grimaced, "Ja, the last year... That fall the bank took our land, every bit of it, to pay for the loans." He spit into the black dirt and hacked angrily at the weeds between the plants.

Jacob shrugged and turned back to his row, his hoe rising and falling with metronome regularity. Three years ago, he'd taken George Junior, his older brother's place, in the fields. He remembered teasing his then sixteen-year-old brother about the fuzz on his upper lip. "Georgie, don't let the cat get too close, she'll lick off those whiskers!"

George Junior had grinned into the piece of cracked mirror hanging on the wall in in their tiny bedroom. "Ha, you're just jealous. Your big brother is now a man."

A few days after he turned sixteen and became a man, Junior had gone to work for the Shumann family on the south end of the valley. Now he only came home on Saturday night and left early Monday morning, and usually spent most of the time drinking and dancing with his friends.

Now, during the week Jacob had the tiny bedroom to himself. Some nights he stared into the darkness and tried to imagine the lives of his friends who had left with their families for America. His imaginings usually yielded only exasperation. He'd never even left Freidorf. His family had just enough money to keep food on the table. Last year his sister Katherine had turned sixteen and now worked as a maid and nanny for the Wiedmer clan across town. If Katherine and George Jr weren't working, Jacob doubted the household would survive.

*   *   *

On this July morning the potato leaves shimmered in the sunshine as Jacob labored in the humid air. Father George's thin shirt was dark with perspiration. The father's thoughts were as morose as his son's but their tendrils crept much farther back into history.

Forty years ago, George had been living with his parents in Kassel, only forty miles northwest of Freidorf. He must have been ten when he heard for first time the story from his father, John Jacob Heupel. John Jacob always leaned back in his chair and puffed on his pipe when he told his adventure.

"This happened about 1800, when I was eight years old living in Nußdorf. One afternoon I went with my father to a meeting at our little Lutheran church. His Excellency, General von Insow, Russia's chief welfare officer for foreign settlers, stood in front of the altar. He held himself straight and stiff, like the pine trees all around."

John pulled the pipe from his mouth and leaned forward, "I can still see the general's crisp, deep blue uniform. His nose was narrow, sharp and long. The General's voice surprised me. He looked cold and stiff, but his voice flowed out like warm honey. He gave an impressive speech."

John lowered his voice and tried to look imperious as he imitated the general, "Your friends in Russia are looking for families that would like to improve their lives. In the southern part of our country we have empty land. Rich land, abundant land. You can almost hear this land begging to be planted and be fruitful.'"

John resumed his puffing and grimaced as he remembered, "Now most of the men sitting on those hard, wooden pews were like my father. They worked on the large estates of the local barons and lived on tiny plots with barely enough room for a vegetable garden.

The General's words painted the picture of an impossible dream. He knew his words floated like a pleasant but fragile soap bubble for these poverty-hardened men. He needed to bring this dream to down to earth. So, he said, 'Do you think this is too good to be true?'"John Jacob pulled out his pipe and laughed, "I can still remember seeing my father and all of the other men smirk and nod their heads. They all thought the Russian was crazy. But this von Insow was a sharp man. He nodded and said, 'I understand your doubts. But brothers listen to this.' Then he dropped his voice so all of us had to lean forward to hear him. He spoke as though it were a secret, 'Our Russian nation desperately wants to see this land in production. We want the Turks to see that we hold this land, that we are using it. We are so eager to see it settled that we're giving special benefits to those who are brave enough to farm it. I know that some of you are brave enough.'"

John Jacob leaned back and his chair creaked. He was relishing the old memory. "You can imagine how all of these German men straightened up and squared their shoulders. Of course, they were all brave. Now the

General raised his voice, 'If you go, you will pay no taxes to our government. You may build your own schools and churches and use your own language. And the land my friends, ahh, the land is a true paradise on earth.'

The general finished his speech and answered questions for another thirty minutes. Then he invited the farmers to give him their names. But my father? Ah, he stood and left, and of course I left with him."

At this point in the story a tinge of melancholy would always creep into John Jacob's voice. "We stepped out into the twilight. I was riding the smooth words of the General out into the blue sky of my imagination. I could already taste the milk and honey of this promised land. I asked my father, 'Will we go to this country, Papa?' He looked down at me and growled, 'My father always said, 'Never trust the Russians.' Who knows if there even is any land out there.'"

Old John Jacob chuckled sadly, "But I was eight and couldn't stop savoring my vision of this Eden. I said, "Papa, if there is land, I bet it's wonderful.' He clucked his tongue at me and said, 'Ach, my child. Do you think your mother could make such a journey? She is so often sick. And if we would get there, how long would my old back last, plowing up new soil? Thousand-mile journeys are for young people, not for old men like me.'"

John Jacob took the pipe out and tapped out the ashes onto the ground. "Maybe my father was right. But this dream of paradise on earth fell like a seed into my heart. It put down roots as I grew up. It sprouted when I saw my brothers join the ranks of laborers sweating on the baron's lands. When I courted Caroline, your mother, I told her, 'If you marry me, be ready to migrate to southern Russian. We're going to build our future there."

Old John Jacob finished his story with a laugh and a wink at his wife, "Well, she had said 'yes' to both proposals and a few weeks after the wedding we left for the Black Sea. And that's how we got here to Kassel."

In 1862, George had been ten when he first heard that story. Now it was 1898, he was forty-six, and the Eden that John Jacob had dreamt of, kept eluding George. He'd grown up and married Elizabeth in the big church in Kassel. Their first child had been born and baptized there.

But George was restless and moved his family a dozen miles southeast to the Klein-Neudorf colony. Then in 1888, he'd bought land and moved his growing brood to the new colony being started in Friedorf. Unfortunately, the land George and his Jacob were now tilling, all the land they worked on, except for their house and the vegetable garden behind it, belonged to other German settlers.

George's glum memories were interrupted by his youngest's excited shout, "Look Daddy, I found a white rock." Grinning little Rudy held up a rock coated with gray white crystals. The rock was a common pebble but the crystals were George's bane.

"Ach, Rudy, this is more saltpeter. It's no good. We had too much of this on our old land. Throw it, boy, throw it far away!" Rudy wound up and flung the rock into the sky, laughing as it sailed over the potato plants. "What's wrong with saltpeter, Daddy? Why is it so bad?" George grinned at his little son's exuberance and simultaneously swallowed the acidic memory of the losing battle he'd fought with his fields.

Like all of the other German colonists, George and his wife had received eighty acres from the Russian government. From a distance the land appeared like all the land in the region. It lay near the little stream that ran along the east side of the valley. For years George, and then he and his sons, had tried to coax crops from the soil. But their wheat fields, their sunflower and barley fields never rippled in the wind, never produced heavy heads of grain. Their land was full of saltpeter. This salt, planted in the soil by nature's whim, greedily sucked up the soil's nitrogen.

The neighbors thought George and his family were lazy, or haphazard in their farming efforts. But saltpeter had starved his plants and finally, he'd been forced to sell the land for pasture, just to pay his bills at the village store.

Now his sweat poured down on the land of other farmers. He worked simply to subsist. He watched other families prosper and still others sell all and travel to America. He grimly attacked the weeds with his hoe. The only traveling he would ever do was to the end of this row of potatoes.

JUNE 1901, FREIDORF

"Sunday! God's day!" Rudy bounded in exuberant circles around his family.

"Rudy, Rudy, you're as crazy as the puppy!" Elizabeth laughed at her youngest son. He was endlessly enthusiastic: exploring, learning, singing, teasing. He relished slurping up every drop of life. Keeping up with him as a toddler had nearly felled her. But now that he attended school she better appreciated his unlimited zest for living. She could savor the Sunday walk with her family as Rudy skipped circles around them.

Sunday was a special day in Freidorf. Sunday was worship day. The plain, unadorned houses lined the one street that ran north and south in the middle of the shallow valley. The solid stone Lutheran church stood near the north end of town.

Though every Lutheran knew pride was a grievous sin, the community felt deep satisfaction whenever they entered their church building. They had carried every stone in the walls from Neu Beresin, nearly fifteen miles away. Buckets of sweat, aching muscles and hours of labor had transformed those stones into a building that not only expressed the builder's faith, but also mirrored the builders themselves: Solid, plain, unpretentious and stubborn men and women who had withstood droughts, floods and political upheavals.

Some still clung to the kite string of hope launched by colony founders who named the village: Freidorf, village of freedom. Lately, traditional Lutheran skepticism regarding the goodness of humanity combined with rumors of turmoil in Russia kept most residents from letting their hopes soar too high.

But on this Sunday morning the sun was still a gentle caress, the breeze but a whisper and the clouds merely a scattered fringe on the horizon.

Suddenly, Rudy stopped in mid-skip, tilted his head back and gazed into the morning sky. The rest of his clan reached him and looked up in bewilderment.

"What're you seeing Rudy?" Jacob stood staring into the empty infinite blue with his hand on his little brother's shoulder.

Rudy spoke with excited reverence. "I just figured it out. God's eyes are blue, just like Mutti's."

Elizabeth, standing behind him, laughed at her son's whimsy. "So, how do you know that, my dear."

"Mutti, that's why the sky is blue. God is always looking at us with big, blue, God-sized eyes. When God sleeps, then it gets dark and we go to sleep too." Rudy grinned in delight at his discovery. The family chuckled at his latest theological musings. They all imagined how deep into their lives the grand eyeball of God could penetrate. Not all of them were as pleased with that image as Rudy apparently was.

They neared the church and other families greeted them. Mothers grabbed the hands of their little ones before they could scamper off, get into mischief and dirty their clothes before the service. The bell in the church tower began ringing as they reached the stone stairs.

Halfway up the stairs Rudy looked around at his family and announced, "Today I'm going to sit with Daddy and Jacob."

Katherine, his 19-year-old sister, snorted, "You? You're still a baby.

You'll sit with us."

Rudy pouted, "I am not a baby," then ran ahead and grabbed onto 18-year-old Jacob's hand. But Katherine grabbed his collar and pulled him back. Rudy squealed and squirmed in the doorway of the church. "Vater…" He began to appeal but his father turned around, scowled down at him and gruffed, "Rudy! Sit with your mother. You're only eight. This side is for the men."

Rudolph dropped his head and silently followed his mother and sister as she slid onto a bench on the left side of the church. He sniffed once and quickly wiped his eyes with the cuff of his white shirt. Big boys did not cry and he was big, even if his family didn't yet know it.

Rudy loved their church. Even in the winter, when the winds howled like the gray wolves and the snow swirled like the dervishes, the heart of the church pulsed with warmth. He admired the white plaster painted walls and the tall glass windows. He marveled at the hush, the moment of silence when pastor Mertz came out of the side door and stood before the wooden altar.

On those rare Sundays when the pastor served the Lord's Supper, he was awed by the way all the men and women, even those who were old and stiff with rheumatism, would kneel on the wooden floor to confess their sins. He was moved by the solemn, pensive looks on their faces. And when the hymns were played on the old wheezing pump organ, oh how he loved to sing along. He'd throw back his head and sing the songs he'd been hearing all his life.

Then, when it was time for the sermon and Reverend Mertz would climb into the pulpit, he was struck by how silent the church became. Sometimes people would fall asleep, he even saw his father's head snap back a few times during a particularly long message. But Rudy never fell asleep, and even though he didn't understand all Reverend Mertz's words, he knew something important was going on. It made him feel important to sit up straight and concentrate, a furrow or two running across his little forehead.

This Sunday, Pastor Mertz was speaking about Jesus calling his disciples. "Jesus said, 'Follow me! And I will make you fishers of men.' And they followed him, right that minute. They put down their nets and followed him. Such faith they had! Such trust. What about you men and women of Freidorf? How is your faith? How is your trust? How is Jesus calling you? Are you listening? Do you trust him enough to follow?"

Rudy tried following Pastor Mertz's words but he got stuck on the picture of Peter and James and John fishing for men. He imagined fishing poles as tall as trees and huge hooks. But what would be the bait? He knew what he'd bite on—a great huge chunk of chocolate! He smiled and licked his lips. Then a sparrow sitting on the window sill next to his mother's shoulder caught his attention and he wondered if God ever gave jobs to sparrows the way Pastor Mertz said he gave jobs to mothers and fathers and children.

Pastor Mertz's "Amen" ended the message and broke into Rudy's musings. He stood with the congregation as they recited the old creed and then sang "Spread Oh Spread Almighty Word." Rudy's father George, and Henry Wiedmer, solemnly and stiffly walked up to the front of the church and the pastor placed into each man's rough calloused hands a heavy silver plate. The two men turned and passed the plates down the rows of pews. The last person in each row would hand the plate to the person behind him and it would be passed down until it reached the waiting hand of Henry or George. Rudy eagerly waited for the plate to reach his row so he could drop in the coin his father had given him before the service started.

When the plates reached the back of the church, Pastor Mertz raised his arms and everyone stood while the two farmers brought the plates full of coins and bills to the front. Rudy knew that now would come the prayers and the final song and blessing. But Pastor Mertz took the plates and then surprised Rudy and, by the expressions on the faces around him, he guessed, most of the congregation too.

"Please be seated, all of you." Pastor Mertz, like his congregation, appreciated the orderly march of the worship service. Deviations were unusual and unsettling. But this one, as it turned out, had happened more than once in the past few years.

"Friends, before we finish our worship today, I want to invite the Reuben Holz family to come forward."

Rudy slid to the end of the pew and watched as the family walked down the aisle. Freddy Holz sat next to him in the second-grade classroom and was one of his good friends. He was slim and his hair was white and thin. Rudy could see where the comb had separated each strand. Freddy's sharp chin pointed down. Rudy couldn't decide if Freddy was sad or scared, or both. He stood with his parents and two older sisters and the baby brother who fidgeted in his mother's arms.

Pastor Mertz stood behind the family looking out at the congregation. "Our dear Holz family will be leaving us this week. They will be traveling to America. Reuben's brother has invited them to join him in a place called Dakota. We know that the journey will be long. I invite you all to join me as we pray for safe travels."

The congregation stood as Pastor Mertz prayed. Rudy kept glancing at Freddy who hung on to his father's hand. He imagined what it would be like to venture out of Freidorf, what marvels he would see. He didn't think he'd be scared, or sad to go to America, especially if his family was going along.

After the service, as the adults gathered around Reuben and his wife, Rudy skittered around the edges of the crowd until he spied Freddy and his sisters.

"Hey, Freddy. Why didn't you tell me you were going on an adventure?"

"My folks told me not to tell. Some people get mad you know."

Rudy, whose days were mostly sunny, couldn't grasp this. "Mad? Why would anyone be mad?"

"I dunno. Maybe cuz they can't go, or maybe, if too many go, the town'll die."

This was a new thought for Rudy. "So...why are you going?"

"My dad says that now we can't talk German in school and when I get older I'll have to serve in the Russian army and the taxes are too high. I don't mind learning Russian and it's a long time until I'm old enough for the army. I just wish we could...."

Rudy heard the choke in his friend's voice. Big boys don't cry and he didn't want to embarrass Freddy. He slapped him on the back.

"Hey, I'm sure you'll have some great times, new friends and a new school." Freddy nodded with bleary eyes and turned away.

Rudy walked home surrounded by his family, holding on to his mother's hand. He imagined the blue-eyed God watching over Freddy in Dakota. Then Rudy wondered who would sit beside him in Freddy's old desk when he started the third grade.

MAY, 1903, FREIDORF

"I hate carrots!" Frustrated nine-year-old Rudy shouted this declaration into the blue cloud-sprinkled sky with all the vehemence he could muster. He was on all fours, thinning the row of pale green fronds that ribboned for twenty feet across the family's backyard garden.

A few feet down the row, Jacob chuckled at his little brother. "No, you don't. You hate choosing which carrot plant will be sacrificed so that the next one can grow fat and long. I know how your little mind works."

Rudy felt a tiny click in his brain. Yes, now his frustration and tension made sense. He did cringe every time he uprooted a tiny plant that had worked so hard to grow. Jacob was right. But Rudy would not admit that to his brother, not today. His throat tightened and his voice rose.

"My mind isn't little and you don't know anything. I just hate this stupid job. Why'd Mom plant so many stupid carrot seeds anyway?"

Jacob kept plucking tiny carrot seedlings. Two cantankerous crows flapped overhead and settled on their apple tree. He spoke quietly.

"Rudy, now you're the one being stupid. You know how small those carrot seeds are, and you know Mutti's eyes aren't all that good anymore. Next spring, you'll probably be the one to plant the carrots. Then you'll see."

Rudy sat back on his haunches and his face flushed with fury. "The hell I will. I'm never gonna plant damn carrots."

Jacob sat up in surprise. "Whoa, Rudy. Since when do you talk like that? Watch your tongue. If Vater catches you, you're in trouble."

Rudy dropped back onto all fours and mumbled into the dirt, "What do you care? You're leaving anyway."

Jacob knee-walked over to Rudy. "Hey, buddy, what did you say?"

Rudy sat up and stared out over the rows of bean plants and cabbage sets. He spoke through gritted teeth. "Why do you have to go to America?"

Jacob lay his hand on Rudy's neck and sighed. "Rudy, you're old enough to see this. I want to be a farmer. That's what I'm good at. But how can I find land here?"

Rudy pushed away his brother's hand and desperately tried to sound angry. "You could… you could farm with Junior."

Jacob folded his arms across his chest. "Ahh, Rudy. Junior got lucky. He married Henry Shumann's daughter. Then both Henry's sons left and now Junior gets the farm. I don't want to be Junior's hired man. I want my own farm."

Rudy knew that men didn't cry but he was losing his brother, the one who'd taught him how to fish and make a kite, the one who'd given him horsey back rides and told him stories. He gulped down a sob and then grabbed a stone and furiously flung it against the board fence.

"Then take me with you. Let me come to America too."

Jacob resisted hugging his hurting little brother. "Rudy, Rudy. You don't even know what you're saying. It costs money to get to America. I saved all my money from when I hired out at last fall's harvest and I still had to borrow some from Junior. Besides what would you do in America?"

Rudy dropped his head and tried not to sound plaintive, "I could help you farm your land."

Jacob sat back on his haunches and laughed. "Rudy, listen. You know Fred Schock, Katherine's husband? He has a clear idea of where they will claim land. I'm following them. I don't even have any land yet. And besides, little brother, remember, I know how your mind works. You'll never be a farmer. A teacher maybe, or a preacher; maybe even a doctor. But never a farmer. It's not in your blood."

Rudy finally risked looking up at Jacob. "But couldn't you stay a little longer? The house will be so quiet, so lonely."

The boy and the young man sat silently as a chilly cloud shadow crept across the garden. Jacob said, "If I could stay one more year I would. I didn't want to borrow money from Junior. If I could stay for one more harvest...but.... Rudy, do you know why the Shumann boys left when they did?

Rudy sniffed. "No, why?"

"Because they were both old enough to be conscripted."

"Conscripted? I don't know..."

"Rudy, you do know. They were both over twenty and old enough to get called into the Russian army. You've been listening. What happens to men called into the Russian army?"

Rudy sniffled again, then murmured, "Sometimes they never come back."

"That's right. And do you know how old I'll be on June twenty seventh?"

Rudy scratched in the dirt and whispered, "twenty, always ten years ahead of me."

Jacob sighed. "Right. Twenty and I swear I'm not going to give one year or one minute to the Russian army. Don't worry, I'll stay for your birthday party in three weeks. But then I've got to go. That's when Katherine and Fred are going. First the train to Odessa then the ship to America."

Rudy did his best to sound strong but his voice squeaked, "And I suppose I'll never see you again."

Jacob returned his hand to Rudy's shoulder. "Who can say that? Do you know God's ways? Maybe someday when you are all grown up and married, you can come and visit me on my farm."

"Married? Yuk. I don't even like girls."

Jacob laughed, stood up and pulled Rudy to his feet.

"We all say that when we're ten. Just you wait. How about I finish thinning the carrots and you go gather the eggs. Then I'll give you a peek at what I'm making for your birthday."

Rudy swiped his sleeve across his eyes, smiled and dashed off to find the egg basket. Jacob watched him scurry across the yard and blinked away the tears that had crept into his own eyes.

OCTOBER 1906, FREIDORF CONFIRMATION CLASS

Rudy could not believe what he was reading: *How graceful are your feet in sandals, O queenly maiden! Your rounded thighs are like jewels, the work of a master hand. Your navel is a rounded bowl that never lacks mixed wine. Your belly is a heap of wheat, encircled with lilies. Your two breasts are like two fawns, twins of a gazelle.*

He closed his eyes and blew out a breath. Such language was almost more than an adolescent boy in this conservative community could handle. That such lurid words appeared right here in his Bible stunned him and set his pulse racing. He'd always assumed such language was sinful and even now felt guilty for not closing the book. But the lure of the forbidden was too much. He opened his eyes and continued devouring the verses.

"Hey Rudy, you crazy guy. You must really love that stuff." Rudy slammed his Bible shut and looked up as his friend Paul climbed the church steps to sit beside him. Rudy was sure Paul would notice his flushed face and gasping breath. But if he noticed Rudy's agitation, he didn't mention it. "You're always the first one here and now your nose is stuck in the Big Book. You afraid of failing confirmation or you trying to impress the new pastor?"

Paul was Rudy's best friend and he wished he could share with his buddy his discovery in the Song of Solomon. But in Freidorf no one ever talked about sex--not parents or teachers or preachers, not even twelve-year old boys.

Rudy simply shot a weak grin at Paul and answered, "Aww, you know my dad. If I stick around too long at home he always comes up with some job for me and I end up coming to class late and sweaty. On Saturdays I always tear out of the house as quick as I can. And since I had nothing to do, I figured I might as well do a little reading."

Paul leaned back with his elbows on the step behind him. He did know Rudy's dad but he couldn't resist teasing. "Admit it Rudy, you just love this stuff so much you can't stay away."

Rudy laughed and said nothing. He did enjoy these confirmation lessons more than his friends did. He was intrigued by the stories, the adventures, battles and miracles. And now that Reverend Berger had come, he relished

13

these two hours on Saturday morning even more.

Reverend Mertz left last year for a bigger church in Bergdorf. Several months later Reverend Berger was installed as their new pastor. He was serious and stern. Evidently that was a pre-requisite for Lutheran pastors. But he was a younger man and even when his face was stern Rudy thought he could see a smile in his eyes. What thrilled Rudy the most was that Pastor Berger allowed you to ask your own questions, not like Pastor Mertz who not only told you what to believe but also made it clear what questions you were permitted to ask.

Helen and Elsie Klein soon arrived with their friend Frieda Shaatz. They were chattering and giggling as they climbed the steps. Willie Bauer and Victor Straub sauntered up, sleepy eyed and dour.

Rudy laughed, "Hey boys, looks like you got dragged out of bed and kicked out of the house." They only grunted and plopped down on the steps.

The crew chattered and teased until they saw Pastor Berger open the parsonage door and walk toward church. He was a short man with a pencil thin moustache. He churned across the yard with his usual nervous urgency.

"Good morning, people. Ready to get started?" He didn't wait for their answer, rushed up the stairs, unlocked the door and strode down the aisle. The class followed him into the chill, damp church. The sounds of the outside world, birdsongs and barking dogs, were muffled by the thick walls and by the blanket of holiness that lay upon this building and all things of God. The class walked to the front of the church in silence.

Old Pastor Mertz had always conducted his lessons with the young people sitting in the front two pews of the quiet, chilly sanctuary. Last year after one interminable session, Paul commented to Rudy as they walked home, "Can you believe that was only two hours? Herr Pastor sounded like the big saw down at the sawmill....oooOOOOoooOOOOooo. And poor Victor reciting the Creed? As slow as a slug oozing across the sidewalk."

Pastor Berger changed that. The seven youths followed his quick strides up to the altar area and then turned right into what was now their classroom. The room once held only one tall wardrobe where the pastor hung his robes and where the chalice, wine and wafers were stored. Pastor Berger had brought in a table and chairs.

Years ago, when the confirmation class numbered in the dozens, meeting in this room would have been impossible. But now, as more and more families moved away, the class of four boys and three girls could sit around the table. And after Pastor Berger removed the heavy curtain from the window, the room was warm and light.

14

"Let us begin with prayer." He prayed, like he talked, in staccato bursts. The group bowed their heads and joined him at "amen." Pastor Berger leapt directly into the session.

"Who remembers what we learned last week?"

Helen, the oldest and prettiest of the Klein sisters, raised her hand. "Herr Pastor, we studied the fourth and fifth commandments."

"Correct. Thank you, Helen. Rudy, can you recite for us the fourth commandment?"

Rudy had been watching how the sunlight seemed to dance across Helen's light brown hair, but caught enough of the question to recover.

"Yes, Herr Pastor. 'Ahh...Honor you father and mother ....so that ...so that your days may be long in the land the Lord God is giving you.'"

"Very good Rudy. Now class, what land is the Bible talking about?"

Paul mumbled to himself and to Willie beside him, "Not south Russia, that's for sure."

"Paul, do you have an answer?" Pastor Berger's ears were sharper than old Pastor Mertz's.

Paul dropped his head "No, Herr Pastor, I..I don't know."

"Come now Mr. Paul, you did have something to say. What was it?" Rudy thought he heard a fleeting chuckle in the Pastor's question.

Paul did not. He lifted his head and muttered in resignation, "I said the land the Lord God is giving sure isn't in south Russia"

The girls giggled and Paul prepared himself for a lashing. The new pastor's tongue was at least as sharp as his hearing. Instead, Pastor Berger asked another question.

"What made you say that? Did you think it was funny?"

"No..yes...I.." Paul dared to look directly at the pastor. "I guess I was just thinking about how so much of the land around here now belongs to the Russians and we Germans, we are... I'm sorry, Herr Pastor."

"You should be sorry for mumbling things. But Paul, what you said isn't wrong. The Lord God was talking about Israel and not south Russia." Pastor Berger paused, tilted his head to the side and asked, "Class, do you think God cares about what happens here in our corner of Russia?"

Rudy and his classmates were stunned by a question that didn't come from the Bible or from the Catechism. Rudy was the first to venture an answer, "I think God cares about us but I don't know if he cares about this land. My brother Jacob just got some land in Dakota. Did God give them that or was it America that gave it?"

The next ten minutes were filled with real conversation. Victor spoke of

15

his parents' decision to move to America next year. Elsie talked about her brother who now worked for a Russian landowner. Pastor Berger brought the conversation back to what the land meant to Israel.

"These people at the mountain had been waiting for hundreds of years for a land to call their own. Just like some of your ancestors. God had promised them a land and they entered that land and held it for a long time. But after they killed Jesus they lost that land. And now these people, the Jews, are without land again, just like some of you and your relatives."

Rudy thought of his father, sweating and growing old as he worked on the land of others. He thought of his brother Jacob, his sister Katherine and her husband Fred in Dakota. He imagined that land flowing with milk and honey just like the Israelites' Promised Land. *Will anyone in my family ever be able to say, 'the Lord gave this land to me'?*

He was pondering those heavy thoughts then Helen Klein looked across the table, smiled at him and he was lost.

JUNE 1903, FREIDORF

When you are a fifteen-year old boy and hear the laughter of the fiddle chasing the scampering notes of the accordion into the warm June evening, and you begin to imagine what the night might bring, naturally your heart expands and your shirt collar becomes a size too small. Rudy tugged at his neck as he and Paul heard the band playing in Ludtke's warehouse even before they saw the dim light of the lanterns seeping into the soft evening.

"Sounds like they're already twirling and swooping," said Paul.

Rudy grinned. "I can hear your dad's flying fiddle."

"He's probably already had a few beers. When he gets loosened up, not even a team of oxen can slow him down."

The two friends lengthened their strides and Paul pulled ahead. In the past two years Paul had stretched up to nearly six feet. When they were thirteen, he and Rudy had been the same height and the tallest boys in their class. But Rudy only inched up while Paul leapt up. No matter. The two were still the best of friends and tonight they were both hoping to hold a few girls in their arms, and swing them around the dance floor.

Earlier in the day, Rudy had decided to practice his waltz steps with his mother.

"C'mon Mutti, let's dance." He'd come up behind her as she washed dishes. She groaned and tried to resist his tickling. But Rudy could always get her to smile and finally she turned toward him, rolled her eyes and let a smile soften her weary face. They circled the kitchen a dozen times while Rudy sang the notes of the Blue Danube waltz. "La, la, lala, La, la, lala."

"Stop Rudy. Enough!" She laughed as she threw herself onto a kitchen chair. Her face was red and, as she fanned herself with a pot holder, she surprised her youngest son.

"You've never seen the Danube, but at least I have a picture in my mind." She spoke wistfully and her face grew younger.

His parents so seldom spoke of their past. Rudy eagerly sat down and leaned toward his mother. "Really? How so?"

Elizabeth silently fanned herself as her breathing slowed. Rudy feared she would get up and go back to her dishes. But she dropped the potholder into her lap and her eyes glimmered as she sailed back into her past.

"My grandmother Richter..oh she could paint pictures with her words. She used to sigh and begin her story, always with these words: 'The Danube. Ah it was so beautiful and... majestic, yes that's what it was.'"

Elizabeth's face seemed to soften as she sailed backward in time. "I was a little girl. We'd be shelling peas together and she'd tell her story. I bet I heard it twenty times. She'd laugh and say, 'Your grandfather was always in a hurry. Only two weeks after we were married, we left Kassel, Germany to begin our new life. I remember how we laughed and sang on the horse cart as we headed south.'"

Rudy held his breath, afraid to break the startling spell that had fallen upon his mother. He'd never heard one story of his mother's childhood, and now, hearing her tell of his great grandmother. Stunning.

Elizabeth continued now, adopting the warbly voice of her grandmother, "I thought everything--every hill, every town--was wonderful and alive. But then we came to the Danube....I had no words. We boarded the boat, I stood there hanging onto my new husband, and I cried."

Now Rudolph, like his mother Elizabeth, began to see the great river through the eyes of that new bride: The ribbon of blue, broad and swift. A sharp stab of longing pricked Rudy's heart. "How long were they on the boat?"

Elizabeth was too lost in her own memory to even hear his question. "Oh, Rudy, they sailed past castles with flags snapping from their high towers. They slipped under bridges that arched over them like frightened cats.... Grandmother said she could have floated on that blue Danube forever."

She sighed and blinked. Her soft smile vanished and the spell broke.

"But then they came to the Black Sea and--" she pushed herself up from the chair and moved toward the sink, "two weeks later, they came to the Kassel Colony. Imagine, they left a Kassel and came to a Kassel. And for the rest of her life she never got more than ten miles from her home. And look at me. I was born in that Kassel Colony and now here I am forty miles away. So much for my great adventure."

She went back to her dishes. Rudy sat dreaming of the great river and imagining his ancestors in love and cruising past lofty castles. When he stood up and went to get dressed for the dance, he heard his mother softly singing as she washed dishes, "La la, lala, la la lala.."

*　　　*　　　*

The two young men sauntered up to the door of the old warehouse. The board floor has been swept clean of onion skins left from last year's crop and all the potatoes had either been shipped out, eaten or sold for the spring seeding. Most of the men, fathers and grandfathers of Freidorf, German and Russian farmers, stood talking and laughing in knots near the far wall where the kegs of beer stood. Their wives sat on benches chattering, smiling and occasionally shrieking with laughter. Little children ran back and forth, along the edges and sometimes skipped across the dance floor, dodging the couples that were kicking and twirling to the sounds of a polka. Long skirts swished and faces were red and smiling beneath the lanterns that hung from the rafters.

"There they are," said Paul as he jabbed Rudy in his ribs with his elbow. He pointed his nose to the distant corner where the girls from their school stood in giggling clusters. As the two friends sidled around the dancing couples, they noticed that a few of their male classmates were already hovering near the gaggle of girls but none of them seemed interested in dancing.

"Looks like we're not the first guys here," Rudy muttered.

"But I betcha we'll be the bravest," Paul said. He didn't slow down as he approached the girls and marched right up to Frieda, grinned, bowed, and held out his hand. She opened her eyes wide in shock and tittered to her girlfriends. But it was all an act; everyone knew the truth. She and Paul had been flirting and eyeing each other for months. She took his hand and they scooted out to the dance floor.

Rudy suddenly felt naked. He was tempted to sidle over to the group of guys. But before he moved, he dared to glance at Helen and she was staring, wide-eyed right into his face, daring him to move in any direction but hers. Like a man in a dream he moved toward her, drawn by her magnetic eyes.

18

He stood before her and his tongue was frozen.

"Hello Rudy, are you going to ask me to dance?" She teased in a warm low voice that finally melted Rudy's tongue and mind.

He clicked his heels together, bowed and held out his hand. "Miss Helen, may I have the honor of this dance?" He laughed as he spoke, Helen laughed back and they hurried out to join the other couples. The music engulfed them and they began to float along with its current. Now Rudy relaxed and reveled in Helen's soft yet strong body as they spun and kicked through the polka. They both grinned as she swung and twirled beneath his upraised arm.

The song finished and they walked back toward the crowd of young people. "Mr. Heupel, I'd say you've been practicing," teased Helen. "Natural talent, pure natural talent," he grinned because they both knew he was not one of the village's most athletic guys.

They had just reached their friends when a shout came from the band, "Chumaky, chumaky!" A roar came from the Russians in the room. Rudy and Helen waved to their friends and led them in the rush to the center of the dance floor.

Decades ago when the Russian farmers moved into the area they brought this dance with them. The girls and women formed an outward facing circle, the men an inward facing one and the music began fast and furious as the circles spun, broke, then reformed. Rudy kicked and stomped but kept his eyes fixed on Helen. She glowed brighter with every spin and swirl. The music ended with a grand flourish and the couples began to leave the floor. Rudy's shirt clung to his back and tiny droplets of sweat shone above Helen's lip.

They took only a few steps when the band, slid quietly into a waltz, the Blue Danube waltz. Rudy turned to Helen. He did not need to ask; her arms were already open. The waves of music swept them around the dance floor and Rudy felt himself falling into her luminous brown eyes. He gasped as all his desires churned through him at once—his libido, his longing to sail beyond this valley, his yearning for adventure, his ache to be a man. The currents of the Blue Danube and the heat of Helen in his arms left him gasping for breath.

The waltz ebbed to a close and without a word Rudy and Helen walked out the warehouse door into the fresh evening air. She stopped with her back against the wall and looked up at him. Without thinking he bent and kissed her and she kissed him back. How many nights had he imagined his first kiss? He'd envisioned it as torrid, burning and steamy. But this kiss was crushed velvet, smooth, and gentle. He took a deep breath, pulled her close to him and in the shadows, with the sound of polkas and dances as background, he told her of the Danube river, the castles and the beautiful bridges arched like cats over the bright blue water.

JUNE 1910, FREIDORF

South Russia's weather could destroy a year's worth of work in a single hail storm. Babies and the elderly suffered, and too often died, in the harsh winters. The people of Freidorf, especially the men, were stoic in the face of life's tragedies.

George Heupel showed his grief more openly than most men. Everyone still remembered how long ago, at the funeral of Lydia his six-month old daughter, his eyes had welled with tears. The icy March wind slapped wet snowflakes against the mourners gathered round the grave. Each member of the family threw a handful of dirt rattling down onto the little coffin. When George wiped his eyes with his dark blue handkerchief, more than one Freidorf man blinked watery eyes and swallowed hard at the lump in his throat.

But today as he sat in the stuffy clinic office, the tears poured openly down the fifty-eight-year-old farmer's weather-burnished cheeks and blurred his view of stocky, bald Dr. Hartz. George's voice was husky.

"Are you saying there is no hope for her?"

"No, Herr Heupel. I am saying that I myself, our clinic here, can do nothing more for her. I recommend you take her to the General Hospital in Odessa. They have the newest treatments, the latest medicines…" His voice trailed off and he swiveled his chair away from George, gathered the test results together, slid them into a brown folder, then stood.

"Here, take these with you and show them to the doctors in Odessa." George reached for the folder as though it might snap at him. When he finally clasped it, Dr. Hartz gently murmured, "George, I urge you to go as soon as you can."

George quietly closed the door of the doctor's office and turned toward the crowded waiting room. Against the wall opposite him, on a smooth wooden bench, Elizabeth sat with her head resting on her son Rudy's shoulder. Her eyes were weak but thirty-two years of marriage allowed her to read her husband's face and his body as clearly as if he were carrying a sign written in giant letters. She sighed and moved to rise. Rudy put his arm around her bony shoulder and helped her to her feet. With Rudy on one side and George on the other, they shuffled with Elizabeth out onto the street.

"Well, Vater, what did the doctor say?" Rudy asked as they neared their carriage.

Elizabeth had lost so much weight in the past months that George barely grunted as he helped her up onto the carriage seat. "He recommended that we go to the hospital in Odessa. They have new treatments there."

Rudy leapt up and grabbed the reins. "Odessa! Of course. They can fix you there Mutti, I'm sure." Rudy clicked his tongue and snapped the reins. The horses lurched forward and Rudy grinned with youthful optimism. On the bench behind him, George and Elizabeth slumped together and stared straight ahead in silence.

*   *   *

"Did you load all of the water?" George looked up at Rudy sitting on the driver's seat of the carriage.

"Ja, Vater, I did." Rudy was impatient. George had asked him the same question twice already this morning. But the son bit his tongue, sensing the pain and worry in his father's voice. He knew George was torn. This was the heart of the haying season and he'd been contracted by several area farmers to make sure their hay was cut and stored before it could be damaged by summer thunderstorms. He could hardly afford to give up these jobs and he did not yet trust Rudy to manage the work. But Elizabeth needed to get to Odessa before she was too weak to travel. Rudy tried to imagine the turmoil in his father's heart. Finally, yesterday it had been decided. Rudy would take his mother to the hospital in Odessa. Elizabeth now sat under the hood of the carriage, wrapped in a blanket despite the warm air of the clear June morning.

Rudy believed it was the tug between his father's need to work and his desire to be with his wife that made George twitch and fret like a nervous horse. He had not heard his parents' many bedroom conversations since the visit to Dr. Hartz.

"No, George, I do not want to die, but— "

"Well then, we will go to Odessa."

"I've already said it's no use, just a waste of time… and money, which we don't have anyway."

"I'll find the money, I've got the haying contracts. Besides, how do you know it's no use?"

"I just know, I can feel it. The thirst in my body…it has no end. The more I drink the more I…And now my eyes are all blurry and the pain in my back and my legs..."

"Lisbeth, my Lisbeth, don't give up. I can't let you give up. If there is any chance at all...I couldn't live with myself if we don't try."

Elizabeth's ravaged eyes could barely see the stricken look on her husband's face but she could clearly hear the fear in his voice. Together they'd made many sacrifices over the decades in the struggle to raise their children and keep the family together. She knew how seriously George took his calling as head of the family and how deeply he grieved over their lack of wealth. She decided to make one more sacrifice. She would go to Odessa for his sake, so that at least he would not have to carry any of that guilt when she was gone.

JUNE 1910, ON THE ROAD FROM FREIDORF

Rudy's hands shook as he held the reins and his heart quivered as though it had been pummeled by a fist. *How could I have been so heedless?*
He and his mother had left Freidorf an hour ago. The morning sky had been a pale blue crystal bowl, the grass had waved slowly as they rolled by, and Rudy had whistled as he imagined the marvels he would see in Odessa.

They'd been traveling for only thirty minutes when Elizabeth murmured, "Rudy, you've got to stop. I need to.... go into the bushes."

He helped his mother down from the carriage and she walked into the low trees alongside the road. He was savoring the sunshine that warmed his back and trying to imitate the songs of the larks when his mother emerged from the shadows.

He gasped. She was the same woman who had walked into the woods minutes earlier, but he was stunned as though he'd never seen her before. Her skin was the dull white of a washed-out flour sack. Her joints bulged like knobs and the flesh hung loosely on her arms. Her steps were jerky and unsteady. She was deathly sick. How could he have not seen?

After helping her back into the carriage, Rudy climbed in and they continued their journey. His hands trembled, he shook his head and berated himself. *Just like me and my stupid garden.* For the past five years, as first Elizabeth's eyes weakened and then her strength faltered, Rudy had been responsible for the family vegetable garden. Seven weeks ago, on a Saturday afternoon, he'd hurriedly planted the rows of beans, beets, carrots, cabbage, potatoes, and other vegetables. Then he'd turned his attention back to outings with friends, final school projects, and preparation for graduation.

In a dark corner of his mind he knew that he should be weeding the garden, but every day was so full of adventures and the garden never clamored for attention. He'd trotted past it dozens of times in the past weeks, scarcely giving it a glance. Then, two days ago, he'd stooped to tie a shoelace on the path and when he stood back up, the reality of the garden assaulted his eyes. The pigweed was taller than the bean plants. The creeper vines were choking the cabbage sets. His garden was overrun. How could he have not perceived what was before him all along?

The neglected garden and now his own mother—Rudy silently bemoaned his selective blindness. *Me, that's all I think about, me, me, me.* Of course, he'd known that his mother was ailing. He'd become accustomed to her slow decline over the past years. And yes, he was aware that lately her health had worsened, but he'd not truly seen her until today. His thoughts were a prayer of confession. *O good God, Mutti is dying and I've been oblivious!* He glanced back at Elizabeth as she gulped down water from one of the many jugs he'd filled earlier. An hour passed and the day grew warmer but still she sat wrapped in the rough blanket. Rudy imagined life without her and a chill quivered through his young body.

"Rudy, we must stop again," she said. He climbed down and looked up into her wan face as he helped her descend. She weakly smiled at him. "Sorry to be such a bother. The water runs through me so fast." She wobbled toward the bushes, this time holding on to Rudy's arm. He stood facing the road and when she came out, he put an arm around her waist. As they walked toward the carriage Rudy noticed a strange sensation. The hand that held his mother's waist tingled. It seemed to pulse with heat. The throbbing persisted until he lifted her back onto her seat. He grasped the reins and stared at his hand. *What's this? Where is this warmth coming from? From her body or mine? I know she is sick but...am I ailing too?* The tingling ebbed away and when he brought the hand to his face, he felt no heat.

All visions of Odessa's wonders faded from Rudy's mind and he snapped the reins to quicken his horse's pace. Now he was desperate to cover the twenty miles to the train station in Emmental. *I'll need to drop Mutti at the depot, then take the horse and rig to the livery stable, and run back to the depot before the train comes. Should I have her buy the tickets while I'm dropping off the carriage or---.*

"Rudy, please. I need to..." Her quiet plea interrupted his stampeding thoughts. He tugged on the reins and pulled onto the side of the dirt road. As he lowered Elizabeth, he again felt the tingling warmth in his hands. He was bewildered and curious at this baffling sensation. After she relieved herself and stepped back out into the sunshine, he walked her back to the carriage and moved his hand up and down her back. As he reached her lower back his hand seemed to throb.

"Ahhh, yes, there, that's the pain. Rub there Rudy, that's so soothing." With her arms braced herself against the carriage she leaned back into his hand and sighed with relief. Rudy was stunned. It was as though his hands could feel her pain—jagged and broken clods of agony beneath her skin. He massaged with his pulsing hands and the clods seemed to diminish and the sharp edges became rounded.

Rudy finally said, "We better keep going." He lifted her up and she settled in to her seat. Her eyes flared wide as she gazed down into her youngest son's face. She managed only a wondrous whisper. "Rudy, I think you have the brauche [the gift.] You have the healing hands of a braucher".

Rudy stared up at her in shock and confusion. He started to protest, then shook his head and climbed into his seat, clicked his tongue and the carriage lurched forward. His thoughts spun like a windmill in a storm. *Mutti said 'brauche', the gift. How can that be? Old Tanta [Aunt] Anna out there in the country, she is a braucher. People ride out to her little house with their aches and pains. She lays her hands on them, mumbles strange words, makes the sign of the cross and brews up teas. Me? A braucher? Crazy.*

His whirling thoughts gradually slowed and then were overwhelmed by that horrific vision of his frail mother stepping out of the woods and by the thunder of his heart as the blunt reality struck him: this journey was a mission of life or death.

JUNE 1910, ODESSA

Cla-click, cla-click, cla-click. The steady rhythm of the train lulled Elizabeth into sleep. She leaned against the streaked window, pillowing her head on her coat. Rudy sat beside her and stared out the window at the rolling plains and small villages sweeping by. Though his eyes saw the fleeting landscape, his mind scarcely noticed. This was his first train ride but he could not relish it. Nausea rippled upward from his belly. They had secured a seat across from the train's water closet which was no more than a hole in the train's floor. As users entered and left the tiny room, stench wafted around them. Rudy smelled his own sweat soaked shirt. He'd had to run nearly a half mile from the livery stable back to the train depot. But

24

beneath this salty tang he sniffed the sour odor of another sort of perspiration: the sweat of fear.

This morning Rudy had set off from home as a boy, relishing his freedom and anticipating adventure. Now his stomach cramped as he recognized the urgency of this trip to the hospital. *Will the doctors be able to help her? What if she must stay a long time in the hospital? Where will I go? Do we have enough money? What if Mutti dies before I can bring her home?* He held his sleeve over his nose and tried to slow his panicked breathing as another surge of nausea threatened to overwhelm him.

And then there was the "gift," the brauche. He remembered Pastor Mertz's harangues, how he'd sternly denounced the brauchers as charlatans, lumping them together with the gypsies who drew on the dark arts; even Pastor Berger frowned when referring to them and their gifts. But Rudy knew that these traditions and his community's beliefs in these figures ran deep. Why else would so many people quietly visit these healers with their ailments? Earlier in spring he remembered seeing his own father and mother, riding west into the golden afterglow of dusk out toward the house of Tanta Anna. His own parents, fervent believers and faithful church goers, had sought out the braucher months before visiting the Freidorf doctor.

Elizabeth's head rocked with the rhythm of the train. A trickle of saliva trailed from the side of her mouth. Rudy remembered his mother leaning her back into his pulsing hands. *Mutti said I have the gift. But how can this be? I didn't ask for any such thing. Pastor Berger says all gifts come from God and are meant to be used for good. But what does that mean for me and...*

The train car jerked and interrupted his troubled thoughts. They were entering Odessa. Elizabeth slowly raised her head and blinked with eyelids weighted by exhaustion and pain. Looking past her, Rudy saw the pillars and ornate fronts of buildings towering higher than the church steeple at home and stretching out for hundreds of meters. The train slowed and slipped next to the begrimed stone walls and pillars of the Holovna station.

They emerged out onto the street. Rudy clutched the small suitcase in one hand and his mother's arm with the other. The noise and swirl of people and movement dizzied them both. An electric trolley clattered up to the depot, squealed to a stop and disgorged dozens of passengers.

Elizabeth's eyes widened and she tugged at his arm. "No, Rudy. We're not going to ride that strange beast." She pointed them toward the horse carriages that were lined up farther down the street. Rudy helped Elizabeth up into the carriage, settled in beside her and gave the driver the address Dr.

Hartz had written out for him. The black cloaked driver was a stocky, Slavic looking man, his face and nose broad and flat. He nodded once, then grunted, snapped the reins and they clattered north on the cobbled streets.

"Look Mutti, look!" Rudy's cloud of anxieties was temporarily swept away by the vistas of this beautiful city. "The steps, the Potemkin steps!" The driver heard Rudy's exclamation and slowed the horses to a walk as they passed the two hundred greenish gray sandstone steps stretching down to the port below. The stairs surpassed the vision Rudy had held in his mind since he was twelve.

The stairs were central to the rioting and death that had swept through Odessa in 1905. 'Revolution, uprising, danger' were the words his parents and their friends had used when discussing the event. They'd debated what threats it presented to their German community. The fact that their school teacher at the time, Herr Leitovsky, had refused to comment about the incident and had forbidden them to talk about it in class had served to inflame Rudy's imagination even more. Now the magnificent staircase stretched below them and he could envision the blood, the gunshots and the screams of the rebels. How soon, he wondered before a new violence erupted and how far would its devastation reach?

The driver clucked his tongue and returned the horses to a swift trot. His mother groaned and Rudy turned to her. Her eyes were squeezed tight; she was breathing deeply. He guessed she needed to relieve herself. He leaned forward to speak to the driver but Elizabeth tugged him back. "No, I can wait. We must be almost there."

Rudy started to protest just as the driver turned into a curving driveway. He reined his horse to a halt in front of an imposing three story building of gray granite with columns, cornices and decorative panels.

"Are you sure this is the hospital?" Rudy asked.

"Ja, the medical university of Odessa," the driver growled in heavily accented German. "The hospital is there inside."

Both Rudy and Elizabeth stood wide-eyed on the sidewalk as the carriage clattered away. "This is a palace," Elizabeth murmured as they moved toward the white columns and the huge doorway. "I'm sure we don't have enough money to stay here for more than two days." Among the many stones of worry she carried she would soon learn that money was a tiny pebble.

It was late afternoon by the time they were led to a room by a heavy, round bottomed nurse who plodded down the hall in front of them. The dim electric lights hanging from the lofty ceilings shone weakly on the asparagus green walls. Rudy could hear sounds of voices and an occasional clatter of metal against metal but he sensed a holy hush hovering over all. This entire vast edifice was dedicated to healing. He dared to hope. *Surely here Mutti can be saved.*

"This is your room." The nurse growled in Russian. The room was a simple box without windows. Two beds stood side by side, separated by a heavy curtain. The nurse pulled back the bed sheet and handed Elizabeth a thin gown. "You're lucky. You have no roommate. Not yet. Dr. Stefanov will send his nurse shortly."

She started toward the door, then stopped and gazed at Elizabeth's thin frame and drawn face. She spoke slowly in German. "Dr. Stefanov is a very good doctor. If anyone can help you, he can." Then turning back to Rudy, she snapped in Russian, "You can stay in the room and sleep in the chair. But don't touch the other bed."

Rudy stepped out into the hall as his mother put on the hospital gown. They had reached their goal and now a heavy cloak of weariness wrapped around him. He leaned for a moment against the wall and watched a young blond nurse moving smoothly down the hall toward him. She was certainly more appealing to the eye than the nurse who'd brought them to their room. She stopped a few meters away from him.

"Frau Heupel's room?" She smiled. Rudy smiled back, nodded and turned to enter the room. She slipped by him. "No, stay in the hall please. I must take a urine specimen." Rudy slumped back against the wall. *Urine? That should be no problem. Poor Mutti is always overflowing.*

The young nurse exited a few minutes later, carrying a pan and bottle. Her face had lost its smile. As she hurried down the hall she said over her shoulder, "You may go in now. Try to have her get some rest."

*   *   *

The night had been endless. Rudy had tried sleeping in the chair but after his head fell forward and jerked back for the fifth time, he rolled up his coat and stretched out on the floor beside his mother's bed. He'd finally dozed off when she slid out from under her sheets and wobbled toward the water closet that lay across the hall. Rudy jumped up to help her. He waited to guide her back to bed then went down the hall to find a nurse and ask for more water.

Four, five, six..Rudy lost track of how many such forays he'd made throughout the night. His eyes felt as though he'd tossed sand into them. His limbs were leaden. He was back now in the chair, facing the door and praying that soon the sunlight in the window across the hall would announce a new day.

He believed his mother had slept more than he had. Each time they'd returned from the water closet, she'd dropped like a stone back into bed and instantly fallen asleep. The tall window across the hall was now a pale gray rectangle and the birds in the trees outside were exuberantly greeting the morning.

"Good morning, son." Rudy jerked in his chair where he'd not so surprisingly dozed off. Elizabeth was lying on her back gazing at him. Rudy saw what he'd noticed yesterday: smiling face and sorrowful eyes.

She nodded her chin toward the suitcase in the corner. "We still have some bread and sausage. How about breakfast?" Rudy's stomach growled at the mention of food. Elizabeth took only a few listless bites but Rudy couldn't help groaning with pleasure as he sunk his teeth into the homemade smoked sausage.

He was chewing with delight when the doctor arrived. He stood in the doorway and glanced at the folder in his hand.

"Good morning, Frau Heupel." Then turning to Rudy, "And you are..?"

Rudy jumped up from his chair and hastily swallowed. "Rudolph, sir. I am her son."

The doctor took two steps into the room, then stopped as he flipped through the pages of the folder from Dr. Hartz that Rudy had given to the nurse when they'd checked in.

The doctor was not a tall man, only a few inches taller than Rudy; but his straight back, and broad shoulders thrown back seemed to give him added height. His hair was dark, neatly trimmed and his moustache was black, frosted with gray. He gazed through a pair of wire rimmed glasses and wore a knee length coat so white it seemed to glisten.

As he examined the pages in the folder, the doctor murmured to himself in Russian, "These people….Why do they always wait so long….?" "These people." Rudy caught the comment, and the words were like the icy winter wind that swept across the steppes. *We're strangers here. What chance do we have? We're the 'other people'.* Yesterday's hope began to freeze and die. Then the ramrod straight doctor splintered Rudy's despairing thoughts. He strode to the chair, pulled it even closer to the bed and turned it so he was only a meter away from Elizabeth.

He spoke in smooth German, "Frau Heupel, I am Dr. Stefanov. How are you feeling this morning?"

Elizabeth shrugged. "Tired….and weak."

The doctor nodded. "And did you need to urinate during the night?"

28

Elizabeth gave him a wan smile. "Ask Rudy how many times we made the journey." The doctor glanced at Rudy who at first shrugged then held up five fingers.

"I see. Yes, that's not surprising." He opened the folder. "You told your Doctor Hartz that you've been having more and more trouble with your eyes. May I have a look?" He pulled his chair closer and pulled back her eyelids. "Hmmm. Yes."

He moved the chair back and then asked, "Have you noticed pains in your lower back?"

Elizabeth slowly turned her head to Rudy, stared woefully into his eyes, and nodded her head. "Yes, a pain that throbs." She sighed. "It never stops."

Dr. Stefanov closed the folder, leaned forward and gently placed his hand on Elizabeth's arm. "Frau Heupel. We did a test last night of your urine and it was laden with sugar. All the signs are there. The eyesight, the failing kidneys. You have what we call diabetes mellitus, sugar diabetes." She turned her head away from the doctor and stared at the heavy curtain.

Rudy stood at the foot of the bed. His eyes shifted from his mother to the doctor. "What will you do? How will you treat this diabetes?"

Dr. Stefanov laid the folder on his lap and turned up his palms. "Son, I'm sorry but we have no treatment. We believe this disease has something to do with the pancreas but we're not sure. We can do nothing."

Rudy's eyes filled with tears and his chin dropped to his chest. "But there is something that you can do, something that your family can do." Rudy raised his watery eyes. "Some people with diabetes have found relief by changing their diet. No bread or sugar. Plenty of meat, eggs, vegetables. I will give you a list."

Rudy nodded. "Thank you, Doctor. You said 'relief'. Is that all we can give her?"

Dr. Stefanov stood. He looked down at Elizabeth, then at Rudy. "I'm sorry. I wish I could give you more. The truth is, we doctors are not God. We're not even little gods, though sometimes we forget that." He reached out for Elizabeth's hand. "God be with you Frau Heupel." He put his hand on Rudy's shoulder. Rudy felt its warm strength. The doctor spoke softly, "I'll make arrangements at the desk for your ride back to the train station. I know you'll take good care of her." He squeezed Rudy's arm and quietly left the room.

Elizabeth struggled to sit up. Rudy moved to help her. "Let's get ready, Rudy. Let's go home."

3 November, 1910
Freidorf, Odessa, Kherson Governate
Dear Jacob and Katie,

Tonight I wish you weren't so far away. I have some very sad news. Our dear mother has died. Mutti passed away on Tuesday, November 1st, All Saints Day. The funeral was this morning. Since Mutti was the letter writer I'm sure she didn't tell you much about her health. She never wanted to bother anyone. I'm afraid you haven't heard much from us for quite a while. I will try to tell you about these past sad months.

Mutti's eyesight was weakening for many years. About six months ago it got very blurry. At around the same time, she became very thirsty. She was always drinking water, gulping it down like she was in a desert. And, of course she had to relieve herself over and over.

Vater and I were often away, at school or work, so we didn't notice at first. But on Sundays when we were all at home, we could see how bad it was. I guess I should say Vater noticed. I was too preoccupied with my own life to really notice.

Mutti tried all sorts of teas made from many different herbs. Nothing seemed to help. One evening she and Vater rode out to visit Tanta Anna, the braucher who lives out west of town. I should have known then how serious things were but... In June they finally went to Dr. Hartz and he told Vater to take Mutti to Odessa. I don't know if he thought the doctors in Odessa could help or if he just didn't want to give her bad news.

Since it was haying season, I ended up taking Mutti to Odessa. I was still hopeful when we left. But that changed during the carriage drive down to Emmental. By the time we got on the train, I realized how seriously sick she was. Mutti was weak and in pain but yet still had her little smile and thankfully could walk. In Odessa, we went to a huge hospital, very impressive-clean and bright. But the news we got there was dark. The doctor said Mutti had diabetes, that her

30

kidneys were failing and that there was no treatment. He gave us a list of foods, what she could and couldn't eat, and then he sent us home.

We tried this special diet and maybe it helped a little, helped her feel better. I don't know. The weeks, then months went by and she just kept getting weaker and weaker. Now the neighbor ladies all came in with their different treatments—hot tea, cold tea, special soups, smelly syrups. It got so bad, that Mutti finally had me tell the neighbors 'thank you but no thank you'. Vater and I did what we could to make her comfortable. I relieved some of her back and joint pain by massaging her. (I have gotten quite good at massage, at least Mutti said so.)

But then harvest time came. Vater and I both needed to work. The trip to Odessa had taken all our money and winter was coming. I don't know what we would have done if Elvira, Junior's wife, had not stepped in. Even though she had her two little ones, and Junior and her father were harvesting too, she came during the day and tended to Mutti. Not only did she nurse Mutti and deal with all her never-ending toilet needs, she would make sure there was a hot meal waiting for us when we came in late from the fields. She was the angel for Mutti and for us all these last months. We should all thank God that Elvira came in to our family.

Harvest was over and the nights were full of frost. Mutti was always cold so we kept the stove going day and night. Her pains got worse so we gave her some tablets that Dr. Hartz had given us. By the middle of October, she couldn't get out of bed. Her head just lay planted on her pillow. Her friends came quietly in twos or threes to say good-bye. I could hear them chattering and sometimes chuckling in Mutti's room. They must have been remembering old times.

Last week we could see the end was close. Mutti was just skin stretched over bones and needed to have pills almost every hour. We called Pastor Berger. Junior and Elvira came and brought along little Herman and Betty. Mutti could hold her eyes open only for a few minutes but when Junior held

31

up Herman and Betty so they could kiss her soft cheek, she smiled her sweet smile. Then Pastor Berger read the Shepherd psalm and we said together the Vater Unser[Our Father]. I could see Mutti mouthing the words but no sound came out.

By the time everyone left, she'd fallen asleep and never woke up again. For the next five days, Vater and I took turns sitting beside her bed. Tuesday morning was clear and cold. About ten, Elvira came to change the bedclothes, Vater was drinking coffee and I was dressing to go out and feed the chickens. Elvira came out of the bedroom.

"You better come in. I think she's close." We stood around the bed. For days, Mutti's breathing had been shallow and steady but now she seemed to gasp, then stop altogether, then suddenly gasp again. I could feel her agony in my body.

This went on for minutes then Vater did a surprising thing. He put his hand over her heart and whispered over and over, "Gott sei mit dir, meine leibste, Gott sei mit dir." [God be with you my dear, God be with you.] Her gasping got slower and slower, she gave one deep sigh, and she was gone. I could sense her leaving without eyes or ears. Once second, four of us were in the tiny bedroom, the next second we were only three.

We knew it was coming, but still, it was a shock. The room flooded with silence as we stood gazing at her body. Then Vater emptied his lungs in a big sigh and Elvira and I hugged him. For a few minutes, we cried and patted each other's back. Then I left to tell Herr Walz, the undertaker, while Elvira and Vater washed and dressed the body.

Herr Walz had already made the coffin so by evening the wake began. The coffin was set on sawhorses in the front room. Herr Walz set a tall candle on each end of the coffin. Mutti's body was dressed in the light blue dress she wore for church. Her long gray hair had spent most of its life in a bun but now it flowed around her face on the dark pillow. Maybe it was my imagination but her mouth seemed to curve in a small smile.

Friends and neighbors came that evening. They brought plates and baskets full of food. The women sat on chairs that we set against the walls around the coffin. The men came in, stood by the coffin with bowed heads for a few minutes then went outside to smoke and talk. About ten o'clock, Elvira's mother, Viola Shumann, sent Vater and me to bed, insisting that she and others would stay the night. We both slept but in the morning Vater still looked exhausted. People came all day to pay their respects. It was another tiring day.

Today we finally had the funeral. We woke up to a fog thick as clotted wool. Herr Walz came with his wagon at 9 o'clock to take the coffin to church. Junior and I had each chosen two of our friends to help us be pallbearers. We moved the coffin from the front room to the wagon. Honestly, it was so light two of us could have carried it. We rode in the wagon up to the church. Once we got there, we followed Pastor Berger up the steps and down the aisle. The church was full as it always is for funerals. We set the coffin onto the sawhorses in front of the altar, Herr Walz opened the lid and Pastor began the service.

I know you've been to enough funerals so you can imagine how the next hour went. We sang 'Jesu, meine Freude' [Jesus my Joy] and Luther's 'Ein Feste Burg' [A Mighty Fortress]. The choir sang 'O Welt, Ich Muss Dich Lassen' [O World I Must Leave You]. Herr Pastor preached on Romans 8:38 and 39, Mutti's favorite verses.

When the service was over, the steeple bell started ringing and we pallbearers carried the coffin back outside. The fog had turned to a thick drizzle. We marched to the cemetery, the bell kept tolling in the steeple, muffled by the fog. Gravel crunched under hundreds of shoes. The water was dripping from the trees around the cemetery and we were all soaked by the time we reached the grave and the dirt piled beside it. Herr Walz and his helper slipped ropes under the coffin and we helped them lower it down. Everyone clustered together and Pastor read the final prayers. Then he picked up a clod of dirt and as he tossed it into the grave he said, "ashes to ashes dust to dust." I've heard those words lots of times, but today they tore open my chest. I stood between Vater and Junior and I cried.

Now it's about 9:30 p.m. I can hear Vater snoring in his room. These last months have worn him down. He looks so old. He still can work like a horse but he has no spark in his eyes. He and Mutti were like one. I don't know how he will handle being alone.

I'll stay here at home, at least until spring. Last year I thought I'd try to leave and go to Odessa or somewhere in Germany after I graduated. But by the time graduation came in June, Mutti was so sick and she kept getting sicker. So, I'll stay with Vater this winter. In the spring, maybe...we'll see.

I pray that you and your families are safe and healthy in Dakota. Please pray for us, especially for Vater, that he can find life again in the middle of his grief.

Your far away brother,
Rudy

FEBRUARY 1911, FREIDORF

The icy knives of February's north wind sliced through Rudy's scarf. He pinched his eyes down to slits as he plodded through the drifts. The sun was a dim silver disk in the milky white sky. He'd donned his thickest and longest coat but the cold was relentless. He was glad he only had to walk one mile from his home to Pastor Berger's home office. He'd requested this meeting last Sunday as he left the worship service. Hopefully Herr Pastor hadn't forgotten.

He gasped with relief when he reached the parsonage and stepped out of the wind's slashing. Before knocking on the door, he unwrapped his scarf and pulled off the bits of ice clinging to the reddish-brown hair of his newly grown mustache.

"Ah, Rudy, come in, come in." Frau Berger ushered him in and the room's warmth dizzied him. She chattered on. "I didn't know if you were going to make it. This weather is brutal. But then, this is south Russia and this is February. Why should we be surprised?" She took his coat, hat and scarf and pointed to the office door. "Go on in, Herr Pastor is expecting you." Rudy was wondered if she always called her husband 'Herr Pastor.'

He tapped on the door and heard Pastor Berger's clipped response.

"Yes, Rudy, you may enter." As Rudy pushed open the door, the pastor came out from behind his desk, greeted his young parishioner and clapped him on the back. "You made the Arctic trek. Such brutal weather. Sit my boy." As he settled in to his chair behind the desk, he asked, "And how is your father doing? I didn't see him in church on Sunday."

Rudy gazed beyond the pastor out into the bleak winter. "Ach, what can I say? On Sunday morning Vater said his legs ached and he wanted to stay out of the cold. He always said we had to go to church unless we were sick with a fever, but these days, he finds excuses..."

"He's grieving, Rudy. I'm sure you know that."

"I know. But it's so hard to see him like this. He was always working, so full of fire. Even in the winter we'd have projects: rebuild the granary, repair the stalls in the barn, make new harnesses. Now, he wakes up and stands for hours looking out of the window, holding his tea mug in his hands. In the evening, I invite him to play checkers and sometimes he forgets which color is his, or that it's his turn. Even when Junior and Elvira bring over their little ones and they climb onto his lap, even then he barely smiles."

Pastor Berger slowly nodded. "Losing a life partner is like having your soul ripped in half. Your mother and father were very close, everyone could see that. Your father is a bit lost. He's trying to find his footing. Keep talking to him..." the pastor chuckled, "and keep playing checkers. Maybe you should let him win a game or two. I'll come to see him later this week."

Then he tipped back in his chair and looked over the top of his glasses. "But Rudy, you didn't come to talk about your father, did you? Sunday, you mentioned something about your future."

Rudy sat back and tugged at the neck of his heavy shirt. The warmth in the room now seemed stifling. "Yes, Herr Pastor. I've been thinking about what I should do with my life. Our family has no land. I don't really like farming anyway. Around here there are no jobs, so I've thought about leaving and.."

"But if there was a job, would you stay?" Pastor Berger leaned eagerly forward, elbows on his desk.

Rudy stammered, "Well, I...I don't know....What sort of job?"

The pastor clasped his hands together. "Rudy, there are going to be some changes in our congregation. With so many of our Lutherans leaving, the smaller churches can't afford to hire a pastor. I have been asked to take on the ministry at Scharowa. More work for me means we'll need someone to lead our youth ministry and work with the confirmation children. I'd like to offer you that position. It wouldn't be a full-time job, at least not at first, but it could grow."

Rudy sat back stupefied. This was as improbable as a thunderstorm in February. Only the serious dark eyes of Pastor Berger kept him from laughing out loud. "Me? Youth ministry leader? I'm not a leader."

"Oh, but Rudy you are. The younger students all look up to you. You speak well, you're thoughtful. When you decide to do something, they follow you, whether you notice it or not."

"But I don't know..."

Pastor Berger raised his hand as if to deflect Rudy's protest. "You know the catechism and the Bible stories better than any student I've ever worked with. I think you'd make a fine teacher."

Rudy looked around the stuffy office like a rabbit desperately seeking a hiding place. "Herr Pastor, this is such a surprise. I mean, I'm honored, of course. But I...Right now I can't even imagine such a thing."

The pastor sat back and nodded. "I understand Rudy. But you must think about it. This is a way to use your God-given gifts. Take a few weeks. This wouldn't start until May and you're my first choice." He folded his arms across his chest. "Now Rudy, I know I interrupted you. What was it you planned to discuss with me?"

Rudy had spent days rehearsing what he'd say to Pastor Berger. But now his planned speech was nothing more than tattered rags snapping in the north wind. His deepest question slipped out before he could restrain it.

"Why does the church hate the brauchers?"

Now it was the pastor's turn to be dumbfounded. His forehead creased as he squinted at Rudy. "What did you say?"

Rudy gulped. "I asked about brauchers. Why does the church hate them?"

The perplexed pastor took off his glasses and rubbed them with his shirt sleeve while he hunted for a response. "I wouldn't say the church actually hates the brauchers. But why do you ask this?"

Rudy ignored the question. "Old Pastor Mertz said we should treat them like the devil's spawn, that the brauchers were pagans just like the gypsies."

"I wouldn't say that, no. I have said that the brauchers could be dangerous and lead believers astray."

Now Rudy leaned forward, "But why, Herr Pastor? Don't they try to help people?"

"Yes, I believe they do. But Rudy, let me ask you this: If the brauchers truly help people, and I'm not so sure they do, is it by their power or by God's power?"

"By God's power; all good is by God's power. That's what you taught us."

"Good. But not all people see this. Some think the brauchers have the power; then they go to them instead of going to Dr. Hartz, or instead of coming to me and letting me pray for their healing. In the Letter of James, chapter five it says---" Abruptly the pastor stopped, sat back and took a deep breath. "Sorry. I'm sure you didn't come for one of my lectures. But Rudy, why are you asking about the brauchers?"

Rudy dropped his eyes and spoke quietly, "Because my mother said I was one."

"Your mother said that? She was a woman of deep faith. Are you sure Rudy?"

In the stuffy office filled with pale snow-screened sunlight, Rudy told Pastor Berger about the journey to Odessa; how his hands had warmed as they touched his mother's back; how his fingers had found and soothed her back pain and how he'd continued to massage and ease her body during her last months.

"And now, Herr Pastor, now Vater sometimes wakes up stiff and unable to turn his neck and my fingers seem to move by their own will to where a nerve is pinched. When I rub and press on that spot, there is a tiny pop and Vater sighs in relief." Rudy turned out his palms and sat back in his chair. "I can't explain this. I didn't ask for this. But I can't believe it's something dark and dangerous."

Pastor Berger had sat listening, elbows on his desk, chin resting on his knuckles. Now he too leaned back. "Well, Rudy...I'm not sure what to say. But one thing I do know. This...this gift is not a danger. It could be one, if possessed by someone else. But I believe I know enough about you. You won't misuse what has been bestowed on you."

At last Rudy poured out his plan. "That's why I came to you, Pastor. Maybe this gift is God's way of telling me that I should help sick and hurting people, maybe become a doctor or a nurse. The hospital in Odessa, I can't explain this, it was filled with a spirit of caring and compassion. It felt like a holy place. Do you know where I could go to learn and use my gifts?"

Rudy's eager words and glowing face softened the pastor's stoic heart. But he was, above all else a pragmatic, rational man.

"Ai, Rudy, you ask a hard question. These are hard times for us all. Any German boy would have a hard time finding a welcome in a hospital or

37

medical school here in south Russia, even if he had the money to pay for the training. More and more we're looked on with suspicion. And in Germany, the schools are even more expensive than here."

Like a dying ember, the glow faded from Rudy's face and he dropped his eyes to his lap. "I see. I guess I was hoping…I've been so mixed up." He sighed and began to rise. "Herr Pastor, I'm sorry I bothered you."

Pastor Berger waved him back into his chair. "Sit down Rudy. Please don't apologize. You can always come to see me. So, you've been mixed up. Plenty of our young German men are confused these days. Every month we see new Russian laws—tax laws, land laws, military service laws. And don't forget Rudy, you're grieving too. It's not just your father who's trying to adjust. No wonder you're perplexed. I hope you'll think about my ministry offer, but I can see your heart is pulling you in another direction."

The pastor sat back in his chair, laced his fingers at the back of his neck and gently rocked in his chair. He sat silently for several minutes. The whistle of the wind and the faint creaking of the chair were the room's only sounds. Rudy longed to escape but was afraid to move. At last Pastor Berger leaned forward and took up a pen and reached for a pad of paper.

"Rudy, I have an idea. It's not quite what you're looking for but maybe it's a step in that direction. And, I don't know if it is possible."

Rudy tried to tether his rising hopes as the pastor spoke.

"Ten years ago, in Treysa, a town in central Germany, the Lutheran Church started a training program for men and women interested in caring for the physically and mentally handicapped. It was called the Hephata Diaconal Center. Do you recognize that word, 'hephata'?"

Rudy shook his head.

"Remember the story in the gospel of Mark where Jesus meets a deaf and dumb man? When Jesus puts his fingers in the man's ears and he puts some of his own saliva on the man's tongue, then looks up to heaven and says, 'Hephata', which in the language Jesus spoke means 'be opened'. The man could suddenly hear and speak. So 'hephata' is a healing word. How about the word 'diaconal'? Do you know what that means?"

Again, Rudy shook his head.

"It comes from the word 'deacon.'

Now Rudy nodded, "That's what we call our congregation's leaders."

"Right. The word 'deacon' means servant and we use it here. But this center trains people to serve people in a more direct way. I know all of this because Frederick Berger, my cousin, was part of the first training group. He's now a deacon and helps administer a small clinic outside of

Frankfurt."

"And you think maybe, possibly, I could go to Treysa and study there?" Eagerness slipped back into Rudy's voice.

"Well, we'll see. I'll write to Hephata directly, also to my cousin. I'm not even sure if the program is still going."

"But if it's still going, how will I pay for it?" Rudy already imagined himself living Germany's heartland, studying and working and meeting new people.

Pastor Berger smiled. "Rudy, don't pack your bags yet. I've got to make some inquiries. I do know that my cousin had very little money. He worked at Hephata and studied there at the same time. So maybe...maybe... Rudy, I'll write the letters today. We could hear something in a month or two."

The pastor left his chair and came around his desk as Rudy stood. He shook Rudy's trembling hand. "I'm glad you came in. You've got lots to think about, don't you? Stay calm Rudy, don't worry. God'll help you sort all this out." He clapped Rudy's shoulder. "Try to be patient with your father. And with yourself."

Rudy murmured a thanks to the pastor and his wife as she handed him his coat, scarf and hat. He stepped outside into the weak sunlight. The hour-long conversation had exhausted him. Sheer surprise followed by plunging despair and then resurging hope---he was drained and yet at the same time exhilarated. He stepped out of the lea of the house into the frigid wind. But now the blast was at his back and it sounded like singing.

AUGUST 1912, FREIDORF

"What the hell are you doing here?" Rudy was sitting on a bench outside the town's grain storage silo and looked up into the face of a tall, sunbaked and whiskered young man. The man's words and the glare in his dark eyes smoldered with resentment.

Rudy looked down, shrugged and murmured. "I suppose I'm here for the same reason you are...looking to be hired for the day."

"You damn Germans. You took our good Russian land and now you try to grab the only work we can find." A squat man, with long, dark hair sauntered over and stood shoulder to shoulder with the inquisitor and joined him in sneering down at the object of their scorn.

Rudy lifted his head and leaned back against the back of the rough board bench. He wanted to remind these two Russians that his ancestors had been invited into south Russian and given the land by the Russian queen herself.

He knew holding that truth up to them would be like poking a stick into a beehive. Yet he couldn't simply ignore these two dolts. He lifted his chin. "Not all of us Germans have land."

"Oh ho!" the tall man cackled and elbowed his pal. "Then this guy must belong to one of those dumb German families who didn't even know how to farm the land they stole."

Rudy leapt to his feet and faced the men. He stood only five feet and seven inches tall but a July full of hauling hay and now an August of shoveling grain had filled out his chest and hardened his biceps. He had a high boiling point and wasn't so impetuous as to start a fight; yet his family's honor had been sullied. He glowered at the two leering Russians.

His words came jagged and splintered through gritted teeth. "You've no right to judge my family. You mind your business and I'll mind mine." He shoved his way between the two and started marching across the street, expecting at any moment to be thrown into the dirt.

That would likely have happened had not Harold Hauck come rattling down the street with a team of horses pulling an empty grain wagon. He jerked back on the reins and stopped in front of Rudy.

"Hey Rudy, a couple of men in my threshing crew didn't show up this morning, maybe sick, maybe hung over, who knows. Anyway, I'm two men short. Can you fill in?"

Rudy scrambled aboard without a backward glance. Harold shouted over to the two Russians who still stood by the depot. "One of you want a day's work?" The men looked at each other, then shook their heads and waved him off. Harold snapped the reins and grunted as the wagon and his passenger rattled out of town. "Those two…joined at the hip…one as lazy as the other."

Rudy's pulse still throbbed as the adrenaline surged through his veins. I can't get out of this place soon enough. As soon as the harvest is over, I'm heading north, no matter what Vater says.

It had been nineteen months since his meeting with Pastor Berger. If he'd been told then that over a year and a half later, he'd still be in Freidorf he might have screamed into that snowy sky.

All through the 1911 spring haying season and the fall harvest season he'd been force fed one of life's most onerous lessons: the deeper your yearning for time to pass, the more sluggishly time moves.

Unfortunately, Pastor Berger's first letter to his cousin brought no response. He'd then sent a letter to another relative who, several months later replied that cousin Frederick Berger had moved. The answer to the

40

pastor's letter to Hephata had been vague, asking for more information and a personal recommendation. Pastor Berger's new responsibilities kept him out of Freidorf for weeks at a time.

It wasn't until January of 1912 that Pastor Berger had sent another set of letters and counseled an increasing disheartened Rudy to not surrender hope. Wintry weeks passed and Rudy chafed, grew irritated with his father, and prayed desperately for good news. But Ash Wednesday and the somber season of Lent plodded in. February's driving snow surrendered to March's slush and freezing rain. Vater George's prolonged mourning slumped into sullen cynicism. Somehow Elizabeth's absence had shrunk the house and Rudy and George were constantly in each other's way.

Rudy had told no one of his conversation with the pastor. He hadn't dared tell anyone of his 'gift' nor of his hopes, not even his friend Paul. March trudged to a close and April's green promise of spring covered the land, but to Rudy the future was a bleary, morose cloud of uncertainty.

On Palm Sunday, the children of Freidorf Lutheran paraded down the church aisle waving paper palm leaves and singing Hosanna, reenacting Jesus' arrival in Jerusalem and inaugurating Holy Week. Rudy and his father sat on the right side of the church with the other men. Rudy remembered how he'd marched down that aisle, full of fervor and enthusiasm, in love with the story and with Jesus. But today as he watched the excited children waving their paper leaves, his heart was sour and his soul skeptical. *Does God want me stuck in this place forever? If I must stay here in Freidorf, I'll shrivel up and turn as bitter as an old radish. Oh God. God, where are you?*

That afternoon, he sat with Helen on a rock above a little stream. Decades ago the farmers had hauled in stones to dam up the small creek to hold water for irrigation. When summer's sun and heat rolled in, the stream turned into a listless and muddy pond. But today it was overflowing with snow melt and as the water tumbled over the rocks it sparkled like silver coins flipping in the sunshine on its way to the Black Sea. Rudy sat staring into the stream and tossing pebbles.

"Why so cloudy on a sunny day?" Helen teased.

Rudy continued to flick pebbles into the water. "Ach, these days living with Vater is like living with a grumpy badger."

"Really?" She chuckled, "And you?"

Rudy turned his head. "Huh?"

"What is living with you like? A polecat or a weasel?" Helen smiled at him and he shook his head and smiled back. She had a gift for breaking through his icy moods.

He picked up a larger stone and flung it into the foaming water. "I'm so tired of this place. I can't think of any reason to stick around here."

"Ohhh, I could think of at least one reason." Helen poked his side and giggled.

Rudy playfully jostled her shoulder. "Aww Helen, you know what I mean. I want to do something with my life but here in Freidorf…" He settled back into glum silence.

"I heard that you could have had a job at the church." Rudy stiffened his spine at her quiet words. Hot irritation flushed his face. This was supposed to be between him and the pastor.

Helen sensed his vexation and quietly added. "My dad's a deacon and they voted to add the salary to the budget. I heard him tell mother….and mention your name. But that was a year ago so I suppose…"

The two sat in silence watching the swifts darting and circling above the splashing stream. Rudy envied their simple life: fly north, devour insects, lay eggs, raise chicks, fly south. Some of them stayed in the air for months at a time. Rudy pulled up his legs, hugged his knees and stared into the foam.

"Pastor sees something in me that I can't see. I'm not a leader. Besides I had another idea and I thought it might even be God's plan but…" He sighed and dropped his forehead onto his knees.

Helen hesitated. Clearly, she'd already breached Rudy's defenses. He was her friend and she didn't want to cause him further distress. But…he was her friend, he was troubled and perhaps she could help. Her curiosity, like the stream before them, was unstoppable.

"Rudy, can you tell me your idea? I mean, if you want to…"

He stretched out his legs and tried, unsuccessfully, to sound nonchalant. "I thought maybe I'd try something in the field of health."

"You mean like a doctor?" As far as she knew, no one in Freidorf had ever become a doctor.

"No, not exactly. Pastor Berger told me about a special program in Germany, called a deacon training program that trains people to work in hospitals."

Helen sat up on her knees. "Rudy, that's great. How did you ever get this idea?"

"Well, Pastor Berger had a cousin who went through this program—"

"No, no. I mean what made you think this was what you wanted to do?"

Rudy wavered. He imagined what a relief it would be to break open the dam of his feelings and thoughts and share them with his best friend. But what would Helen think when he described his 'gift'? He didn't dare ask her what she thought of the brauchers. Would she think him weird and laugh? He doubted that. And yet… Finally, he settled on a safe answer.

"I guess it was during the last months taking care of my mother. I felt that I could bring her some relief and comfort and, and she said I was good at it. So, I thought maybe…but…" He shrugged and threw another stone into the creek.

"Last year, at the end of February, Pastor sent out letters to his cousin and to the deacon program, but there was some mix up. Now he's sent another batch of letters, but we've heard nothing. It's probably not going to happen. I guess I'm stuck here, like everyone else. Until I hit twenty, then the army will grab me."

"Rudolph Heupel, how can you say that?" Rudy winced as if the scolding words came from a teacher. Then, irked by his own reaction, turned sharply to retaliate but noticed glittery tears in her luminous eyes. He leaned back in surprise as she continued.

"How can you give up, lay down like a whipped dog just because one door hasn't opened? You sit there feeling sorry for yourself. What about the rest of us?"

"What do you mean, 'the rest of us'?"

She shook her head and her voice quavered with emotion. "You can buy a ticket and get on a train to anywhere anytime you want." She clenched her fists in her lap and bitterness flavored her next words. "Do you think my parents would let me do that? An unmarried young woman traveling alone? Ha. The whole colony would condemn me."

She threw up her hands in frustration. "You're smart. You can study and work at so many things. I'm smart too. But how many doors are open for me? Look around you Rudy. You're not the only one feeling stuck." She jerked to a stop, swallowed the rest of her searing words, then dropped her head and stared at the grass between her feet.

Rudy's cloak of self-pity had been rudely ripped from his shoulders. The afternoon air turned chilly. Once more he'd been so absorbed by his own circumstances, so immersed in his own situation that he'd ignored the hurts and struggles of his friends. He shivered and sadly remembered Pastor Berger's oft repeated declaration: Man's greatest sin is to be curved in upon himself. *Will I ever find a way to escape my old Adam?*

Helen started to rise and Rudy leapt up to help her to her feet.

"Helen, hold on. I'm sorry. You're right. I just never thought about how

---

43

tough girls have it." He had to hurry to keep up with her. Finally, she slowed her charging steps but kept gazing straight ahead.

"No, Rudy, I'm the one who should be sorry. I dumped my frustration on you. This is just the way things are here in the colonies. It's not your fault. I don't want to talk about this again."

The murmuring of the creek dimmed as they walked toward the town but Rudy's emotions still tumbled and surged. He was sorry that he'd never recognized how constricted life was for women in south Russia. It was as though Helen had torn blinders from his eyes. He thought of his mother and how bound her life had been. He wondered if his sister Katherine in Dakota fared any better. He was ashamed of his own obliviousness.

But as they trod back home, Rudy's disquiet included more than shame. Here in Freidorf people didn't spill out their feelings as Helen had just done. Emotional outbursts were shameful signs of weakness. People of suspect character, like the gypsies who wandered through the region, those were the ones who flaunted their emotions. Rudy was embarrassed for Helen. He longed to defend and protect her, but did not know how.

When at last they arrived at Helen's house, Rudy reached for her hand, squeezed it, and looked deep into her eyes. She caught his look, then dropped her gaze to the ground. He sighed, released her hand and turned toward home.

*   *   *

The letter came the day after Easter. Rudy and his father were in the vegetable garden, wielding spades and turning over the damp dirt, preparing for seeding. They heard the rattle of an approaching carriage, then the snort of horses being reined in. A shout came from the front of the house. "Hello, Rudy, George. Are you home?"

Rudy dropped his spade and trotted around the side of the house, just at Pastor Berger clambered down from his seat. He was grinning and holding up a letter. "Rudy, Easter is not the only good news for you this day!" He extended the letter as Rudy wiped his hands on his pants. Rudy's entire arm was shaking as he grasped the envelope.

The pastor climbed back into his carriage. "I can't stay. Mrs. Walz is failing and asks for prayers. Come by my office tomorrow and we can make plans." He rolled off just as George came around the side of the house.

"What was that all about? What did Herr Pastor want?"

Rudy was deaf to his father's question, all attention consumed by the inked words on the sheet that trembled in his hand

March 1, 1912

Hephata Center
Treysa, Germany
Dear Pastor Berger,

We have received your letter and are pleased to report that our Hephata deacon program in Treysa is thriving and continues to draw Christian men and woman from throughout Germany and beyond.

We have received correspondence from one of our fine graduates, your cousin Frederick, who informed us of your candidate. On the basis of your high recommendation, we invite Mr. Heupel, to enroll in our deacon program to prepare him for care giving hospital work. He would be part of our work-study program, allowing him to work part time in our institution to pay for his studies. Our program is year around and semesters begin in June and January.

We look forward to receiving him as soon as he can enroll.

Sincerely,

Dr. Alfred Baum, Director

George came alongside his son. The stunned look on Rudy's face alarmed him. "Rudy, Rudy, what is it? Bad news? Jacob or Katherine in Dakota? Are they all right?"

Rudy puffed and gasped for breath. "No, Vater, not bad news. Good news. Great news for me." Rudy turned toward his father, looked at his creased and aged face. Rudy's soaring joy plummeted to earth. He'd mentioned nothing to his father of his plans, afraid of the reaction he'd get. Why risk upsetting him if it all came to nothing. But the nothing had now become something and he could no longer hide his intention.

"Vater, let's go inside and I'll explain it all." Rudy followed his father into the kitchen and pulled out a chair for his father to sit. Then he sat across from him with his letter before him.

"Vater, I'm not sure where to start…"

George shrugged, "Why not just tell me what's in the letter?"

"No, that would confuse things…. Vater, you know the last months before Mutti died? You know how I would massage her back and bring her relief? And how now I can crack your neck and make it feel better?"

"Yah, I know all this but what does that…?"

"These things made me think about what I might do with my future."

"Your future? But you are here with me. We work in the fields, take care of the animals, tend the garden."

"Yes Vater, but, but I'm looking at my calling."

"Calling? What are you saying? You want to leave me? Leave Freidorf?"

"The Russian law says the youngest son gets the land, but since we have no land I need to learn a profession, I need to—"

"The Russians? We are Germans and you need to stay here and take care of me."

"What? What do mean?" Rudy had never imagined his father needing care. He definitely never imagined caring for him.

"You're the youngest. That's your responsibility." George shrugged as though this were self-evident

Rudy was flummoxed. "Who decides this? Since when—?"

George threw out his arms. "Since when? Since always. This is the custom. The oldest follows his father's footsteps and the youngest takes care of his parents."

Rudy felt his face burn and his chest tighten. He never confronted his father, but these words, these ideas were absurd. He desperately tried to lower his voice.

"Vater, Vater, this makes no sense. Jacob and Elizabeth, they left. Your grandparents left Germany to come here. Why can't I—"

George shook his head. "Jacob and Elizabeth were in the middle, I was in the middle. Those of us in the middle must find our own way in the world. But the oldest and the youngest, their futures are set."

Rudy sat back, smacked in the face by a tradition as rigid and rough as a pine plank. He mentally visited the many families he knew in Freidorf. He trembled as he realized that his father was right: the oldest son inherited the farm, the youngest tended the parents in their old age and the others fended for themselves. How did I not see this? Why was this never mentioned?

"But Vater, you had no farm to give to Junior."

George winced at this reminder. "But he is a farmer, like I was. And when Elvira's father dies, the farm will be his."

Rudy grabbed at this straw. "You see, already this custom is broken. Elvira's brothers all left for Dakota." He set his jaw and did his best to sound resolute. "Junior and his family can take care of you. I am going to leave Freidorf."

George snorted. "And where will you go? Will you beg in the streets of Odessa? No one is going to hire a soft German boy."

Rudy ignored his father's caustic words and held up the letter. "I am going to Treysa, near Frankfurt and I'm going to become a deacon."

"A deacon? Treysa? Who put such ideas into your head?"

Rudy breathed deeply and pretended to reread the letter. He looked up and tried to meet his father's gaze. "After Mutti died, Herr Pastor wrote a letter to the Hephata Deacon Training Program in Treysa and recommended me for—"

George sputtered, "Pastor Berger? Pastor Berger did this? Wasn't he the one who taught you the 4th commandment? You do remember it, don't you? Or have you already forgotten?"

Rudy leaned back in his chair and tried to avoid his father's sarcastic, venomous words. But they seared his heart and he could feel tears accumulating in his eyes and shouts clamoring to burst from his chest. Before saying or doing something he would regret, he leapt up, spun out the door and began to run out of town. As he pounded on the dirt road the words of the fourth commandment in Luther's Catechism thundered in his ears.

Thou shalt honor thy father and thy mother that it may be well with thee and thou mayest live long upon the earth.
What does this mean?--We should fear and love God that we may not despise nor anger our parents and masters, but give them honor, serve, obey, and hold them in love and esteem.

His lungs bellowed, his feet pounded on the dirt road and the tears skimmed off his face as he ran into the wind. If he could have sworn at his father, perhaps he'd have felt better, if he could have cursed God maybe his anguish would have diminished. But these options were taboo in his world and so he ran and ran until his legs were leaden. His run turned to a shuffle. His thoughts whimpered. *I'm trapped. God's word, my traditions--I've been snared. I can't escape.*

He slogged along the road, up a small rise, until he reached the low white picket fence surrounding the Lutheran cemetery. He stopped and turned around. Greening fields swept back toward the village. The church steeple stood guard over the cluster of houses. To his right lay the hills that bordered Freidorf. The day was peaceful and quiet, except for the rasping of Rudy's breath and the raging turmoil in his mind. *Freidorf, the village of freedom...my prison.*

A sound floated across the fields from the town a half mile away. Someone's hound yelped in pain. Helen's words from a week ago pummeled his brain. 'You lay down like a whipped dog.'

But how can I stand up against God and custom? How can I say no to

Vater? Rudy tipped back his head and gazed into the pale blue bowl that rested lightly upon the emerald landscape. His legs carried him through the cemetery gate and down the path between the stone markers. The dirt on his mother's grave had sunk after the first spring thaw. A simple granite headstone now marked her resting place. Rudy remembered how hollow her face was in those last months, how her eyes held the only sign of life.

Didn't Mutti say I have a gift? Doesn't Herr Pastor teach that all gifts and talents are God-given and should be used for His glory? The eddying thoughts buffeted him. His frantic breathing slowed even as his confusion grew. He trudged back toward town, his mind in a haze. He passed his home and the church and on the far edge of the village, moving as one in a trance, he knocked on the sturdy door of Junior's house. Elvira opened the door.

"Rudy, what a surprise." When he stood unmoving before her, her voice tightened with concern. "Are you all right? Has something happened to your father?"

Rudy vigorously shook his head. "No, no. Nothing like that. But, well, maybe I…. I need to talk to Junior."

At that moment, Herman and Betty scampered across the room, exuberantly shrieking. They adored their uncle Rudy and ran into his arms. He grabbed first Herman then Betty and tossed them into the air. They giggled and each grabbed an arm and led him into the kitchen. Rudy smelled the rich warm scent of baking bread and waves of hunger and longing for his mother swept over him. How often he'd been greeted by that scent when he'd returned from school and sat with her as they ate a slice thick with creamy butter.

Elvira followed them into the kitchen and Rudy sat at the table. "Junior will be in for lunch in a few minutes. He was getting the seeder ready to plant wheat. Would you like some tea? Or, wait…"

She called to Betty and spoke softly to her. The girl smiled and nodded then ran out of the kitchen door. Rudy sat in a cloudy stupor and paid no attention to the creak that meant the root cellar was being opened. But then little Betty walked across the room toward him, smiling and holding a mug of beer as though it were a great treasure. His emotional fog began to lift and he grinned as she proudly handed him the glass.

Elvira chuckled as Rudy gulped down the golden brew. "We don't usually drink beer at noon. But I had a feeling you needed some stronger medicine."

Rudy sighed as the beer warmed his stomach and massaged his cramped

48

muscles. Elvira was washing vegetables with little Herman standing on a stool helping her. Betty was carefully setting out plates on the table and humming to herself. Rudy's chaotic thoughts cleared as though a crystalline mountain river overpowered a sluggish muddy stream.

Freidorf is no prison. Life can be blessed here, IS blessed here. For those who embrace its rhythms, make peace with its fickle weather, sink roots deep into its soil, this place is home.

Rudy smiled as Elvira and Herman giggled and elbowed each other at the sink. The anxious band around his chest snapped and he breathed in the sumptuous aromas of a farm house kitchen. The sweet current of a long-denied conviction sluiced to the surface of his thoughts.

I was born in this place but I was not born for this place. If I leave, no WHEN I leave, I'm not escaping prison nor abandoning home. When I leave, I'll be on my way to discover the home God has in mind for me. I'm not running away, I'm running toward my future.

*　　　　　*　　　　　*

Junior and Rudy were sitting outside on the stone steps digesting their lunch. On the lilac bushes bordering the porch, the pale purple blossoms hung limp in the midday sun. The barnyard chickens had all retreated to the shade and were clucking softly in their sleep.

Elvira had insisted the men eat first and discuss later, away from the ears of the children. Rudy had seldom discussed anything with Junior, partly because Junior looked so much like Vater, only younger and better fed. Also, because of their twelve-year age difference, Junior seemed more like an uncle than a brother. But this was a momentous family matter, so Rudy poured out the entire story of his plans, along with his father's reaction. Junior did not interrupt or do anything more than gently nod when Rudy told of George's rage. Rudy ended his story with a deep breath. Junior chewed silently on his toothpick and Rudy began to wonder if his taciturn brother would ever respond. When he spoke, Rudy was stunned.

"Rudy, you can't leave this spring. I hope you see that."

"But, but why can't I leave now? I can make it for the spring semester? I've got to go, don't you understand, I--?"

Junior put his calloused hand on Rudy's knee. "Calm down, Rudy. I know you're aching to leave here. I'm not surprised at that. Didn't expect you'd work things out so quick, but I understand, I do."

"Well, then, why can't I pack up and move out?"

"Rudy, what you're not understanding is what this all means for Vater."

Against his will, a bitter whine slipped into Rudy's mouth. "Huh. He just doesn't want me to escape his prison."

"No, no, Rudy. You're only looking at all of this from your side of the fence. Sure, Vater lives by the rules of his past. Don't think it's easy to ignore those; they're in your blood and bones too. Someday you'll see. But there's more going on here. Vater is afraid."

Rudy leaned back and glared at Junior, doubt twisting his face.

"Ja Rudy, he's afraid. Vater says, 'If you go away, who'll take care of me?' But think about this: When you go away, who will Vater take care of? For over thirty years he's been sweating and working to make a life for his family. Mutti is gone and now you want to leave. Who will he live for then?"

"But I can't stay here, I can't." Rudy shifted anxiously on the steps.

"I know, I know, you're ready to bolt like a jackrabbit. But you've got to slow down. You've got to give Vater some time to swallow and digest all this news."

Rudy drew a breath in protest, but before he could utter a word Junior stood and looked down at his young brother with a grin on his face.

"Tell me, got enough money to travel to this town in Germany?"

Rudy turned his face toward the chicken scratched dirt at his feet. "Not exactly. I was wondering if you…"

"Ach no, Rudy. You'll need to pay your own way for your own journey." Junior reached down, grabbed Rudy's arm and pulled him up. The two stood looking out toward the field beyond the fence: brown, soft earth, open and waiting to be planted. Junior began walking toward his seeder and Rudy followed.

"Rudy, here's what we can do. I'll talk to Vater, do my best to convince him that Elvira and I will be here for him, tell him that whatever happens he'll have a place with us. Then you'll ask him, not tell him Rudy, you'll ask him if he'll let you hire out to other farmers for haying and harvest. He'll have some weeks to think about that. If he says 'yes', you should be able to make enough money for your trip by the end of summer."

Junior stooped and began tightening the bolts on the seeder hitch. Rudy stood nervously shuffling his feet.

"And what if he says 'no'?"

Junior looked up and grinned at his brother. "Well, then I guess we'll have to find another way to get you on the train to Germany! Think positive, Rudy and try not to see Vater as your enemy."

Rudy walked back through the town. The beer, the dinner with family, and Junior's words had all served as a balm to his scorched young soul. He walked with a lighter tread. He pledged himself to patience in his dealings with his father. Nonetheless, as he walked, he began to rehearse the request he needed to make to his father. When he asked his father's permission to hire out his labor for others, what would he say? What would the next months bring? A declaration of war or a season of peace?

*   *   *

Late September was a golden season in south Russia. The spring and summer hay cuttings were safely stored in barns or in pillowy stacks outside, the grain was all harvested and either sold or in sacks waiting to be milled into flour, the nights whispered of the winter to come but the days still shouted summer. Rudy pressed the last of his shirts into the battered valise that only a couple of years ago had carried his mother's clothes into the hospital in Odessa. As he tied shut the small suitcase, he sighed with relief that the uneasy truce of the past four months was nearly over.

In the middle of May, he'd finally approached his father and asked for permission to work for others. He'd not been met with a volley of stinging words. Vater had glared at him, muttered under his breath, then cleared his throat and proffered, what for Rudy was the second most feared response, "We'll see." Neither fight nor flight, but wait: a dire test of Rudy's pledge to patience.

For the next two weeks, the house was home to a brooding stillness. The atmosphere was charged as though a thunderstorm lurked beyond the horizon. George and Rudy worked together in garden and field and spoke only when needed. At home, George sunk into gloomy silence and Rudy hardly dared speak lest he inadvertently offend his father.

One evening, as they finished their supper, George pushed his soup bowl to one side, put both elbows on the table and leaned forward. Rudy's throat tightened with fear and anticipation. George spoke and his voice was husky; from disuse or from emotion, Rudy couldn't tell.

"Junior and I, we've talked about your plans. We think it would be best if…" George coughed and Rudy's heart stuttered. "We think it would be best if you stayed here until the harvest is over. You can hire out to work. At the end of summer, if you have enough money, you can travel up to Germany. But it will have to be your money."

Rudy choked down the joyful, relieved shout that filled his chest. He remembered Junior's words and recognized how much these words were costing his father. He dared not gloat. He lifted his eyes, glassy with tears. "Thank you Vater, I am so grateful."

With that, the tension ebbed out of the atmosphere. The two now talked about the events and doings of the town, the gossip from the neighbors. As the days grew hotter and haying season began, Rudy dared to tell his father the gossip about the other farmers he was working for and even how much money he was making. But around the topics of leaving, of traveling, of forging a new life, around anything beyond the end of harvest, a tall, dark wall had been built. They declared a truce and the truce had held.

And now at last the day had arrived. Rudy stood in the doorway of the house where he'd been born and lived his entire nineteen years. If he'd been a few years older he might have turned around and swept his eyes over the solid furniture, the faded pictures on the wall, the marks on the door frame marking the heights of all the Heupel children. He might have tried to take a mental photograph of it all. But he was nineteen so without a backward glance he stepped out into the sunshine.

Junior waited for him in his wagon, ready to carry him to Emmental to catch the train. Rudy would have liked to ride a boat up the Danube, retracing in reverse the journey his great grandparents had made a century earlier. But that trip was slow and his summer wages couldn't stretch to cover the cost. He barely had enough to pay for a seat on the train. The rail line ran from Odessa to Hamburg was over 1000 miles. He would embark at nearby Emmental, and after a three-day journey, disembark at Frankfurt, Germany. He hadn't yet worked out how he would traverse the eighty-five miles north from Frankfurt to Treysa, but this morning that detail could not derail his excitement. He'd face that challenge when the time came. His confidence was as bountiful as the fall's harvest.

"Endlich! [Finally!] There he is." A laugh went up from the people surrounding Junior's wagon. These sorts of farewells from Freidorf were usually quiet, reserved affairs, marked with melancholy; mostly composed of young men off to serve in the Russian army, or of entire families leaving for another continent. Not so today. Pastor and Frau Berger stood chatting with George; Helen and Paul were teasing Junior's little Herman; Betty clung to her mother Elvira's hand. Rudy's throat tightened and he felt the threat of tears behind his eyes.

"Such a send-off party. Thanks for being here." He tossed his valise into the wagon. Trying to keep his tears at bay, he hurried to say his goodbyes.

Elvira kissed him on both cheeks and squeezed his arms, "Rudy, you make sure and take care of yourself. Get a warm coat, it's cold up there." He smiled and nodded because he didn't trust his voice.

Betty and Herman stood before him with outstretched arms. He grabbed his nephew, tossed him into the air and then hugged him until the little boy grunted. "You be good now and don't tease your sister, OK?" Herman laughed and ran behind his mother's legs.

Rudy picked up Betty and as he hugged her, she leaned back and said, "When will you come back?" Rudy grinned. "I haven't even left yet and you're wanting me to come back. We'll see how long it takes to me to finish my training. Maybe by then you'll be a big girl." She giggled as he set her back onto the packed dirt of the roadway.

"Rudy, we're proud of you and we'll keep you in our prayers." Pastor Berger shook his hand and Frau Berger held out a brightly wrapped package and spoke with tears in her voice, "This Bible comes from your church family. Keep reading it. Find a church in Germany." She kissed his cheek as she murmured, "God bless you, Rudy."

Rudy's resolve was fading and his eyes were filling with tears. He turned to Paul and Helen. Paul slapped his hands onto Rudy's shoulders and gave him a sideways grin, "Now don't go all weepy on us like some girl."

"Hey, not fair," Helen laughed as she wiped the tears that trickled down her cheeks. "You better study hard, Rudy. We're counting on you." She gave him a quick kiss on the cheek and whispered, "I'll miss you, please write to me."

The three friends shared a quick embrace, then Rudy turned to his father. George's eyes were dry, his face sober, and he held out his strong, sun-darkened hand and gripped Rudy's hand until it trembled.

"Be careful, son. Do a good job." He released his grip, inhaled and murmured as he released his breath, "Make your mother proud."

Rudy could only nod, dared only whisper, "I will, Vater. I will. And thank you, thank you."

He scrambled up onto the wagon seat beside Junior who slapped the reins and set the wagon rolling before anyone could see Rudy's tears, tears composed in equal measure of relief, sadness, and joy. That composition might have changed had Rudy been able to gaze into the future. Never again would he see any of those people whose smiling faces sent him on his way. Never again would he return to South Russia, in fact the entire region would change hands. And, never, ever again would Freidorf be his home.

But Rudy could not see beyond his present moment. He had not even the faintest intimation of the trials and triumphs, the delights, sorrows and, strife that awaited him in Germany.

PART TWO-GERMANY

SEPTEMBER 1912, ON THE TRAIN

Rudy closed his eyes and rested his head against the train car's window. The afternoon sun beams permeated his eyelids, he smiled in their orange glow and remembered when he was ten years old.

He and Paul had invented a new game. The spring melt had turned the little creek into a surging river. The two boys sat on a flat rock above the stream where the banks narrowed and forced the gushing waters into a narrow pass. The restricted waters formed an eddy that swirled near the bank beneath the two boys. They each had gathered a pile of sticks and now took turns tossing a stick into the whirlpool. They counted how many circuits each stick made in the eddy before being shunted to the shoreline, where it was doomed to bob listlessly in the backwater. The stick making the most orbits was the winner. But occasionally, a stick would surprise them. Instead of circling until shoved to shore, the audacious little twig would slip out of the eddy, shoot out into the rushing waters and zoom downstream. The boys would watch it disappear and delightfully imagine its wild ride into the unknown.

Rudy sat back in his seat, took a deep breath and slowly let it seep from his lungs. The adrenaline from the goodbyes and the rush to the train ebbed away and a delicious lassitude wrapped itself around him. He was on his way, riding joyfully to his future.

"Excuse me, young man."

Rudy's eyes snapped open. A thin man with a shock of gray hair stood in the aisle, gazing down at him through thick lenses that gave his eyes a bulging, fish-eye appearance.

"My sleeping berth is not yet ready. It looks as though we must share a seat for a few hours." He spoke Russian and Rudy responded in Russian.

"Yes, sure. Please sit down."

The man took off and folded his long gray coat, sat down, then set his black briefcase on the floor between his feet. He extended a gloved hand.

"My name is Misha."

Rudy shook it and answered, "Rudolph."

Misha examined Rudy through his round spectacles.

"So, young man, how far north are you going? All the way to your homeland?"

Rudy's face fell and he gave his seat mate a sad grin. "Has my accent betrayed me?"

"Your Russian is excellent. No, it's not your tongue, it's your clothes."

Rudy protested. "My clothes? But I bought them in the store owned by a Russian"

The gentleman laughed. "They're fine and I'm sure no one else would notice. But I'm a clothes buyer for the big stores in Odessa and I know what sorts of styles and fashions the German colonies prefer. Therefore, I guessed. And I guessed right, I think."

Rudy laughed, relieved that he hadn't simply been marked as a country rube. "You're right. I'm from the Freidorf colony."

The man nodded in satisfaction and settled back in his seat. The rattle of the car muffled the chatting of the other passengers and Rudy thought their own conversation was over, but the clothes buyer spoke again.

"I'm on my way to Krakow to examine some of the fabrics and styles that are being sold there. How about you?" Now he spoke in German with no trace of a Russian accent.

Rudy was eager to share his news. "I'm going to a training center north of Frankfurt. I'm seeking a profession in the health field." He was exhilarated by how adult he sounded.

"Ahh, that sounds ambitious. Excellent. And you are going at the right time. Though I suppose some might say you're jumping from the hot kettle onto the cook stove itself. "

Rudy blinked in confusion. The gentleman dismissingly waved a gloved hand.

"Ach, an old expression from my grandmother. 'From trouble to bigger trouble.' But excuse me. I'm just spewing out my own grim thoughts."

"But, from trouble to bigger trouble? I don't understand." An anxious mist began to creep over the dreamy landscape of Rudy's imagined future.

Misha turned his head away, then turned his magnified eyes back to Rudy and spoke softly. "Look, you're traveling to a new place with great hopes, I can see that in your face. I imagine your soul is bursting with expectations. Don't let an old fool like me spoil that for you."

The train rattled forward as Rudy felt the anxious mist thicken. His first instinct was to close his mind to anything that might threaten his rosy dream. But his German blood and Lutheran faith told him that life's darkness could never be avoided. At last, he sighed and spoke.

"I think…I think I should know what troubles you see, both behind and ahead of me."

Misha shrugged. "Well, I don't know how things are in your town, but in much of south Russia, the temperature of the blood is rising among the Russian peasants who are against the German farmers. Even the landed Russians think the Germans are buying up too much land, and have too many privileges."

Rudy protested. "But I …our family has no land, only an acre around our house."

Misha shrugged. "Well, the fever that is rising may never infect your town. But it is contagious and affects everyone who is German. Who knows how fast or far it will spread? I only can tell you what I see and hear in on the streets of Odessa."

The anxious mist hovering over Rudy's dreams was now congealing into a brooding thundercloud. He'd never thought of faraway governments or the hot passions of entire groups. Though he was intelligent and knew his geography, he was a small-town product and could not help but see the entire world as like an extension of his known world into larger spaces. What sort of future was he rushing toward?

"But, sir, Germany, you don't hear about Germany on the streets of Odessa, do you?"

"No, of course not, or at least not very much. But we have newspapers in Odessa and they report that there are stirrings within Germany's people, feelings against the government, some unrest because of the Kaiser's preferential treatment of the military, some business with the French in Africa, and then of course the stock market crash in Berlin earlier this month."

Misha saw the concern pooling in Rudy's eyes and hastened to add, "But I'm sure this has not much to do with the daily life of the people. I'm sure it would never affect your school or your training. You probably don't even know what the stock market is. This is all just news of the day. Newspapers must fill their pages with something you know. Please, don't be upset. I'm sorry I mentioned this. You must look forward with hope."

Misha stooped and pulled a newspaper from his briefcase, a signal that the conversation was over. Rudy sat silently and watched the sun slowly pull night's gray blanket over the passing plains. He stared out into the darkness and considered the reality to which he'd been blind: not all troubles were personal, not all conflicts were familial. He was stepping into a much vaster world, a world where everyone could be buffeted by storms of protest, anger, resistance and rebellion. As the train clattered northeastward, he never could have imagined what tempests he would encounter in the land of his forefathers.

*   *   *

Rudy's growling stomach roused him. Sometime after dark his seatmate had left for the sleeper car and Rudy had lain down on the leather seat that smelled of every bottom that had ever sat upon it. He'd been exhausted but his mind had churned—bright dreams now mixed with brooding dreads. He'd pulled up his legs and pillowed his head on his arms and doubted he'd be comfortable enough to sleep. But the rhythmic clicking of the wheels on the tracks had managed to rock him into a fitful rest. Now his stomach rumbled, the pale light of morning filled the train car, and he imagined he smelled food.

He sat up, began to stretch, then gasped at the vista flashing past his window. Freidorf nestled on south Russia's plains—largely treeless, softly rolling fields. Yesterday they'd traveled northwestward across that terrain. This morning trees streaked past the train and in the gaps between their trunks Rudy could see purple peaks stretching into the brightening sky. He sat mesmerized. The train seemed to be traveling at lightning speed.

As he zoomed forward into this beautiful morning, his thoughts slipped back to his first train ride: how sick his mother had been, how overcome he'd been with panic. He smelled again her medicinal breath as she leaned against the cloudy window of the train car. It struck him that he'd registered nothing of the countryside they'd traveled through that day on their way to Odessa. He wondered at how a person's inner thoughts and feelings could dominate and dampen one's senses.

His stomach growled again and overpowered his musing. Thought gave way to physical need. From the valise beneath his seat he pulled out the brown grease-soaked paper bag that held the bread and sausage he hoped would last until he reached his destination. He chewed and watched as a few of the other passengers moved forward toward the dining car. A kitchen on a train, tables with tablecloths and plates— he decided he had to see this marvel for himself. He finished his breakfast, tucked the bag back into his valise, wiped his hands with his handkerchief, and lurched forward to the door at the front of the car.

He passed through two cars and opened the door to the delicious smells of toast and coffee. Before he even had a chance to savor the sights of this spectacle, he was met by a bow tied, white shirted, portly man who sniffed like a portentous hound.

"Good morning, ahem…'sir'. Do you have a reservation?"

Rudy stammered, "No, I was just..ah, sorry, excuse me."

He began to back out when a bass voice, soft yet commanding said, "Bring the young man to our table, please."

Without turning around the maître d' sighed, "Of course, Herr Einstein."

He stiffly waved his arm to Rudy, "Please be seated."

Rudy hesitated, but the slight mustached gentleman and a smiling woman gestured to him and he slowly sat down on the velvet cushioned chair. The man was dressed in a dark suit and tie and the woman wore a light blue dress with a large lace collar.

"You look hungry. We've already exceeded our stomach's capacity. Here is toast and an egg. My name is Albert, and this is Mileva, my wife. And you are?"

"Rudy, ah Rudolph Heupel." Rudy slowly pulled the plate of food toward him.

"Heupel, a south German name, isn't it?" The man asked.

Rudy nodded, chewed then swallowed. "I think so, but I was born in south Russia."

The woman spoke German with an accent Rudy could not identify. "That name 'Heupel'…did you know it means 'bold thinking mind'?"

The man chuckled and nudged his wife, "Mileva, if that is true, then your name should be Heupel. How did you ever come across that bit of information?" Then turning to Rudy he asked, "So, how long have you been traveling?"

"One full day."

Then the man asked, "What changes have you noticed?"

Rudy thought the question peculiar but tried to answer. "Well, the countryside has obviously changed. My homeland is all open plains. This morning I woke up to trees and I have the feeling that we're moving faster than we were yesterday. Everything seems to be flying past our windows."

The man leaned forward, propped his elbows on the table and a new eagerness entered his voice. "Now, if you are a truly a quick and a bold thinker, surely you can tell me what gives you this feeling."

Rudy's mind, still groggy from his fitful sleep, cringed at this challenge.

"Albert, there's no need to quiz this boy. He's not one of your students."

The woman shook her head in annoyance.

The man barely noted his wife's complaint, and as impatient teachers are wont to do, quickly answered his own question. "Yesterday, when you left south Russia, your eyes were focused on the vast, distant plains and it took a long time to note any changes. Today, your eyes focus on the nearby trees that flit across your window. Your view changes so rapidly that you conclude the speed has increased, when in fact the train's velocity is the same. Everything, even time is relative so—."

"Enough of your lecture, Herr Professor." Mileva stretched out a hand and touched Rudy's arm. "Excuse my husband, Rudy, he can't stop thinking about time and velocity and all things physical. Please, eat this good food before it goes to waste."

She sat back, stared out of the window and murmured, "The answer is not simply a matter of physics but also a matter of the mind and heart. When I traveled in Serbia, my home country, I paid little attention to what was around me because it was all familiar. But when I am traveling to a new place, where everything is different, then I try to absorb it all, drink it all in with my eyes and ears and nose. My senses are overwhelmed, it all slips by too fast." She turned to Rudy and her eyes held sadness and concern. "Are you going to a new place? Beginning a new life?"

This breakfast and strange conversation were discomfiting Rudy. He merely nodded in response to her question.

"Then, be prepared to be overwhelmed. At least at first. Everything will seem to rush at you. You'll be exhausted at the end of every day, simply because you are trying to drink in that new place, new people, new sights, sounds, smells…even the air will seem different." She glanced over at her husband. "Believe me, I know this first hand. I and my boys have suffered this experience many times."

The man turned his head toward the aisle and the woman returned her gaze to the trees that flew past their window. Rudy quickly swallowed the fried egg that was as chilly as the air between the couple. He pushed back his chair and stood.

"Thank you both for the breakfast and the…conversation." The couple acknowledged his departure with faint smiles before once again turning their faces away from each other. Rudy wove his way back through the cars, trying to match his steps with the swaying of the train. He slid onto his seat and shook his head, bewildered by his encounter in the dining car.

He'd tried to imagine what his life would be like in Germany but he'd never envisioned being overwhelmed and exhausted. And 'everthing is relative'? To Rudy, or to anyone who'd grown up in the confines of Freidorf, that smacked of blasphemy. He wondered what other sacred values would be challenged in the years ahead.

———

OCTOBER 1, 1912 TREYSA, GERMANY

"Even time is relative." Rudy remembered those words as his train chuffed its way toward Treysa. He'd been riding on trains for only three days yet the gentle cradle rocking and the rhythmic clacking already had become a natural part of his world. He felt as though he'd been journeying for a month.

Earlier in the day he'd disembarked in Frankfurt, found his way to the ticket window and spent three fourths of his remaining money on a ticket to Treysa.

"Three p.m., gate seven," the agent had said as he handed Rudy his ticket without looking up. Since he had two hours until departure, Rudy decided to reawaken his cramped muscles. As he walked toward the main exit of the station he gaped at the vaulted ceiling and the windows stretching three stories high. Outside he was struck by the ornate towers flanking the building's entrance. Each one stood twice as high as the church steeple back home.

In a shop tucked in the shadow of the towers, he bought a bun and piece of cheese and sat down on a bench to eat. He watched the policemen on horses patrolling the square. The horses' hooves clattered on the reddish cobblestones. He marvelled at the flurry of people crisscrossing the plaza.

He got up, arched his aching back, and strolled past the many stores that ringed the square. He lingered in front of a clothing store and was disheartened by the prices. When he looked up to check the time on the huge clock on the station front it was 2:55 p.m. Two hours had disappeared with the speed of light. Time, it seemed, was indeed relative. He'd taken his seat just in time.

Now, an hour after boarding, the train slowed and the tan brick walls of the Treysa station appeared, and with jerks and clatters, the train squealed to a halt. Steam and smoke from the engine swept over Rudy as he stepped out of the car onto the platform.

He stood for a moment, raised his nose and tested the air. A bit of smoke, a hint of pine--yes, the air did indeed smell different. He strode through the depot to the street and saw a line of carriages waiting to carry disembarking train passengers to their destinations. He approached the nearest one and asked the driver, a mustached old man with the red nose of a veteran beer drinker, "How much for a ride to the Hephata Center?"

The driver glanced at him, barely shifted his head and mumbled words that were swallowed up by the gray brush on his upper lip.

"Excuse me sir, I didn't hear you."

The old man turned and grunted, "I said, 'you sound like a Russian.'"

"No, no I'm German. I'm here to study at the Hephata Center. Please, how much?"

The man surveyed him from head to toe. "It'll cost you three marks."

Rudy wondered if it was only for him that it cost three marks. No matter. He did not have even two marks to spare. He dared to ask the sour driver one more question. "Which way to the Center?"

The man snorted and pointed his florid nose to the north. Rudy's spirit quavered at the driver's rudeness. *Does this man represent all of Treysa's citizens?* Rudy thanked the gruff man, grabbed his valise and began walking. Twice more he asked directions: first from a woman locking up the door to a dress shop and then from a young man carrying school books. Both smiled and cheerfully pointed Rudy along his way. His step and heart lightened.

The streets were lined with solid two-story houses covered in white stucco. They had dark wooden timbers that outlined the corners of the walls and made inverted vee's up to the peaked roofs. The stucco glowed in the last of the sun's fading light. An occasional carriage clattered by on the clean, gray cobblestone streets.

Within fifteen minutes he stood before a heavy, dark red-oak door, deep-set into a wall of large gray stone. Near the top of the door was a rectangular metal plate engraved with the words, "Jesus said, 'Hephata—Be Opened.' Mark 7:34". Below the plaque, affixed to the door with sturdy black bolts hung a knocker in the shape of a heart. Beneath that, in the center of the door was a black metal knob. Rudy set down his valise, took a breath so deep it lifted his shoulders. He banged the knocker twice against the solid door. He could hear his heart pounding in his ears.

The doorknob turned, the heavy door swung open, and a deep, smiling voice bellowed, "Welcome to the Hephata Deacon Training Center." The tall man threw out his arms and if Rudy hadn't picked up his valise and held it in front of him, he would have been hugged. "Come in. You must be Rudy. My name is Heinrich Siebold. I'm the Headmaster."

The headmaster was tall and thick in the middle. He reminded Rudy of a long sweet potato. When Headmaster talked, he boomed and when he smiled, he beamed. He led Rudy to the dining room and even though meal time was over, he found some potato salad for Rudy. As Rudy ate, the headmaster chattered on about fall weather and Rudy's anxiousness slowly melted. When Rudy finished his meal, Headmaster stood.

"Well Rudy, time to go the Emmaus dormitory and meet your new roommates, classmates, and I hope, friends."

They walked across the street to a three-story gray stucco building. They walked down a hall lit by a few electric lights. Rudy was impressed. Obviously, the Center had electricity day and night. Before the dormitory door was opened, Rudy heard the buzz of voices.

The buzzing ceased when the two entered and twenty faces turned their way. Headmaster threw his arm over Rudy's shoulder.

"Gentlemen, here's a new roommate who's come to take this last top bunk in the corner. He'll be your classmate when classes start in January. He's early, but we'll put him to work, won't we?"

"Oh yeah," the guys groaned and laughed.

"His name is Rudolph Heupel and he's from south Russia." The laughter died away and Rudy thought he heard a few snorts. The Headmaster continued.

"Rudy and his parents live in one of the German colonies north of Odessa. What's the name of the town?"

Rudy was tempted to drop his eyes but forced himself to look up. He pasted a lopsided smile on his face and croaked, "I'm from the great metropolis of Freidorf."

No one laughed at his joke. But a black-haired boy, about Rudy's height, strong in the shoulders and thick in the legs, rolled off his bunk and stuck out his hand.

"Hi, I'm Marvin Becker. My family lived in south Russia until two years ago. They moved to America and I came here to study. My colony was Bergdorf. Have you heard of it?"
They began talking and soon several other boys came up and introduced themselves. Most of them simply returned to what they'd been doing. Marvin pointed to the boy lying in the top bunk across from Rudy's bed. "That guy there is Vernon Steuber. If he starts snoring, just whack his big snout with your pillow."

Vernon gave Rudy a lazy grin, rolled his eyes at Marvin and snorted, "I barely get any sleep at all with you down below, dreaming of girls and shaking the bed all night long."

Then Marvin pointed to a lanky blond fellow stretched out on the bunk below Rudy's. He hadn't moved since Rudy came in, just lay there in the shadows with his hands behind his head.

"And that overly friendly, ambitious guy is Fred." Fred made no move to rise, only stared at Rudy with a peculiar smile on his face. Finally, he nodded, yawned and rolled over facing the wall. Marvin shrugged. "Fred is

Fred. Don't let him bother you."

The headmaster clapped his hands. "Gentlemen, I suggest you finish your homework and get some sleep. Remember what the Psalmist says, *I lie down and sleep; I wake again, for the Lord sustains me.*"

He turned to go and most of the boys said, "Goodnight, Headmaster." Fred, whose face was still turned toward the wall, just groaned.

Rudy stood looking up at the ladder. He feared he'd have trouble falling to sleep. Bunk beds and dormitories were novel experiences. But when he crept up the ladder and lay down, his exhausted muscles and nerves went limp and he soon felt himself melt into the straw stuffed mattress. Vernon may have snored but Rudy never heard a thing.

Treysa, Germany,
November 23, 1912
Dear Helen,

How are you? How is your family? I am fine.
Let me begin with the hardest words. 'I'm sorry.' I got your letter almost a month ago. When I left, I said I'd write to you and I didn't mean to wait two months. I could give you a list of reasons for my delay. (I know you would call them excuses?!) Instead I'll give you only one: I've simply been engulfed by this new life.

From the moment I open my eyes in the morning to my last sigh when I hit the pillow, I'm swamped by new sounds, new smells, new places, new buildings, new words, new customs, new rules...so much newness sometimes threatens to drown me. Only in the past few days I've finally started to feel like I can keep my head above water. I'm not completely exhausted at the end of every day so I'm writing my first letter, and it's to you.

I'm living in a dormitory with twenty boys. Across the field, there's a building with some female staff but that's off limits to us. The spring semester started in June and the new semester doesn't start until January. I showed up in the middle so naturally I got the leftover bed: the top bunk in the corner closest to the toilet and shower room. Every morning and evening I get to endure the noises and smells that twenty guys can make. I've gotten to know quite a few of the boys but the ones closest to being friends are Fred who has the bunk below me, and Vernon and Marvin who have the top and bottom bunks next to mine.

Even though my classes won't begin until January, I've already learned quite a bit about the Center and how it works. The Center has a huge garden and depends upon the vegetables to feed the students. I helped harvest the carrots and pack them into sand-filled crocks down in the cellar.

I picked and cleaned beets so the kitchen staff could can them. I dug and sacked the potatoes. I did all that fall garden work, just like back home. Late in the afternoons I scrub the floors in the classroom buildings so I sometimes see the professors leaving their offices and I stare at the notes on the blackboards.

One day I was sent to help clean the surgery room in the hospital. So much shiny equipment, sinks and tables and lights. In one of the classrooms there's a complete skeleton all held together with wires, standing on a pedestal. The first time I walked in I almost dropped my bucket of soapy water. It's amazing how many bones we have in our bodies. My fingers itched and I longed to touch every bone.

Well, I could write another ten pages. I could tell you more about the guys who are my buddies and how Fred has somehow become one of my best friends here in Treysa. But my eyelid muscles are weakening so I will close and leave some stories for my next letter.

I miss your smile and our conversations. You always helped me see things in bigger and better ways. I hope you are finding good use for your great energy and intelligence. Say hello to Paul and the rest of our gang.

Thank you for your letter and thank you for being my friend. Please greet your family from me.

God's blessings, Rudy

DECEMBER 3, 1912 TREYSA, GERMANY

"That preacher rattles on worse than the Treysa streetcar. I thought Professor Schatz was bad, but that guy—Whew." Fred whistled his disgust.

He, along with Rudy, Marvin and Vernon had just left the big downtown church where they'd sat through an hour-long Sunday evening Advent service. Vernon laughed and said, "Oh yeah. Taka-taka-taka-taka." Marvin hooted at his bunkmate's streetcar imitation.

Rudy, whose idea it had been to go to this special worship service, laughed along with the rest but said nothing. In Freidorf, the beginning of the Christmas season was always marked with reverent holiness and joyful anticipation. For the past two months, he'd been too busy to miss his home.

But as December began, he realized his spirit was yearning for that sense of transcendent wonder which had always been part of this season for him and his family. When he'd learned of the Sunday evening Advent celebration, he convinced his buddies to join him.

Sadly, the entire worship service in the cold cathedral had been stiff, formal and lifeless. Everyone seemed to be merely fulfilling an obligation. The preacher never attempted to speak to the heart. Rudy was not only embarrassed for dragging his friends out into the night but felt dejected and soul hungry. Yet the whispered voices of his parents and his heritage would never allow him to criticize one of God's ministers. That's why he appreciated Fred's observation. Fred said what Rudy scarcely allowed himself to think. It was Fred's audaciousness that always captivated Rudy.

That allure had started in early October, during the first week of his life in Treysa. Rudy had been out in the Center's garden digging up potatoes when Fred appeared.

"Hey Roosky, mind if I join you?"

Rudy looked up at his bunkmate's smirking face, then stomped his spade into the dirt with a grunt. "My name is Rudy... and I'm German. Aren't you supposed to be in class?"

Fred shoved his spade into the dirt next to the dead potato stalks in the row across from Rudy. "Ach, old Baldy, Professor Bachmann was lecturing about statistics but everything he said was right in the textbook. I thought, 'why should I have to sit there and listen to stuff I can read about and probably will never need?' So, I started talking out loud and laughing until he got pissed off and kicked me outta class."

In his entire life, Rudy had never been kicked out of a classroom. He'd been bored, sleepy, and frustrated but he'd never even imagined purposely trying to get booted out by a teacher. He didn't know how to relate to someone who apparently did not worry about the approval of teachers, or, it seemed, of anyone else. He was confused. Should he object to or admire his bunkmate's attitude? Strangely, he wanted to do both.

"Come on Roosky, I bet I can dig more taters than you!" Fred grunted and began shoveling and dumping potatoes into the bushel baskets.

Rudy ignored the slur and began digging as furiously as he could. For fifteen minutes they flung dirt like a pair of frantic badgers and pitched potatoes into their baskets. Rudy kept glancing at Fred, hoping he'd soon tire but Fred's wiry arms kept working like pistons. Just as Rudy was about to drop, Fred whooped, tossed his shovel into the air, and flopped onto the ground.

"Woowee, good diggin' Roosky!"

Rudy dropped to the ground alongside Fred. Muscles exhausted, bathed in sweat and coated in dirt—he'd left Freidorf to escape all of that. But at that moment, lying in the soft dirt of the potato patch, smiling up into the October sky, he had felt at home.

Now, six weeks later, as he and his friends walked home from church on this first Sunday of December Rudy smiled to himself at that October memory. Those crisp sunny fall days had disappeared into the clouds and drizzle of November and two weeks ago Treysa had its first snowfall of the season.

"Look out below!" shouted Vernon as he launched a snowball straight up into the air. The boys scattered as the icy sphere splatted onto the sidewalk.

Marvin hooted, "Better watch out or Rudy the Snowball King will attack!"

With a whoop, Rudy scooped up a handful of snow and dashed after Vernon. For the past two weeks, his dorm mates had jokingly bowed to him and intoned, "Greetings oh great Snowball King!" Fred had dubbed him with that name after one of their misadventures.

That first snow had fallen on a Friday night in mid-November. The young men awoke to a landscape painted with a crisp new palette. The dismal, murky clouds had evaporated and been replaced by an intense blue sky. The grays and browns of autumn, cobblestone streets, dull rooftops— all were now covered with a coat of crystalline white. The leafless tree branches were etched in ivory.

As the young men gazed at their transformed world they were carried back to their carefree, exuberant boyhood. But this morning, as on all Saturday mornings at the Center, was set aside for cleaning the dorms and the bathrooms. On this first snowy morning of the year the boys laughed, teased and splashed and scrubbed their way through the work.

At the lunch table, while his jaws worked on his schnitzel, Fred announced to his tablemates, "Guys, this afternoon let's go to the Witch's Tower. Whaddya say?"

Though their mouths were stuffed, Vernon and Marvin vigorously nodded their approval. Rudy wondered if he'd heard right. Witches? His thoughts fluttered back to his hometown where some of the brauchers had been called witches. His own mother had suggested he was a braucher. A chill crept into his chest, but he tried to sound merely curious.

"Witch's Tower? What the heck is that?"

"It's an old stone tower in the south part of town. They say it's about thirty-five feet high. I bet the view from up there would be great today." Fred's enthusiasm had already infected the other two boys.

Rudy held back. "But why is it called the 'witch's tower'?"

Fred swiped his hand in dismissal. "Ach, four or five hundred years ago, some woman was thrown into the dungeon that's in the bottom of the tower."

Rudy risked another question, "But why was she called a witch?"

Fred shrugged, "Who knows? Maybe she tried to turn somebody into a black cat. Maybe she gave a sick man some special tea and he got sicker and died. Hell, maybe she had red hair, red lips and got caught in bed with the mayor." The other boys roared at Fred's effrontery. Rudy chuckled and tried to shake off his unease.

The boys didn't walk the three miles to the Witch's Tower. They cavorted, skipped, and frolicked down the snow-covered streets. When they reached the tower, their cheeks were red with cold but they were sweating beneath their wool coats.

The tower walls were made of irregular reddish stones; bits of plaster seemed to be splashed haphazardly in the seams. High above their heads the boys could see openings covered with weathered wood planks held together by rusted metal straps. The very top of the tower was crenelated and the four boys could imagine fierce warriors firing arrows at the enemy below. And if arrows, why not snowballs?

They scuttled around the base of the tower looking for a door. They found one but it was closed.

"Look, the bottom hinge is busted." Fred was already tugging at the weathered wood. He managed to tip the bottom edge outward. "Guys hold this out for me will ya?"

The others hesitated but Fred's look of disdain cracked their restraint and they held onto the heavy door as Fred scooted inside the tower. One by one they entered, with Rudy entering last as the other three pushed the door from the inside. The boys gazed about in the silence. Light from a high-up half-shuttered window lit the circular room. The air was stale and as cold as an icebox. A worn stone stairway hugged the wall, disappearing upward through a hole in the first ceiling twelve feet above them.

"C'mon guys." Fred had no patience for observation. He began climbing the smooth steps and the others followed him. They were all puffing by the time they reached the top. They leaned against the wall, puffing their frosty breath into the azure sky. Fred had been right. The view was spectacular. Sun rays sparkled and danced off the glistening rooftops. The snow on the tops of the furrows in the distant fields had already begun to melt, giving them a striped zebra look. The pine trees' bold green branches sliced sharply into the snowy backdrop.

"OK. Let's see who's got the strongest arm." Fred was already packing a snowball, squeezing out as much fluff as possible. He took two steps away from the wall, then ran and flung his missile. The four watched it arc out and down and splat onto the street below. Vernon and Marvin formed their own icy projectiles and whipped them out into the air, but they fell short of Fred's mark.

"Rudy, you're our last hope. Give it all ya got." Rudy squeezed with both gloved hands until his ball was nearly ice. It felt solid and heavy. He backed up, took two steps forward and hurled his ball. The boys watched it arcing out and out; and then, before they could even gasp in horror, they saw a black vehicle crawling on the street toward the plummeting missile. Thwack! Even from their aerie they could hear the impact. Then they saw a hole in the fabric ceiling, the vehicle wobble and slide sideways into a small tree.

"Christ, Rudy, you hit a motorcar." Fred gasped in admiration.

"It was an accident, an accident." Rudy sputtered.

Three people emerged from the car, wiping snow off their clothes and examining the damage to their canvas roof.

"Get back," hissed Marvin. "They're looking up here. If they catch us, we'll be in deep…"

"Time to run," Fred whispered gleefully and dashed for the stairwell. The others followed him and skittered down the stairs faster than was safe.

"Hurry, hurry, hurry. Hold the door." Fred was already on his hands and knees scampering under the door.

The three boys all scooted out and were holding the door up for Rudy to escape when a fur-coated man shouted, "Hey you. Stop right there."

Rudy scrambled to his feet, dared one look back at the red-faced man, then turned and galloped after his fleeing friends. The four boys took a long circuitous route back to the Center, running most of the way. They stood panting outside the entrance door, trying to laugh between their gasps.

"Whoowee! Now that was a real kick!" Fred slapped Rudy on his back. Rudy gave a wan smile. Fred was ebullient. "No, really, I haven't had so much fun since... Roosky, you dress like a Russian, your haircut looks Russian, you use German words that only my gramma uses. But you know what Roosky? You are a good shit." And then, he bowed deeply before Rudy. "And today, today I dub you the Snowball King."

So it was, that for the rest of November, every time Rudy entered the dorm, someone would shout, "hail to the Snowball King."

Now, on this first night of the Advent season, after the disappointing church service, Rudy lay in bed, staring up into the darkness, hands behind his head, contemplating the past two months. The Hephata Center's buildings and grounds now felt familiar. He knew the names of most of his dorm mates, and even though they teased him and called him 'Snowball King,' he felt they had accepted him. Only Fred continued to call him 'Roosky,' and Rudy had resigned himself to that moniker, because, as everyone knew, Fred was Fred.

He mused about his near future. He still was a month away from the start of his classes. In a few weeks, most of the students would travel home to their families for the holidays. The cafeteria would be nearly empty, the dorm would be a lonely cave. Advent was supposed to be a season of preparation and growing anticipation. But Rudy worried he would be overcome by homesickness and boredom. His worries were incredibly misplaced.

SUNDAY, DECEMBER 17, 1912 TREYSA, GERMANY

The students had escaped just in time. On Friday noon, under glowering gray skies, most of the young men and women of the Hephata Deacon Training Center had hastily packed their bags and scrambled toward the train station to go home for Christmas. That evening snow began to fall—first in huge fluffy flakes that floated like feathers, then as the temperature dropped and the wind arose, in small pellets that stung the skin. Throughout the night and into Saturday the wind had raged and the snow fallen until drifts piled high. Saturday evening the sky had cleared, the thermometer's mercury plunged, and the wind increased. In the campus courtyards, white snow dervishes spun in the brittle cold.

Sunday morning, Rudy was still dozing when Headmaster Siebold swung open the dorm door.

"This is the day that the Lord has made! Let us rejoice and be glad in it! Good morning boys." His booming voice echoed in the near empty room. Four groans emerged from beneath four different mounds of blankets. "I know its early, but we need your help. Gentlemen, isn't that what deacons do—they help?"

Heads emerged from quilts and fists rubbed bleary eyes. Rudy propped himself up on his elbows.

"This blizzard has blocked the roads. Some of our nurses and orderlies at our Krankenstation [Infirmary] won't be able to get here today. We need some muscles to help us attend to our residents."

The Infirmary was a two story, red brick building on the far corner of the campus. It was the oldest of Hephata's buildings. Rudy had never enteit, but he knew that it housed men and women with physical and mental handicaps. The headmaster stood waiting as the four boys threw aside their blankets and hastily slipped into their chilly clothes. They followed him out into the blinding white morning. Thankfully, the wind had died overnight, but the air was frigid. Rudy could feel it slice like a chill knife through his wool coat. His breath created clouds that quickly coated his thin mustache with icy crystals.

After a five-minute walk, they stepped into the Infirmary's steamy warmth.

"Gentlemen, this is Nurse Heinitz. She's your boss for today. You'll eat here in the dining room and stay as long as she needs you." Headmaster Siebold grinned and gave an exaggerated salute to the nurse before spinning around and marching back out into the cold.

Nurse Heinitz had dark hair topped by a white round hat. She was tall, and though she stood as stiff as her white starched smock, her smile was warm. "Boys, you don't know how glad I am to see you. We're very short-handed this morning. Let's get to work. Follow me."

The boys hurried to keep up with her as she led them down the hall and into a ward with dozens of beds separated by curtains. She talked as she walked.

"Our residents all have disabilities, either mental or physical or both. This ward is for men who suffer from some form of paralysis caused by different things—palsy, polio, birth defects. You need to get them into their wheelchairs and down to the dining room." She turned and winked at them.

70

"Boys I'll warn you. Some of them are cranky. It's past their breakfast time. Hurry now."

Each boy went to a curtain and pulled it aside. As Rudy slid open the white divider he was greeted with a snarl.

"About damn time. I need my coffee for Christ's sake." The skeletal man was lying on his side. Evidently someone had already tended to him this morning for he was wearing a blue shirt and a pair of loose-fitting gray trousers. Obviously, the attention had not improved his mood.

"Who the hell are you, anyway? Every damn day its someone new."

Rudy's family never swore, but he'd grown used to the rough language in the boy's dormitory. Still, he was taken aback to hear it from an old man—and in Rudy's eyes this man was certainly old.

Rudy tried to smile. "I'm Rudy and I'm here to take you to breakfast." "Well, whoever the hell you are, I guess I'm glad you're here," the man grunted, then grudgingly added, "I'm Willy. Let's eat."

Rudy helped the man sit up on the edge of the bed and through Willy's shirt he could feel a hump on his back. A wheelchair stood beneath the window and Rudy rolled it alongside the bed and lifted Willy into it. Though he appeared to be only skin and bones Willy was a dead weight in Rudy's arms. After setting the old man's feet on the rests, Rudy set off down the hall toward the cafeteria.

His eyes abruptly fixed on Willy's neck just as his hands began to tingle. Willy's head was permanently bent sideways. His right ear nearly touched his right shoulder. His neck was a white arc of stretched ligaments, muscles and skin. Rudy stared and watched his own left hand as it moved from the wheelchair handle and lay itself softly on Willy's neck.

"Hey, what're doin', you young..." Willy's sputtering protest ended in a deep sigh. "Jesus. Your hand is warm, feels damn good. Where'd you learn how to do that?"

Rudy kept pushing the wheelchair with one arm and softly massaging Willy's neck. He didn't know how to answer. He hadn't learned what he was doing, and he certainly couldn't explain how his hands seemed to have their own ability to sense pain. He finally laughed weakly. "Sir, it just looked like your neck might be a little stiff."

As they wheeled down the hall, Willy rocked his head back and forward a few inches. "Every year it gets a little stiffer. It's worse in the cold. Nice warm hands you got there. That's my table over there."

Rudy rolled the chair up to a table where three other men in wheelchairs sat slurping coffee. Before he left the old man asked, "What'd you say your name was?"

"Rudy, sir, Rudolph Heupel."

"Rudy, yes. And no need to call me 'sir'. Willy will do. Thanks Rudy. Come again tomorrow." He chuckled, "Maybe if you come earlier, I won't be such a nasty bastard."

Rudy walked back down the hall, grinning at his encounter with salty tongued Willy. He helped four more men get to breakfast. The last one was a stout man. His left arm and leg flopped uselessly as Rudy strained to get him into the wheelchair. One side of the man's face seemed frozen. His mouth chewed desperately as he tried to speak but the words were too shredded for Rudy to understand. At last the man gave a snort of disgust and surrendered to silence. Out of curiosity, Rudy touched the man's left shoulder. Instead of a tingling warmth there was a chill shiver.

"Ah, you're bringing Adolph. He's the last one to breakfast this morning." Nurse Heinitz came up alongside Rudy. "Adolph suffered a stroke five years ago that paralyzed his entire left side. His family tried to take care of him at home, but his wife passed away and his children...well, with children of their own and work, it became impossible. Lifting and moving him...he's not a small man. So now he's part of our family, aren't you Adolph." She squeezed his good hand and a smile tugged at half of his face.

Rudy pushed Adolph's chair to his table and returned to the head nurse's side. She swept her gaze around the room and murmured more to herself than to Rudy. "Our Germany...so busy building and buying and trying to prove how great it is...These little ones with feeble bodies, feeble minds... 'hide them' they say, 'remove them from our sight, so we can build our nation.' So here we are, the only home they'll ever have."

Rudy's heart felt her sigh. He thought of his distant cousin Herbert, one of the 'little ones' back in Freidorf. Herbert would never be able to read or write, his words were jumbled and he could do only the simplest of tasks. But he lived with his family and wasn't hidden from the community.

Rudy conceded that Freidorf wasn't Treysa and boisterous, busy crowded Germany wasn't south Russia. Maybe things had to be different here. He looked out over the dining room, brightly lit by the winter sun. Thirty men and women sat at tables. Some fed themselves, others were being fed by white-clad aides. Some were engaged in conversation, others slumped in silence. Though the signs of pain and brokenness were everywhere, calmness pervaded the room. The words of Jesus came unbidden to Rudy's mind. *'Come to me, all you that are weary and are carrying heavy burdens, and I will give you rest.'*

Nurse Heinitz did not let the boys linger. After breakfast, they helped move some of the residents to their rooms, others to the bathing facilities, and still others to an activity room where residents worked on knitting projects, exercised with small weights, or read books. Then the boys helped move them all back to the dining room for lunch before they sat down to their own meal.

Rudy was just using his bread to sop up the last of his potato soup when the head nurse stopped at their table and smiled.

"Boys, you've been a great help this morning. A few more of our staff people have managed to break through the snow drifts so I'm releasing you from duty. Thanks again for stepping up."

The four stood, politely bowed and thanked her for the meal, then they turned toward the entrance area to retrieve their coats. But just before leaving the dining hall Rudy paused, then turned and briskly returned to Nurse Heinitz. He stood with head lowered.

"Excuse me, Nurse. I'm not going anywhere for Christmas and I haven't started any classes so I've no homework to worry about. I was thinking… that maybe if you need any extra help for the next two weeks…"

His voice trailed off as he realized he might be overstepping some school rule or regulation. If he'd lifted his eyes, he'd not have been so hesitant. The nurse was grinning and her eyes were glittering.

"What's your name?"

"Rudy, Rudolph Heupel."

"Rudy, most of the young men avoid the Infirmary. They act as though our residents are contagious. They're afraid of their own mortality, I suppose. Of course, we can use your help here. You'll have to request permission from the headmaster, but you can tell him that I will welcome you."

"Thank you, thank you." Rudy bowed gratefully, and scurried after his friends. A half hour later he stood in Headmaster Siebold's office. The training center's leader leaned back in his chair and stretched.

"Rudy, already out of a job?" Rudy nodded and opened his mouth, but before he could speak, the headmaster continued. "So, I'll bet you're itching to start your training. You've had quite a long wait, but I've seen that you're a hard worker and dependable. You'll do fine in the classroom. Are the other boys treating you well? No fights or bullying?"

"Oh no sir. They've all been decent fellows."

"Great." He thumped his meaty fists on his desk in exclamation. "Now,

---

what can I do for you on this Arctic afternoon?"

Rudy had rehearsed his request carefully. "Nurse Heinitz says she could use some extra help; and since I'll be here for Christmas and I don't have any homework yet, I'm asking for permission to work at the Infirmary for the next two weeks."

Headmaster Siebold cocked his head in thought. "Hmmm. I was planning on setting all four of you boys to work shoveling the snow off our sidewalks. But three of them will do... And you'll surely learn new skills at the Infirmary. You probably already know how to shovel snow, right?" His boisterous laughter filled the office and Rudy nodded.

"Oh yes, sir, I've had plenty of practice with that."

"Very well. Beginning tomorrow morning, report for duty at the Infirmary."

Rudy ran back to the dormitory laughing until his teeth grew cold in the icy wind. He did not yet realize how fruitful and fateful the next two weeks would be.

CHRISTMAS EVE, DECEMBER 24, 1912 TREYSA, GERMANY

If we Lutherans honored saints, Nurse Heinitz would be the one I'd honor. Rudy smiled to himself as he lit another candle and set it on one of the dining room tables. In the previous weeks as he'd helped dress, bathe and move the residents of Infirmary, he'd listened to the complaints, laments, and grumblings from those who realized that Christmas was approaching. Only a few of them could look forward to being taken out by family for a Christmas Day dinner or worship service. Most of them knew that while their families and friends sang and feasted, they would be sitting in their rooms staring out into the gray wintery sky.

"Well, I'll be damned. It almost looks like Christmas Eve," growled a voice from the dark corridor.

"That's gotta be you Willy. You're the first one here." Rudy laughed. One of the aides rolled Willy in and set him in the space Rudy had cleared for the Christmas Eve festivities.

For two weeks, Rudy had listened day after day to the melancholy words of the residents and found himself not only empathizing with them but admitting that he shared their same sense of grief. No family, no delicious sense of mystery and delight. No warm group singing the old familiar carols.

On Wednesday it had struck him. *They can't do anything about this*

74

sadness. But I can. That night he'd written down his thoughts and the next day he shared them with Nurse Heinitz.

After glancing at his notes, she said, "Rudy, are you thinking of becoming a pastor?"

"Oh no, I'm here to study caregiving. I don't think I'm the pastor type."

She laughed. "I don't know what type that is. I'm just saying that you've put together a very nice outline here. I know the Infirmary family will love it. I'm leaving tomorrow and won't be back until January first. We'll be short staffed on Christmas Eve, but I'll leave word of your plan and make sure you have all the support you need."

Now it was Christmas Eve and Rudy rubbed Willy's neck as they both examined the scene. The small pine tree that had stood in the reception area had been moved into the dining room. Rudy and some of the residents had decorated it with colored paper, gold and silver foil and carefully placed candles. Its faint forest scent filled the room. Alongside the tree was a crude manger filled with straw that Rudy and the other boys had made the day before. A doll, provided by one of the nurses lay wrapped in a blanket atop the straw.

On the other side of the tree was a box filled with small wrapped packages. Back in Freidorf, Christmas Eve was when presents were given and received and Rudy couldn't conceive of celebrating without gifts. But as he planned for the evening festivities he'd been stymied. How and where was he supposed to find dozens of gifts? He was reluctantly preparing to relinquish his dream.

Then, at Friday morning's breakfast, he saw the cook who ran the house kitchen coming toward him. She was a short lady who rolled toward him on short legs. Her cheeks always reminded Rudy of white bread buns. She seldom smiled and when she spoke her mouth barely moved. Rudy could never read her mood. She put her hand on his arm, leaned in and spoke conspiratorially.

"Nurse Heinitz tells us you're planning on a special Christmas Eve celebration. Our staff would like to make up some small presents for everyone. Would that be all right?"

Rudy blinked, gasped and then stammered to this rotund angel, "All right? It'd be magnificent. I'm so grateful."

"We'll have them ready by noon on the 24th. Stop by the kitchen and pick them up." Without another word, she trundled back to her ovens and stoves.

True to her word Rudy had found a colorfully decorated box filled with small gifts, each one wrapped and tied with a bow. Now as the other residents came in, some walking with an aide, others being wheeled in, the room filled with soft oohs and aahs and childlike laughter.

The tables had been pushed back into a semi-circle. The candles on the tables created a friendly island of light. The residents sat with their backs to the darkness and gazed at the glowing tree and the manger.

Rudy waited for the last of the residents to arrive. He stared at the candles on the tree until his eyes blurred and his thoughts grew wings. *Vater—I wonder how Christmas will be for him? And Junior and Elvira with Betty and Herman—how excited those two little ones must be! I bet they'll eat plenty of snowball cookies tonight...Helen, Paul and the old gang...I imagine they all have parts in the church's Christmas Eve program. Jacob and Katherine in Dakota, so far away. How will they celebrate Christmas?*

A tug on his elbow brought him back to earth. "We better begin before some of them fall asleep," said the night nurse who was wheeling in a woman so bent and twisted she had to be belted into her chair.

"Yeah, sure," answered Rudy. For a moment he'd nearly forgotten that he was in charge, that this was his program. He stepped out in front of the tree, facing the three dozen men and women who'd gathered. "Merry Christmas!"

The response was a mix—some clear and emphatic 'Merry Christmas's' and many slurred, stuttered, and groaned sounds that only by a charitable leap of the imagination could be considered as 'Merry Christmas.'

Nevertheless, Rudy was moved by their enthusiasm. He began the program by leading them in the singing of familiar Christmas carols. He was amazed that Adolph and others who seldom could express a thought, sang the words without hesitation. He saw smiles on faces that he'd thought were frozen in permanent grimaces. Then he opened the Bible given to him by his Freidorf congregation.

"I've heard this story since I was a little child. I'm sure most of you have heard it before too. Here is what the gospel of Luke says about the birth of our Lord."

Rudy read the Nativity story, closed the book and dropped his eyes. He'd worked on a short message, had even practiced it out loud as he walked around the campus, but now a band of panic tightened across his chest. *Who am I to speak? I'm no preacher, just a lonely guy far from home.*

At last he dared to look up. Friendly eyes reflecting the light from tree looked to him. Hungry and expectant eyes. The band loosened as Rudy

76

sensed their need, his own need. He didn't need to worry about performing. He was not being judged. He began to speak, mixing his prepared words with the feelings flowing from his heart.

"Imagine those shepherds, out there on the hills. All the other people in Bethlehem were at home, eating a late dinner or sleeping in their nice warm beds. Most people turned up their noses at shepherds; they smelled like sheep and they were poor. And these shepherds were the nighttime shepherds and that means they were the lowest of the low. Even the other shepherds looked down on them.

"But when God's angels came to announce the coming of the Lord, who did they come to first? That's right. These poor, humble shepherds. God has a special place in His heart for the little ones, the weak and broken ones. Other people might forget about them, or turn up their noses at them, but not God. God sends angels to give them good news, the best news ever."

Rudy saw silvery tears trickling down the creased cheeks of some of the residents. He blinked his own eyes and finished his thoughts. "Many of us are far from our families tonight. Many of us feel weak or broken. Some of us feel forgotten. But God never forgets. God gives us this family right here, and sends angels who help us make it through our days. And angels who bring us gifts to remind us of the greatest gift of all."

The night nurse and her aides began to hand out the little gifts. Some residents needed help untying bows and tearing paper. Some squealed in child-like delight as they unwrapped their presents--gingerbread men trimmed in frothy white icing. The smell of fresh ginger mingled with the pine aroma.

Rudy laughingly interrupted their excitement. "Before you start eating your gingerbread, let's sing our last Christmas carol, 'Silent Night, Holy Night.'" Dozens of voices, some wavery and weak, some rusty from disuse, others little more than deep throated groans, sang the words to the familiar song. Rudy sang and was a child again, on Christmas Eve, in the Freidorf church, sitting on his mother's lap and gazing up at the sparkling pine tree stretching into heaven.

The carol ended and the nurse and her aides began wheeling their charges to bed. A few residents hobbled up to Rudy. They reached out their twisted and withered hands to grip his and they thanked him. Lydia, wispy haired, bent and frail, edged toward him with her two canes, stopped before him and murmured, "Thank you, young man, for giving us a Christmas."

Once the hall was empty, Rudy picked up wrapping papers, extinguished the candles and dragged the tables back to their places. Then he stepped out into the crisp night and walked back to his dormitory. If anyone had asked what he was feeling he'd have spoken of Christmas joy and a touch of homesickness. For a nineteen-year old young man that was as close to the truth as he could get.

But there was more. Beneath Rudy's Christmas joy lay a sense of fulfillment. When he was twelve years old, he'd helped his father make a new door for the boy's bedroom. He held the measuring tape as his father marked the boards and the locations of the hinges. He steadied the boards on the sawhorses as his father sawed. He watched his father chisel out thin slivers of wood for the face plate. He helped carry the door into the house. When his father lined up the door, slid it into place, and dropped in the hinge pins, when the knob mechanism slid smoothly into the face plate with a quiet click, Rudy experienced a shiver of accomplishment. His father had grinned in satisfaction. Click—their efforts had filled the door frame's need.

This evening's program, trimmed and shaped by Rudy had not only fit the need of the Infirmary. It satisfied Rudy at a depth he had not fully perceived, tapped into gifts he did not yet know he possessed. He walked back to the dormitory wrapped in a warm blanket of emotion. But there were layers to this blanket, concealed layers, hidden even from Rudy. They were layers that were to shape his future.

Rudy slipped into his quiet, empty dormitory and burrowed under the quilts. He thanked God for his family, prayed that their Christmas would be blessed and that God would guide him as he began his study. Then he took a deep cleansing breath and floated gently down into a contented sleep.

MAY 1, 1913 TREYSA, GERMANY

Rudy muttered without lifting his head, "Go ahead without me."

Vernon stood over Rudy's desk and watched him underlining in his text book. He poked Marvin in the ribs, "Our buddy Rudy must adore that management class."

Rudy raised bleary eyes. "Adore? More like hate. But, it's a required course so…" He shrugged and returned to his reading.

"Damn it Roosky, what's happened to you?" Fred grabbed Rudy's shoulder. "You always used to be ready for a little adventure. But lately you're as much fun as an old stick in the mud."

Rudy jerked his shoulder away. "Just leave me alone."

The three boys fell silent, unsettled by the vehemence of Rudy's response. Then Marvin quietly spoke up.

"Rudy, maybe if you take a little break the studying will go better. Always works for me."

Rudy sat back, sighed and closed his book. He grinned reluctantly up at his friends. "Okay, you win." He stood and playfully punched Fred's shoulder. "But if I fail that final test, I'll whoop your ass."

Fred hooted, "Rudolph Heupel fail a test? Ha. That'll be the day. Come on let's get going. The parade starts at 10."

Though still blocks away from the town center, the boys could hear the notes of the brass band soaring like silver birds into the cloudless blue sky. The May Day parade was just beginning as they reached the plaza. The smell of sizzling sausages and tang of sauerkraut drifted upward with the charcoal smoke.

Up the main street came three dozen chestnut horses gleaming in the bright sun. Ribbons hung from their harnesses, flower wreaths were woven about their ears. Their riders sported fiery red jackets and hats that sprouted white plumes. Marching behind the horse troop was the Treysa city choir. The crowds encircling the plaza joined in their anthem. Even Rudy and Marvin, who'd grown up in south Russia, had heard the song often enough in the past months to sing along.

Germany, Germany above all things,
Above all things, in the world,
When, it's for protection and for our defense
It stands always in brotherhood.

German women, German loyalty,
German wine and German song
In this world it always will retain
Beauty and it's ancient resound
Inspiring us all to noble deeds
All throughout our lifetime.

Unity, justice, and freedom
For the German fatherland!
Towards these let us all strive forth
Brotherhood in heart and deed
Unity, justice, and freedom:
The foundation of happiness;
Flourish in the glow of this happiness,
Flourish, German fatherland!

Beer steins were raised and shouts rang out along the streets as everyone shouted the last line, "Flourish German fatherland."

Marvin was standing beside Rudy and after the choir passed, he asked, "When I grew up in Bergdorf my family never talked about 'fatherland.' Did yours?"

Rudy shook his head. "Not that I remember. I suppose Freidorf would be my fatherland. That's where my father is." He sniffed and shook his head. "But we don't have any land there."

Marvin nodded. "Now my family is in America. I guess they have settled on some land in Dakota. But——."

A spark ignited in Rudy's mind and he interrupted his friend, "And what about 'homeland'? Did you ever talk about 'homeland'? Lately, every day I hear 'homeland this' and 'homeland that.' Even Professor Beck says we are studying so we can be of use to the homeland. Back in Freidorf 'homeland' was a simple ordinary word, but here, whenever people say it, they make it sound, I don't know…"

Marvin nodded, "yeah, they make it sound romantic, even religious."

Then the brass band swept into the plaza. The trumpets, trombones, and tubas set the crowd clapping and whistling. The four boys bought beers, toasted each other and joined in the exuberance. Rudy did his best to ignore classroom anxieties and melancholy thoughts. After another horse troop clopped past, a hundred school children marching in lederhosen, the choir from the Treysa Gymnasium, entered the square waving small German flags and singing. They sang with bright eyes and enthusiastic grins.

I have given myself
With heart and with hand
To you, country full of love and life,
My German Homeland

My heart was enlightened,
Loyally turned towards you,
You land of the free and faithful,
You glorious Homeland!

I will hold and believe
In God faithfully and freely;
I will, Homeland, remain
Forever strengthened and loyal to you.

Let me gain strength
In heart and hand,
To live and to die
For the holy Homeland

The choir marched past to the cheers of the crowds. Despite the frothy brews he'd just drunk, a melancholy mist clouded Rudy's spirit. He was surely a man without a homeland. Neither the tiny island of Freidorf in the great south Russian sea, nor this burgeoning, industrous, self-confident Germany was his homeland.

Later, as the boys wended their way back to the Center, Rudy's thoughts churned. He recalled the words he'd read the night before. Since he'd come to Treysa, he'd tried to read a chapter in his Bible before sleeping. Last night's words from the letter to the Hebrews now stood alongside the day's events: *For here we have no lasting city, but we are looking for the city that is to come.* He guessed that Marvin might agree, but doubted that the others in his dormitory or even in the entire school would accept what he was thinking: nowhere on earth, not in France or Russia or Dakota or Germany was there such a thing as a 'lasting city' or a 'holy homeland.' A grim smile crossed his face. *Best keep my heretical thinking to myself.*

The sun was slowly dying when they reached their dormitory. Rudy stopped outside the door.

"Guys, thanks for the day. You were right. I needed to get off my butt. Fred, I owe you for the beers. I'm going to put in a few more hours of study for that test. See you tomorrow."

As he turned toward the library and steeled himself for more grinding reading, Fred shouted after him, "Roosky, tomorrow morning, before the test, if you let me look at your study notes, we'll call it even for the beers."

Rudy trudged on and waved without looking back.

JUNE 14, 1914 TREYSA, GERMANY

Rudy and Fred stood on the bank of the Schwalm river north of Treysa. They'd been walking in the balmy spring air and now stood watching the wheel of an old grist mill wheel spinning as the churning water sparkled and spumed.

"Roosky, look there. The water hits the paddles, the wheel spins. It's a natural reaction. And that's how I feel about enlisting. Nobody's forcing me. It just seems natural."

Rudy laughed in mocking surprise. "Whoa, look who's getting philosophical."

Normally Fred would have thumped Rudy's shoulder with a friendly punch or countered with a barb of his own. Today he clasped his elbows as though he were chilly, despite the warm sunlight filtering through the trees.

"Yeah, well...I know I'm not as smart as you. But I can tell what direction we're moving and I want to be where the action is."

"But Fred, you'll graduate next week and then you can—"

"Can what?" Fred interrupted. "Scramble for a job in a hospital or a poor house or a school? C'mon Rudy, can you really see me as a deacon anywhere in the world?"

Rudy wanted to chuckle and agree, but one look at Fred's wrinkled brow stifled that response. Instead he asked, "But you finished the entire course. Why did you keep—?"

"Because my dad's a stiff-necked, bull-headed old Prussian Lutheran and he swore that if I left the deacon training school, he'd stop supporting me, even cut me off from my inheritance. So, I plowed through, didn't exactly enjoy it though, as you may have noticed."

Fred picked up a dead branch that lay on the path and threw it into the frothy current. Rudy had never glimpsed the inner workings of Fred's mind. He was moved and honored that Fred trusted him with thoughts that were obviously painful.

"But a soldier? Is your dad OK with that?"

"Ah Roosky, you don't know very much about Germany. Prussian men, like my dad, have bayonets for backbones. The only thing more important than defending their Protestant religion is defending their Holy Fatherland. Last October, the Kaiser called for over 100,000 men to sign up for the army. We'll have an army of 800,000. War is on the horizon. Everyone in Prussia is saying it. So, I'm enlisting and not only is my dad okay with my decision, he's overjoyed, though he'd never tell me directly. I bet he'd secretly do cartwheels if he wasn't such a sour, stiff-necked s.o.b."

Rudy heard a mix of bitterness and pride in Fred's rant. Though Rudy himself had gone through troubled times with his own father, he never would have spoken of him in the terms Fred was using. But as he'd learned during the past three years, Fred was Fred. The half-opened door to Fred's feelings slammed shut and he turned to Rudy.

"What about you, Roosky? You've got one semester left. I suppose by next January you'll be working in some Lutheran institution somewhere."

For a few minutes they ambled along the riverbank in silence listening to the gurgling stream. Rudy scuffed his shoes in the gravel path, his thoughts swirling. Fred's frankness emboldened him and he found himself saying aloud words he'd scarcely dared whisper even to himself.

"Fred, maybe this'll sound crazy to you, but I'm afraid to finish school."

Fred threw a laugh into the blue sky, then turned and saw Rudy's somber face. "My God, you're serious. Afraid? Afraid of what?"

Rudy suddenly wished he had a net to recapture his words and restore them to the dark caverns of his mind. But his innermost thoughts now fluttered in the sunlight like the dozens of copper-shot butterflies that danced over the river. And as sure as this river ran to the ocean, Fred would not relent until Rudy explained himself.

"C'mon Rudy. What can you be afraid of? You always get good grades. You turn in all your assignments on time. All the teachers love you. If you can't make it out there in the world, who can?"

Rudy puffed up his cheeks and emptied out his lungs in a long suspiration. "It's more complicated than that. It's…I don't know if I can…I'm not sure I've figured it out myself.

Fred tossed an arm over Rudy's shoulder. "I've got all day. Just talk."

Rudy replied,"Your dad made you come here. I had to fight my dad to let me leave home. I thought I had some talent for helping people but I didn't have any money. I didn't have many choices if I wanted to study. I came to Hephata because here I could study and work to pay my way."

Fred chuckled, "Well, I'd say you've worked your butt off. You make the rest of us, me at least, look like a slacker."

Rudy shook his head, "But for what? The closer I get to finishing, the clearer I see the truth."

Fred poked an elbow into Rudy's ribs. "The truth? As Pilate said to Jesus, 'What is truth?' Who's getting philosophical now?"

Rudy smiled, "OK, OK. Not THE truth, a truth. In the almost three years that I've been here I've learned a truth about myself: One part of me likes to study, read, take tests and please teachers. But another part of me just wants to work with people. How can I best use what talents God has given me? You don't know how many nights during this past year, I've lain in my bunk, staring up at the ceiling and asking myself questions. And the answers are always the same."

"So why didn't you change courses? Try out some other track?"

They walked out into brighter sunshine as Rudy struggled for an answer. "I suppose because I didn't know what direction to go. I didn't want to be like those butterflies flitting from one flower to another. Vater says, 'finish what you start.' So now I'm close to finishing the general course and I'm afraid. I don't know what I'll do or where I'll go when I graduate."

Fred dared to grin at his friend, "The Kaiser always needs more soldiers."

Rudy grinned back, "I don't think I've got the mettle for that. Besides, does our Lutheran Kaiser want a boy born and raised in Russia?"

"Oh, I never thought of that. The enemy, that great brutal Russian bear…. No soldiering for you. Roosky, I never figured I could give you advice, but here's my recommendation: You've got six months 'til graduation. Think about it, talk to Headmaster or some of the teachers. Tell 'em what you told me. A lot can happen in six months. Hell, the whole world could end by then."

The two meandered along the river. Where the river widened, they skipped stones across the placid water. They startled up ducks from the reeds, laughed, told jokes and returned to the Center with lighter souls. Their conversation had revived youthful buoyancy to their spirits.

Rudy and Fred did not know that at that very moment, a thousand miles away in Sarajevo, a nineteen-year old Serbian man's spirit was smoldering with rage. Within weeks he would kill a prince and light a fuse and explode the world. Within a month all of Europe would know the name of Gavril Princip.

JULY 28, 1914 TREYSA, GERMANY,

The two young men stood on the hot sidewalk in front of the Hephata Center.

"Forget the taxi. If I carry one of your bags, we'll be at the train station in twenty minutes." Rudy hefted Marvin's leather suitcase. "Save your money for when you get to America."

The two began their hike under a mid-morning sun that sent shimmery waves up from the cobblestones. Three weeks earlier Marvin had received money from his parents living in South Dakota. After selling their farm in Bergdorf, they'd traveled to the middle of America and claimed their 320-acre homestead. Unlike Rudy's brother who arrived in his new home nearly penniless and still struggled to pay his bills, Marvin's parents were able to purchase equipment and seed and build a solid home.

"I never knew you planned to go to America after you graduated," Rudy said as they trudged down the sidewalk.

"My folks have been pushing it since they've gotten settled. I resisted them. I always thought I wanted stay in Germany." Marvin grunted and transferred his heavy suitcase to his other hand. "But now with all the rumbling and shouting since that killing in Sarajevo…. I've lost my enthusiasm for Germany. As for south Russia, you couldn't pay me to go back there."

They reached a street corner and stopped to catch their breath. "When Vater cabled the money to buy a ticket for passage to New York I had to rethink everything. I've got to start my life somewhere, so it looks like it'll be in America."

"Good luck, boys." They looked up to see an elfin, gray-haired woman leaning out of her upstairs window. She was smiling and enthusiastically waving at them.

Rudy and Marvin shared puzzled looks then waved to her with their free hands as they crossed the street.

"What do you suppose that was all about?" Marvin asked.

"No idea. Maybe she was overwhelmed by our good looks and couldn't resist." Rudy grinned.

They were three blocks from the train station when they noticed a distant murmur filling the air.

"Sounds like the crowd at a soccer game," Marvin said.

"Too early for that, besides there's no field around here." Rudy stepped aside to let an elderly man with a handlebar mustache pass.

As the gentlemen moved past them, he gave a deep nod and growled, "Give 'em hell boys, and God bless ya."

Marvin looked at Henry and Henry looked at Marvin. The veil slowly lifted and their smiles faded.

"Damn, they think we're off to Frankfurt to enlist," Marvin shook his head.

Rudy wiped the sweat from his brow. "No need to say anything. Just get on the train and go."

They turned the corner and gaped at the scene before them. The street in front of the station was swarming with people. A dozen German flags snapped in the breeze and cheers rippled through the crowd. In the middle of the throng was an open circle. At its center stood two dozen young men, faces flushed from heat and emotion, smiling, waving and saluting. Their friends, families and neighbors shouted and whistled passionately.

"Hey, here's two more." Burly arms grabbed Rudy and Marvin. Before they could say a word, they were swept through the crowd and into the center circle. Rudy was chagrined to be standing alongside these young patriots. He didn't share their passion and couldn't appreciate their desire to go join the army.

He recalled the times he and his family in Freidorf had said goodbye to young men who'd been drafted into the Russian army. Instead of cheers and flags, there'd been tears and quiet, solemn embraces. Rudy felt like an impostor standing alongside these ebullient young men. But as he looked out at the adoring crowd, he had to admit to himself that he coveted the affection they were receiving.

The shrill whistle of the approaching train triggered another round of cheering. The engine squealed and the cars clattered to a stop. The circle dissolved as the soldiers-to-be received last hugs from family. Marvin and Rudy hurriedly escaped to the platform. They set their suitcases down and awkwardly embraced, slapping each other on the back.

"Rudy, thanks for… for everything. Stay safe."

"You too. Don't get lost in America. It's a big place."

Marvin picked up his bags and swung up into his train car. His voice was husky. "If you ever get to South Dakota, make sure and look me up. Just go to Ipswich and ask for the Beckers."

Rudy waved and hurried away. He didn't want the crowd to see him and think he was a deserter. He didn't want Marvin to see the tears that glinted in his eyes. Today it was Marvin. A month ago, he'd said good bye to Fred and tomorrow Vernon was interviewing for a position in Marburg. His closest friends were gone. The July vacation was almost over. He was already dreading the start of classes. But within days his personal dread would be obliterated by horrific events that would script and sculpt the next eight years of his life.

AUGUST 2—9, 1914 TREYSA, GERMANY

"It's about damn time." Rudy heard Willy growling behind the curtain and smiled to himself. *Old Willy's in his usual cheery mood.* Transporting Willy to breakfast had been part of Rudy's routine for three years now and the old man's spirits usually hovered between barely tolerable to blackly bitter. Rudy assumed Willy had heard him coming.

Rudy pulled back the curtain, "Sorry to keep you waiting, my friend."

Willy was already in his wheel chair, and painfully turned his neck. "What? Oh, is it time for breakfast? I wasn't talking to you, Rudy. I was reading the Frankfurt Sunday paper. Look at this."

With trembling hands, he held up the newspaper. Two-inch letters screamed across the page: GERMANY DECLARES WAR AGAINST RUSSIA. Willy folded the paper and lay it on his lap.

"About damn time. For years those conniving bastards have been plotting to get their filthy paws on our land. But old Kaiser Wilhelm beat 'em to the punch this time. Kill 'em all I say."

Over the past few years Rudy had become inured to Willy's dark mood but today's vehemence stunned him. Rudy grabbed the wheelchair handles and tried to humor him. "That would take a lot of bullets and swords, Willy. Don't know if we've got enough iron to do the job."

"Hell, they can melt down my wheelchair for bullets if they need to. Time to teach that dirty bear a lesson. Don't mess with Germany."

Rudy pushed the chair down the hall in silence. *I was born in Russia. I grew up in Russia. I speak Russian. Vater lives in Russia. My brother and his family... I have friends who are Russian. They're not bastards. How many Germans think like Willy? Maybe he's just a crazy old fool.*

If Rudy thought Willy was crazy, then his first sight in the dining room suggested the entire world had gone mad. All the residents already in the room held tiny German flags. The same little flags lay on every yet-to-be filled space at every table. Some of the residents seemed bewildered by the new objects before them. Those with gnarled fingers could not pick them up. Those who could waved them with glee. As Rudy wheeled Willy to his usual table, Nurse Heinitz reached into the pocket of her white apron and handed a flag to Rudy. She chuckled at his stunned look.

"The wholesaler at the store where we buy all our flour was handing them out to his customers. He gave fifty of them to our driver this morning. Most of Germany seems excited that we are finally attacking our enemies."

Rudy looked down at the little bit of cloth glued to a miniature flag pole. He was quite sure the nurse did not know of his roots nor of his feelings about Russia, but nonetheless, he chose his next words with caution.

"Most of the country? Not all of it?"

She pursed her lips and for a long moment peered into his eyes, then pulled her gaze away and looked out over his shoulder. "My father was in the Franco-Prussian War. As children, we were taught that because of that war our Germany became one nation, the best and strongest nation in Europe. We were taught to honor the heroes who created our Fatherland."

She paused and lowered her voice. "My father was in the battle of Gravelotte. More than twenty thousand of his comrades died there. Dad survived but his right leg was blown off. He never spoke of the war unless he was drunk. Then he'd curse and cry and smash furniture. I grew up with a father who seldom smiled and hid inside a shell for most of his life. He died last year. Today, I dare say I'm glad he's not here to see his Germany marching into another...." She shifted her gaze back to Rudy. "Pardon my rambling. I think it'll be wise for us all to keep our thoughts about the war to ourselves." She turned away so swiftly that her starched uniform rattled.

Rudy's usual warm attentiveness to the residents of the Infirmary was absent on this Sunday morning. He helped with moving and bathing the men, he lifted them into and out of bed. But he worked as an automaton, without will or feeling. His emotions had commandeered all his energy. Fear for himself and for his family, aching loneliness, confusion about the present, anxiety about the future—this maelstrom plagued him throughout the morning, into the afternoon and tossed and tumbled him throughout the endless night.

Rudy was not ready for Monday morning. After three years at Hephata, he had one of the better bunks in the room, quiet and dark, far from the bathroom and from the eastern windows. Yet on this morning, he was the first one to sit up and put his feet onto the cement floor. His head was leaden, his mouth tasted like the inside of an old shoe, and his nightclothes were sticky with sweat. He groaned at the thought of going to class. *What will I say if anyone wants to talk about the war?*

Only half the seats were taken at the 8 a.m. class. Rudy slid into his desk, folded his hands atop his books, closed his eyes and prayed that God might pacify his tumultuous spirit. At the same time, he strained to hear the comments of his fellow students. He was stunned.

"Have you read this chapter?"

"No, I played cards until midnight. Did you?"

"Only the first half, then Martin and I went out for beers. We met a couple of girls and...."

Normal Monday morning pre-class chatter. Evidently not everyone's world had been upended. Though Rudy had chosen to ignore it, war and talk of war had been in the air for so many months that its arrival was no shock. When bald-headed, portly Professor Bachmann strode into the room, the students all rose as usual, the teacher nodded to them as usual and, as usual, the students sat down and readied themselves for an hour of tedious lecture.

"Gentlemen, this morning, many men of our Fatherland are fulfilling their patriotic duty in distant places. We are here, and our duty is right here and I expect you will be as fervent in fulfilling your obligations. We begin with a summary of Chapter seven. Who can tell me a key point from this reading?"

Rudy's tumultuous spirit of Sunday was calmed by Monday's mundane routine of lecture, essays, and reading. He concentrated on his assignments and so the day passed. He managed to hold his anxieties at bay until Tuesday noon. A sign on the cafeteria door read: "All student meeting, 1:00 p.m., in the auditorium."

The cafeteria was abuzz with conjectures and speculations. "Rudy, what've you heard? What's this all about?" Rudy didn't risk opening his mouth. He shrugged his shoulders, shook his head and kept his dire thoughts to himself.

By 1:00 p.m. the auditorium was full and as steamy as a Finnish sauna. Headmaster Siebold dwarfed the tiny podium standing in front of him on the narrow stage. He cleared his throat and every student hushed. His voice boomed into the silence.

"Brothers and sisters in Christ, thank you for coming. You all know that our Center is devoted to bringing healing and hope to those most in need. You also know that on the first of August our Fatherland declared war against Russia. Some of you may already know that yesterday we declared war on France."

Whispers fluttered through the crowd. This was news to many. The headmaster raised his arms for silence.

"But there is more. Early this morning I was informed that Great Britain has declared war against us."

The whispers now became murmurs and small conversations spread through the crowd.

"Please, people. Silence."

The steamy air now competed with the chilling news. The noise slowly died and the headmaster came out from behind the podium and came to the edge of the stage.

"What will all of this mean for Germany? What will it mean for Hephata Center? What will it mean for each one of you?" He paused, shook his head and slowly spoke. "I do not know. A spirit of war has brooded over our country for two years. Is this a righteous spirit? Again, I confess I do not know." Now he began to walk back and forth across the front of the stage.

"What I do know is this: Hephata Center will continue to teach and serve and fulfill our Christian calling to the best of its ability for as long as our Lord permits us. We will maintain all classes and projects and services. You will continue to study and learn and prepare yourselves to serve our Lord through your deacon work. Now more than ever, our homeland needs God's

---

healing spirit. If any of you have concerns or questions, and I'm sure some of you do, please come and see me.

"Friends, do not forget your prayers and your reading of God's holy word. Remember the words of the Psalm writer, *'Though an army encamp against me, my heart shall not fear; though war rise up against me, yet I will be confident.'* Thank you for your time. Go with God's peace."

The students sat in silence as the headmaster marched off of the stage and left the building. Rudy sat for a moment as his fellow students shuffled out accompanied by muted conversations. *War, war, war on every side. What will become of us? Of me? Of my family? I can't even send them a letter. If I go to the post office with a letter for Freidorf, will they think I'm Russian? Or worse, an enemy spy? Even if they took the letter, it'd never get delivered. And what if Hephata closes? Where will I go? What will I do?*

He walked out of the auditorium. Beads of sweat trickled down his forehead and an icy snake coiled around his heart.

SEPTEMBER 1, 1914 TREYSA, GERMANY

Rudy was taking the long route to Headmaster Siebold's office. He walked past the potato patch and grieved at the sight. Two nights earlier a deep, unexpected early frost killed all of the garden plants. The potato plant leaves, instead of using their green surfaces to swallow sunshine and transform it into plump potatoes, were blackening and shriveling. The Center would be lucky to get half as many potatoes as last year.

"Come in Rudy, come in." The headmaster met him at the door and put his arm around Rudy. "You're not looking well. Circles under your eyes. Worry I suppose. Can't blame you. Sit, sit please."

Rudy eased into the straight-backed chair in front of the dark wooden desk. He needed to talk but could not find a way to begin. The threat of tears tightened his throat and he silently berated himself for such weakness.

"It's alright Rudy, take your time. Can I get you some tea?" The headmaster arose and went to a pot setting on a small hotplate under which a blue gas flame flickered. While he fussed with the cups, Rudy tried to reassemble his thoughts.

Rudy took the tea cup and when the headmaster sat, he haltingly began. "Headmaster, I've got so many—No, too many things to worry about. My family, back in Freidorf. What is happening with them? Nobody knows. I got a letter last week from my brother in America. He asks me, 'how are Vater and Junior and his family?' As if I would know anything. It would be foolish to send a letter to Freidorf, wouldn't it? My stomach aches every time I think about what might be happening to them."

The headmaster nodded sympathetically. "Ach ja, Rudy. I know it's hard. But you should know, the Russian and German armies, if and when they fight, won't be in south Russia. I don't think the war will get that far south."

"I sure hope not. But my family is German and they're living in Russian territory."

Now the headmaster leaned forward in his chair. "That is true and no one knows what that means. And you, Rudy are Russian born and living in Germany. And we don't know what that will mean either in the months ahead. We don't know if hatred of all things Russian will grow. The newspapers all say our generals expect victory within months. We can only hope they know what they're talking about."

"But Headmaster, what can I do? I'm German, not Russian."

"Yes, of course I know that. I also am one of the few around here who knows that you were born in south Russia and have a Russian birth certificate. We will keep it that way. Don't talk about your family to others. Don't go out too much into the city."

Rudy nodded then dropped his head. "I understand. But in four months I'll graduate. Where will I find a job? Where will I go?"

Headmaster sat back and stroked his chin. "Ja Rudy, I know. I've been thinking about your situation. Here's a proposal. I'm guessing we'll be losing some of our students and some of our workers to the conscription. We'll need help in the gardens, with cleaning, with maintenance and care in the Infirmary. You could stay here and work until the war is over. And, to make your position safer, you could take some classes so you'd still be considered a student. What do you think?"

Rudy's eyes widened. The chaotic swirl of his thoughts slowed and stopped. He stammered. "You mean I can stay? And I can study?"

"That's what I mean. We'll need your labor. I know you're finishing your course but maybe you can find a class or two that—"

Overwhelmed by his runaway enthusiasm, Rudy interrupted the headmaster. "Oh, thank you sir. You don't know... I planned to tell you today how unsure I was about the course I was finishing and how I so wished I'd taken a different direction and how I was so sorry that I'd not taken other classes and now...now, this is... you are an answer to my prayers."

Headmaster stood and exploded into one of his fulsome belly laughs. "I

---

don't know if I've ever been anyone's answer to prayer. Rudy, I try to help all of our students. You're a solid faith-filled young man. I'm sure we'll weather these next months just fine."

Headmaster Siebold may have been able to answer a prayer, but he was not able to foresee the future.

OCTOBER 10, 1914 TREYSA, GERMANY

Rudy stared at the envelope in disbelief. It was a letter from Freidorf, sent at the end of July, only days before the declaration of war—over ten weeks ago. The fact that it had arrived at all was a miracle. He turned it over. Small tears, smudges and sloppy glue marks—the letter had already been read, probably more than once. Rudy tried to open the envelope carefully but his hands trembled so violently that he tore off the flap. The letter slipped out. Dirty fingerprints around the edges proved that others had perused it. The letter was signed by Elvira, his sister-in-law. She had written the letter in Russian. He was flabbergasted. *Elvira is no writer. She even has a tough time writing German. Look at how heavy she pressed, how slow she must have written. Why Russian?*

Rudy had received the letter from the Center's office and now sat on a bench outside of the classroom, away from prying eyes.

Dear Rudy,

How are you? Here we are doing very well.

I have been practicing my Russian in speaking and writing. Even Vater is speaking Russian since that is what we now speak in the stores and in church too. It is a beautiful language, don't you think?

Junior is busy with harvesting. He sold the fields southeast of the house to Mr. Sokolov for ten rubles an acre. We all thought that was a fair price.

Your friend Paul left last month for the Russian army. He was honored to serve his country.

Herman and Betty are growing like Russian thistles. They often ask about you.

Vater and Junior send greetings and we all hope you will find good work in Germany.

Blessings,
Elvira

Rudy reread the letter and gulped down the sob that threatened to escape. Elvira had strained to write in Russian but she was clever enough to hide within the words her true meaning, a meaning only someone who knew Elvira and Freidorf would perceive. He reread the words of the letter and imagined hearing her voice.

Dear Rudy,

I hope you are doing better than we are.

We are now forced to write and speak only in Russian. Vater is lost in his grief and anger. He misses Mutti and his children and now he can't sit outside and chat with his friends without getting reported for speaking German. Our poor pastor struggles to preach a decent sermon. Russian is a foul and ugly language.

The Russian council forced us (and many other German families) to sell our land to Russian peasants. We were given only ten rubles per acre. These Russians are filthy thieves.

The commandant came for your friend Paul and dragged him away to the army. He was terrified and his parents are forlorn.

In all our other letters we said, "come home when you graduate." But now we tell you, "stay in Germany. This part of Russia is sliding into hell."

Your angry and worried sister-in-law,

Elvira

Rudy stuffed the letter into his pocket. Now the local post office, and surely the local officials knew of his Russian background. Since the declaration of war against Russia he'd grieved knowing he wouldn't be able to communicate with his family until the war ended. This tattered letter, at least as he decoded it, reinforced his worst fears. And yet he wondered.

Am I reading between the lines, or am I reflecting my own dread? Who knows if what is written here is true? Can we trust anyone to speak openly? All through August the Frankfurt Newspaper announced victories and declarations that Paris was within range of German cannons. We were told that soon the enemy would surrender. In the past few weeks there has been a strange silence. Lately all we are given is an abundance of words about our brave, honorable soldiers and their great courage in battles on the Marne River. Who controls the news?

Rudy stood and walked to his next class. He lifted his collar against the afternoon damp. Since the early frost in September, the skies had been a dismal gray. Today banks of bruised purple clouds ringed the horizon.

Bitter rain was on the way. He shivered and thought of Fred. *Is my friend in France? Is he safe? Is he staying warm in this icy weather?*

FEBRUARY, 1915 TREYSA, GERMANY

"I've heard about riots in Berlin. Can't imagine them in Treysa. Still…" Headmaster Siebold shrugged and frowned. His customary smiles were now a rarity as this speedy war dragged into its sixth month. He had called Rudy into his office on a frigid Sunday evening.

"Riots over potatoes. Here in Germany. It seems impossible. But here we are. The Center's sacks are almost empty too."

Rudy wasn't sure why he was sitting in the headmaster's semi-dark, damp office on this winter Sunday evening but he wasn't surprised by the news. He had helped dig and store the Center's meager potato harvest. He nodded, "The frost killed our plants at the worst time."

The headmaster folded his hands on the desk. "Tomorrow the potato warehouse opens at eight in the morning. I don't expect any trouble but I don't want to take any chances. Normally one of the kitchen helpers goes every week with the hand cart and buys a fifty pound sack. That's our standing order. Tomorrow, I'd like you and Ida to take the horse cart and get two sacks, three if possible. We don't dare run out. We've got people in our Infirmary who can't lose any more weight."

"Sure, what time should I go?"

"I want you at the warehouse by 7:00. There may be a line. But you'll have to pick up Ida first. I've told her to be waiting outside the women's residence at 6:30."

"Ida…? I don't think I know her."

The headmaster smiled wearily. "Ida Loock, from up north near Hanover. She's been here longer than you. Quiet girl, works in the kitchen and sometimes does night duty at the Infirmary. But don't worry. There won't be too many young ladies outside of the women's dorm at 6:30 tomorrow morning."

Brittle darkness still filled the streets of Treysa as Rudy slowly rolled up to the women's dorm at 6:30 on Monday morning. A small figure, bundled in coat and scarf, stood under the dim light of the lone streetlamp. Rudy stopped the cart but before he could descend, the figure clambered up and sat on the seat beside him.

"Let's go, I'm cold." The words were clipped and insistent.

Rudy opened his mouth to speak but instead clucked to the horses. As they clattered over the cobblestones, he turned to his passenger, "Good morning, I'm Rudy."

"I know," came the soft reply.

It was still too dark to see clearly but Rudy thought he detected the gleam of an eye emerging from the scarf enwrapped face. "You must be Ida."

"Who else would be standing out in this cold?"

Is she angry or is she teasing? Rudy couldn't decide and it was too early for banter anyway. So they rode down the dark streets in silence. They turned the last corner and the potato warehouse hunkered darkly against the gray pre-dawn light. A half dozen dark cloaked figures were lined up on the sidewalk in front of the building.

Rudy steered the cart to the side of the street, climbed down and tied the reins to a post. Ida was already walking across to the line. Rudy caught up with her and grumbled, "Old Headmaster is getting panicky. He was afraid there'd be a horde out here."

"It's early. Just wait." Ida stepped up to the end of the line. Rudy stared at her back. She was short and even with her heavy coat Rudy could tell she had a slight figure.

A tall man with a fur coat in line in front of Ida turned around and growled, "This is the sacrifice we make for the Fatherland. Freeze our asses off for a sack of potatoes so our boys on the field can eat."

Rudy only risked a tight grin and nod. The man turned back toward the front.

A few seconds later Ida turned around, leaned toward Rudy and in a harsh whisper said, "My roommate got a letter from her brother. He's a soldier fighting in the Vosges mountains. He said the rations are lousy and the potatoes are half rotten."

Rudy was pleased and surprised by Ida's passion. He snorted in agreement. "I'm sure that somewhere in Germany those with enough coins are eating beautiful solid spuds." Then, before she could turn back, he quickly added, "By the way, who's your roommate? Maybe I know her."

Perhaps Ida didn't think Rudy's attempt at conversation was feeble, or maybe she was as lonely as he was. For whatever reason, she answered his question and the two spent the next hour chatting about school and work and, in subdued voices, about the war.

A few minutes before eight o'clock, four women dressed all in black, including black veils, arrived and resolutely marched to the front of the line.

"Soldier's wives," muttered Ida. "Because their husbands are out of the home, they get special treatment. They look strong and healthy to me. What about the poor helpless ones we take care of?"

Rudy heard murmurings running up and down the line, which by now had grown to nearly thirty bundled up Treysan citizens. Evidently Ida was not alone in her opinions.

The door swung open and a broad-shouldered mustached man wearing an apron stepped out and stood with arms crossed. He boomed out his announcement, each word accompanied by a white cloud. "Today we have received a new order. This week we can still honor all standing orders. By next week expect something different. If you have no standing order, you may buy no more than ten pounds. Don't complain or whine to me. The law is the law. We're at war so tighten your belts. Come in, one by one. If you start pushing or shoving, I'll slam the door and send you all home."

"He must have heard what's been happening in Berlin," Rudy said as they inched forward. He knew Headmaster would be disappointed with only sixty pounds. The servings on the plate would be smaller this week. As they neared the door, Rudy began to worry. How could he help Ida get her fifty pound bag out of the store and into the wagon without losing his place in line? He'd just begun to suggest they trade places in line when the door in front of them opened. Ida entered the building and minutes later came out with the potato sack across her shoulders and her mouth set in a determined grin.

"Meet you at the wagon," she grunted as she passed Rudy. A few minutes later, when Rudy neared the wagon with his potato sack, Ida was already perched on the seat clapping her mitten clad hands together to keep them warm. Rudy dropped in his sack, climbed aboard and clucked to the horses. The feeble winter sunlight stirred up a morning breeze that brought tears to Rudy's eyes. He glanced over at Ida and her eyes were pinched tight. How could he compliment her without offending? He tried a playful tone.

"Ida, good job with that potato sack. How'd you get so strong?"

She kept her eyes closed against the icy breeze but answered him with words muffled by the scarf across her face. "It started at home. My brother Klaus was born with a very twisted club foot. Ever since I was a child, I helped him get around. I sometimes carried him, even when he grew bigger. When I came to work here at Hephata I was ready for heavy work. On weekends, I help move and bathe our residents. During the week…well, if you ever came to the kitchen and saw the heavy kettles and pots we handle every day you'd see that a few kilos of potatoes can't slow me down."

Rudy smiled at her bravado and saw that her eyes were laughing back at him. This Ida…she was fun. He wondered if he dared wander into the kitchen someday this week. He already planned to volunteer to make next Monday's potato run.

Rudy found no time to visit the Center's kitchen during the week. He was so engrossed by the material in his new courses that he scarcely thought of Ida during the days. But sometimes, at night, as he slipped wearily into slumber, he'd smile inside as he remembered her laughing eyes.

On the following Monday, Rudy arrived at the girl's dormitory at 6:30 a.m. Ida stood beneath the dim street light. Last week's icy cold had receded and been replaced by a more seasonal thirty-five degrees. This morning he could see Ida's smile. She swung up to the seat next to him.

"So, you got stuck on potato duty again?"

Rudy grinned, "Would you believe, I volunteered?"

"You must be crazier than you look!" She giggled.

"No, I just like to watch you lug potatoes on your back."

Ida laughed but then softly muttered, "If we have any potatoes to lug… Now we're having trouble getting bread too."

Rudy resisted the serious turn in the conversation. "Oh, there'll be potatoes today and next week too. Come on, breathe deep, enjoy this warm February air."

She smiled and threw back her head and filled her lungs then emptied them in a long whoosh. "Are you always such a positive thinker?"

Rudy yearned to charm this girl and was tempted to give her a glib 'of course'. But deception, in himself or others, was deeply offensive. He was silent for a few seconds as the horses' hooves clicked on the cobblestones. Then he chuckled softly and said, "Not always, but I try."

Ida must have sensed the hesitancy in his answer. It opened the door to her next question, one that took him by surprise.

"Rudy, why are you still here?"

"What do you mean?" Rudy feigned innocence but suspected where this conversation was headed.

"You graduated in December. I was at the ceremony. So many graduates went to the army, some are working. But I hear you're still taking classes. How come? I mean, that's OK if you are. I'm just, well..people talk and…I'm curious, but it's OK if you don't want to tell…." Ida looked at him with a crinkled 'excuse me' expression on her face.

Rudy couldn't help smiling at her consternation. "Don't worry, I'm not offended. An honest question deserves an honest answer. OK?"

Ida gave a tiny shrug and smiled in agreement.

"Let's just say it's not a good time for a young man born in Russian territory to look for a job in Germany. Or to go off fighting, for that matter. Thankfully Headmaster has invited me to stay and work here—and study."

Ida nodded thoughtfully. Rudy wondered if she'd known he was Russian born. He hoped that fact was not widely known, but people, especially women, always talk....

Rudy pulled the reins to turn the corner and gave a low whistle. A line of figures snaked from the potato warehouse door all the way to the corner. A half dozen police officers with hands on their nightsticks strode up and down the sinuous chain of people.

"We should have started earlier," Rudy said as he tied the reins to secure the carriage. He and Ida hurried across the street.

Ida turned to him as they reached the end of the line "The head cook told us that the Federal Council froze the price for potatoes all across the country. Now the farmers are protesting, feeding the potatoes to the pigs instead of selling them to the market." She huffed, "Everybody only thinks of themselves."

The queue seemed subdued. There were no shouts or loud conversations, but Rudy detected a low deep murmuring. It struck him as more ominous than angry outbursts. He was glad the officers were there, though he wondered what six men could do if all of these perturbed men and women decided to rush the door.

When the door finally opened, the line only oozed forward. Ida stepped out of the line and into the street, peering up ahead. She returned shaking her head. "There's a government man sitting at a table and everyone has to sign in and then they get some sort of papers."

"Ration cards, potato ration cards." The woman in front of them muttered disgustedly. "We still have to pay for the potatoes but every time we buy five kilos, we have to give up a stamp. I've got three boys at home. I hope my stamps last until the end of the month."

Ida sighed, "I just hope they don't run out of potatoes today. At the Center, we're already cutting back as much as we can."

Rudy did not repeat his earlier optimistic opinion. Treysa was surrounded by agricultural country and was not a large metropolis. If the situation was difficult here, what must it be like in Berlin and the other large cities of Germany? What would happen to them all? What was happening to his family? As he had done so many times during the past seven months, he lifted his shoulders in a deep breath, mentally slammed the door on his grim, fatalistic imagination and forced himself to concentrate on the moment and the person in front of him.

He reached for Ida's hand and squeezed it. "Let's hope and pray." She looked up at him. He could not read her face, but she didn't withdraw her hand.

SUNDAY, APRIL 11, 1915 TREYSA, GERMANY

"Seven million killed in one month? Sounds impossible." Rudy shook his head in disbelief.

Ida nodded in agreement. "I know. But Cook says it's in all the newspapers. And her family out in Saxony wrote that every farmer's hogs were slaughtered. All by government order. The papers call it the "Great Pig Massacre.""

Rudy had at last summoned up enough courage to ask Ida to join him for something more than potato purchasing. They were walking to the worship service at the Hephata church. Ida's gruesome news was a stark contrast to Rudy's soaring spirits and the brisk spring morning. He unsuccessfully tried to scrub the bizarre scene from his mind.

"But this massacre…what's it supposed to accomplish?"

Ida shrugged. "I guess the government figured the pigs were competing for the potatoes. No pigs, means more potatoes for the troops…and maybe for us."

Rudy snorted. "Back in Freidorf we used the pig manure to fertilize the potato fields. No pigs means no manure. No manure means a lousy potato crop. Maybe we'll see more ham and bacon for a while but I doubt we'll see more potatoes."

Ida looked straight ahead and murmured, "Even the pigs must make the ultimate sacrifice for the Fatherland." Then she tilted her head and looked up at Rudy with the slimmest hint of a grin on her face.

Rudy chuckled as he and Ida approached the Hephata church. The red-bricked hexagonal steeple soared into the clear April sky. The hopeful spirit of last Sunday's joyful Easter celebration still animated the worshippers as they entered, and the brilliant stained-glass windows cast rainbows over the pews. Rudy's spirit recovered its verve. Memories of past Sundays in Freidorf and longing for this day's good news infused his heart. He and Ida slipped into a pew just as the pastor began the service.

Pastor Preus was as thin as a pitch fork handle with a sharp beak of a nose. He had a severely trimmed grey moustache that perched haughtily

---

above a narrow-lipped mouth. He wore the typical black gown and white double-winged collar that emphasized his substantial Adam's apple. He marched the congregation through the opening liturgy and read the Bible lessons designated for the day. He motioned for the worshippers to be seated and climbed the steps into the oaken altar that towered ten feet above the pews.

He looked out over the faces gazing up at him, smoothed out his moustache and for the first time that morning, allowed his mouth to bend into a brittle smile. He then spoke in a stentorian voice that reached the farthest corners of the room.

"Our master Jesus was slandered and called a devil. How shamefully he was treated. On this Lord's day we could say that as Jesus was treated, so also have the German people been treated. We have quietly and strenuously done our duty, complied with the will of God to the best of our knowledge and as far as it was humanly possible. We have worked not only for ourselves and our own welfare but for the welfare of mankind, for its moral and religious progress. We have worked for the Kingdom of God on earth. We Germans have always valued ideal aims more than earthly gains."

He paused and swept his eagle eyes across his audience, daring anyone to disagree. Then he lowered his voice and spoke slowly."And what thanks have we received from the people to whom we have ungrudgingly given our best? The other nations suddenly compare us to the devil. They declare that we incited and precipitated this war, they charge us with shamelessly assaulting peaceful neighbors."

A dark chill swept through the chancel. Like a butterfly struck by frost, Rudy's Easter joy plummeted to earth.

The pastor stopped, shook his head, then pounded on the pulpit with his fist. "And yet, they know, they all know perfectly well how good natured and peace-loving we Germans have been. They thought they lulled us to sleep with their hypocritical songs of peace. They thought that once we were sound asleep, they would fall upon us and murder us."

Now he leaned forward as far as the pulpit would allow him and shot a baleful glare at his congregation."And the saddest thing is that even in our German house there are many brethren who have sided with our peace-loving opponents."

Rudy and Ida joined the congregation in absolute stone-like stillness. No one dared move a muscle lest the pastor's invective fall upon them. He snorted in disgust and continued.

"Well, we know we're in good company when we're slandered like this.

Our master was called the devil, why should we, his imperfect disciples, be treated any better." Now the pastor leaned back and raised his eyes as though gazing into heaven.

"But what is the will of God in this war? Some things are very clear: to hire assassins and murder princes is not His will. Nor is it His will to help assassins and protect them from their well-deserved punishment. Nor can it be His will to deceive a trusting friend and then try to thrust a poisoned dagger in his heart all the while saying, 'Let's have peace.' To murder men because of their honesty or because their work and reward is better than one's own, that is not the will of God. No, that is the will of the oh so pious British." He lowered his gaze back to the congregation and raised a long, lance-like forefinger.

"One thing is clear. God must stand on our side. We fight for right and truth, for culture and civilization and human progress, and true Christianity. We stand against untruthfulness and hypocrisy and falseness and unculture and barbarism and brutality."

He shouted the next sentence. "All human blessing, even humanity itself, stands under the protection of our bright weapons." The pastor sighed, his fire flickered and his voice dropped as he closed his message.

"Someday, when our army returns wearing the laurel leafed crown of victory, the words of the psalmist will be fulfilled, 'Mercy and truth meet together, righteousness and peace have kissed each other.' Thanks be to God. Amen." [i]

Pastor Preus descended from the pulpit, led the congregation in the closing prayers, then raised his arms and dismissed them with the blessing.

Rudy and Ida stood and shuffled down the aisle with the rest of the silent crowd. Once outside, most people began smilingly greeting friends and neighbors and standing in small circles to chat.

Rudy and Ida walked silently back toward the center of the campus. Waves of sadness and anger buffeted Rudy. The brisk wind now bit with icy teeth, a pale filmy cloud covered the sun. More rain was coming. Ida broke the silence.

"At least we've no doubt where Herr Pastor stands."

Rudy shoved his hands into the pockets of his coat, plodded ahead, then finally spoke. "When I was a little boy, I accepted some things as simply true. My father was the hardest worker in the world, my mother made the best kuchen in the world, and the preacher always spoke God's word."

"And now?" Ida asked.

Rudy shrugged and grimly smiled at her. "The verdict is still out on my father and mother, but for me that last truth has crumbled. How can a pastor, a Lutheran pastor at that, make the claims that Pastor Preus made today?"

Rudy's voice rose, his stride lengthened and he continued his harangue. "He makes us Germans sound like saints. All people, all nations are sinners—every Lutheran learns that in catechism class. His words are totally—."

Rudy chopped off his words and dropped his arms as two men appeared on the path in front of them. He nodded as they passed then gulped and shook his head. *What am I doing? I've got to keep my mouth shut. War fever is everywhere. If the wrong people hear me…. I shouldn't even say these things to Ida. Who knows what she thinks…or who she talks to.*

Rudy glanced at her as they walked. He saw no hint of her feelings on her face.

She looked up at him, then asked, "I hear you've been taking preaching classes at the Center."

This non-sequitur completely baffled Rudy. "What? Oh..yeah, I am."

Ida nodded and smiled up at him. "Preaching courses. About time I'd say."

"Why would you say that?"

"Everyone knows you're a good preacher. About time you saw it too."

Rudy was puzzled. "Everyone? What…? Who?"

"Well, at least the staff at the Infirmary says it. Don't you do the Christmas programs there every year?"

"Sure but…"

"I went home for Christmas the first year you did it. When I came back the residents and the staff were all raving, how nice it was and how well-spoken you were. I go home almost every Christmas, but this year with the war going on, I stayed here and worked. I helped bring the residents from second floor down for the program. I heard you preach. I'm just saying it's about time you see what others have seen years ago."

Ida's words warmed Rudy more than she could have imagined. His first months in the preaching and pastoring classes had delighted him and fed his hunger more than all of the previous three years of classes combined. Because of his upbringing, he sometimes felt a twinge of guilt for enjoying this work so much. Ida's affirmation assured him that he was on the right path. Her next words again caught him by surprise.

"My new roommate is a nursing student. She tells me you're taking anatomy and physiology courses too. Can I ask why?"

Now Rudy flinched. He hadn't fully acknowledged, even to himself, his interest in these courses. He hadn't dealt with the conflict between his religious tradition and his mysterious healing gift. He wasn't prepared to share with Ida what for him was still a confusing mixture of awe and longing.

"Oh, I'm taking those classes mostly out of curiosity. Bodies, bones, organs—things that can be seen and touched. They balance out all my study of words and texts."

Ida nodded her head. "So, it's balance you're after." Then she playfully poked Rudy in the ribs. "I'd say ol' Pastor Preus threw your balance out of whack this morning."

Rudy blushed and sputtered. "Look, please don't repeat my words. I can't afford to get in any trouble."

Ida grabbed his hand and then hugged his arm and spoke softly. "Rudy, Rudy, don't worry about me. I don't know much about preaching, but I hate this war as much as you do. We're cutting food to our residents. It's insane. I haven't told you, but my family up north says that their food shortage is worse than ours. I just pray that Germany's old generals wake up before we all starve. I'm with you Herr Heupel, and glad that I am."

Rudy smiled, put his arm around her shoulder and the frosty edges of his years-long loneliness began to melt.

JULY 20, 1916 TREYSA, GERMANY

"Come in Rudy," Headmaster's voice sounded sandpapery and raw. The dim light from the lamp on his desk made the wrinkles on his face look like deeply etched ink lines. Rudy had never seen him look so old.

"Sit down. I've got some sad news. I'll tell the assembly tomorrow but I thought you should know…" He rubbed his eyes and sighed. "Your classmate Fred was killed in France a month ago."

Rudy gasped, dropped his head and whispered, "Oh God, oh God."

"We received a letter yesterday from his parents with the news. Thousands and thousands have been killed at Verdun. This war, this war…. Rudy, Fred's parents also sent this."

Rudy raised bleary eyes as the headmaster slid a smudged and wrinkled envelope across his desk. "They found this letter in his pack. Written the day before he was shot."

Rudy stared at the battered envelope and at his own name scrawled across it. Even on the battlefront Fred wrote with a flair. Unbidden, an image of Fred's grin frozen in death's rictus flashed into Rudy's mind. He shivered and with a trembling hand picked up the letter.

Headmaster Siebold stood with a groan and came around his desk. He wrapped his long arms around Rudy. "I'm so sorry Rudy. I know you were good friends. I'm afraid we'll be getting more notices like this before the war is over."

Rudy left and sat in the courtyard and by the feeble light of the street lamp read Fred's last words.

JUNE 12 1916

Dear Rudy,

I don't know if this will get to you. They claim that our mail gets delivered. Some guys have gotten letters from their families. I haven't gotten any, not that I'm too surprised about that.

Maybe you'll send me a note if you get a chance. I'm sending this to Hephata because I don't know where you went after graduation. I figure they'll send it along to you.

I've been in France for almost six months, in a place called Verdun. We have moved forward and backward more times than I can count. We've captured and been driven out of one little town a dozen times. This is the sort of war we fight.

What can I say about being a soldier? I've shot my rifle and been shot at. We've launched our sausage bombs and gotten our share of French fireworks shot back at us. Not much chance to be a hero out here.

We spend days and nights down in trenches which we share with rats and mice. The worst are the fleas. If you have a chance, send me some powdery fine sulfur. Guys put it in a bag around their necks, that seems to ward off the little bastards.

I have had buddies get blown up alongside of me. Yesterday we buried some boys and then this morning the bombs hit their graves and a hail of body parts filled our trench. You get numb after a while. That is another scary part of this war...that numb feeling. Our officers tell us we are winning the war. (You know how much I have always respected and trusted the ones in authority!)

I remember the day I told you that enlisting seemed like

the natural thing for me to do. Would old Dr. Altmann say that what is 'natural' for the sinful man is not what God intended? Are you surprised that I'm now asking a religious question? You shouldn't be. Every day here in France we stand on the edge of hell!

I can't tell you how much I miss my time at Hephata. I know I bitched a little(!!) while I was there. I guess I didn't appreciate how good I had it. When I think about our gang, our adventures and late night talks I get homesick. Homesick for a dormitory? Sounds dumb. But living with you guys was the first time I really felt unafraid to be myself. Isn't that what home is supposed to be?

Well, we'll be moving out soon, trying to claim another few meters of territory. I hope your days are safer, happier, and cleaner than mine are. Write when you get a chance.
Your friend, Fred.

Rudy closed tear-filled eyes and saw Fred's jaunty step, his grin-- saucy and sardonic, his eyes full of roguery; he heard his lost friend drawing out his own nickname, "Roooosky". Rudy gulped down a sob as the images dissolved into the sultry night air.

But as he lingered on the bench more apparitions appeared. He was fifteen again and dancing with his mother in their kitchen, and then seventeen standing beside her grave, he was ten and hugging brother Jacob and sister Katherine as they left for Dakota, he was nineteen shaking his father's hand, embracing Junior and his family, saying goodbye to all his friends and to his past, he was twenty-one seeing Marvin off on his way to America….

Gone, gone, all gone. Fred had said he was homesick. Rudy wondered if there would ever be such a thing as 'home' in his own future? A wave of grief rolled toward him, threatening to drown him in despair. He dared not sit here any longer lest his tears erode him completely. He stood and went to look for someone to share his pain. He went in search of Ida.

AUGUST 13, 1916 TREYSA, GERMANY

He guessed there were two of them. Rudy could barely make out their crouched silhouettes against the darkening twilight. If he crept quietly, he could probably get close enough to grab one of them. But then what would he do? Instead Rudy yelled.

"Hey! Get outta there" He began sprinting angrily toward the Center's garden. The two figures kneeling amidst the plants scrambled to their feet, grabbed their baskets and dashed out across the street and into the gloaming.

In the gathering darkness Rudy surveyed the loss. Another half a row of carrots had been dug up. "In another month they'd have been twice as big," Rudy muttered to himself. Of course, then the loss would have been twice as painful. He wondered how much of the garden would be left by season's end. He knew the two thieves were not pranksters raiding the garden for a lark. They were hungry people trying to feed their families.

The Center's garden had always been a supplemental food source and a way to keep young students working. Most of Hephata's food had always come from local markets. But when the harsh whispers of war began sweeping Europe, even before Rudy arrived, Headmaster Siebold had taken action that now seemed prescient. He'd gleaned the records of students and Infirmary residents in search of families that had nearby farms. He contracted with those that could provide food supplies the Center needed.

The Center still bought food in local stores, but now as shortages and rationing had become the norm it relied more and more on its own suppliers, and on its disappearing garden.

The last of the evening glow was extinguished, the crickets had begun their evening concert. Rudy shuffled back to the dormitory. He chewed on the questions that most of Europe was asking. How long will this war go on? What will happen this winter? How long will we last?

JANUARY 15, 1917 TREYSA, GERMANY

"Every mouthful? Are you insane?" Werner, one of the new aides in the men's ward, rolled his only functioning eye.

"Every mouthful. Chew every mouthful one hundred times before you swallow it. That's what my grandmother said," Sophia from the women's ward responded between chews.

She, Werner, Ida and Rudy were eating dinner in the Center's cafeteria. They'd just finished bringing the residents in for the evening meal and now were trying to choke down their own meals. To conserve energy, half of the lights had been turned off and the thermostats were set down to fifty-five degrees. Many of the residents shivered even though they were bundled up in frayed blankets.

"What's the point? Why bother chewing this crap a hundred times?" Rudy asked.

"Yeah, if you chew this war bread that much it turns to paste in your mouth," Werner smacked his lips.

Ida slowly chewed, then nodded to Sophia, "My grandmother gave that advice too. When food is short, chew more. Your jaws work so hard they convince your stomach that you're full."

"Well the food is short, no doubt about that. The late blight wiped out everyone's potatoes. Even the ones in storage turned into a rotten, smelly mess. I should know, I had to shovel 'em out." Werner shuddered at the memory.

Rudy held up a spoon piled high with white pulp. "Behold, the lovely turnip. Back home it was the what we fed the pigs when we ran out of good feed. Now it is all that stands between us and the graveyard. Get ready for one hundred chews." He ceremoniously slurped the mashed turnip from his spoon and began chewing.

"If you think its tough for us, you should see what it's doing to our residents," Ida said. "Last week, Hilda Krause died and no matter what they put on her death certificate, it was lack of decent food that killed her."

"I know this is crude, but it's funny too." Sophia leaned in and lowered her voice. "Yesterday, old Bertha Kautz said, "I don't mind eating rat, but I'm having a hard time getting used to the imitation rat they've been serving in the cafeteria." The four chuckled and then Werner lowered his voice further.

"This is even cruder, but sitting here eating these turnips…it just fits. So, one day last week Chancellor Hollweg comes into the Kaiser's office and says, 'Kaiser, I have bad news and worse news.' The Kaiser says, 'Well, start with the bad news.' The Chancellor says, 'The food situation is so bad that people are eating shit.' The Kaiser says, 'That's terrible news. What could be worse than that?' The Chancellor looks him in the eye and says, 'Kaiser, there's going to be a shortage.'"

The girls slapped their hands on their mouths to stifle their laughs and Rudy who was on the fifty ninth chew of his turnips, sputtered and nearly choked as the joke hit him. *Dark humor…that's all we have in this bleak winter. Still, I'm glad we can laugh. If we lose that, then hope's demise is not far behind.*

After downing their turnips, they carried their plates into the kitchen. Ida said to Rudy, "I'm going to the meat market tomorrow at eight o'clock.

Want to join me? It's only a six blocks."

"Not tomorrow. I've got a big anatomy test at eight. You want someone else to go with you? Will you be okay?"

Ida shrugged, "Oh sure, I'll be fine. I just thought you might like a bit of winter exercise. I'll see you at lunch tomorrow." She and Sophia began helping the women residents toward the elevators. Rudy smiled as watched her quick, purposeful steps and her gentle touch with the women. *Ida... a strong woman, a dear friend.*

The next morning all of Treysa lay under a blanket of winter fog. The evergreens were frosted, the leafless tree branches were coated in rime, the air itself was crystalline white. Somewhere above, a feeble sun tinged it all with a pearly glow. It was nine o'clock and Rudy was the first one to finish the anatomy test. He stepped out into the gelid air and decided to see if Ida had already returned from the meat market.

"No, she left a little before eight and isn't back yet," said one of the kitchen aides as she scrubbed out a kettle. "Usually she's only gone twenty minutes, but who knows…maybe there was a long line."

A swift prickle of apprehension skittered across Rudy's mind. He tried to keep his voice light. "I think I'll just walk out to meet her."

The aide smiled a bit too broadly, "Oh I'm sure she'd really like that."

Rudy ignored her teasing tone and stepped out into the white shroud. He'd gone two blocks when he heard swallowed sobs from within the fog. He broke into a trot just as a tattered apparition emerged from the haze.

"Ida, my God, what happened?" He ran up to her. She was holding a bag against her chest with both hands. Her cap was gone, her light brown hair, usually in a bun, was in disarray with a few strands pasted to a bloody cut on her cheek. One of the sleeves of her coat was torn. Ida looked up at him, dropped the bag, sobbed and leaned into his embrace.

"Oh Rudy, Rudy. It was terrible. I thought she was……" She began it gasp and tremble.

"It's okay, slow down, deep breaths, slow, deep breaths." Rudy rocked side to side with Ida in his arms. The distant sounds of voices and motorcars were muffled by the fog. The two of them stood in the center of a white world. Bit by bit, Ida's breathing slowed and her trembling eased.

Rudy stepped back and looked into her smudged and tear-tracked face. "Want to tell me what happened or want to go home first?"

Ida sighed, then stooped and with a grunt picked up the bag and handed it to Rudy. "I'll tell you on the way." They headed toward the Center and Rudy waited patiently as Ida grappled for words. She grew stronger as she spoke.

"She was a big lady, large—and with an ugly, large voice. She was right in front of me in line at the butcher shop. Complaining loud enough for everyone to hear. Her husband was dead, her son was in the army, her daughter-in-law and two boys were living with her, and she had only one ration stamp left for meat. When she got her five pounds of meat she snarled at the butcher. I thought she was going to bite his head off. She stood by the door and kept grousing.

"I took her place at the counter with the Center's ration stamp booklet and got our twenty five pounds of meat and five pounds of soup bones, then put the bag into my cart. I guess...I suppose... she must have been watching me the whole time." Ida shuddered at the thought.

"Anyway—I pushed my cart out into the fog. I'd gone about half a block when this same lady—the big one, appeared out of the fog right in front of me. Her head was lowered and without a word she charged like a mad cow into my cart. I fell backwards but I didn't let go of the cart and it tumbled on top of me.

"She stood over me with her fists on her hips and started sputtering about how I'm stealing from hungry children and that she was going to take her share of my meat. She snatched the cart but I grabbed onto the bag. As I got up, I told her that the meat was not for me, but for Hephata. Then she really went crazy and started screaming about cripples and retards getting food while her grandkids go hungry. What could I say?" She looked up at Rudy and he shrugged in commiseration.

"I was holding onto the bag, staring at her. She tossed the cart aside and caught my coat sleeve and ripped it. I jerked away and she roared out and scratched my face. I felt the blood running down by cheek and then I guess my anger swallowed my fear. I held the bag in front of me with both hands and barreled into her. She fells backwards onto the cart and totally crushed it. She must have hurt her back too. As I ran into the fog, I heard her groaning and swearing. I ran for a block and then, I guess my nerves...well, I started crying and couldn't stop."

Rudy shook his head. "If I'd gone with you, like you asked...."

Ida hugged his arm. "Don't be silly. How could you've known? I never thought such a thing could happen here in Treysa. But this winter, everyone is hurting."

"Speaking of hurting, you got banged around. How're you feeling?"

Ida's voice was almost back to normal. "Oh, I'll be okay. My back and neck are sore and I've got a headache, but I'll be fine."

When they reached the Center's kitchen, Ida had to tell and retell her misadventure to the other kitchen workers.

Rudy finally interrupted. "Ida, I think you should get your scratch cleaned up and get some rest. Let me take you to your room." Then turning to the kitchen staff, he asked, "May I borrow a kettle full of hot water?"

The kitchen aides tittered as they filled a teakettle and Ida blushed but just nodded as Rudy took her arm. He helped her up the stairs and once inside her small apartment, told her to sit on a chair. He took a towel and soaked it in hot water, wrung it out and lay it across her neck and shoulders. Then he found a clean dish cloth, wet it, crouched before her and gently washed the gash on her cheek.

"There's some ointment there on my dresser," Ida said. Rudy got the ointment and softly applied it to her wound.

"You act like you know what you're doing," Ida smiled weakly at Rudy's serious face.

"I haven't been taking all of those anatomy and health courses for nothing." He allowed himself a grin. Then stood and went behind her. "Now relax your neck and shoulders." He removed the warm towel and began to gently massage the tight muscles across her shoulder blades and up into her neck.

"Ohh, that feels good. Your hands are so warm."

Rudy moved his fingers up her spine until he came to a spot just below her skull. "Ah, here's the problem." He pressed with his finger on a vertebra. "Is it sore here?"

"Ouch. How did you know that?"

Rudy did not answer, but kept rubbing the tender spot. "Now dear, I want you to sit very still, very relaxed."

He put a hand on each side of her jaw, tilted her head to one side, then gave a sharp twist. They both heard a distinct 'pop.'

Ida gasped, then swiveled her head from side to side. "My headache is gone. Rudy, what did you do?"

Rudy came around and stood before her smiling. "You had a nerve that was pinched. Probably happened when you got shoved over."

Ida sat back, looking up at him. "But, how could your hands find that nerve? How did you know what to do? Who taught you this?"

Rudy sat down on the edge of the bed. "Ida, no one taught me. My hands just seem to know what to do."

"How can your hands…? Ida's face held a hundred questions.

Rudy leaned forward and stared down at the faded rug on the floor.

Finally, in a voice scarcely above a whisper, he said what he'd only spoken once before, "My mother believed I had the gift of healing. She said I was a braucher."

"Braucher? Never heard of that word."

Rudy sat up straight and shrugged. "Oh, I guess braucher is one of those south Russian words. I suppose you'd say volksheiler, [folk healer]."

Ida began rubbing her still aching neck and asked, "Why do you seem so, I don't know, embarrassed or ashamed about being called a folk healer?"

Rudy gazed at her with rueful eyes. "It's scary having some sort of power or ability that nobody can explain. It makes me feel strange, or freakish."

Ida leaned forward in her chair. "But, Rudy, what about the Bible? Doesn't it say that Jesus and his disciples healed lots of people?"

"Sure, sure. But that was long ago. And they were special. Me? I'm nobody." Rudy shook his head. "Besides, our Lutheran church today says, 'Stay away from folk healers, they're in bed with the devil.'"

Ida arose from her chair and sat down beside Rudy and took his hand and laid it on her lap. They sat for a minute in the quiet room.

Then Ida declared, "You are not a nobody. And you're special—to me you are. Maybe the church is just jealous." And then, to Rudy's complete surprise, she giggled. "And as far as being in bed with the devil…well, unless you see horns on my head, I think you're OK."

Her giggle swept away the worries from Rudy's befogged mind and the reality of his situation burst upon him a meteor tearing through the night sky. *I'm here in Ida's bedroom. Sitting on her very own bed. She is gripping my hand, holding it in her lap. The room smells of soap and perfume and woman…And she has just told me I'm—."*

Finally, mercifully he managed to stop thinking, put his arms around her, leaned down and discovered that her lips were already waiting for him.

MARCH, 1917 TREYSA, GERMANY

Winter was only grudgingly surrendering to spring. In the courtyard, Headmaster Siebold wrapped his long arms across his barrel chest. One hand clutched the official order. He stood with Pastor Preus and a few dozen students—all of them staring up at the Hephata church tower.

The workers had nearly finished the scaffolding and pulley system they would use to lower the bell onto the horse drawn wagon waiting below.

111

The pallid headmaster sighed. "It was only a matter of time. All the churches in Berlin and Frankfurt had their bells confiscated last month."

The pastor continued gazing up at the workmen on the steeple but cleared his throat and growled. "Siebold, the word 'confiscate' suggests you are against this. That's not true is it, Herr Headmaster?" Herr Preus let that ominous question hover for a moment in the bleak morning air before continuing. "You should think of this as Hephata's contribution to the war effort. Our boys need bullets to defeat the forces of evil."

Rudy was standing in the midst of the group of students. A vision of Fred, crumpled and broken in a trench passed in front of his eyes. Then he saw the headmaster open his mouth in response to the pastor's comment, slowly close it and shake his head. Rudy had to clench his own jaw to keep from shooting off a volley of angry words at the pompous pastor.

But the new aide, Werner, either less intimidated or more naïve, blurted out what they all were thinking, "If we have to melt down church bells to get bullets for our soldiers then Germany must be in deep trouble."

The rest of the students gasped as one body and froze in place as Pastor Preus spun around and shot a frigid glare at Werner. The pastor's words crackled like thin ice under heavy boots.

"And who are you to say Germany is in trouble? What are you doing to defeat the pagans who assault us?"

Werner's face turned as white as the frosty ground. His eye frantically looked for a snow bank he could dive into. But all the banks had melted into gray, misshapen icy lumps and he was affixed to his spot by the pastor's stare and biting words.

"You young people…your hearts are weak, your faith shallow. Out there in the trenches and on the battlefields…those are our strong hearted heroes, they know they are part of a righteous army and that God will bring them victory. You young people should—"

Rudy could not stomach anymore of the pastor's vituperative tirade. He spun on his heel and stalked off to class. *I swear I will never enter that building again as long as that man is pastor. And if this is what my church preaches, then, then I…what will I do?*

APRIL 15, 1917 TREYSA, GERMANY

How does it happen that I become friends with people who are so unlike me? Rudy was reflecting on that mystery as he entered the Infirmary. He'd walked across campus remembering his bunkmate Fred but now as he strode down the corridor of the men's ward, he thought of foul-mouthed and bitter Willy. *How is it that I've come to looking forward to my encounters with this old man whose spine is as twisted as his spirit?*

"Good morning Willy, are you ready for breakfast?" Rudy pulled back the curtain and waited for the usual spate of invectives. Willy was lying on his side and groaned without looking at Rudy.

"You sick, Willy? Should I call Nurse Heinitz?" Rudy bent down over the hunched slight figure.

Willy sighed, "Ahhhh. I'm sick all right but there's nothing any nurse can do. Help me sit up."

As Rudy lifted Willy into his wheelchair, the old man muttered, "The whole damn world is ganging up against poor Germany."

Rudy massaged the tortured muscles of the paralytic's neck and began pushing the chair toward the dining hall. He slipped in to the bantering tone he often used with Willy. "You mean you've finally gotten fed up with the kitchen's breakfast war rations: rye bread and rat meat?"

Willy was in no bantering mood. He spoke over his twisted shoulder with growing vehemence. "I'd eat that crap for every goddamn meal if I thought it'd help our boys. But as of last week, they've got a whole shitload of new enemies to deal with. Not only the Frenchies and the Brits and the bastard Russkies, now the filthy Americans are coming at us too."

Rudy was so stunned he jerked the wheelchair to a stop. "What are you talking about, Willie?"

"What the hell? Why're you stopping? I'm talking about the war, for God's sake. What else is there to talk about?"

Rudy slowly started pushing the chair. "Sorry, I just…what did you mean about the Americans coming at us?"

"Jesus, Rudy, are you living under a rock? Last week the president of the United States of America declared war against us. Before long, our boys will be taking bullets from those asshole American soldiers."

Without another word Rudy rolled Willy's chair up to the table and headed off fetch his next resident. He went about his morning duties in a murky haze. *So now America declares Germany an enemy. And what about Jacob and Katherine and all the Germans who live in America? Are they enemies too? Have they been arrested? Put into prison? Killed? And Vater and Junior and his family in Freidorf? How can it be? Everyone in my family is living in a country at war with Germany. What am I doing here? If only I could run and hide…but where? The world is going mad and dragging me along with it.*

MAY 23, 1917 TREYSA, GERMANY

"Today is an auspicious day." Rudy said to Ida as they walked hand in hand along the Schwalm River.

Ida swung their joined hands. "Today the sky is blue, the breeze is cool, the grass is green-- a normal spring. Today I look at you and I'd say--," she looked him up and down, "you've lost about twenty pounds since January. That's a bit more than me, but none of that makes today auspicious."

"Ahh, but there's one thing you don't know." Rudy raised his free hand into the clear spring air. "Today, I'm twenty-four years old."

Ida dropped his hand and put her hands on her hips. She tried to sound angry but her laughing eyes betrayed her. "Rudolph Heupel. Why didn't you tell me sooner? I would have planned a party. Baked something special."

Rudy grabbed her hand and laughed. "With what? Rye flour and mashed turnips?"

She smiled, "Oh, I could've found something, I'm resourceful you know." She couldn't resist adding, "Although, I don't know...I don't usually bake for such old men."

Rudy gleefully poked her with his elbow. "Yeah, well, I don't know if I'd trust eating food cooked by such young girls. How old are you, anyway?"

"Dumkopf, don't you know it's not polite to ask a lady her age?"

Rudy chuckled, "I wasn't asking a lady, I was asking you."

"Youuuu...!" Ida laughed and gave him a shove in the back that made him stumble forward.

They laughed and joined hands again, strolling along the sun-dappled path, savoring the momentary illusion that they were living in a beautiful, peaceful world.

Abruptly Ida stopped and turned toward Rudy, "I just had an idea for your birthday present." Her enthusiasm tickled Rudy.

"Whoa, you are resourceful. What is it?"

"It's a surprise. I can't tell you. Are you free on Sunday morning?"

Since he'd made his vow regarding worship at the Hephata church, Rudy had taken over the Sunday morning shift at the Infirmary. But for a birthday surprise....

"I can be. What time?"

"Meet me in front of my building at seven. Put on your good clothes." She giggled with excitement as they walked along the sparkling river.

MAY 27, 1917 TREYSA, GERMANY

Rudy hadn't sauntered in a long while. But today as he crossed the campus to meet Ida, he was sauntering. He'd gotten up early, trimmed his reddish-brown moustache and spent extra time combing his wavy hair. Because of the weight he'd lost, the collar of his white shirt was loose around his neck, but he'd tied his only cravat a bit tighter to compensate. He brushed his dark gray wool suit and after dressing, looked into the mirror.

He caught his own serious look in the glass, stuck out his tongue at himself and left the dorm laughing. He whistled back at the sparrows that greeted him and silently thanked God for the beautiful day.

Ida was waiting for him. The spring breeze gently ruffled her white blouse and rippled her dark blue skirt. "You look like an excited little boy going to a birthday party," she said as she grabbed his hand and began walking westward.

"It's been a long time since I've had any kind of birthday celebration. And I've never shared a birthday with such a lovely 'lady'." Rudy laughingly bowed and emphasized that last word.

"About time you recognized me for what I am," she giggled and then quietly added, "I just hope you'll appreciate the surprise."

"Oh, I'm sure I will. Whatever it is, I'll like it."

Ida shrugged, "Guess we'll soon find out."

They chatted and laughed as they walked down the quiet streets for thirty minutes, passing shuttered stores and a few families walking to church. They reached the last of the houses, the cobblestones ended, and a graveled road stretched out into the countryside.

Rudy gave Ida a quizzical look. Before he could speak, she said, "Only fifteen minutes more. Don't tell me you're already exhausted?"

"Ha-ha. Lead on young lady, lead on." *A blue sky, a just warm enough day in May, a smiling, wonderful woman holding my hand—this is already more of a birthday present than I could have imagined.*

They reached the crest of a small rise and saw up ahead a low, white building with several horse carts alongside it. As they approached Rudy noted a cross set on the roof above the doorway.

"Is this a…. Are you taking me to—?"

"Yes, Herr Heupel, I am taking you to church." Ida smiled and looked up at him. She saw a cloud shadow of dismay sweep across Rudy's face and hastily added, "I know you made a promise to yourself, but this church is different and today's preacher—I've heard him before. Please give him a chance."

"Sure, I will. Of course." Rudy smiled broadly, trying to camouflage his disappointment. This definitely was a surprise, but it certainly was not on the list of enjoyable surprises he'd imagined. He and Ida reached the doorway and several people welcomed them with warm handshakes. The hands were rough and calloused; farmer's hands, Rudy guessed.

An elderly couple walked in ahead of them and separated, the man sat down in a pew on the left side of the aisle, the woman joined other elderly women on the right side. Rudy paused for an instant as the warm memory of the Freidorf church coursed through his heart. Ida tugged him forward to the pews where younger couples and families sat together.

An elderly man was softly playing a pump organ as the people entered. Once Rudy and Ida had settled in their pew, she leaned over and whispered, "Today's preacher is from the Hermannsberg Mission. The Seminary is at Hermannsberg, close to my home. I think you'll…" She patted Rudy's knee. "Let's just see."

The small church was nearly full when the pastor stood and the organist stopped playing. The quiet conversations ceased and for a moment the joyful warbling of the birds outside in the trees filled the room. The pastor welcomed everyone, then motioned them to stand and led them in singing a hymn.

The last notes of the song still echoed in the small room and the pump organ bellows slowly wheezed to silence when the pastor bade everyone sit.

"Brothers and sisters in Christ, we are blessed today to have with us Reverend Heinrich Behrens of the Hermannsberg Mission. He's been a missionary in the Transvaal Colony in Africa since 1898. Two years ago, because of the war he and his family were forced to leave their mission work. But he intends to return when this horrible conflict ends. He's visiting churches in the area to raise support for this important work of reaching God's African children who haven't yet heard the Christian good news. I now invite Reverend Behrens to speak."

As the missionary stood up, Rudy noted that he was not wearing the typical Lutheran robe. He had a dark suit and a tie that was only loosely knotted. He lacked hair on the top of his head but more than made up for it with a dark full beard. He smiled, ran his hand through his beard then spoke in a strong baritone voice.

"I am honored to be with you on this Lord's day. Thank you for giving me this time to speak to you not about my mission but about God's mission. But first I must say a very hard thing. I must say some words that may upset some of you."

116

Rudy, Ida and the entire gathering leaned forward, anticipating and dreading what might come next.

The smile left the missionary's face. "War is a horrid thing. War is not part of God's plan for this world." He swept his gaze across the room. "Now I know that some of you here have sons and other family members fighting in this war. Maybe some of you here have lost dear ones in the battles. I am not questioning their honor or bravery, I think we should all recognize their sacrifices and pray for them and their families every day."

He paused and moved down the aisle until he stood beside the first pew. "But friends, I am simply reminding all of us that all war, any war, including this war, is the result of a broken, sinful world. Our own Lord said, 'Blessed are the peacemakers for they shall be called children of God.' This war, all war, hinders the God's mission."

Rudy felt the muscles in his chest relax as he realized the verbal assault he'd expected was not coming. He found himself silently mouthing, 'Amen', as Reverend Heinrich spoke.

The missionary pastor took a deep breath, then smiled broadly to the congregation. "But brothers and sisters, we know that God's mission cannot be hindered forever. Let me tell you about the Hermannsburg Missionary Society and our work.

"Our founder Reverend Ludwig Harms never let us forget Christ's word: we should always be servants and never lords. In Africa we've founded a center that reaches out to the black people of that land. We call it the 'farmer's mission' because we're raising most of our own food through farming and because most of us pastors once were farmers."

He paused and grinned, "Friends, like many of you, I've shoveled my share of manure."

Soft chuckles filled the little church and the pastor's warm voice filled the ears and hearts of the congregation. He spoke for thirty minutes, evoking for the rural German men and women the massifs and plains of the Transvaal of exotic Africa. Out of the corner of her eye Ida saw Rudy's profile. He sat statue still and she could not begin to guess what he was thinking.

Reverend Heinrich opened up his Bible. "I will close by reminding you of the last words spoken by our Lord before his body ascended into heaven: *Go ye therefore into the world, making disciples of all nations, baptizing them in the name of the Father and the Son and the Holy Spirit. And remember, I am with you always, to the end of the age.* May those words inspire all of us. Amen."

Five minutes of walking and still not a word from Rudy. Ida struggled to keep up with him as they hiked back toward town on the gravel road. After the sermon, the local pastor had led them in prayers and then they'd all stood and closed the service with the hymn 'Alone in you I Trust.'

Confirm in us your Gospel, Lord,
Your promise of salvation.
And make us keen to hear you Word,
And follow our vocation:
To spend our lives in love for you,
To bear each other's burdens too.
And then at last, when death shall loom,
O Savior come,
And bear your loved ones safely home.

Ida had looked up at Rudy and winced when she saw he wasn't singing. As they left the church, she and Rudy had shaken the hand of the guest preacher and Rudy had murmured a subdued 'thank you.' They'd spent a few minutes chatting with some of the worshippers. Then Rudy had fixed his gaze upon some invisible point on the horizon and begun marching silently home.

The larks sang in the fields as they passed, the gravel crunched beneath their shoes, the breeze sighed in the grass in the ditch, and Ida's heart sighed in disappointment. Unable to restrain her tongue any longer, Ida murmured, "Well, at least I tried."

Rudy took a few more strides before slowing and asking, "Sorry, did you say something?"

Ida grabbed his arm before he could hurry off again. "I said, 'at least I tried.' I know it wasn't much of a birthday present and not what you expected or hoped for, but, well I…"

Rudy came to a complete stop and turned toward. His eyes brimmed with tears and fire. He put his hands on her shoulders. "Ida, what are you saying? Your gift..This morning…That man's words, a gift from God; I hardly dare say it…I've been given a revelation. I think…I believe God wants me to be a missionary to Africa."

Ida felt the weight—of Rudy's hands upon her shoulders and his words upon her heart. She was thrilled that her gift had inspired Rudy and awestruck by what it might mean for his, or did she dare hope, their future.

Rudy slowed his pace and his arms and hands punctuated his words.

118

"Soon, soon this war has to end. I'll go to that seminary in Hermannsburg. I'll work too. I wonder how long the course is? Maybe my work here at Hephata will count too. How far is it from your home? Maybe we could…"

Rudy's enthusiastic chatter carried them all the way back to Treysa and to the Center. His excitement delighted Ida. She'd given him more than she'd imagined.

But hidden from the sunshine and warm optimism of the day, Ida felt an ache with every step. Like a pebble in her shoe, she could not ignore the hard facts: they were hungry and poor in a country sinking ever deeper into the quicksand of a never-ending war.

OCTOBER, 1917 TREYSA, GERMANY

It was a miracle it hadn't happened sooner. After years of fearing what had never come, he'd almost forgotten the danger.

Rudy whistled as he walked back toward Hephata. Earlier in the evening he'd walked with Ida to her friend Hertha's apartment near the train station. Hertha was hosting an anniversary celebration for her parents the next day and Ida was staying overnight so she could rise early to help with the baking and cooking.

They'd all had a few glasses of wine, laughed and joked into the night. At last Ida decided it was time for Rudy to leave so the girls could get some rest before the next day's festivities. Now Rudy strolled down the moon-dappled sidewalk, whistling and savoring the vision of Ida's wine flushed cheeks.

"What the hell you whistlin' about?" The slurred and sour question came from one of the two men who now stood a mere six feet in front of Rudy. The reek of cheap beer drifted to Rudy's nostrils and a chill slithered down his back.

They were both unshaven and wore battered army caps. The shorter man had a large bandage covering one cheek and side of his jaw. By the pale moonlight Rudy could see it was gray with grime. The two men swayed and glared at him.

"I said, 'What the hell you whistlin' about?" the short man growled.

"Nothing, no reason…I'm, I'm just going home." Rudy took a step to his left to pass the pair, but they moved to block him.

The taller of the two grabbed Rudy's arm, "Whoa, what's yer fuckin' hurry? 'Fraid a talkin' to a couple of the Fatherland's finest soldiers?"

The bandaged soldier burped and laughed. "Yeah, pretty boy. We've

---

119

been up to our asses in mud and duckin' bullets for years. That takes the whistle right outta ya." He lay his hand on his bandaged cheek. "I took a hit in the face. Ain't never gonna whistle again." He lurched to within inches of Rudy's face. "Where've you been hidin' during this war, you cocksucker?"

Rudy tried to pull back from the ravaged visage in front of him, but the tall soldier swung him around and grabbed his other arm from behind with a steel grip. Like nausea, a wave of panic flooded his senses. He frantically tried to think. *I can't say I'm Russian born. I dare not say I'm against the war. Then they'd kill me for sure.* His thoughts were a flock of frantic caged birds. He blurted out in desperation.

"Gentlemen, I've…ah..I've been working in the hospital." He tried to force authority into his voice. "Yes, yes. I'm taking care of Germany's finest men."

The tall man behind him growled in his ear. "You tellin' us yer a fuckin' doctor? I say bullshit. You're too young." He pulled Rudy's elbows toward each other.

Rudy suppressed a groan. A note of desperation slipped through a crack in his voice. "Not a doctor, no. I'm a doctor's assistant. I, I, I help——"

"Goddamn liar." The bandaged man grabbed Rudy's shirt. "I just spent five weeks in the city hospital and there weren't no such thing as doctor's assistants. Shit. All the hospitals are so damn short-handed—every mother's son is out fighting this war."

He jerked savagely at Rudy's shirt; fabric ripped and buttons flew. "So, tell me, candy ass, how'd you escape getting called up? Didja hide under your mutti's skirts?"

"My mother is dead," Rudy muttered, secretly relieved that at least he could stop lying.

"And asshole, that's what you should be," screamed the drunken, bandaged soldier as he drove his knee into Rudy's groin.

Rudy's breath left him in a deep groan as he fell. He curled into a ball with his arms covering his head. Three years' worth of fears congealed into an icy ball in his stomach. The kicks began.

Once, when he was ten, he and his friend Paul, on their way home from school, had gotten caught in a hailstorm. At first, as the walnut sized stones had fallen straight down, they'd held their notebooks over their heads and laughed. But when the wind began blasting and the stones flew sideways against their backs and legs, they shouted in pain and ran in terror for shelter. They had bruises for days.

Now as the frenzied kicks went on and on, Rudy wondered how long the

120

bruises would last. Then as boots kept thudding against his back and head, he began to fear he'd never rise again. Finally, in an instant, the overpowering pain, frantic fear and savage kicks vanished into complete blackness.

*　　*　　*

He floated in a dark violet ocean of pain. He dared not move a muscle, twitch a toe or wriggle a finger. The tiniest movement would sink him like a stone into an endless depth of agony. So he floated, stiff and motionless, on the violet sea. But tears flowed unabated down his cheeks and trickled into the gloomy waters. Tears flowed in response to a deeper wound: shame, remorse.

He had stood on that dark street and lied, quickly and deftly. And if allowed, he would have kept lying, desperately, endlessly. He'd always clung to a secret pride, a kernel of superiority rarely admitted even to himself. But still… He had coveted it, cherished his absolute honesty as though it were a pearl of great price. Now, floating on this violet sea of suffering, even with eyes pinched shut he was forced to gaze into his deepest self…a liar, a self-serving, self-saving coward, a sinner as guilty as everyone else.

He rolled his head from side to side in sorrow. An electric flash of lightning seared his brain and he sunk into the violet sea.

*　　*　　*

A distant voice slipped through the ringing in his ears, "Rudy, can you hear me?" He thought it was a question from his own bewildered, mangled dreams. "Rudy, can you hear me?"

There it was again, cutting through the pulsing hum that filled his brain. The smell of bleach and a faint waft of urine filled his nose. Now he felt a pressure upon his shoulder. He focused all of his will and energy to his eyelids. His face twisted and trembled as though he were lifting a hundred pounds.

At last he opened his eyes. A blurry silhouette seemed pasted upon a bright background. He blinked as his eyes focused. Nurse Heinitz, hand upon his shoulder and brow furrowed with concern, looked down at him.

"Rudy, Rudy….you heard me. Can you talk?"

Rudy's voice echoed distantly in his own ears. "Where am I?" He turned his head and the room began to whirl.

"Lie still, Rudy, it's OK. You're in the Infirmary. You've been unconscious for almost eight hours." The nurse pulled a chair alongside his bed and returned her hand to his shoulder. "Your back is badly bruised, you

121

probably have some broken ribs, maybe you have a concussion. We won't know if you have kidney damage until you…We'll wait until you have to use the bedpan."

Rudy lay back, trying to recover contact with his body. Wherever his mind probed he cringed with pain. But the humming in his ears was fading and his vision was clearing. "How…how did I get here?"

Nurse Heinitz sat back in her chair and shook her head. "Quite a story, Rudy. You know Sophia our new aide?"

Rudy gave the tiniest of nods, afraid of setting off another wave of nausea.

"Sophia and her friend came out of the bierhaus just as the soldiers were kicking and cursing you. She says she recognized you on the ground—I don't know how—and she started screaming. The men looked at her but didn't stop.

Her friend started screaming too and then people started pouring out of the bierhaus and the two drunks ran off down the street. The bar owner came out and since the two guys had come out of his bar, he was afraid he'd get in trouble. He brought around his car and was going to take you to the hospital but Sophia convinced him to bring you and her to Hephata. You got here about midnight."

"What time is it now?" Rudy asked.

"It's a few minutes after seven. Dr. Meinz, our on-call doctor, checked on you when you arrived. Said your pressure and heart rate were normal and he'd be back around eight."

"Rudy..ohh. You're awake. Thank God. Sophia told me—" Ida burst into the room, red-faced and panting. Then she caught herself, remembered her nurse's aide training. She stood for a moment and caught her breath, then walked quietly to the bedside. Nurse Heinitz smiled and left the two of them.

"I was so scared when Sophia showed up at Hertha's. I ran all the way." Her eyes welled with tears. "Why would anyone do such an awful thing?"

With heavy eyes Rudy gazed at her, then turned away. "They suffered in the war and I didn't."

"Oh, that's ridiculous. They were drunken beasts."

"Yeah, I know. But they were soldiers who'd fought for their country and they were pissed that I hadn't."

"But to assault you….they might have killed you if Sophia hadn't—"

"I lied to them, Ida. I tried to lie my way out of their grasp."

"So? Who wouldn't do anything to stay alive." She grinned, "Besides,

122

looks like you didn't do such a good job of it. Maybe you need more practice." She saw at once that her attempt at humor had not only nosedived but had wounded him.

He winced, closed his eyes and muttered. "I'd always promised myself I'd never, ever lie."

Ida stretched out her hand and touched his cheek. "Oh, Rudy, I'm sorry. Please don't beat yourself up over one lie. You've been beat up enough."

He slowly opened his eyes and smiled weakly. "You've got flour smudged on your cheek."

She chuckled as she wiped her cheek. "I was in the middle of making küchen dough when Sophia showed up. She took my place and I ran here as fast as I could."

Rudy lay in silence, staring at the ceiling. He turned to her and his look was solemn. "Ida, I'm glad you came. Really. But, right now I think I need to sleep. Maybe you can see me tomorrow." He closed his eyes and slowly turned his head away from her.

Ida sighed and stood. She wanted to believe that what Rudy said was true. She stopped at the door before leaving the room and looked back at him, staring at the wall.

Maybe Rudy was still in shock, or maybe she was imagining it. But inside, in a place she could not touch, she felt a tremor and she could not escape the sense that in the landscape of their relationship a fault line had appeared.

NOVEMBER, 1917 TREYSA, GERMANY

Rudy sat wrapped in a rough woolen blanket on a bench next to the Infirmary. He watched the beech trees surrendering their last leaves to the frisky breeze swirling through the Hephata campus. High goose feather clouds sailed across the crisp blue sky. It was a beautiful autumn day. But to Rudy, the entire scene, even life itself, was draped in gauzy gray. He cringed at the thought that soon they'd all be forced to surrender to another bleak winter.

His broken ribs ached with every breath. Five days ago, tall, thin Doctor Meinz had examined him and given him the results of his sidewalk beating: deep contusions on the back, forearms and buttocks, three cracked ribs, no discernible kidney damage, but quite possibly, a slight concussion.

After the examination, the perpetually weary doctor stood beside Rudy's bed and shook his finger. "Young man, you're fortunate. This could have been much worse. But still, you need to take some precautions. No heavy lifting for at least three months until the ribs are healed, get plenty of rest, no running."

A suggestion of a smile swept across his creased face. "And maybe worst of all, no beer. It slows down the healing."

Now Rudy tugged the blanket closer around his shoulders, hunched down and sighed. *Here I sit, on a tiny island in a sea of violence. Going through the motions, waiting, waiting...for what? How do I escape this never-ending circle? No one'll rescue me from this sameness. If Hephata weren't so kind, I'd have starved ages ago. Where do I belong? What kind of man have I become? What if this war goes on for another ten years? What if my ribs never heal right? What if Vater saw me now? All this time, all these years...and nothing so show for it. That is, if Vater is still alive...or Junior and his family...or Jacob and Katherine...*

Rudy groaned as he lifted his bruised body from the bench. He'd slept ten hours last night, but weariness clung to him like a leaden overcoat. He trudged off to bed. The more time he spent sleeping the less time he had to think.

*   *   *

"Ida, what's so captivating out there? You've been standing at that window for ten minutes." Sophia came up beside Ida and followed her glance to where Rudy sat on a bench. "Ohh. Why don't you go out and talk to him?"

"He's not in the mood for talking these days."

"Rudy, not eager to talk? Now that's strange. Was his jaw so beat up that it hurts him to talk?"

"No, I don't think it's because of the beating, not directly anyway." Ida shrugged. "It's as though while his body was getting pummeled his spirit got kicked and punched too. And even if his ribs are healing, his spirit is still wounded. And it refuses to heal."

Sophia nodded. "That sounds like melancholia. My mother, after my little sister was born, dragged herself around the house for weeks, stopped taking care of herself. Only talked when you talked to her. And then her talk was nothing but gloom."

"Oh, that's Rudy these days." Ida's eyes were dry, but her words held tears. "Yesterday he called himself a 'shallow fool'. When I protested, he started ripping apart his own idea of being a missionary to Africa."

Sophia said, "A missionary to Africa? Sounds exciting."

"Ja, a couple of months ago that's all he could talk about. But now he

124

claims he's a liar; that he was lying to himself and to me. Yesterday he whined, 'Africa? I don't have enough money to take a trolley across Treysa. Besides, how can a broken shell like me carry any good news to anyone?'"

"Have you tried cheering him up?"

"Sure, but it usually backfires. I say, 'think happy thoughts' and he rolls his eyes and mutters that he'd just be telling more lies to himself. It's as if he doesn't want to, or can't, stop looking at the darkness."

Sophia put her arm around her friend, "That's melancholia for sure."

"Did your mom ever get over her dark mood?" Ida asked.

"Eventually, ja. We didn't do anything special. Just never left her alone and tried to help her out. Gradually, she seemed to come out of her cloud, until one day she actually laughed, you know, a deep belly laugh. She started to fuss and coo and love the baby. She hadn't done any of that for weeks."

The two women watched as Rudy slowly raised himself from the bench. "I wonder if there's anything I can do for him?" Ida mused.

"Don't know. All I can say is, don't give up on him." Sophia squeezed Ida's shoulder.

"Don't worry. I'm a long way from that." Ida gazed at Rudy as he plodded to his room and she murmured a prayer. "God, let his spirit find rest and his heart be healed."

DECEMBER, 1917, TREYSA, GERMANY

Rudy sat and looked around at the dozen people in the circle. *Well, at least this is better than writing numbers in account books.* For six weeks since his beating, Rudy had been working in the Hephata administration office. At first, he'd been taken aback by the meticulous attention the staff devoted to record keeping. Every bit of information was recorded, sometimes in triplicate. He wondered if his being born outside of Germany had spared him from the fanatical attention to details that seemed such an integral part of the German character. Nevertheless, as best he could, he applied himself to the work. Headmaster Siebold had reminded him, "Rudy, if you can't lift and bathe the patients in the Infirmary, you'll need to put in some hours elsewhere."

During the first weeks, the drudgery of the office work had fit with his dour attitude and melancholy spirit. But gradually his patience had eroded, and he'd accepted the headmaster's latest assignment with as much anticipation as his own persistent glumness allowed. Last week Headmaster Siebold had interrupted Rudy's accounting work. "Rudy, some years ago, we had a regular Bible study with our Infirmary residents. I want you to restart it."

Maybe this was just another bit of busy work to keep him occupied but Rudy had to grudgingly admit he'd enjoyed the preparation and now looked forward to the gathering.

He sat and looked at the dozen residents sitting around the circle in the activity room of the Infirmary. A few seemed eager, a few curious, and some seemed ready to fall asleep. He recognized all of the faces and knew some of the names. There was Lydia, a tiny wisp of a woman; Greta who seemed always to be staring at her feet; Lizette, who wore fiery red lipstick every day; Christoph who had only one leg and often laughed at odd moments; and Adolph, paralyzed on the left side of his body.

Rudy smiled, cleared his throat and…in rolled one more resident. Willy, his wheelchair pushed by a grinning Sophia, stared at Rudy with what seemed a defiant air. Rudy almost greeted him with his usual banter. But considering how Willy often responded, he checked that impulse and simply nodded and welcomed him into the circle.

"I'm glad you all decided to join me today for this Bible study. We haven't had a study time like this for a long time and I don't know how many of you have been to one before. That doesn't matter. We'll learn and study together? Ok?"

Lydia and Christoph smiled and nodded. The rest of the group looked at him with...with what? indifference? curiosity? Rudy swallowed and began. "The Bible is full of great stories. Today we're going to look at some stories in the Old Testament, the stories of Jacob. Do any of you know of anything about Jacob?"

Stampeded by his own nervousness and enthusiasm Rudy was only able to allow a few seconds of silence before he began to answer his own question. "Jacob was—"

He detected a murmur from Greta and leaned forward. "Did you say something, Greta?"

Without lifting her head, Greta spoke in a voice so soft and inflectionless, it almost sounded like a character in a dream. "Jacob was the third patriarch, after Abraham and Isaac, fraternal twin brother of Esau."

Rudy sat back, disconcerted and humbled. He'd always seen Greta as mentally deficient, a victim of dementia or some other malady of the brain. How many other preconceptions about the people in this group would he need to jettison?

"That's right Greta. Have you studied the Bible a lot?"

Greta raised her head slightly, "I taught Sunday school for twenty years when I was younger."

Rudy grinned, "Then you're way ahead of me, Greta. How about the rest of you? What stories do you remember?

"Wasn't there one about a ladder to heaven?" Christoph asked.

"You're right, Christoph. God came to Jacob in a dream. In the dream angels were going up and down the ladder and God descended and promised to bless Jacob. Anything else?"

After only a moment of silence, Willy growled, "The bastard was a liar and a cheat."

Rudy dropped his eyes to his lap to keep the group from seeing his smile. *Leave it to Willy to zero in on the worst.*

"Well, Willy, technically he wasn't a bastard. But he did lie to his father and did cheat his brother out of his birthright."

Rudy shared with them the story of how Jacob with the help of his mother, deceived his father Isaac and received the blessing and inheritance meant for his brother Esau. Then he asked, "Any other stories of Jacob?"

Once again Greta murmured, "His sons became the twelve tribes of Israel, after he wrestled with God and had his name changed to Israel."

"That's right. And why was he wrestling with God?"

Willy spat out, "Because the lying, cheating bastard was a damned coward."

Apparently, the others in the group knew Willy well enough to not be shocked. But Rudy pushed back. "Willy, no need to swear. Besides, he wasn't damned he was blessed by God. He was—"

"Don't need to lecture me. My dad was a pastor and I've read the stories more than once. In the end Jacob was blessed but he still was a damned coward."

Willy's dad—a pastor? Another shocker. Rudy sat back. "OK. Herr Willy, tell us why you think he was a coward?"

Willy snorted and shook his shoulders. "Jacob has a pissed off father-in-law behind him, so he can't go back. And Esau, the brother that he cheated is on the road ahead, coming to meet him with four hundred soldiers. So, what does he do? He sends his wives and kids and herds across the river, puts them between himself and Esau. Damned cowardly thing to do if you ask me."

Tiny Lydia chirped, "I think the poor man just wanted to find a place he could call home. But he'd betrayed so many people that he couldn't go back and he couldn't go forward. He was stuck and he was afraid."

Lydia's words were another gentle slap on Rudy's face, a reminder of how easily he'd labeled the residents as slow and simple thinkers. He nodded to the group.

"So, Lydia sees Jacob as a poor fellow who's made mistakes and now is desperate to find a home and Willy sees him as a cowardly...let's use Willy's words, 'a cowardly bastard.' How about the rest of you?"

Rudy spent the next few minutes listening and encouraging the quieter members to speak. He was gratified to see that most of them were willing and able to express an opinion. He decided to ask the question that he himself had not been able to answer.

"Let's think about this: Jacob lied and cheated; he often used other people for his own gain; he was a broken, flawed man. And yet, God chose to bless and make him an important part of God's plans. Why?" The silence that followed was broken only by the clanking of the radiator pipes.

Finally, Lizette, who up to now had been mostly quiet, spoke with quiet intensity. "Why? Forget it. Nobody can figure out why God does what he does."

Then Greta, whose voice had grown stronger and her gaze lifted, responded, "The story reminds us that God can use broken people to do God's will."

Rudy nodded, "And we need to remember that all of us are broken."

"Aww, that's bullshit," Willy snarled. "I can't get out of bed by myself, or even wipe my own ass. You can walk and run, chase girls and plan for tomorrow." He slapped his hands on the armrests of his wheelchair. "You're free, I'm a prisoner. Don't give me this 'all of us are broken' shit."

Rudy's first instinct was to rebut Willy's tirade and talk about his own, and humanity's brokenness. But then something happened, something that hadn't happened to Rudy since the beating. His perspective shifted.

For a brief moment, he was pulled out of himself and was deposited into Willy's wheelchair and he experienced the world through Willy's life—felt Willy's pain-wracked body, sensed his aching loneliness, cringed at the crusty edge of his anger.

Rudy spoke softly, "I'm sorry Willy. You've got a point. I didn't mean to say our realities are equal. You Willy, all of you here, have had to face challenges I can only imagine. I apologize. Let me try again: if God can use Jacob to do good, then God can use any of us, all of us to do some good in this world. How does that sound?"

Willy sat in silence. Most of the others murmured their approval. Rudy finished the study with the story of how Esau, the sinned against one, had received his brother Jacob with open arms and forgiveness. Rudy closed the gathering with a prayer and the group slowly dispersed.

After the room was empty, Rudy sat with arms folded and legs crossed as he reflected upon the gathering. The melancholy mood of the past weeks was now penetrated by swirls of light. He allowed that feeling of empathy he'd had for Willy shift to someone closer to his heart: Ida.

She hasn't abandoned me. That's a miracle. I've been as responsive as an old fence post. When she tried to cheer me up, laughed and teased me—I snapped at her. She could've turned her back on me, just walked away. She didn't. Crazy, she stayed. She got quieter, gentler. Stopped telling me to 'be happy'. She didn't stop dragging me to her small gatherings, like those after work bierhaus parties, even when I couldn't drink beer. I hope it's not too late to tell her how much she means to me.

JANUARY 15, 1918 TREYSA, GERMANY

An entire week passed before the irony of the situation struck Rudy. One wintry day, two battered military trucks ground up the hill to Hephata and rattled to a halt in front of the Infirmary. A lanky grizzled man in a rumpled tan army uniform stepped down from the first truck as Headmaster Siebold lumbered across the yard toward them.

"I am Sergeant Schultz. We have fifteen soldiers that need attention and the hospital in town is full. By the High Command we are ordering your facility to provide care." The soldier's words were hard, but his face was lined with fatigue and his voice raspy with weariness.

The Headmaster nodded. "Yes, of course. We were told you'd be coming. No need to order us, Herr Sergeant. It is our calling to care for those in need."

Rudy and a dozen other students had already gathered around the trucks. They dropped the tailgates and were met with eyes: some dark and wary, many narrowed in pain, and a few blankly staring. Rudy and the others helped lower the men who were on crutches. Because of his still healing ribs, Rudy allowed his fellow students to lift out the litters holding the severely wounded.

"Take them into the first floor of the education building, the large classroom," the headmaster ordered. He turned to the Sergeant, "We've turned that space into a hospital ward, basic but clean and with good light."

The soldier grunted, "Probably get better care than at the City Hospital."

Inside the room, Rudy walked down the rows of cots recording the names of the young men. Though a few of the soldiers barely whispered their names, most spoke in flat, inflectionless voices, as though they were being interrogated by enemy forces. Except for Johannes.

"My name? What the hell difference does it make to you?" He was leaning against the back of his cot. With his high cheekbones and long jaw, he reminded Rudolph of a wolf. His eyes were smoldering coals.

Rudy began patiently, "First, we'd like to use your name instead of saying 'hey you'. Second, if you need any medication, we need to make sure we're giving it to the right soldier."

"And, don't forget if I die, you'll need to fill out the death certificate," the young man snapped.

Rudy tried to smile at the bitter soldier. "We're going to do our best to keep that from happening."

"I've been so close to Gevatter Tod [Grim Reaper] so many times, I figure my luck is gonna run out one of these days." He sighed, "My name is Johannes, Johannes Bierwagen. You can add to your notes, 'the poor bastard with only one leg.'"

Rudy couldn't avoid staring at the grimy bandage wrapped around the stump of Johannes' leg which ended above his right knee. "How long has that bandage been on?"

"A week? Two weeks? The days are all smeared together since the damn Frenchies stole my leg."

Rudolph shuddered, "As soon as I finish getting everyone's names, I'll be back to change that filthy thing."

So began Rudolph's work with Johannes and the rest of the wounded troops. He spent the next week, every waking hour, changing bandages, giving injections, distributing medicine. At night, he fell into bed exhausted but every morning he woke up eager to see how his men were doing. He began to see flickers of light in some of the blank eyes. Conversations increased as the young men comprehended that they truly were in a safe place surrounded by caring people.

One morning, a week after the soldiers had arrived, Rudy entered the room and heard Johannes' call out, "Hey Doc, can you come over here?"

Rudolph began walking across the room when the irony twisted his face into a rueful grin. *Three months ago, I tried to escape a beating by baldly lying, claiming I was a doctor tending wounded soldiers. If only these young men had shown up last September... I might still have gotten beat up*

130

but I wouldn't have had to compromise my own moral integrity. I should admit it..in this war, in this world, sooner or later everyone's shiny integrity gets tarnished.

"What's so funny Doc?" Johannes asked as Rudolph drew near.

Rudy shrugged, "Not funny really, just thinking about how crazy this world can be."

"Crazy. You talk about crazy." Johannes threw his arms in the air, "Doc, don't think I'm losing it, but I swear to God, my leg hurts like a Hurensohn [son of a bitch]."

Rudolph leaned over to examine the soldier's leg.

Johannes dropped his voice now, evidently embarrassed, "No, no. My other leg, the one that's not there. I can feel it. It feels like someone's shoving needles into it."

Rudy was fascinated. He'd read about phantom pain. Some believed it was a psychological reaction to losing a limb. Others wondered if it might be related to damage in the spinal cord or nerves. He pulled a chair next to the bed. "Have you felt this before?"

"No, not really." Johannes shook his head, then looked quizzically at Rudy. "Well, awhile back, I think when I was in the truck, I felt something like this but I figured I was delirious and getting ready to die."

"How long did it last?"

"Christ, Doc, how the hell should I know? We were bouncing and banging in the back of that old clunker, I didn't have the chance to check my gold-plated pocket watch."

Rudy grinned in appreciation of the sarcasm, "Dumb question. Forgive me. Johannes, you're not going crazy and you're not the only one who's felt what you're feeling. It's called phantom pain."

"Phantom? Damn it, this pain is real."

"Ja, ja, it's real pain. But it feels like it's coming from a leg that isn't there. Your lost leg is the phantom."

Johannes' face lost its harshness, "Doc, is there something you can do? Some drug you can give me?"

Rudy leaned forward and spoke quietly, "Johannes, understand this, I'm not a doctor, so I can't give you any medicine. Besides, I don't think there's any medicine that can treat phantom pain. But I do know that when nerves are damaged or hurt, they cause pain. Nerves from your legs run into your spinal column." Rudy dropped his voice even more, "If you'll allow me, I'd like to massage your back."

"You're asking me for permission?" Johannes rolled his eyes. "First time that's happened since I got drafted. Sure, Doc, if you think it'll help."

Rudy stood, "I can't promise it'll help, but I'm convinced it won't hurt. I'll be back in a few minutes with some warm towels."

An hour later, Rudy straightened up and rolled his shoulders. Johannes was sleeping on his belly. Rudy had rubbed and kneaded the muscles of the wounded soldier's back. He'd located several painful knots and hot spots. As he'd massaged, he'd felt Johannes' muscles relax and the soldier had groaned in satisfaction. Rudy had no way of knowing whether his massaging and manipulating had alleviated the pain but he took Johannes' soft snoring as evidence that he'd helped and not harmed the patient.

By the next morning when Rudy arrived at the ward, every one of the soldiers had heard some version of Johannes' experience. Though Rudy still did his morning duty with the residents, from that day forward, for as long as Hephata received soldiers, Rudy not only cleansed wounds, gave injections, and distributed medicine. He also spent hours every day probing aching joints, stretching aching muscles, and realigning displaced vertebrae. His discovered that his innate capacity to locate pain was growing with practice and his ability to alleviate pain with massage was increasing the more soldiers he treated.

He was so immersed in this daily routine that he could not have foreseen how these skills would shape his future.

APRIL, 1918, TREYSA, GERMANY

"Looks like an ordinary carrot to me," Ida shrugged as Rudy held up the dirt-smudged, long, thin root. They were walking across the campus square under a sunny spring sky.

"Ah, but looks can be deceiving," Rudy grinned. "This carrot survived intact in the garden dirt all winter long."

"You mean you forgot to harvest it?" Ida playfully chided.

"No. Well, let's just say it was buried deeper than the others so I missed it. But what makes it special is that the early snow covered the garden, insulated the soil so that this carrot didn't freeze. It's as fresh as if I'd plucked its green top this morning." Rudy popped the tip of the carrot, dirt and all, into his mouth and bit. The carrot crisply cracked, and Ida cringed.

"Eww, all of that dirt."

"Ach, a little dirt is good for the body," Rudy said as he took another bite.

Ida smiled and said mostly to herself, "I'm glad that more than that

132

carrot survived the winter intact."

Rudy, with his mouth full, mumbled, "What are you saying?" But before Ida could answer he swallowed and said, "Oh, look, look. There in that tree." He grabbed Ida's shoulder and pointed up into the branches. "See right there, a nest. I think it's a dove. Oh, see the mother is coming back, look at that little beaks wide open, praying for food. Can you see them?"

He turned to Ida. But she was not looking into the branches. She was gazing up at him, smiling with shimmering eyes.

"What?" Rudy smiled back at her. She said nothing but tugged his hand and they continued walking.

"A couple of months ago, I didn't know if I'd see you excited about anything ever again." Ida said quietly.

Rudy shook his head and gripped her hand tighter. "I know, I know. I wondered too…I felt trapped or…I didn't know what was happening."

"Sophia called it 'melancholia', said her mother went through it once," Ida said.

Rudy chuckled. "'Melancholia' ---sounds about right. How can I describe it? When you have a bad cold and you're all stuffed up, you know how you can't smell and everything you eat is tasteless? Well, it was as if my entire body and mind had a cold. Everywhere I looked I saw dismal gray, every sound was a hollow echo, every thought was a dull slug. My life was flavorless. I don't know how many mornings I'd lay in bed and say to myself, 'I don't think I can get up today. Why should I bother?'"

"But you did, every morning," Ida hugged his arm.

Rudy nodded. "That's because some people wouldn't stop pestering me. Between Headmaster Siebold, and Nurse Heinitz and a certain Miss Ida Loock—." He tickled her side and she squirmed and laughed. He continued, "And then, when the soldiers came, I started feeling better. But for three months before that, I was in quite a hole."

"We didn't know how to get you out of the hole you were in, but we weren't going to let you sink out of sight." Ida said.

They'd reached the edge of the campus and Rudy gazed down the hill leading into town. He seemed to be considering whether or not to keep going.

"I didn't sink completely, but it got awfully dark for a long time."

Ida pulled him away from the street and back onto the campus sidewalk. "Let's stay here on campus. It's nicer."

"You mean safer," Rudy corrected her as he reluctantly turned back. "One of the weights that dragged me into that pit was this load of guilt. I can't say that treating the soldiers has taken that away. I'm cowering like a rabbit here while every other young man is fighting."

Ida's reply was swift and sharp. "Don't exaggerate Rudy. You know it's more complicated than that. You read the Frankfurt Zeitung article last month. In January a million workers in the war industries were on strike. You're not the only one trying to stay alive in this madhouse. Honestly, ask your injured soldiers. I think the whole country is exhausted and fed up with this stupid war. In the news articles the generals keep saying 'the Fatherland is nearing victory.'" She snorted, "What a pack of liars."

Rudy sighed, "Lying comes naturally when you're afraid. I always thought I was a strong—"

Ida stopped walking, put her fists on her hips and glared at him. She spoke with more vehemence than he'd ever heard from her. "Stop it, Rudy. Don't start moaning again. You, you…Let me ask you this: if I was running away from some evil men and you saw where I went, and they came up to you and asked, 'which way did she go?', would you tell them the truth or would you lie?"

Rudy, a bit chagrined by her intensity, replied, "I'd lie of course, to save you, I'd lie."

"So, to save my life you'd lie, but lying to save yourself is somehow this great sin."

"Yes, no,..but—"

Ida shook her head and started walking down the sidewalk. Rudy caught up with her and grabbed her arm. Like a swiftly passing rain squall, her intensity was gone. A misty smile hinting of distance and longing graced her face. "Have you ever seen the ocean?" He shook his head and she continued. "I think we need to see the ocean. It would do us both good."

"The ocean? Why?"

She slid her hand into his as they walked between the Center's buildings. "The ocean reminds me of home. Our family would go there for holidays and we would camp. For me the ocean is connected with laughing and relaxing and family. Ohh, how I miss all of that."

Rudy nodded, "Yeah, I see how the ocean would be good for you. But me?"

Ida smiled, then raised her chin and looked pensively skyward. "Don't take this wrong Rudy, but… if you would sit on a sand dune by the ocean shore, and look out over the waves, rolling, rolling, endlessly cresting and falling, you'd be reminded of how small you are, of how small we all are and of how short our time is on this earth. I think it would help you…help you take yourself less seriously."

Rudy tightened his grip on her hand and silently nodded. In his mind the picture of the ocean Ida had painted thinned, grew faint and was replaced by the endless waves of grass on the plains of south Russia. He was a boy again, skipping through the grass under God's eternal blue sky. He was small and all of life's worries fit into the tiny pocket in his pants...and the pocket had a hole.

"Ah, my Ida...I'd love to see your ocean. And your parents too. Should we ask Herr Siebold for a two-week vacation? Or maybe three? How about a four-week paid vacation?" They strolled, swung their hands, laughed at their own ridiculousness and their laughs joined the songs of the wheeling birds in the springtime sky.

AUGUST 1918, TREYSA GERMANY

The angel of death takes flesh in many forms. Werner Klein barely noticed the young soldier sitting next to him on the seat, leaning his head against the window. As the Frankfurt to Treysa train slowly clattered along into the afternoon, Werner was envisioning Sophia back at the Infirmary. I wonder if she's on duty, if I'll get a chance to see her yet this evening. Not that she'll be eager to see me. With my one dead eye and bald pate, what chance do I have. But her smile—so warm, magnetic—

"Bitte, excuse me." The young soldier got up, squeezed by Werner and, for the third time since they'd left Frankfurt, wobbled down the aisle to the water closet. Within minutes he returned and with a groan collapsed onto the thinly padded seat.

"Looks like you're not feeling well," Werner said.

"Sheiss [shit], that's how I feel, and that's all I've been doing in the WC. Must have eaten some bad sausage. Just my luck...to be sick on my one week leave." The soldier rolled his blood shot eyes.

"Where've you been fighting?" Werner asked.

"France, France, always France...if you can call what we do fighting. Scurry like rats from one trench to another, shoot and duck, take cover behind dead bodies, then—" The soldier coughed twice, began to speak, then coughed over and over again, a deep gurgling bark.

Werner looked with pity as the young thin soldier's head bobbed back and forth. He'd heard about mustard gas and wondered if his seatmate's lungs had been seared.

"Damn, this crazy cough, just started this morning," the soldier said as

135

he wiped the tears from his eyes with a crumpled gray handkerchief.

"Maybe you should see a doctor before you go home," Werner suggested.

"Nah, I'm just going to crawl into bed and sleep for a week. Rest is all I need. That and my mother's cooking." The wan and weary soldier leaned his head against the window and closed his eyes.

Werner felt a surge of pity for the young man. If his mother's pantry was like that of most German households it was most likely nearly bare. *Hopefully the poor guy can get some rest at least.*

As they pulled into the Marburg station, the soldier stirred and shakily stood. Werner stepped out into the aisle to let him exit and as he passed Werner felt a wave of heat. *He's burning up with fever. He really should see a doctor.*

The young man left the car, the train jerked back into motion and Werner's thoughts returned to Sophia. He was so caught up in his reverie he did not notice the tickle far down, deep inside his throat.

*   *   *

Rudy pulled open the Infirmary door and nearly collided with Nurse Heinitz.

"Stop, Rudy, and put this on." The white cloth mask across her face muffled her voice. Her outstretched arm held a similar mask.

"What's this all about?" Rudy asked as he tied the mask around his face.

"Werner Klein came back from Frankfurt yesterday afternoon. This morning his roommate brought him here. He's got a fever, he's coughing and has diarrhea. I'm sure it's the flu."

Rudy growled through his mask, "Dumbkopf! If it's the flu, why'd he bring him here to contaminate others?"

Nurse Heinitz shook her head. "I'm afraid it's too late to worry about that. Werner came in last evening. According to him, he just wanted to say 'hi' to Sophia. They talked for a few minutes, then he went home."

"Ach, Gott. Is Sophia sick too?"

"No, but we've got her in the isolation ward too, just in case. The worst thing is that she was on duty until midnight so if she's infected..." The nurse's voice trailed off.

"Are you sure it's the flu? Maybe Werner just—"

"We can't take a chance." Her eyes flashed above her mask. "The government doesn't talk about it, but I've heard rumors that the flu back in March and April killed thousands in Germany alone. Now if its back on the battlefield, who knows."

136

"The battlefield? None of our wounded men have the flu. You mean Werner—"

"Sat beside a sick soldier all the way from Frankfort. The young man was coughing and shitting the entire journey."

Rudy grinned behind his mask at her unexpected crudity. But Nurse Heinitz was in no mood for humor.

"Enough. Keep your mask tight and wash your hands after every resident."

Rudy stepped past her and moved down the hall to take his men to breakfast. Nurse Heinitz stood guard at the door, her hand full of masks.

*   *   *

Rudy had grown weary of the bland message he'd repeated all morning long to every resident he'd met. "Just a precaution, trying to stay healthy, don't want to give you any unfriendly germs." Most of them shrugged and fell back into their own tiny worlds. But of course, Willy was one of the exceptions. He squinted up at Rudy.

"C'mon Rudy, don't try bullshitting me. You didn't wear that rag yesterday so what's changed? What's going on that we're not supposed to know?"

Rudy rolled his eyes behind his mask. He knew Willy wasn't one to gossip but still he hesitated to say anything. Rudy lifted Willy's skeletal body into the wheelchair and the old man growled.

"Is somebody sick out in the town or already here in the house?"

"Ach, Willy, you stubborn old coot. One of the aides… He came in and isn't feeling good this morning. You know what Nurse Heinitz always says, 'Better safe than sorry.' But Willy, don't go flapping your jaws now and telling all your buddies."

"Buddies? Ha. Just so you know how bad things are for me, you're the closest thing to a buddy I've got in this damn place."

Rudy grinned behind his mask. "I don't know if I should be flattered or offended." He rolled Willy and his chair toward the dining room while he massaged the old man's twisted neck.

"Either way's fine with me," Willy snorted. "Just keep that sick aide away from me. You can send around that cute nurse though, that Sophia. She brought me my pills last night. She can warm up even a dried-up old fart like me."

An hour later, after he'd gotten all of his residents back to their rooms or to their afternoon activities and before attending the wounded men, Rudy slowly descended the basement stairs to the isolation ward.

———

137

"Can I see Werner?" he asked.

The young, dark haired nurse seated behind the counter looked up. Her eyes flashed.

"Most certainly not. He's in isolation."

"But—"

She cut off his stammer with an upraised hand and dropped her voice. "And, he is very, very," her eyes widened, "VERY sick." She lowered the temperature of her gaze and a tremulous quaver infected her voice. "His room is over there. Just take a peek into that window. But I'm warning you, do not open the door."

Curiosity and dread drew Rudy across the hall to the door. The window was a small square, barely larger than his face. But he saw more than he wanted to see. Werner lay flat on his back and his chest was heaving as though he could not breathe. A nurse wearing thick gloves and mask was wiping red froth from his mouth. He had dark, almost black, splotches on his cheeks. Even through the thick glass Rudy could hear Werner's groans. He backed away from the window and his hand moved reflexively to make sure his mask was in place.

Rudy returned to the nurse's station. "And, please, tell me, is Sophia down here too?"

"Yes. But she's in isolation too. I can't let you in to see her."

"I understand. Can you tell me, is she…?"

"No, she's not sick like Werner. So far, she's just complaining of a headache. You can peek into the window of room twelve."

Rudy nodded his thanks and hurried to room twelve. Sophia had her back to him, sitting on the edge of her bed, looking up at the patch of sky in her tiny basement window. He tapped on the door's tiny glass portal. She jerked and without rising turned her head to the door. When she saw who him she rose and came walked across the room. *Does her smile seem forced? Is their pain behind her eyes? Mein Gott, I pray…*

Sophia's voice barely penetrated the door. "Hello Rudy, you look important in your mask."

"Oh, you know Nurse Heinitz…" He hesitated for an instant. "Sophia, how're you feeling?"

"Oh, I'm OK. Just a little headache." She shrugged and dropped her voice so that he barely heard her next words, "And a tickle in my throat." Then she turned her head in the direction of Werner's room. "How is Werner doing?" Her words were steady and stiff, without their usual lilt.

Rudy wished he hadn't descended the stairs. Too late to run away now.

He gave a tiny shake of his head. "The nurse says he's quite ill. He's being tended to."

Sophia swiveled her head back to him. Her eyes said it all. 'Rudy, I know you know more, but I won't ask you to tell me.' The only thing she did say before returning to her bed was, "Tell Ida 'Hi.' After I get out of this place, we'll all go to the bierhaus."

Rudy hurried down the hall, ran up the stairs two at a time and hustled outside. He pulled off his mask and drew in a lungful of the bracing fall air. *I wonder how soon any of us will get to that bierhaus?*

*　　　　*　　　　*

By the next morning Werner Klein was dead. Rudy was given the news by one of the aides handing out face masks at the door. Rudy tied on his mask as he walked down the hall in search of Nurse Heinitz. The August heat and humidity had infiltrated the building and everyone moved sluggishly. Rudy felt as though he were swimming upstream. The head nurse emerged from the basement stairwell.

"Rudy, shouldn't you be getting the residents to breakfast?"

"Yes, I know. I wanted to find out—"

She stepped close to him and spoke quietly. "Werner died around midnight. I've never seen anything like it. So fast. We tried everything. But his lungs..they filled up with bloody fluid. He literally suffocated to death."

"What about Sophia?" Rudy asked and watched the nurse's face stiffen.

"I'm afraid she's got it too."

"Mein Gott," Rudy murmured.

"But we did start treating her sooner. We're trying to keep the fever down. She's a strong girl. And...we'll just keep praying." She sighed and waved Rudy toward his assignment.

*　　　　*　　　　*

Willy was last on the list for breakfast this morning. Rudy yanked back the curtain expecting the usual muttered blue curses. But Willy lay curled up and silent, still in his nightclothes.

"Hey, old friend. Time for breakfast."

Willy groaned from beneath his pillow, "Stop yer damn shoutin'. A bad-assed blacksmith is bashing his anvil inside my head. Earlier I sent the aide away. Now you can leave me alone too."

Rudy tightened his face mask and moved alongside Willy's bed. He lay his hand on an exposed arm. "You've got a fever, Willy. I'm calling the nurse."

Ten minutes later, Rudy eased Willy onto a bed in the isolation ward.

139

Willy's twisted limbs now shivered and continuous groans replaced his curses. Rudy looked down at Willy's pain-wracked face. The nurse was already shooing Rudy out of the room.

"You stay tough. And mean, Willy. You've got to fight this flu. I'll be praying for you."

Willy paused in his groaning. "Don't waste your time on me. If it's my time to go, you can't change nothin'." He rolled over curled up and the groaning returned.

Rudy climbed the stairs to the main floor, hurried to the sink in the men's room and began scrubbing his hands. He was rubbing them with soap for the second time when he remembered the hospital in Odessa. Seven years ago, he'd been there with his mother. He saw again the white walls, the crisp nurses' uniforms. As he'd walked down those halls he'd been convinced the hospital was a sacred space, especially imbued with God's healing spirit.

Now as he finished washing and drying his hands and stepped out into the stifling hall, his feelings clashed with that long-ago memory. Today this place exuded a dark foreboding spirit. The hallway seemed narrow and life-constricting. The walls radiated stale heat. Rudy fought the panic that threatened to seize his legs and send them running toward the door. Though he knew it was ridiculous, he kept his breath shallow so as not to inhale any lethal germs. He held his breath as he walked the last few feet to the door. He stepped out into the muggy morning and tiny pearls of sweat trickled down his forehead.

*   *   *

The day's heavy air had spawned a late afternoon thunderstorm that had swept through Treysa and left behind cooler, drier air. Rudy listened to the last drops dripping from the trees as he stood outside the kitchen waiting for Ida to finish the evening kitchen clean-up. The only news he'd been able to get from the isolation ward was that no new patients had been admitted. He cautiously cleared his own throat. *No scratch or tickle there. No headache either. Stop being such a coward.*

"Hey Rudy, thanks for waiting." Ida emerged from the kitchen waving a hand in front of her face. "Whew, hot in there. Let's walk so I can cool down."

They walked in silence for several minutes, avoiding occasional puddles.

"Have you heard anything more about Sophia?" Rudy asked.

"One of the nurses told Silvia that Sophia's fever hadn't risen since noon. They hoped that was a good sign."

140

They entered the faint circle of a street light and Rudy grabbed Ida's arm and led her around several long earthworms that had been washed out of the grass onto the path.

"I saw Werner before he…I pray Sophia doesn't have to suffer what he did." Rudy shuddered.

"Sophia is tough. We've all got to keep praying." Ida paused, then quietly added, "the nurse also told Silvia that they could hear Willy's coughs all through the ward."

Rudy shook his head. "I'm afraid Willy's spirit is a lot tougher than his body. He told me not to pray for him. Says if his time is up, prayer can't change anything."

"Do you believe that?" Ida asked as they reached the corner and turned down the next block.

"No…I don't think I do. If God is listening to us, then…anyway, the Bible says we should pray."

"But will our praying change God's mind?"

Rudy realized that like a moth drawn to a flame, Ida had homed in on the heart of the matter, and to his own deepest question.

"Ai, if only we knew that. But then, we don't even know if Sophia getting the flu is part of God's plan at all."

"Oh, how can that be? What kind of a God would want that?" Ida protested.

Rudy sighed, "And yet…in my catechism class we memorized God's omni's: omniscient, omnipotent, omnipresent."

Ida's voice thickened with tears. "All I know is that I don't want Sophia, or Willy, or anyone to die. All I can do is keep pounding on God's door."

Rudy put his arm across her shoulder and they continued walking into the quiet evening. Again, Ida had clearly and simply voiced what he'd also concluded. Still, like a tongue pressing on an aching tooth, his mind could not stop probing painful thoughts. *If God is merciful, how can he let His children suffer? If God is all powerful why does He not stop this madness? If God is not all powerful, what hope is there for any of us? …God, Oh God, hear the prayers of your little people.*

SEPTEMBER, 1918 TREYSA, GERMANY

The afternoon sun magnified the gold in the three glasses of beer standing on the small table under the beech tree. Sophia walked slowly between Ida and Rudy who loosely held her arms. They eased Sophia into

141

her chair and took the other two seats.

"This isn't the bierhaus, but the air is fresher and the beer is…" Rudy tasted a sip from his glass, "not bad, not bad for a wartime brew."

Sophia smiled at her two friends. Her face was still pallid, but the impish sparkle had returned to her eyes. "Why do I see only one glass for me? Is that my wartime ration?"

They laughed because they still could. Though the war churned on endlessly beyond Germany's borders, and those within the country, including themselves, endured countless privations, these three friends relished their beer on the autumn afternoon.

Ida chuckled, "This is your reward for defeating the enemy. Get your strength back and we'll see about adding another glass."

Sophia took a long swallow. "Ahhh, sehr gut." She looked across the table. "Honestly though, I can't claim any credit for my victory. I didn't do anything more than Werner and Willy did."

Rudy dropped his eyes at the mention of Willy. The poor man had died two days after the symptoms appeared. Like Werner, his lungs had filled with fluid and he'd died from lack of oxygen. The fearful authorities had quickly removed the body and buried it hastily without any ceremony. Rudy still felt a peculiar emptiness every time he passed what had been Willy's bed. He wondered if he'd have felt different had he been able to say goodbye to his cantankerous friend or at least attended his funeral. He sighed as he sipped his beer, never imagining that he'd experience that forlorn emptiness many more times throughout his life.

*   *   *

They had walked Sophia back to her room and now watched the sun slipping behind the roof of the Hephata Center church. Rudy's thoughts brooded over the absence of Willy, pined for his distant family, rejoiced at the restoration of Sophia and relished the closeness of Ida. Out of that strange mélange he spoke words that surprised himself and stunned Ida.

"Let's get married."

"What? Rudy, are you..? Are you proposing to me?"

Rudy sputtered, "I guess, well…I… Seeing Sophia and realizing how close she was, how close we all are, to dying, I just figured we should spend whatever time we have left together."

Ida turned and smiled up at him. "Ach Rudy, you're not very romantic but you're sure dramatic."

Rudy smiled back, embarrassed by his own uncharacteristic emotional words. "I guess I didn't think about the romantic part, but I, we're romantic together, I mean—"

Ida put her arm around his waist. "Rudy, Rudy, I know what you mean, and I love you for offering, but…"

Rudy put his arm around her shoulder and apprehensively waited for her to continue. They walked slowly into the shadow of the church.

"Rudy, I've thought about us getting married. Maybe more than you have. And I'd say yes in a heartbeat but…But I'm always bedeviled by the same question: Do I want to bring children into this desperate, insane world? How would we feed them? What if they get sick? What if this war pours into Germany and enemy soldiers fill our streets? Every day I fret about the safety of you and my friends. If I had to worry about my own baby, I'm afraid I'd—" She shuddered and leaned deeper into Rudy's embrace.

Rudy turned and wrapped her in his arms. He looked out over her head into the dying evening light. "Ja, Ida, you're the wise one, the Christian one. I was only thinking about us, really, just about me. Children, of course we would have children. Bringing children into this hell? That would be a sin, wouldn't it? So, I'll wait, we'll wait and pray for this damned war to end."

NOVEMBER 11, 1918 TREYSA, GERMANY

Can we hold our breath for more than a month? The dying sunlight flickered out as Rudy joined the remnant of the student body, the Hephata professors, and the staff as they shuffled into the large lecture hall.

Early in October, the government's censorship blockade had crumbled. The vague official news of distant victories and valiant battles fought by heroic soldiers which had filled the newspapers for over four years abruptly disappeared. The pages were now full of grim reports of defeats, desperate retreats and distressing death tolls. Everyone was shocked, though Rudy imagined, some more so than others.

Since early October Rudy, and he supposed, the entire country walked through their days with bated breath. Will we ever breathe again and what sort of air will we breathe?

Rudy climbed the stairs to the back seats where Ida had saved him a seat. Before the war, this room would have held only a third of Hephata's population. Now scattered seats reminded them all of the toll these years had taken. The professors and the pastor took up the front rows and then Headmaster Siebold entered. How these years had worn out this man. Rudy still could remember the great brawny bear of a man who'd welcomed him

---

143

with open arms. Now the headmaster shambled in like an underfed, mangy bear. His jowls sagged and his red-rimmed eyes drowned in dark pools. He straightened up and waited until the room hushed.

"Today, the eleventh day of the eleventh month, at the eleventh hour, an armistice was signed between Germany and the Allied forces. The Great War has ended."

He paused and the breath everyone had been holding for weeks, months, and years filled the room with a sighing like the wind in a nighttime forest. Then, most sat in silence, but a few turned to their companions and began whispering. The headmaster held up his hand and continued.

"These years have brought horrific suffering for so many. I have no doubt that in the weeks and months ahead we will see many more men and women in need of care and consolation. Hephata too has been wounded. We need only look at the empty seats. But even in our weakness I am convinced that our ministry will be needed now more than ever, and certainly we've not been abandoned."

He stopped and pulled a small worn book from his pocket. "I urge all of you to stay close to the Scriptures in these uncertain days. Here is the word I would have you ponder tonight. Psalm 9, verse 18. *For the needy shall not always be forgotten, nor the hope of the poor perish forever. Rise up, O Lord! Do not let mortals prevail; let the nations be judged before you. Put them in fear, O Lord; let the nations know that they are only human.*"

The headmaster closed his psalter and silence settled on the room for a few heartbeats. Then Rudy heard harsh whispers from the front row and saw Pastor Preus leaning his head toward Professor Wierre. Even from the back row, Rudy could see the back of the pastor's neck flushing deep red. The clergyman began to speak from his seat but with every word rose up higher and thundered louder.

"Herr Siebold, of course we all know that the nations are human. But in this war, the other nations attack God's Kingdom. The pagan enemies attack our Christian virtues, offend the Fatherland, and the faith of our valiant men. Abandoned? Perhaps God has not abandoned us. But our government, the cowards of this nation, have abandoned our brave men."

Headmaster Siebold stood stunned by the vitriolic words. Some in the crowd murmured what sounded like agreement. Rudy could only conjure up the faces of the two soldiers who had pummeled him mercilessly. Valiant, brave men? He snorted in disdain. Then he reviewed the faces of the poor wounded men he'd tended. Sad and broken boys. He sighed.

Then Professor Wierre leapt to his feet and turned to the assembly. "The

144

cowards in Berlin were hypnotized by the enemies' propaganda. They are rabbits hypnotized by a snake. The government has stabbed our soldiers in the back."

The buzzing in the room began to swell. Then from the highest corner came a loud taunting laugh. All eyes swiveled to Sophia who stood and began waving her arms.

"Stabbed in the back? Ha! Who's been stabbed? What about us? We were forced to feed on turnips, give up butter, give up bread, sacrifice our health, put our lives on a leash—all because our boys supposedly were winning one great battle after another, teaching the world's pagans a lesson."

She was flushed and panting and began to sit down. Then with a swallowed sob, stood again. "Some of us... some of us... we got letters from those soldiers. They were dying in filthy trenches full of rats. They hated it, they didn't think of themselves as Christian knights. Stabbed in the back? How many soldiers died and how many of us suffered because some generals wanted to show the world how big Germany was?"

Rudy began to applaud but Ida grabbed his hand. "Not here, not now," she murmured. Pastor Preus was firing arrows with his eyes at Sophia and appeared ready to run up the stairs toward her. The room filled with screeching voices, hisses and cheers.

"Silence!" Headmaster's voice rattled the window panes. From the depth of his weary soul he'd dredged up a bit of his old vibrancy. He swept his gaze over the entire room and settled on the front row.

"Are we Christ's people or not? If we fight and tear each other apart what good are we to God or the world? The war is over. What is done is done. None of us knows what will come tomorrow. But I guarantee we will need forbearance, compassion and the strength to build peace. Go home now. All of you. Go home and pray for wisdom." He began marching out and motioned for the professors and pastor to follow him.

The rest of the assembly moved toward the door in embarrassed silence. Rudy followed Ida down the stairs. He glanced at the darkling night beyond the windows and an ominous premonition skulked across his thoughts. *Germany's war against the world has ended but Germany's war against Germany has just begun.*

JULY 1919, TREYSA, GERMANY

"Is it worth the risk?" Ida asked.

"I can't bear to spend another Saturday night playing endless hands of schafkopf with my dreary roommates. Let's go out and live." Sophia stood in the doorway as Ida finished getting dressed.

A voice boomed up from the bottom of the stairs. "So, you call drinking a beer in Treysa's bierhaus living? Where's your imagination?"

Sophia turned, looked down and laughed. "Rudy, if you can come up with something better, I'm all for it."

The women descended the stairs and Rudy introduced them to Harold, a shy, blond haired young man who'd recently come to Hephata from the rural south. He reminded Rudy of his own shy, lost self who'd arrived almost eight years ago.

The four young people walked toward the city center in the warm evening. In mid-conversation, Rudy stopped the group.

"Sophia, you asked for it. I just thought of something that might be fun and…maybe even educational for our young friend. Are you all ready for a little adventure?"

He led the way down the dark streets and, despite teasings, ticklings and threats, refused to reveal their destination. They turned the last corner, Rudy stopped and pointed across the plaza at the black oblong thrust up against the dark sky.

"What? You bring us to stare at up at the Witch's Tower? C'mon Rudy," Sophia chided.

Rudy cuffed her shoulder. "You underestimate me. We're going to stare down from the top of the witch's tower."

"But it's not open, is it?" Ida asked.

He remembered asking the same question of Fred years ago. "Not yet it isn't. But real adventures include some risks, don't you think."

He led them to the base of the tower. During the war years, the area had gone completely untended; weeds grew up against the stone walls and the wooden door was tied shut with only two strands of rusting wire. Rudy undid the wire latch and swung the door open with a flourish. A whoosh of wings flashed by their heads and the girls screamed.

"Shhh. It's only a few bats. They won't hurt you." He ducked his head and stepped into the tower. The smell of bat dung mixed with dusty air. It was pitch black, but Rudy couldn't resist bragging, "The bats are new. Otherwise it's just as I remembered it."

"You can't see any—wait—you've been here before? When?" Ida asked.

"I'll tell you on top. Hold onto my shirt and let's go." He led them to the stairway that spiraled up the inside wall and they crept upward.

They emerged from the stairwell and, between gasps for air, giggled with childlike excitement.

"Gott, my lungs aren't what they used to be," Sophia complained as she leaned against the balustrade. "But this view…ai, it was worth it."

For Rudy, the vista wasn't nearly as spectacular as the glorious winter morning of years ago. But the warm breeze, the dark cotton clouds floating lazily past the moon, and the faint glimmer of lights in the homes below merged to produce a languorous atmosphere. All four of them relaxed and leaned into the night's amiable embrace.

"Now, Mr. Heupel, what's this about being here before?" Ida wriggled her fingers into his side.

Rudy smiled as the memory of how he, Fred, Marvin and Vernon and scaled the tower on that blazing white snowy day. He began telling the tale, embellishing every step of their adventure. Just as he was describing the arcing trajectory of his snow ball missile, Harold exclaimed, "Guys, look, look."

Coming toward the tower from a side street was a crowd of men carrying torches and shouting. By the crackling flickers of the torches they could see rifles carried by many of the men.

"Get down, don't let them see us," hissed Ida.

"They're turning. They have some other target in mind," Sophia said as she peeked over the edge.

"But who are they?" Harold's voice trembled.

Rudy glared at the crowd marching down the street. "They call themselves the Freikorpss. They're soldiers back from the war. But they still have the battles inside of them."

Through gritted teeth Sophia spoke, "If my brother hadn't died on the Russian front, if he'd come home, I wouldn't let him run in the streets."

Harold now stood against the stone balustrade and stared fascinated at the retreating mob. "In our country village we never heard of this. Why are they out here? What are they doing?"

Rudy grunted in disgust. "They are hunting for enemies. Up in Bremen they killed four hundred people whom they claimed were communists. In Berlin when some of the workers went on strike, these Freikorps barbarians attacked and killed over a thousand people."

The torch-lit crowd disappeared around a corner and the shouting faded. The four moved closer together and Sophia shook her head. "They're like roving bands of wolves. They swagger and curse and claim that they were betrayed by soft civilians like us."

Gunshots splintered the evening stillness and then the red glow of flames lit up the sky on the street the Freikorps had entered.

"Someone's store, or home. Someone they've decided deserves to be punished." Rudy shook his head in disgust. "Let's get out of here before those lunatics come back this way."

They hurried down the dark stairs in silence. Rudy, Ida and Harold had reached the floor and Sophia was only two steps from the bottom when her foot slipped and she thudded down, seat first, on the stone stair.

"Ow. Verdammte dunkleheit. [damn darkness] Help me up." She groaned as Harold and Rudy helped her stand up and descend the last step.

"You alright?" Rudy asked, "You crashed down hard."

"Ach, I'm sore but I'll be fine." Sophia seemed more embarrassed then hurt.

They scurried across the plaza and into the darkness of the street. They replaced their earlier carefree strolling with brisk, stiff steps toward the Center. They were within a few blocks of home when Sophia spoke.

"Can we slow down now? I guess I did get banged up when I fell. I've got a sharp pain in my back with every step."

They eased their hurried pace and supported Sophia's limping stride. When they reached her apartment, Ida pulled Rudy aside and quietly asked, "Do you think you could..? Could you help her back pain?"

Rudy cringed. He wanted to help his dear friend but was loath to reveal his gift to someone who could not keep a secret. He hedged. "Maybe it's just a bruise. Let's see how she is in the morning."

He watched Ida help Sophia to her room, then walked with Harold back to their dormitory. Adventures…they always seem to end in misadventure.

The next morning Rudy had not yet reached the Infirmary for his morning duties when Ida intercepted him. "Sophia is worse this morning. She's so stiff she can barely walk. She says every step is a stab in her back."

Rudy ran his hand through his sandy hair as he took in the worried look on Ida's face. He spoke to himself, barely loud enough for her to hear. "Ja, sounds like she jammed some vertebrae when she fell."

He swept his hand across his jaw, took a deep breath and spoke with new authority. "Is there a firm surface in her room, big enough for her to lie on?"

Ida nodded, "She has a big kitchen table."

"Good, put some sheets or a blanket on that table. Have her lie face down. Heat up some towels and put them on her back. Keep her back warm.

I'll be there as soon as I take my residents to breakfast." He hurried off to his job and Ida hastened to follow his instructions.

An hour later, he knocked on Sophia's thin wooden door. "Hello. I'm here." Ida opened and motioned for Rudy to enter.

"Is that you Rudy? I hope you know what you're doing. Ida has me stretched out here on the table like a butchered pig. 'Face down,' she says. It's killing me. Do you have a plan or what?"

Rudy chuckled as he moved toward the table. She lay with her face between her arms, still dressed in her nightshirt, "Well, Sophia, I can see that at least your tongue is still in fine condition."

He removed the towel and began to massage her lower back through the damp night shirt. Then he moved his hand slowly up and down her spine, feeling each bone.

"Mein Gott, Rudy. Your hands are warm, even warmer than the towel. Mmmm." Sophia gave out a muffled groan as Rudy touched a vertebra in her lower back. "Ow, that is so sore."

"Ja, I know," said Rudy. Then he positioned his hands flat upon her back and stooped and spoke softly, "Now, Sophia, listen. I'm going to press down on your back right here, but first I want you to breathe out all of your air."

"But, what--?"

"Sophia, just breathe out, please."

Rudy listened for the whoosh of air leaving Sophia's lungs and just as it stopped, he rapidly pushed down and twisted his hands counter-clockwise. They all heard a rippling, clicking sound, like the rattling of dice and then a sharp 'Unh' from Sophia

For a few seconds silence hovered in the air like a silvery soap bubble. Then Sophia pushed herself up on her elbows. "Christus, Rudy. What did you do? Were you trying to break me in half? Wait…"

Ida helped her sit up on the edge of the table. She shot a puzzled look at Rudy, slid her feet to the floor and took a few steps. "I'm still sore, but the pain is gone. Is this a miracle?"

Rudy grinned and began moving toward the door. "No, no. You had a few vertebrae that got out of line when you fell. They were pinching your nerves. I just put them back in place."

Sophia put her fists on her hips "But Rudy, I want you to tell me who taught you—."

Rudy held the door and laughed, "I've got to get back to work, Sophia. Don't do any heavy work for a few days. Wiedersehen." He took the stairs down two at a time and ran out into the summery sunshine.

JANUARY, 1920 TREYSA, GERMANY

Rudy stepped off the train. The station was empty but he was too excited to notice. Once he had feared that he'd never see Freidorf again, now he was only a mile away. He could not see the sun, yet the endless plains and even the sky were suffused with a pale, yellow glow. *I never would have expected it to be so warm and so green...Isn't it January?*

Sooner than he expected the village stood before him. He was puzzled as he gazed at the houses and shops lining the streets. They were unfamiliar to him, yet their paint was faded and their shutters sagged as though they'd been standing there for decades. He walked down the middle of the street and saw no one, only the swift shadows of faces withdrawing from windows as he passed by.

What's happening here? Rudy's throat constricted, the blood pounded in his temples. He was about to spin around and dash back the way he had come.

Then he saw the steeple of the Lutheran church looming over the roof of a store. He gasped in relief. Home was only eight blocks south of the church. In an instant he stood before its familiar rusty gate. Does Vater still live here or has he moved in with Junior and his family? Is this now another family's refuge?

The iron wrought gate stood half open, and he entered the yard. Once the yard had been hard-packed earth that his mother had swept clean every day. Now it was full of sickly, drying weeds. As he stepped up to the door, the sky's yellow glow was replaced by a muddy umber sheen. He knocked lightly, once, twice. Then he rapped with force three times more. Bang, bang, bang. He was ready to pound with his fist when the door slowly creaked open.

A chill filled his lungs and a groan escaped his clenched teeth. The house was gone. The wall holding the door was all that was left of his old home. Everything else was gone—pots, pans, curtains, pictures, rugs and every stick of furniture. Except for the kitchen table. There it stood, a desolate island amid the pieces of plaster and litter covering the floor.

Rudy could see again his mother sitting at that table delighting him with the story of her ancestor's Danube trip; his father's stony glare when he told him of his plan to leave Freidorf; so many meals, moments, and memories. The table—so lonely, so sad.

Rudy felt tears burning his cheeks. His eyes moved beyond where the back wall had been, and he walked toward what had been the garden. He gasped. Now, where vegetables had once been, where he might have expected more weeds, he saw graves, dozens of them. The dirt was still mounded over each plot. New burials, fresh graves. There were no headstones, but at the head of each mound was a white placard affixed to a stick. He could see writing but could not read the words.

He was paralyzed with dread. Were these the remains of his family? His neighbors? His friends? Was this all that was left of his past? He began walking toward the nearest mound just as a low moaning wind swept out of the now greenish yellow sky and rattled the leafless branches of the ancient twisted apple tree. He stood before the nearest grave and was bending to read the inscription when he heard a snarl behind him.

Two huge dogs, mangy red, slavering and foaming at the mouth charged toward him. He tried to run but his legs would not move. He strained to shout but could only manage weak grunts. The beasts were upon him now, he could see their bloodshot eyes and smell their rotten breath. With one final effort he freed his legs, kicked with all of his force, shouted at the top of his lungs, and….

Rudy woke up on the floor beside his bunk. His heart was a steam engine pounding in his chest. He stared up at the ceiling and tried to slow his breathing. The shadow of Harold in the top bunk cut into the darkness.

"Rudy, you OK? What's all the shouting about?"

Rudy slowly eased up off the floor and climbed into bed. "I'm alright Harold, just a nasty dream. Sorry to wake you."

Rudy lay in bed, hands behind his head, reliving his terrifying dream, praying that it didn't foreshadow reality. He'd written a letter to his family in Freidorf six weeks ago. The post office had insisted that mail service was back to normal. Even if that was true, he had no way of knowing what service was like outside of Germany's borders. Day after day he waited for a response. He'd read newspaper reports of the revolution in Russia, of the Red Army and White Army clashes, of the Ukrainian nationalist movement declaring independence from Russia. What did all of this mean for the German settlements like Freidorf? What was this chaotic maelstrom doing to his family? He had no way of finding out. He drifted into a fitful sleep beleaguered by the disturbing visions of his nightmare.

151

OCTOBER 1920, TREYSA, GERMANY

"I assumed I'd find you here."

Rudy was on his knees in the garden, scooping up the potatoes in the soil he'd just turned over. He looked up in surprise at the headmaster.

"Herr Siebold, what brings you out here?" Rudy stood and pounded the dirt off his knees.

The headmaster's arms, so often widespread and world embracing, now were clasped behind his back.

"News, Rudy. News you need to hear."

The sweat on Rudy's back turned to ice. "Is it my family? Have you heard something?"

The headmaster unclasped his hands, swung out his arms and put his large hand on Rudy's shoulder. "No, Rudy. I'm sorry, it's not that. My news is more…personal, closer to home."

Disappointment, then relief surged through Rudy. The headmaster wrapped his long arms around himself as though he too were chilly.

"I will be leaving Hephata in a few weeks, Rudy. The administration and the teachers already know. You're the first of the students to find out. Well you've been here the longest so…" he shrugged.

"Ach, Herr Siebold, I don't know what to say. What will Hephata do without you? You're too young to retire."

The headmaster tipped his head up and sighed as he returned his gaze to Rudy. "Let's just say retirement was the best of the options put before me." He held up his hand as Rudy tried to speak. "No, no, let's just leave it at that. What's more important is what this means for you."

Ever since he'd been beaten by the soldiers, Rudy had contemplated the various scenarios that would thrust him out of the ceaseless whirlpool that had become his life at Hephata and back into the turbulent currents of history. He straightened up, put both hands on his shovel and waited to find out.

"Rudy, I'm not sure who'll be my successor. But the board has made it clear that whoever takes over will have to undertake major consolidation of our programs. Given the direction of the German economy, many positions will be eliminated. And you…, well, I've valued your presence here but now…" He stopped and looked at the garden soil at his feet.

Rudy let the shovel drop and reached out and gripped the headmaster's arm. "Herr Siebold, I understand. I've been so lucky…no, so blessed by my time here. I know you've bent rules to let me stay as long as I have. If it weren't for you and Hephata, I don't know what I'd have done. You're right. So right. It's time for me to face my future."

The headmaster nodded, "Ja, I assumed you'd understand." He gave Rudy a brief smile. "I've also been doing some searching on your behalf. I have a friend, Andreas Lichtenfeld, who is the administrator at the German House in Halle, a home for the elderly and the disabled. He has an opening for someone with care-giving and chaplain experience. I told him about you. I gave you a good recommendation. Of course, you're not obliged to follow up but…"

Rudy chuckled, "You're too kind to me Herr Siebold. And if I have to leave Hephata, why wouldn't I seek to go somewhere run by a friend of yours?" Now Rudy took off his gloves and with both of his hands, grabbed the headmaster's hand. "Thank you, thank you for everything."

Herr Siebold turned the handshake into a long bear hug. Wordlessly, he turned and headed back to his office. Rudy watched him retreat, then dropped to his knees and began filling his basket. While his hands were busy with the potatoes before him, his thoughts were soaring elsewhere. *How do I begin this leave-taking? What do I do first? How will I tell Ida? Will she still have a job here? I wonder what this will mean for us? For our future, our life?*

HALLE, GERMANY JANUARY, 1921

Rudy raised the collar of his coat. The morning breeze skimming in from the River Saale sent a shiver across his shoulders. Halle, hopefully his new home town, was brightly dressed in a fresh dusting of snow. He picked up his luggage and began striding to his job interview.

In his right hand he carried the same battered valise he'd brought from Freidorf ten years earlier. In his left, he carried a new suitcase, a thank-you gift given to him by Nurse Heinitz and the staff at the Infirmary. It held his Bible, the books he'd used in his theology and anatomy classes, and two pairs of new clothes he'd bought with his slim savings.

He turned onto Breite Street and caught his first glimpse of the imposing three story building, that housed the German House. Rudy set down his suitcases and caught his breath.

He'd arrived late last night on the train from Treysa and stayed in a dingy hotel near the station. Though the bed clothes were clean and the room quieter than he'd expected, his sleep had been shallow and fitful. Like a child who surpasses his exhaustion limit, Rudy hadn't been able to relax. Packing had been simple and swift, the two-hundred-mile train ride had

153

been smooth. It was not physical exhaustion that had kept him awake.

Emotionally he was completely spent. When he'd left Freidorf so many years ago he'd been young and naïve. The exhilaration of launching into a new and wonderful life had cushioned him from the sadness of departure. But he was no longer that starry-eyed boy.

Since that distant day, he'd lost friends to enemy bullets and to ravaging disease; his ribs ached from his beating whenever the weather changed; he still had no word from his family; the Freikorpss still prowled throughout Germany; a new political group, the National Socialist German Workers' Party, led by a fiery speaker named Adolph Hitler was inflaming passions; but the worst attack upon his emotional reserves, from Rudy's perspective, was the fact that Ida—his heart friend, the one he could count on to listen to his complaints, cheer up his moods, challenge his ideas—was not here with him.

Before he left, they'd cried and prayed together. They'd consoled each other with platitudes: 'this time apart will help us see our relationship more clearly'. Neither of them had believed that, but they'd strained to convince themselves. The sum of all these things had left him emotionally drained and restlessly dozing for hours in the dingy hotel.

Finally, mercifully, the night had given way to dawn. He'd risen and splashed his face with icy water, combed his hair and set out for the German House and Herr Lichtenfeld.

Now, the striking building, more elegant than any edifice at Hephata, loomed before him. He took a deep breath, picked up his suitcases and looked for the administrator's office.

*   *   *

I wonder if I'm too early? Rudy climbed the stairs to the office building. But the door was open and a receptionist was already at her desk. She welcomed him, he identified himself, and asked for Herr Lichtenfeld. She nodded, offered to take care of his suitcases, and then pointed across the hall to a door that stood ajar. Rudy smiled to himself. Just like his friend Herr Siebold, this director is already at work.

Rudy tapped on the door, heard a soft, 'come in' and entered. Andreas Lichtenfeld was pencil thin and short, his elbows barely cleared the edge of his desk. He did not rise as Rudy entered; instead he silently gestured to a stiff wooden chair and then continued to read from a folder on the desk before him. Rudy slowly sat and for a moment was mesmerized by the director's hair. Every blond strand was in perfect alignment as though lacquered in place. Inexplicably, the more he stared at the top of this small

154

man's head, the more apprehensive Rudy felt.

"So, you are Herr Rudolph Heupel and you came from Hephata I presume."

"Yes sir, I arrived in Halle last night."

The director flipped some pages in the folder and briefly looked up over the top of his wire-framed glasses. "Your records show that you were at Hephata since 1912."

"Yes sir, I came in October of that year and began classes in 1913."

Herr Lichtenfeld returned his gaze to the papers before him. "Hmm…Eight full years of classes." He shook his head and read from what Rudy supposed was his Hephata transcript. "Hospital administration, Bible, preaching, anatomy, basic medical practices…"

Rudy shifted uneasily in his chair. "Yes, I…I changed my career goals and also…well, the war came…"

The director removed his glasses and held them in one hand, cocked his head and blinked his pale gray eyes. "Tell me, Herr Heupel, how did you avoid conscription?"

The unexpected question struck a painful nerve. Rudy tried to dampen his defensiveness. "I didn't avoid conscription. I…the fact is..I…well, I wasn't eligible."

Herr Lichtenfeld said nothing but continued his inquisitional gaze. Rudy felt compelled to continue.

"I was born in what is now the Ukraine." The director, still staring, sat back in his chair. Rudy hastened to add, "But I'm fully German. My ancestors moved from Germany to south Russia and I was born in a little German colony called Freidorf. So, I am German, but my only document is my birth certificate and it says I was born in Russian territory. So…" Rudy's voice trailed off. *Maybe I've said too much already. Have I already forfeited my chances here?*

"In the Revolution, whose side did your family take? Did they favor the Reds or the Whites?" The words had the icy feel of a trap.

Rudy's exasperation overwhelmed his anxiety. "No, Herr Director. No. My family is not Russian. We do not like the Russians. Besides I haven't heard from my family since the war began."

A tiny smile crept onto the director's face. "Everyone knows that the Russians conscripted south Russian Germans into their army."

Rudy vehemently shook his head. "Not my brothers. One of them is in America and the other… he fought against the Russian peasants trying to take his land." *That last bit is close enough to the truth, not really a lie.*

155

The director pursed his lips, closed the file and folded his hands atop it. "Very well, Herr Heupel. Siebold tells me you do good work. You know, we went to school together many decades ago." He sniffed and tapped the folder, "and even though he committed his life to that backwater Hephata Center in Treysa, I still believe he's a decent judge of character. So…"

Rudy gritted his teeth at the insult of his mentor and of the Center.

"Herr Heupel, like most institutions in Germany we're strapped for money and yet we have work that needs doing. We are combining two positions into one: a social worker in the center for the disabled and a chaplain for the senior home. We've always had an ordained minister as a chaplain for our senior home. But since the war, so many of them have been disillusioned and have left the ministry."

The director cleared his throat, pursed his lips and at last directed his full gaze at Rudy. "According to Herr Siebold, you have experience in both of our areas of need. I am willing to offer you a provisional position for three months. At the end of that time we will evaluate your work and consider you for a more long-term position."

Rudy dropped his gaze to his lap. *This man is the opposite of Herr Siebold. Five minutes and I already detest him. God forgive me. What can I do? Do I have a choice? Mein Gott help me.* He raised his head and took a deep breath. "Of course, Herr Director. I accept your kind offer and look forward to working with you and the rest of the staff of the German House. I am ready to begin."

JUNE, 1921, HALLE, GERMANY

Rudy walked through the park as the sparrows, finches and jays praised God for the Sunday morning sunshine. They seemed to be daring Rudy; 'Enough of your dour plodding; stop suffocating your spirit; allow yourself to be happy.'

He couldn't help but grin at one boisterous tiny finch that kept flying ahead of him and warbling a good morning. It had been an arduous six months of work at the German House. The work itself had not been so different from the tasks he'd had at Hephata. What had made the labor so onerous here had been his attitude. He'd carried his animosity toward Herr Lichtenfeld with him every hour of every day. As a result, the same sort of caring and serving of others that had so deeply satisfied him at the Center irritated him here at the German House. Nevertheless, the values he'd learned from his parents had not allowed him to shirk his tasks. He'd performed competently enough to pass his three-month evaluation and be hired for the year. But he'd experienced no fulfillment and very little joy.

Rudy passed beneath a blossoming apple tree and filled his lungs with its sweet aroma. It would be a sin to refuse happiness on such a beautiful Lord's Day. *Thank you, Ida for helping me see that. Thank you, God, for Ida.*

Rudy's complaints and frustrations had spilled out in torrents in the letters he wrote every week to Ida. In her letters she never chided him; she gently encouraged and sympathized but never scolded. But a month ago she'd closed her letter with some words that he'd memorized because they'd served to snap the emotional tourniquet he'd tied around his own heart.

> *Rudy, I miss you so deeply and there is sadness in that missing. But I don't think God would be pleased if we allowed that missing to completely swallow all of our joy and convert every day into a gray, heavy obligation. Yesterday I heard something that might apply to you and that director: 'Carrying a grudge is like drinking poison and hoping the other person dies.' Rudy, can you stop carrying that burden?*
>
> *I wish sunshine for your spring! All my love, Ida*

The first time he'd read those simple, truth-laden words tears had sprung to his eyes. He'd breathed slowly, deeply for the first time in months. And he began, haltingly and gradually, to relinquish his burden. That is why, on this warm June morning, Rudy was able to smile and whistle a tune as he walked through the park on his way to church.

DECEMBER 20, 1921 TRAVELING TO CADENBERGE

How often are fiery desire and shivering anxiety two sides of the same coin? Rudy asked himself that question as the train passed through Berlin on its way to Cadenberge and the Christmas holiday with Ida and her family. That coin kept flipping within him as he envisioned the week ahead. His heart ached to hold Ida and he was obviously nervous about meeting Ida's parents but his disquiet went beyond that.

In July he'd spent half of his savings on a round-trip train ticket for a three-day visit to Ida in Treysa. He'd written to her of his trip, so his coming was not a surprise. In his mind he'd imagined their reunion—embraces and kisses, laughter and joy. But their coming together had been more convoluted.

While the six-month absence may have made their hearts grow fonder, it also had produced a shyness, a hesitancy that both of them sensed. Rudy tried to break through this curtain by joking and playful teasing. Ida had smiled but definitely had not warmed to his antics. The time had been too short for them to reestablish the comfortable harmony they'd both cherished. Their farewell at the train station had been full of passion tinged with sadness.

Now Rudy stared out of the window as the train pulled out of the fortress-like Hamburg station for the final leg of his journey. Will we ever recover our togetherness? Rudy had dared to write that question to Ida in a letter shortly after his return to Halle. Her response had encouraged him but not completely eased his anxiety: 'I want us to, and I truly hope we will.' Then she had added that chilling phrase, 'Only time will tell.' Time...Six months ago, Rudy had celebrated his twenty-eighth birthday. Increasingly he'd been plagued by the notion that his time was hurtling ever faster into an unknown tomorrow.

DECEMBER 25, 1921 CADENBERGE, GERMANY

"Rudy, are you serious? You've never eaten Klaben before this week?" Ida's seventeen-year-old brother August, with his mouth full of the dark, raisin-laden holiday cake, teased a grinning, stuffed Rudy. "You really are uncultured."

From the comfort of the overstuffed couch in the Loock parlor, Rudy patted his stomach. "Herr Loock, I've eaten enough Klaben these last few days, to have reached the cultural heights, not to mention having gained a few pounds."

Ida, snuggling next to Rudy, pinched his arm. "That's why I brought you here, to fatten you up."

Katie, Alma, Johanna and Helene—Ida's four sisters giggled not only at their older sister's comment but also at the infatuated look she bestowed on Rudy.

Most of the Loock family was in the parlor, recovering from the bounteous Christmas dinner. Klaus, born with a club foot, was quiet like his father Fred and both of them smiled at Ida's remark. Brother Herman and his wife Ann were still in the kitchen helping Ida's mother finish the dishes. Brother Frederick sat next to Ida on the couch. His eyelids drooped and his head tipped forward.

Rudy felt the soporific effects of the banquet too, but the tingling pleasure he felt at the welcoming warmth of the Loock family kept him smiling. The enjoyable chaos of Christmas preparations in the midst of a large family had dissolved the distance and reserve he and Ida had experienced in July. They had recaptured their comfortable togetherness. Being surrounded by a family for the first time in a decade had slaked a thirst he'd kept hidden even from himself.

The only damper on his delight was the prickling reminder that tomorrow evening he'd be back on the train toward Halle and Ida would be heading toward Treysa. They'd talked about Ida moving to Halle. But Rudy had no sense of the job situation outside of the German House and he dissuaded her from even thinking of working under Herr Lichtenfeld. Added to this, since Germany's first war reparations payment of fifty million marks made to the Allies in June, prices had spiraled upward. Leaving a job where at least food was available, would be extremely unwise.

But tomorrow was tomorrow. Today was Christmas, God's entry into this broken and confusing world. Rudy remembered the pastor's words in the morning sermon: Since God was willing to enter into this world as a vulnerable baby, we can be assured that He is with us when we are vulnerable, that He sustains us as we walk into our unknown tomorrows. Rudy believed that message. Nonetheless he hugged Ida and wistfully prayed that today would never end.

APRIL 16, 1922 HALLE, GERMANY

"No better place for a Lutheran to celebrate Easter than right here," Rudy whispered as he and Ida slipped into a pew into the famous Market Church in the center of Halle. The brilliant morning sun flooded through the towering windows and sent everyone's vision soaring to the vaulted ceiling.

Ida, who'd come to Halle for the holiday two days before, smiled at his enthusiasm and whispered back. "I thought you said once you were unimpressed by magnificent Gothic cathedrals."

Rudy was unfazed. His eyes glittered, his knee bounced with enthusiasm and he barely contained his whisper. "You hear that organ playing the prelude? Handel had his first lessons on that organ and Johann Sebastian Bach played it and his son Wilhelm was the organist here for twenty years. And see that pulpit? Martin Luther himself preached...."

Before he could continue his commentary, the organist pulled out the stop knobs and the stirring notes of Ein Feste Berg ist unser Gott [A Mighty Fortress is Our God] cascaded into the vast cathedral. The congregation stood and sang together Martin Luther's most famous hymn.

159

The last notes reverberated in the heights above him and Rudy closed his eyes to keep the tears from escaping. He reached for Ida's hand as they sat down. The worship service had just begun but through the words of that magnificent hymn, the Easter good news already flooded his soul with light. 'We will not fear for God hath willed His truth to triumph through us'; 'The Spirit and the gifts are ours'; 'God's truth abideth still. His Kingdom is forever.' These phrases and their truth pierced his trepidation. *Why am I so apprehensive about my future? If I have been claimed by God what have I to lose? Why should I let this sinful world determine my possibilities?*

For the next hour, as the choir praised the risen Christ, and as the pastor preached on the resurrection and God's victory over death, Rudy's conviction intensified: Now was the time to seize his future.

*   *   *

After the worship service, Rudy and Ida walked through the park. Now he led her to a bench on the bank of the Saale River that shone like a silvery snake in the spring sunshine. "Ida, let's sit for a minute."

Rudy sat for a moment staring at the water, then turned and took both of Ida's hands in his own. Her eyes widened at the serious look on his face. He cleared his throat.

"I know we've talked about this before…But today, today's message..Today I'm convinced that I, you and I, we need to be bold, we need to have faith in the future, no matter what the world looks like." He swallowed hard, "Ida Loock, will you marry me?"

APRIL 22, 1922 HALLE, GERMANY

Who gets married at nine o'clock on a Saturday night? A couple who has decided to marry simply and quickly and is obligated to take the last available time slot of the week.

Rudolph Heupel and Ida Loock stood in the tiny side chapel at the Market Church on the Saturday after Easter. The weariness of the assistant pastor was matched by the fatigue of the bridal couple. Finding and furnishing a tiny apartment, making a hasty trip to Treysa to fetch Ida's few possessions, and finally, despite Rudy's misgivings, securing a job for Ida at the German House—the flurry of events of the past week had drained them. But tonight, their hearts were buoyant and their faces shone with delight.

The candles on the altar glowed warmly in the darkened chapel. Sophia, who had arrived by train that very morning, stood a step behind Ida, beaming with happiness for her two friends. A step behind Rudy stood a slightly bewildered Wilhelm, a fellow aide recruited by Rudy at the last minute to serve as witness.

At the pastor's command, they now turned toward each other, and the young clergyman spoke to Rudy, "Please repeat after me, 'I Rudolph, take you Ida, to be my wife.'"

Rudy repeated the words while gazing into Ida's glistening eyes. His voice grew thick with tears, "I Rudolph take you, Ida to be my wife."

The pastor went on, phrase by phrase, and the tears slid down Rudy's cheeks as he spoke the words that would forever change his life: "To have and to hold from this day forward, for better, for worse, for richer, for poorer, in sickness and in health, to love and to cherish, until we are parted by death. This is my solemn vow."

When it was Ida's turn to repeat the words, she spoke in a voice that to Rudy's ears mirrored her soul: quiet and strong, gentle and steady. Her gaze was clear, her grip was firm. And though Rudy's heart was shouting an ardent prayer of thanksgiving, like most newlyweds, he had no way of realizing how profoundly he would come to depend upon this slight woman who was now his wife.

AUGUST 17, 1922 HALLE, GERMANY

The tiny apartment on the second-floor radiated heat like the inside of an oven. The breeze which usually blew off of the river was suffocated by the sodden night air. Rudy and Ida were trying to sleep on the sticky sheets. Rudy was mentally rehearsing the message he would be presenting at tomorrow's chapel service for the residents of the elder care center. He was drifting close to slumber when Ida touched his arm.

"Rudy, quick, put your hand here."

Rudy snapped awake and reached out his hand to Ida's swelled abdomen. At first, he wondered what he was supposed to feel. Then beneath his hand, beneath the stretched skin of Ida's belly, he felt a movement, the slow sliding of a tiny body, readjusting itself inside her womb.

"Did you feel that? Isn't it amazing? We've made a new life." Ida whispered, and Rudy could hear the smile in her voice. She was four months pregnant, the morning sickness had already passed and her skin held the luminous glow of mothers-to-be. Soon her breathing was slow and steady, but Rudy now was fully awake. For months he'd been able to submerge these occasional disquieting thoughts, but now they bobbed to the surface of his consciousness: *Am I ready to be a father? Will I be able to support a family here in Germany? What about my dream of being a missionary? Have I been moved by faith or by my own unrealistic dreams?*

He spent the next hours physically and mentally tossing in his bed. As he'd feared, Germany's internal battles continued to rage. Last month, the foreign minister who happened to be Jewish had been assassinated outside of his home. Strikes and counter strikes were often bathed in bloodshed. The Freikorpss still roamed the country and only weeks ago had assaulted a well-known journalist.

Like most Germans, Rudy worried about the future of the nation. But on this night, the specter that haunted him was at the door of their apartment. Food prices were climbing. Last week landlord had risen the rent again. Their wages were losing value day by day. *We can barely feed ourselves now. If this inflation continues, how will I feed my family?* Rudy tried to pray, pleaded for assurance that he was doing God's will. But the only sounds in the tiny room were Ida's quiet breathing and his own restless sighs.

*   *   *

The next morning Rudy's eyes felt as though they'd been bathed in sand. He blinked and tried to smile at the two dozen elderly men and women who'd come for the Friday morning chapel service. He opened with a prayer and then led them in a a familiar hymn:

> Well He knows what best to grant me;
> All the longing hopes that haunt me,
> Joy and sorrow, have their day.
> I shall doubt His wisdom never, --
> As God wills, so be it ever,--
> I to Him commit my way.

Rudy's strong tenor voice led the quavering choir of this aged congregation. As he sang, he could see in their faces and their bodies the joys and sorrows they'd endured. He recognized that this morning his own faith was wavering. *'As God wills, so be it ever'*—*O my God, give me the strength to embrace that declaration.*

Rudy looked out at the creased and wrinkled faces before him. "Dear Friends in Christ, listen to the words Jesus spoke one day before his crucifixion: ***Do not let your hearts be troubled. Believe in God, believe also in me. In my Father's house there are many dwelling places. If it were not so, would I have told you that I go to prepare a place for you.***

162

"Jesus says, 'Do not let your hearts be troubled.' And yet, my friends, our hearts are often troubled by the uncertainties of the future. We all long for a lasting home. Ten years ago, I left my family home in south Russia. I thought it was secure, but now I don't know what has become of it or of my family. All of you left your homes to come here. And yes, you do have a home here at the German House. But we all know that this isn't a lasting place."

Rudy saw many heads nodding at that declaration and knew that some of them were longing for their lives to end. He finished his message with words that carried his own longing.

"We all hunger for an abiding home, a place where we are accepted and loved, where we are safe and secure. Some of us may spend our entire lives looking for such a home. The truth is, all the homes we have here on earth, are only faint reminders of the eternal home we will have with God forever. Jesus assures us that the Father is preparing for us an eternal dwelling place. Let us rejoice and take comfort in his strong promise. Amen."

As Rudy finished, he turned to pick up his hymn book. When he looked up, his body stiffened in shock. Standing behind the chairs, arms folded across his chest was Herr Andreas Lichtenfeld. The director had never appeared at the chapel services before. Rudy nervously cleared his throat and led the singing of the final hymn. As the men and women slowly moved back to their rooms the director remained rooted to his spot, riveting Rudy with his pallid eyes. Rudy's stomach ached with apprehension. Before the room had been stuffy, now it felt like a sauna.

When the last resident left the room, the slight man spoke bluntly, "Herr Heupel, come to my office." He spun on his heel and marched out of the room. A hot flush of fear swept over Rudy as he followed the director's staccato steps.

"Sit, Herr Heupel." The director pointed to the same straight-backed chair Rudy had sat in eight months earlier. The director leaned back in his cushioned office chair with his arms once again folded across his chest. The shades had been drawn against the hot sun. In the dusky silence Rudy could hear the blood pulsing in his ears. Director Lichtenfeld now leaned forward and picked up a document from his desk.

"Do you know what Herr Lenin in Russia did last year in December?"

Rudy shrugged his shoulders in bewilderment.

The director pasted a stiff smile across his face. "Herr Heupel, you should pay more attention to what has happened in your native land."

Rudy began to protest, "Excuse me, Herr Director but I am—"

Lichtenfeld held out his hand to halt Rudy's objection. "Last year the Reds defeated the Whites. Many Russians chose exile instead of submitting to the victors. So, on December 15, Lenin declared that all Russians in exile were no longer citizens. Legally, it would appear you are now a stateless person."

Rudy sputtered, "But I…I'm German. I'm not in exile."

The brittle smile left the director's face. "And yet, the only document you have says you were born in Russia. We know you are Russian born, but we have no proof that you are German, other than your word."

Rudy sat in stunned silence. *When will this tyrant let his hammer fall?*

"I've asked you into my office today because I have some good news for you." The tenor of the director's voice belied his words. Rudy waited with dread.

"Certainly you've heard of the League of Nations?"

Rudy could only nod.

"Good. Five weeks ago, the League of Nations decided that all member countries could issue identity cards to Russian refugees so they can work or travel freely. I would encourage you to apply immediately for such a card."

Rudy's frustration now outraced his dread and he bristled "So you consider me a refugee?"

The artificial smile returned to the director's face. "If you were a German you would've been conscripted into the army. Since you weren't…" The slight man shrugged and simpered. "Of course, you could return to Russian territory then you'd no longer be a refugee."

Rudy threw out his arms, "Ach, Herr Director. Why are you telling me all of this? What do you really want to say?"

Andreas Lichtenfeld lowered his head, peered over his wire rimmed glasses and his words were as sharp and cold as an ice pick. "Your contract with us ends on December 31. We will not be renewing it. You'd best apply for that identity card so you can travel and look for work. You may go now."

Rudy's legs trembled as he stood and shuffled out of the office. Before long Ida would have to give up her job. In late December she would deliver the baby. The baby's father was now a refugee and would soon be unemployed. He stepped out into the blistering sun, but he shivered with angst. Once again, he would be without a home. Despite Jesus's promises, Rudy's heart was deeply troubled.

September 1, 1922
Halle, Germany
Dear Jacob,

How has your summer been? Have you finished the harvest? I pray God blessed you with bounty.

In my last letter I wrote about my marriage and my work at the German House here in Halle. Now I can announce that we'll be parents before the end of the year! All goes well with the pregnancy. Ida had several weeks of morning nausea, but now is eating well. She's especially craving the strong vinegary pickles they sell in the market.

The rest of my news isn't as joyful. My contract at the Foundation is over at the end of the year. I won't go into the reasons. I'm beginning the hunt for a new job. But things aren't going well here in Germany. Prices are rising by the day. Our wages are adjusted only at the end of the month so we're always thirty days behind. I'd hoped to save some money to enroll in the Lutheran seminary here in Halle but that now seems impossible.

Here's the most ridiculous news: I've just been informed that I am considered a stateless 'refugee' here in Germany. Have you ever heard of anything so crazy? I only have my birth certificate and supposedly that's not strong enough proof that I'm German. I'm told that I can get a special identity card allowing me to travel and work in Germany. But why should I stay in this country if it doesn't really want me? Since the war I don't know if Germany will ever feel like home.

I have to make some decisions soon. Before I do, I'd like to hear your opinion. Should I try going back to Freidorf? I haven't heard anything from our family there in so long, but I know that our whole region is now part of the nation of Ukraine. Maybe things are better there.

Should I try coming to the United States? How expensive is it to live there? Are there any Lutheran seminaries close to North Dakota? Everything always seems to depend on money.

Our Lord said "Do not worry about tomorrow, for tomorrow will worry about itself. Each day has enough trouble of its own." If it were just me, I might be able to do that. But now, like you, I've got a family. I have to think about our future.

I look forward to hearing your opinions. Keep us in your prayers.

Blessings to your family and Katherine's family,

Your brother, Rudy

JANUARY 7, 1923 HALLE, GERMANY

"Isn't she the most beautiful thing you've ever seen?" Ida could not take her eyes off her tiny daughter.

Sophia stood with her arm across the shoulder of her friend. "Baby Ida is as beautiful as mother Ida." She paused then grinned and whispered into Ida's ear, "She's so big for a baby born four weeks early...or maybe the wedding was a month too late."

Ida blushed and playfully poked her friend in the ribs. Nothing was going to spoil this holy day. Along with three other families they had marched to the front of the Market Church's chancel, and now were gathered around the large bronze baptismal font embellished with relief carvings of the twelve apostles.

Rudy stood alongside Ida and was awash with emotions. He still hadn't completely absorbed the miracle of Ida Maria, who in only eighteen days had reconfigured his world. To stand now in this cathedral, before the very font where Handel had been baptized, to hear God's promise to welcome his daughter as a beloved child of the kingdom—his heart bowed in humble reverence for this undeserved blessing; to open his mouth and promise to raise up this child as a disciple of the living Christ—his breath caught at the weightiness of that responsibility.

Sophia, Ida Maria's godmother, held her as the minister poured icy water over her tiny head. She whimpered but did not cry. Rudy and Ida held hands as they returned to their pew. The congregation sang a hymn, and as they sat down the cathedral was filled with the words of the chorus: 'On Christ, the solid rock I stand, all other ground is sinking sand.'

Ever since the baby's birth, Rudy had done his utmost to build a barricade around this day, permitting only joy and light, love and gratitude to enter. But as the words of the hymn reverberated up to the pinnacles of the steeples, a fissure appeared in his precarious construction. *O God, where am I standing? My faith says if I trust in Christ, I'm on solid rock. But I feel the sand beneath me, up to my ankles, my knees. I want to do right, fulfill my vows as a husband, my promises a father. But tomorrow we must move again; the future is hidden in swirling clouds. I want to trust you, I do. Don't let me sink dear Father, don't let me sink.*

Thanks to his Hephata friend, Vernon Steuber, Rudy had a job. Beginning on January 15 he would be an assistant chaplain at the Deacon Hospital in Marburg where Vernon was personnel

---

administrator.

Vernon was doing him a great favor; the current chaplain was several years from retirement, but Vernon had convinced the board that it would be good to have someone trained and ready to step in. Unfortunately, the hours and the pay were less than he'd had at the German House.

Rudy hoped he might find a second job once he got to Marburg. Since Ida had to stay home with the baby, he simply had to find another job. He fell into bed each night exhausted by his never-ending struggle to keep the prowling wolves of panic at bay. On an extremely personal and intimate level Rudy was facing what the entire nation of Germany would confront in the years ahead.

FEBRUARY 20, 1923 MARBURG, GERMANY

"I think she's smiling at you," Ida said as she held the bundled-up baby on her lap in the cramped basement apartment. Rudy had just arrived from work and sat down on the only other chair at the table.

"Kleine Puppe, [Little doll] are you happy to see me?" With her big blue eyes and porcelain skin she did look like a little doll, at least to her father's eyes. He smiled back at her and held out a letter for both Ida's to see. "Papa Rudy has a letter from America. Should I read it?"

Without waiting for a reply, he carefully cut open the envelope and took out the two onion skin pages. He scanned the first page until Ida interrupted. "Out loud dear, I need to hear this too."

"Ja, of course, sorry." Rudy straightened out the pages and began, "Dear Rudy and family (I am guessing you have a baby by now!)," Rudy smiled up at Ida who was bouncing the baby on her knee. "I am writing this on Christmas Day. We had planned to have dinner with Katherine and her family but this morning the wind started howling like a lonesome coyote and then it started snowing, so we are all sitting close to the coal stove."

Rudy paused and murmured, "I wonder if they pay as much for coal as we do." He returned to the letter. "We got your letter about two months after you sent it. I think it took a long while to get from New York out here to New Leipzig. Anyway, I'm slow in answering because the harvest was late, and then we had to finish the fall plowing and cattle shipping. Also, I had some long talks with Katherine about your questions. You asked for my opinions so here is what your big brother and big sister think." Rudy chuckled and nodded his head, "They always make sure I remember I am the baby of the family."

He returned to the letter. "You mentioned going back to Freidorf. In October we got a letter from Elvira, the first one in many years. They are alive but she said conditions are horrible. 'Sehr beschissen' [terribly shitty] were her exact words. Their daughter Helen got cholera and died last year."

Rudy choked and looked up at his own little girl. He shuddered and continued reading. "When Elvira wrote, Vater was still alive, but she said that by the time we read the letter he would probably be buried next to Mutti. He couldn't keep anything in his stomach and was all skin and bones.

"She also said there wasn't much food to put into anyone's stomach. They've had a bad drought for a couple of years and harvests are way down. To the north the crops were fine, but the government confiscated almost all the grain and shipped it to Russia. Hundreds of people in the area have starved to death.

"We'd read some things about the famine in our local newspapers but didn't think it could possibly affect Freidorf. It always was such a breadbasket. Elvira says she and Junior and Herman are as thin as scarecrows. They are praying that there will be plenty of winter rain so that next year's crops will be better.

"Rudy, you don't want to bring your wife and newborn to the Ukraine. Things seem very dark there and so many of us German Russians here in North Dakota are praying that our relatives who stayed behind will survive."

Rudy put the letter into his lap and sighed. "Little Helen—I still imagine her little—gone, Vater gone, people starving to death. Mein Gott, it all seems like a dream."

He sighed again and continued reading. "Now to answer some of your other questions. You ask if it's expensive to live here in America. I don't know about all of America but here in Dakota, we have a garden and with our pigs, chickens and milk cows, we have enough to eat. When the price of grain is decent and enough rain comes in the spring, we can make a good living. "About the seminary: I talked to the pastor at Zion Lutheran in Elgin and he said there is a Luther Seminary, College and Academy in St. Paul, Minnesota founded by German Lutherans. He attended there and said it is a good school. I don't know about costs but…."

Rudy muttered under his breath, "It always comes down to money." He shook his head and read on. "My Katy and I have been talking to Katherine and her husband Frederick about you and your future. What we hear about Germany is not good and the Ukraine seems worse. We would like you to come to America."

Rudy's eyes flashed across the page. "We can pay for your tickets to cross the ocean and take the train out to North Dakota. First, we will have to get our seeds and fertilizer paid for in the spring and then we can wire money for the tickets. It would be sometime in May."

Rudy's voice shivered with excitement. He did not notice the cloud on Ida's face. He read on, "I can't make any promises about the seminary. But we do need pastors out here for all of our German Russian folks. If the harvest is good, we can help with that and there might be others in our congregation too. Talk it over with your wife and let us know if you will accept our offer. Christmas blessings from our family to yours, Jacob."

Rudy dropped the letter onto the table, closed his eyes and whispered, "Thank you, Lord." His most secret prayer had been answered. Then he opened his eyes. Ida's face held a forlorn smile and a trickle of tears on each cheek.

He pulled his chair closer to her. "What's wrong Leibe?"

"Rudy, this is what you've longed for, I know. And yes, it's the best choice for us. For you.." Ida swallowed, "for you it means moving close to your family. For me…"

She sniffled, then sighed and hugged the baby. "What do you say, kleine Ida? We'll just have to make our own family in America, won't we."

The baby gurgled in Ida's arms and Rudy knelt beside her chair and hugged them both. "Kleine Mutter,[little mother] how can I thank you for understanding. We'll be a family wherever we go. You'll like my brother and sister. We'll be surrounded by good people."

He stood and took the baby and began bouncing her in his arms and pacing in their tiny kitchen. "Finally, something to look forward to. Mein Gott, what a miracle. I'll write back today. And then I'll write to my old friend Marvin Becker in South Dakota. He was from south Russia too but moved just before the war. I'll see what he says about living expenses and seminaries. Then I'll check on the costs for passage to New York. I'll have to tell Vernon at work…No I'd better wait until things are all set." He continued chattering to himself.

Ida smiled at his enthusiasm. *At least I can be happy at my husband's excitement.*

MAY 21, 1923 MARBURG, GERMANY

"Well, look who's come to walk me home." Rudy had just finished squeezing out the mop in the hospital's janitor storage room and was locking the door when Ida came pushing the dilapidated baby carriage he'd rescued from the junk heap. Five-month-old Ida Maria looked up at him and waved her arms in delight. Rudy had gotten the janitorial job soon after their arrival at Marburg. The pay was minimal but the hours were flexible so he'd been able to juggle both his chaplaincy and janitor jobs without too many late nights.

"The day was so beautiful, and yesterday's sermon about the great and mighty wind of Pentecost made me hungry for some fresh air." Ida beamed and held out a white envelope. "And…you got a letter from your friend Marvin. The baby and I want to hear what he has to say."

"Oh ho. You're getting as impatient as I am." He took the letter as they left the hospital. They stopped and sat on a bench near the street. Ida kept gently pushing the carriage back and forth.

"Let's see what Marvin has to say." Rudy pulled out a single thin sheet, written only on one side. "Hmm. Evidently he doesn't have too many words." Rudy pressed the flimsy paper onto his knee and read.

"Dear Rudy, Ida and baby, What good news that you are coming to America. The news we hear about Germany and Ukraine is very dark. I am writing this late at night because we are in the middle of planting season and I'm too busy to even think. I don't have time to answer your questions in this letter.

"But I do have a very big request. I have moved from South Dakota. I had a chance to get some land of my own and so now live in Golden Valley, North Dakota. Can you believe it? After all of my study I am now a farmer. Here is my request: Out here there are no young German women available and I am not a happy bachelor.

"Do you know of a strong youngish German woman who would be willing to come out to North Dakota and marry me? You know that I'm a serious, God-fearing man. I have my own farm and my house is small but solid. Maybe your wife has a friend who is brave enough to come along with you to be my bride. I look forward to seeing you again my friend, to meeting your family and hopefully a nice German woman. God's blessings, Marvin Becker."

Rudy looked at Ida and they both laughed. Rudy shook his head, "Marvin's a character. Well, like the pastor said yesterday, 'the Spirit blows where it wills.' Today here comes a blast from America."

Ida sat back, closed her eyes and let the spring sunlight bathe her. "So, husband, what brave, strong, youngish German woman comes to your mind?"

Rudy chuckled. "Oh no. I don't want you to think my eyes have been roving. You go first."

Ida giggled, "Okay. But I'm going to tell you who you are thinking of. It's Sophia isn't it?"

Rudy smiled and nodded, "If anyone would say 'yes' to such an invitation, it would be her. Marvin and Sophia—husband and wife...Now that would be a lively household. Now who were you thinking of?

Ida shrugged and smiled back, "Of course Sophia. I think she's just the perfect one to do it. And wouldn't it be nice to have my best friend in America too? I'm going to write her tonight. You'll have to describe Marvin to me. You better make him good-looking."

JULY 24, 1923 HAMBURG GERMANY

The wind skipped off the chill North Sea waters and ruffled Rudy's hair. Most of the passengers had already crossed the gangplank and stood against the railing of the ship that would take them to America. Rudy and his family still lingered on the wooden weather-beaten planks of the pier. He gazed ruefully at his League of Nations issued 'stateless person' passport.

Stateless, homeless, penniless—I will leave this continent without regrets. When he opened the simple cardboard cover, he couldn't help but grin at the photo inside. Three faces: his own, with the light burnishing his wavy hair, his moustache in shadow and the bridge of his nose straight as an arrow; his daughter's face, with her round head leaning against his left temple, her cheeks chubby and her eyes wide with curiosity; and behind and above them both with half smile and high forehead hovering like an angel, the face of his wife Ida.

172

I'm penniless but not poor. A beautiful healthy daughter, another child on the way, and a strong and wise wife. Blessed, I'm doubly blessed. And soon, a new beginning.

Seven-month-old Ida Maria was squealing with glee at the multi-colored pennants snapping in the wind up on the deck of the SS Resolute. Her godmother Sophia bounced her playfully. Rudy imagined that some of Sophia's jouncing was due to nervous energy and an eagerness to begin the journey.

He was anxious too. As a ten-year-old he remembered when Jacob and Katherine had traveled to America. They had written of the horrible conditions in steerage: the stench of vomit, the horrible food, the ruffians who prowled through the ranks of open bunks at night. When he went to buy the tickets for their journey, he was dismayed to discover that his money barely covered the cost of the cheapest passage.

The ticket agent had tried to assure him. "Things are much better now. We even have small separate rooms for families. And you can all come up on the main deck. Ever since that British ship sank ten years ago, we've been forced to make below decks more livable."

Rudy had no choice but to hope that the agent's words were true. He was anxious to see for himself.

They all were waiting for Ida to say her farewells to her parents. Ida had said goodbye to her brothers and sisters yesterday in Cadenberge. Her parents, Ida and Frederick, had traveled with them by train up to Hamburg's port of Cuxhaven.

Ida, already five months pregnant, had her arms wrapped around her mother. She embraced her until the ache in her arms matched the ache in her heart. The two Ida's murmured to each other. Their cheeks were damp with tears when finally, mother Ida stepped back.

"I know, this is hard, but you go where your husband goes, that's the Lord's will." Rudy could hear in her voice the source of his Ida's practical levelheadedness.

Ida then turned to hug her father. To Rudy's surprise, the usually stoic, taciturn man burst into tears. "Ida, my Ida you're going away forever. I'll never see you again." His face grew red as he sobbed. He would not release his daughter.

Rudy stepped toward them, "No, Herr Frederick, we'll come back. In five years, maybe ten years, we'll come back to visit. I promise."

The tears dripped off of the old man's moustache, he looked over his daughter's shoulder and he shook his head, "Nein, nein, nein. This is really goodbye."

His wife put her hand on the shoulder of his black wool suit. At her touch he released the grip on his daughter. He heaved a quavering sigh, stepped back and strained to compose himself. Rudy solemnly shook his father-in-law's hand and gently hugged his mother-in-law. He took the baby in his arms, led his wife and their intrepid friend Sophia up the gangplank, and together they stepped into an uncharted future.

PART 3 AMERICA

JULY 30, 1923 ABOARD THE SS RESOLUTE

Rudy leaned his elbows on the railing of the ship. Thankfully, the nausea he'd felt the first days of their voyage had passed. Ida and Ida Maria were taking an afternoon nap below deck on the bunk in their tiny third-class room. Ida's first months of morning sickness had evidently inoculated her against the seasickness still afflicting many others.

The ticket agent had been right about the conditions in steerage. Though the air was stuffy and the space cramped, it was not the hellhole he'd imagined.

Up on deck, the air was sultry, the sea and sky were a metallic gray, and the waves languidly rose and fell. The SS Resolute, its three backswept stacks belching smoke, plowed steadily westward across the Atlantic. Sophia was chatting with a group of women from the single women's third-class quarters. Clumps of men were seated on the deck playing cards or chess. Rudy, like dozens of other men, stood alone at the railing, pensively staring at the rolling seas. As had happened often in the past weeks, Rudy's musings mixed with his prayers.

Ida was right. Gaze long enough at this vastness and you begin to realize how infinitesimal we all truly are. My endeavors won't alter the world. These waters will roll on and on long after I'm gone. I suppose there's some comfort in that…But Lord, my life, my work, my family, my tiny world…it still matters to you, doesn't it? We all have a reason for being here, don't we O God?

Twelve years ago…the first time I set out to make my life..such a boy I was, so naïve. I climbed aboard that train expecting to be transported to a new world, transformed into someone new. Mein Gott, how the world has changed since then. And definitely not in the ways I'd imagined. Me? I'm different now in lots of ways. My brain has more knowledge, my body too. I've relished sex, tasted hunger, smelled death, endured beatings and blood. No boy left in me. But none of us can escape who we are, can we God? You know me… still stubborn, still wrestling with my ego, still wondering if I'm ever good enough. Today as I travel, I see how much I need You and others if I'm going to be anything at all.

The afternoon sun began to puncture holes through the gray blanket and drop dollops of light onto the waves. Rudy straightened his back and gripped the rail until his knuckles were white.

Gott, mein Gott, help me be strong enough, man enough to do what must be done to feed my two Idas and the new baby. Help me put them first. If that means my dreams must…What will I do in America with no land, no money? Ach, Lord, forgive my weak faith. Help me to trust in You.

AUGUST 3, 1923, NEW YORK HARBOR

Rudy pointed, "Look püppchen, [little doll] see the big lady?" Ida Maria had awakened in their tiny room and roused her mother and Rudy before sunrise. The weary parents tried to quiet her, but she was determined to squeal and laugh. Rudy had decided to take her up on deck and now, one hour later, they had a prime spot at the rail as the statue many called the Mother of Exiles came into view. She glowed in the rising sun. Next to Rudy an old gentleman wept and hugged his stoop shouldered wife. All along the railing, people cheered and waved.

Ida Maria, too young to follow her father's pointing finger, simply giggled at her father's excitement. She touched her pudgy finger to his cheek and said, "Papa." Rudy laughed and hugged her. "Let's hope America is like that lady and welcomes papa and baby and your mama. Let's go wake her and get ready to go." He hurried below deck as his daughter cheerfully babbled, "Mama, mama, mama."

Jacob and Katherine's letters had warned Rudy of the organized chaos of the next hours. Before they left the Resolute, the ship's officials pinned a name tag with a printed number on every passenger in steerage, even the babies. Rudy held on to Ida Maria and Sophia helped Ida shuffle along with the horde onto the Manhattan pier. They watched in envy as the first and second-class passengers boarded taxis or buses and escaped into the freedom of the New York streets. For the steerage passengers the day was only beginning.

Men in navy blue uniforms began shouting instructions to the passengers. The cacophony reminded Rudy of the gospel story of the first Pentecost. The instructions were shouted in dozens of

---

languages. Finally, they heard words they understood.

"You will board these barges in groups of thirty. Your baggage will be stowed below the barge decks. Stay with your family group, make sure they all get on the same barge. You will be taken to Ellis Island for processing. "

Rudy's spirit sagged. How long would it take thousands of hungry, weary, grimy immigrants to travel to the island in groups of thirty? How long would the processing take? "Patience" his sister's letter had read. "Patience and calm. Don't push, don't hurry. Don't draw attention to yourself." Rudy sighed and tried to swallow his impatience. Ida was able to nurse the baby while they waited, but since everyone had left the ship before breakfast, most everyone else's stomachs were grumbling in complaint.

Two hours later their turn arrived. They tried to swallow their apprehension as officials stowed their precious baggage below decks. Their group was herded onto the barge and plowed through the choppy waters to the island that was the doorway to America. When they landed, another group of uniformed interpreters met them, shouting out instructions. Rudy and everyone else who spoke German followed the German speaking interpreter into the main room and up a steep stairway. At the top stood an official with a clipboard. Rudy saw him stare at an elderly gentleman dragging himself up the steep incline. When the gasping man reaching the top, the official glanced at the number pinned to the man's jacket and wrote on his clipboard. *We are being tested already. I hope he realizes that Ida's short breath is because she is pregnant.* He was tempted to stop and explain this to the officer, but Katherine's words rang in his ears. "Don't do anything to draw attention to yourself." Rudy held himself erect and marched past the man without a glance.

Once their group had reached the Registry Room, the interpreter announced, "Now, women and children will go to the line on the left, men will go to the right. You will meet again after the health inspection."

A flicker of fear swept across Ida's face, but Sophia gave her a hug and Rudy reluctantly handed her the baby. He could hear the child whimper as he stepped into the line of men scuffling toward an officer seated on a high stool. Rudy watched as the officer examined each man. Occasionally he would take a piece of chalk and scrawl a mark directly upon an immigrant's clothes. Rudy tried to moisten his dry mouth. *That can't be good. What if one of us is marked? Sent back to Germany? What will we do?*

Thankfully the line moved quickly before panic had a chance to overwhelm him. The official gave a cursory overview of his face, swept a gloved hand through his hair, ordered him to swivel his head back and forth, glanced at his hands, and then motioned him forward.

Rudy moved ahead and as he recovered his breathing, he realized how quiet the crowd had become. All of the men, like Rudy himself, were cowed by the perilous gauntlet they were traversing. What defect, misstep, blemish would cause America's door to slam in their faces? How could they explain to their wives and children that this long, exhausting journey had been wasted?

Up ahead Rudy saw the figure of an officer who seemed to tower over all of the European men. The German interpreter told them that the doctor would now check them for trachoma. He ordered each man to tip back his head as he stepped forward. Rudy whispered a prayer as he tilted his head. The doctor pulled back his eyelids and ordered him to roll his eyes. The man grunted "Good" and the interpreter pushed him forward.

Now the line slowed as men were ordered to unbutton their shirts. White-coated medics slapped stethoscopes onto the men's bare chests and backs, listening for rattling lungs or murmuring hearts. Once again, Rudy saw a few men marked with chalk. He quietly prayed for them and their families and fervently thanked God that he remained unmarked.

At last, after hours in the line, he stood before a tall desk. A German speaking interrogator, sitting on a lofty stool began asking him questions. Some of them were clear and obvious: "What is your full name? Who paid for your tickets from Germany? Where do you intend to live? How much money are you bringing with you? How many years of schooling have you had?"

Some questions almost made Rudy smile: "Are you a polygamist? Are you an anarchist?" And several questions gave Rudy pause: "What skills do you have? Do you have a promise of work here in the US?" *I could say that I'm a lay preacher, but I speak only German and no one has promised me a position.* Rudy hesitated long enough for the interpreter to raise his eyes and stare questioningly at this thin German man before him.

Rudy stammered, "Yes, sir, of course, ahh…I have worked as a hospital aide in several places in Germany and many years as a farm worker. My brother and sister both have farms in Dakota and I will be working with them."

The man gave an exasperated sigh, marked the paper on his desk and waved Rudy on. Rudy hurried past him, stepped through the high doors out of the examination room and into the dining room.

Unlike the hush and tension behind him, in the cafeteria he was surrounded by excited voices and even quiet laughter. These relieved men and women had passed their examinations, and though they yearned to shout for joy and relief, their celebrations were muted. They all knew that this was only the first step on the long journey toward a secure life in a new land.

"Rudy, here, here!" Sophia's cheerful shout cut through the noisy cafeteria. He headed toward the table where his family sat. His jaw dropped and his legs froze. Ida had a chalk mark on her blouse. He gasped in alarm, but before he could say anything, Sophia elbowed him in his ribs. "The letters are Pg. It means she's schwanger, "pregnant" in English. You're responsible for that fact, dummkopf." Ida grinned up at him and the baby waved her arms and giggled.

Rudy chuckled in relief and let himself drop onto the bench. "Preg-nant. I guarantee I'll never forget that English word."

It was nearly two in the afternoon and they had more tasks ahead but first they needed to eat. They devoured the stew which was warmer and thicker than any they'd had on board. Rudy gulped down his meal, then gathered his family and moved to their next stop: the money exchange.

The money Jacob had sent for the tickets was gone, but he had managed to save some German Marks from his last few paychecks. Sadly, the value of his Marks had shriveled. One look at the blackboard above the six cashiers' windows told him the sad news of German's shattered economy: "1 US Dollar= 3,500,000 Marks".

Thankfully, before they'd left, Ida's brothers and sisters had quietly given the couple some Swedish Krona. How they'd gotten them they would not say. Then there was Sophia. She had paid for her own passage, whether with her own money or with money sent by her prospective husband she would not say. Now she unwrapped the belt around her waist and pulled out a sizeable bundle of bills. As they stood in line before the exchange window, she handed the money to Rudy.

He flipped through the bills. "Sophia, looks like my friend Marvin is going to be marrying a rich lady."

She laughed, "By the time I get to Golden Valley, all of my gold will be gone. Then I'll see if he's willing to marry a destitute woman."

They found a cashier who spoke German. He not only quickly exchanged their money for dollars but helpfully pointed them toward the room where they could reclaim their baggage. The attendant opened the door to a room crammed with trunks, boxes, suitcases, and crates. Obviously, many immigrants had to deal with baggage that needed to be managed, carted and shipped to final destinations.

Rudy and his family had no such worries. In Europe they left behind few possessions and took even fewer things to America. Their bags held only clothes and a half dozen of Rudy's theology books. They were entering their new life unencumbered by things.

But like most of their fellow immigrants, Rudy and Ida carried other sorts of baggage: psychological wounds from years of wartime privation, emotional scars from anguished relationships, aching fears of the future. Yet these two believed, or at least hoped, that because of their faith and the community they expected to find, they could cope with this baggage and thrive in their new land.

AUGUST 6, 1923 NORTHERN PACIFIC RAILWAY CAR

Ida's grip on the baby remained strong. But the grip on her spirit was weakening. Baby Ida slept on what was left of her mother's lap as the Northern Pacific rail car continued its clattering run westward. For forty hours Ida, Sophia and Rudy had taken turns holding, bouncing and playing with the baby.

Ida had been cheered by the trees, green fields and tidy towns as they'd traveled across the land from New York to Chicago. She'd been encouraged by the hills and forests of Wisconsin and Minnesota. They had reminded her of Treysa and of the verdant lands of her home in northern Germany.

Early this morning, as the sun began replacing the gray dawn with pastel colors, Rudy had announced, "Great day! We've crossed the Red River of the North, we're pulling out of Fargo. We're now in North Dakota."

His enthusiasm did not send Ida's spirit soaring. Instead his excitement dragged it closer to the train car's gritty floor. She stared out at the countryside. Where were the trees? The hills? The trim, neat towns? And what had happened to the green?

180

Tan grain and stubble fields, gray brown dirt, endless undulating land and empty pale blue sky. Not only was she moving mile by mile away from her family, she now found herself in a landscape as foreign to her as the surface of the moon.

Rudy's eyes danced as he saw the terrain. It reminded him of the vistas surrounding Freidorf: fields rolling off to the horizon, wheat fields—some waiting to be cut down, some laid out in windrows, and others already harvested and stubbled waiting to be burned off so they could be plowed before the winter. Soon they would arrive in Bismarck, North Dakota's capital, named for the devout Lutheran who'd been the first chancellor of the German Empire. Surely these wide-open plains could become what he'd long hungered for: a true home for him and his family.

AUGUST 6, BISMARCK AND NEW LEIPZIG, NORTH DAKOTA

The hot summer sun danced off the red tiled roof of Bismarck's Northern Pacific depot. Rudy and Ida stood on the wooden platform with their bags at their feet.

Sophia's eyes shone with tears as she hugged and kissed the baby. "You be good, kleine Prinzessin" [little princess]. She handed her back to Ida, then awkwardly hugged all three of them. "You'd better be ready for company. If Marvin isn't the gentleman you've described to me, I'll be showing up at your doorstep."

She wiped away her tears and laughed as she boarded the Northern Pacific rail car that would cross the Missouri, go north to Washburn and then turn west. Within hours she would be in Golden Valley and meet her prospective husband.

Thirty minutes later, Rudy and his weary family clambered aboard another NP train: four freight cars and one passenger car. They settled onto the dark leather seats, stiff with grime and sweat. Ida Maria fretted, infected by the intensifying excitement and anxiety of her parents. She stopped in mid-whine and her eyes grew large when the train jerked to a start and began rattling over the Missouri River bridge. Rudy held her next to the window.

"Baby, look at the big muddy water. We're almost done with the train. A few more hours, then you'll see cousins and uncles and aunts."

The train turned south and Ida's spirit rebounded a bit as she saw the bluffs and trees along the great river. Then the conductor shouted, "Next stop Cannonball," and after halting for a few minutes the chuffing engine turned, left the green cottonwoods behind and rolled west.

Hills and mesas now scalloped the horizon, crop land now competed with miles of prairie carpeted with short grass parched buffalo bone white by the relentless sun. Every few miles the train stopped at small, one-story, brown painted depots to take on coal and water and unload passengers and freight.

Tall grain storage bins, taller and uglier than Germany's castles, loomed over the tracks. At every stop they saw villages: one or two dusty streets haphazardly lined with stores surrounded by rows of houses: Solen, Parkin, Timmer, Gall, Flasher, Lark, Carson....

When the conductor announced, "Next stop, the village of Heil", Rudy hugged his exhausted wife. "We must be close now. We're coming to 'Heil.'" [Salvation]

Ida tried to smile and leaned her head back against the seat. She could not share her husband's excitement, but she most definitely was eager for the journey to end.

When the train pulled out of Elgin, their next to last stop, Rudy's knees began bouncing. The tracks headed straight into the late afternoon sun, then curved gently south before swinging back westward. A range of hills jutted up to the north and to the south the plains were an endless ocean rolling to the horizon.

As they passed over a black wooden trestle, the conductor shouted, 'Next stop New Leipzig', the train sliced through a cut in a bluff, the whistle blew, the engine braked, and one by one the train cars clanged together, and then stopped. They had arrived.

Rudy and his family were the only ones leaving the passenger car. He picked up the baby and helped Ida to her feet. They paused in the doorway of the train, looking down in wonderment at the flock of people smiling up at them. Rudy felt the breeze ruffle his hair and for five seconds the entire world held its breath.

"Bruder, bruder, little brother," a stout, tanned man in overalls shouted and marched forward, followed by a short woman wearing a faded blue sundress and a plump-cheeked smile. Jacob Heupel and Katherine Heupel Schock held out their arms and swallowed up the little family in hugs.

Ida Maria, stunned by the noise and embraces began to whimper, followed by Rudy's tears of joy and Ida's soft exhausted weeping.

182

Rudy looked over his brother's shoulder at the young people who stood quietly smiling. Rudy smiled to himself. *Not so much shouting, not too many tears. Even here in Dakota we are Deutsches-Russisches Volk [German Russian people].*

More than a year of anxious planning, eight days of exhausting travel, over five thousand miles away from Europe…Before long, Ida's pining for Germany's green would return and Rudy's hibernating dream of mission to Africa would reawaken, but now, at this moment, on New Leipzig's wooden depot platform, warmed by the August sunshine, caressed by the eternal Dakota breeze, Rudy and even Ida relaxed into embraces that smelled of sweat and earth, baking, babies…and home.

AUGUST 11, 1923 SCHOCK FARMSTEAD

Katherine Schock was teaching her sister-in-law how to make kuchen. She was forming the sweet dough into a ball as she chatted.

"Ja, Ida, I know they make kuchen in Germany. But in Russia, we made it different." She put the ball into a bowl and grabbed another handful of dough. "You make this recipe and I guarantee Rudy will fall in love with you all over again." Katherine glanced down at Ida's growing belly and giggled, "though it looks like that's not a problem for you two."

Ida blushed but couldn't help laughing. She was learning that her inherited relatives had a broader, earthier humor than her family in Germany. She dared to respond, "By the size of your family, it looks like your kuchen works extremely well on Fred."

Katherine smiled as she mixed the cream and eggs and sugar in a saucepan. "We've been blessed with nine healthy ones. But just between the two of us—" She winked at Ida, "I'm thinking I might stop making so much kuchen."

The laughter of the two women in the kitchen mixed with the outside noises: the clucking of chickens looking for grains of wheat in the dust around the grain bin and the shouts of children playing in the shade behind the house. Eighteen-year-old Magdalena was tending Ida Maria, her own baby brother Ruben, and also making sure her other four siblings stayed out of trouble.

Drifting in on the dry summer air, muted by distance, came the chuff of the steam tractor and the clatter of the threshing machine. Fred, Rudy and the older boys were out with the neighborhood

183

threshing crew harvesting the last of the wheat fields.

Out in the field, Rudy's muscles screamed for deliverance as he pitched the bundles of wheat onto the horse-drawn wagon. Back in Freidorf, a decade ago (though it seemed like a lifetime) he'd had enough brawn and endurance to do this work all day for weeks at a time. But these last few days, as he tried to keep up with his brother Jacob, brother-in-law Fred and the neighborhood men and boys, he realized how flabby he'd become.

After their long journey and days of restless sleep on the ship and train, he could have slept for days. But he did not want his family to think he was ungrateful for all they had done, or that since he was now a Christian deacon, he was exempt from such labor. So, for the last three days he'd stifled his groans as he arose before sunrise, joined the other men in gulping down the steaming coffee, eating the eggs and home-cured bacon and then riding out to the fields, all the while gritting his teeth, prodding his reluctant muscles back into action, and praying he'd survive another endless summer day.

Today, the sun was still two hours above the western horizon, when the steam tractor stabbed a piercing whistle into the air and brother Jacob shouted, "Gott sei dank! God be praised!" Brother-in-law Fred and the entire crew whooped and waved their pitchforks. The last grain bundle had lurched up the conveyer belt into the dark innards of the thresher, the last blast of chaff had spewed out of the spout, and the last handfuls of wheat had fallen into the grain box.

The incessant whine of the flywheel that spun the twenty-foot belt powering the awkward threshing monster gradually slowed, then stopped. Everyone's ears relaxed and they all unconsciously sighed in relief at the silence. Water jugs passed from man to man, a few of them tugged off their hats and dumped the now tepid water over their dusty heads. They all climbed onto the horse-drawn wagons and headed home. The younger ones hooted and joked. Rudy and the rest of the older men grinned in anticipation of a relaxing dinner and tomorrow's day of rest.

Two hours later, the men pushed back their chairs from the table in the Schock dining room. The younger children were already in bed and Jacob and his boys had left for home. The rest of the threshing crew had devoured mounds of potatoes, green beans, and roast beef. Fred looked around the table and nodded with pleasure. "Good work today, all of you. I didn't think we'd finish this week, but here we are, Saturday night and done with the wheat until next year."

He leaned back and slapped his belly, "And such a supper. You ladies are going to fatten up all of us. And that rhubarb kuchen to top it off!" He grinned at his wife and winked. He began to rise from the table, then grunted in pain. "Ai, my back...." He dropped onto his chair, then hesitantly stood up once more. He put his hands on his lower spine and tipped back his shoulders with a groan.

Fifteen-year-old Freddy, his father's namesake, chirped, "Vater, are you getting old and swaybacked like our old mare Duchess?"

Fred grimaced, "I had a full fork load--" he paused and smirked at his son, "--a man-sized fork load, three whole bundles--and just as I was pitching it into the wagon, I stepped into a gopher hole. I felt something pop. It bothered me all afternoon and tightened up when I sat down. Mein Gott, it hurts."

Rudy felt Ida's hand on his elbow. He turned and read the question in her eyes. *Are you going to help or not?* A bundle of questions churned within his own heart: *If I respond to this hurt, how will they look at me? What might it lead to? I want to be a missionary, a pastor, not a healer. But if I sit here quietly how can I claim to be the Lord's servant? A true deacon?*

Rudy slowly stood, walked around the table and murmured to Fred, "Let's go out to the benches. Maybe I can help." Fred gave him a puzzled look then hobbled out the door to the east side of the house. Katherine and Ida followed the men outside. As usual, the day's heat was quickly disappearing, and the cooling evening air was aglow from the last golden shards of the setting sun. The two women stood in the shadows and watched.

Rudy went to the picnic table and pulled two benches together side by side. "Here, let me help you lie face down."

Fred groaned as he lowered his stocky frame onto the wooden benches. His face was turned to the side and his arms hung down to the hard-packed dirt. He grunted, "What are you planning to do to me, Rudy?"

"Just lie still and let me check your back." Rudy ran his hands slowly up and down on both sides of Fred's spine. He reached a spot low on the spine, almost between the farmer's hips. "Ah, here, this is where it hurts, ja?"

"Ow, ja, ja, that's the spot. How did you know?"

Rudy did not answer. "I'm going to massage it, try to relax." With a circular motion he began to gently rub Fred's lower back.

185

"Ahh, warm hands…how come you've got such warm hands?"

Rudy ignored the question and said, "Now, I want you to roll over on your left side."

With more grunts and groans Fred managed to roll onto his side. Rudy stood in front of him.

"Now, Fred, crook your right leg. Take a deep breath and then blow it all out." Rudy put his left hand on Fred's bent knee and his right hand on Fred's shoulder. When the last bit of air whooshed out of Fred's lungs, Rudy pushed downward on the knee and backward on the shoulder. The twist produced an audible "pop" from Fred's back and a sharp yelp.

Rudy smiled, "Ja, a little pain. I didn't warn you because then you wouldn't have relaxed. Just roll back onto your stomach now and let me massage a little more."

After a few minutes, Fred sat up, then cautiously stood and slowly twisted his torso. "This is ein Wunder. [a miracle]"

"Nein, nein. No miracle in this. I just put those bones back in place." Rudy lay his hand on Fred's shoulder. "Now, getting that rowdy crew of men all working together today, that was a miracle." Rudy and Fred walked back into the house sharing stories of the day's work.

Ida turned to follow but Katherine grabbed her hand. Her eyes were round with awe. She whispered, "Ida, do you think… do you know…is my brother Rudy…is Rudy a braucher?"

Ida glanced toward the house then back at her sister-in-law. "We didn't use that word in Germany so I'm not sure if I know exactly what 'braucher' means, but one thing I do know: Never, ever use that word around Rudy."

AUGUST 12, 1923 TRINITY CHURCH

Rudy sat on the wagon seat with his family as the horses trotted up the hill toward the country church. The cross seemed to be tugging the steeple upward into the endless heavenly blue sky. This church was smaller than the stout stone church in Kassel where his parents had married. But it was larger than the small church he'd cherished back in Freidorf and its white wooden sides glistened in the morning sun unlike the gray stone of Freidorf's church.

Fred slowed the horses as the wagon rolled into the church yard and came to a halt. Rudy's heart had wings as he helped Ida out of the wagon, then swooped the baby out of his sister Katherine's arms. Ida Maria shrieked with delight.

"You have to be a good girl now. We're going to church and you have to be verrry quiet." Rudy tickled under her chubby arm. "It's been awhile so maybe you've forgotten." She giggled and tugged on his moustache. At the church door, Ida took the baby. Along with the other women and their children she sat on the right side of the aisle where the sunshine cascaded through the open windows.

Rudy joined Fred, Jacob and the other men on the left side. Other than the occasional whimper from one of the children, the only sound was the intricate melody of the meadowlarks already singing their hymns of praise from the surrounding prairies. Rudy looked around at his fellow worshippers. The rough-hewn faces of the men, their square shoulders and sturdy sun darkened necks; the women, most with their hair pulled back into buns, wearing their modest print dresses; he felt as though he'd leapt a decade backward in time and thousands of miles eastward across the ocean to Freidorf.

A pump organ began playing and tugged Rudy's eyes forward and upward. Written on the arch that curved over the altar area were the words, Allein Gott in der Höh' sei Ehr. [Only to God in the highest be honor]. All those gathered beneath that phrase were reminded every Sunday to whom they owed their lives. On this day, as Rudy read those words, he felt both judged and summoned. *How often, O God, in these past turbulent years full of fear and frustration, how often have I forgotten to give you honor. But I am here in this new land with new hope, and I honor you this day, thank you and pray that you will reveal to me how best I may honor you.*

The service began. Hymns, readings, liturgy and sermon—all of them in the German-Russian dialect he'd grown up with. For the first time in years, Rudy was drawn out of himself and fully immersed in worship. At the close of the service, everyone filed out and shook the pastor's hand.

Jacob grabbed Rudy's elbow as they approached the door. "Pastor Affelt, this is my brother Rudolph. He finally made it here from Germany. And here is his wife Ida and their baby."

The pastor gripped Rudy's hands with both of his. "Herr Rudolph, and Frau Heupel how good to see you. Jacob has spoken of you. He said you were in Germany during the war. And you were studying there?"

Rudy was conscious of the line of people behind him waiting to

---

187

leave the church, but the pastor hadn't yet released his hand. "I studied at Hephata Deacon Center in Treysa, north of Frankfort."

"He studied nursing and preaching," Jacob added.

The pastor's smile widened, his eyes danced, and he tightened his grip on Rudy's hands. "Truly God works in wondrous ways. In one month, we'll have our yearly Mission Fest. The missionary who was supposed to come contacted me this week and said he had a recurrence of malaria and so he was canceling. Herr Heupel, I am sure you have many experiences you could share with us. Would you be willing to preach here on September 16th?

Rudy forgot the line behind him, his brother and wife beside him. *Would you be willing, would you be willing?* The words reverberated in his ears. Was God answering the prayer he'd murmured only an hour ago? He'd only been in the country one week, his mind and body were still reeling, how could he say 'yes'? But here it was, an invitation, a door blown open by the Spirit. How could he say 'no'?

With a half laugh that could have been a gasp, he said, "Well, if you believe this is God's hand at work, how can I turn you down? Pastor Affelt, I'll do my best."

"Ausgezeichnet, [Excellent]. I'm going to New Leipzig tomorrow and I'll stop in and we can talk about the Fest."

Rudy descended the three stairs onto the graveled church yard. He tried to take a deep breath but his suitcoat seemed to have shrunk. The conversations of the men, the laughter of the children and the chatter of the women were all muted by the humming in his mind. Fred Schock was talking excitedly to his neighbors, rubbing his back, swiveling his shoulders and pointing to Rudy. Ida Maria stretched out her arms for Rudy as they walked toward their wagon. *O God, everything is so fast, too fast. Keep my feet on the ground, my mind clear. Show me your way.*

AUGUST 13, 1923 THE SCHOCK FARMSTEAD

Pastor Affelt's horse cart had rolled in to the Schock's farmyard at 11 a.m. Naturally Katherine had invited him to stay for dinner. She'd poured each of the men a glass of cool water and now they sat in the shade of the house.

"Herr Pastor, thank you for coming. I didn't sleep much last night. I may have said 'yes' too quickly..."

"Nein, nein, Herr Heupel. Our people are your people. We will be

188

glad to hear one of our own speak. Last year we had a missionary from New Guinea. He did a good job but he was an outsider. There was a distance…"

"But, I'm not a missionary, not yet. Maybe someday… I haven't been to exotic places, I don't have great stories to tell."

"Rudolph, may I call you Rudolph? You have been studying and working in Germany, ja? You lived in Germany during the Great War, ja?"

Rudy shrugged and nodded, "Ja, but—"

"Listen, Rudolph: We live out here on the prairies. We've no massive mountains, no roaring rivers, no grand forests. Our daily life? It's as plain as our landscape. Our families labor every day to put food on the table. They don't have much time or energy to lift up their eyes to a bigger world. The Mission Fest is when we stop, raise our heads and remember that God is at work around the globe. Germany is an exotic place for our people. Tell them the story of what God is doing through the Deacon Training School. Help them see that world."

Rudy grinned, "You're very persuasive, Pastor. I guess I'm nervous because everything is so new to me. I haven't even had time to plant my feet in this country. I wake up in the morning and I still can't believe I'm here. I have so many questions."

Pastor Affelt took a swallow of water and nodded, "I'm sure you do. Maybe I can answer some of them."

"Well, this is maybe a silly question but, why is the church nine miles north of New Leipzig?"

The pastor laughed. "You should ask 'why is New Leipzig nine miles south of the church?' Do you know when your family moved here?"

Rudy closed his eyes and cocked his head, "Well, I know I was ten, so that must have been 1903."

"That was twenty years ago. Trinity congregation already existed and there was no such town as 'New' Leipzig."

Rudy caught the pastor's emphasis. "You mean there was an "Old" Leipzig? Ida and I've been to Leipzig in Germany and it's old, but--."

The pastor waved his hand, "Our countryside may be simple, but our history is more complicated than you can imagine. Your relatives who lived in the Black Sea area came from Germany, ja?"

"My father said that his relatives came from Nußdorf in

Germany."

"Well, early in the 1800's people from Leipzig, Germany came to south Russia, southwest of Odessa near the Black Sea. They built a town and named it Leipzig. About fifteen years before your sister and brother got here, some of those Leipzigers left the steppes and came out here to this part of North Dakota. One of the first things they did was organize a congregation."

"Sounds like they were good Lutherans," Rudy laughed as he finished his water.

The pastor smiled in agreement. "Ja, well, life was hard. They figured they'd need lots of God's help. About the same time, a couple of miles east of the church, a settlement started with a post office, a creamery, a flour mill and houses. And, by now you can guess what they named it."

Katherine had come out to refill their glasses and couldn't resist interrupting. "Obviously, 'Leipzig'. When Fred and I and Jacob came here in 1903 Leipzig had about a hundred people and Trinity congregation was getting ready to build its first building. The men all helped haul lumber in from Glen Ullin up north, lots of wagon loads and lots of labor."

Pastor Affelt raised his glass, "Danke, Frau Schock. So, by 1907 Trinity Church was built. About that same time, rumors started floating around that the Northern Pacific Railroad Company was going to lay tracks out of Bismarck heading west across this part of Dakota. Everyone hoped the line would run close to Leipzig. But in 1909 both the Northern Pacific and the Milwaukee railroads started grading and laying tracks eleven miles south of Leipzig."

Rudy asked, "So what did the people of Leipzig do?"

"What could they do? They saw the writing on the wall. In the spring of 1910, before the tracks were even finished, they started to move their town south. They put beams under the houses, set the beams on wagon frames and slowly transported them. They even took the flour mill and lifted it, got four steam tractors and dragged it to the new townsite. And Leipzig was reborn as 'New Leipzig.'"

Rudy mused, "So that's how Trinity was stuck out there in the country."

"Nein, don't say that. Trinity belongs right where it is planted. Some of the earliest homesteaders are buried in the cemetery. Most of our families live around here. There's a Lutheran church in the town but the German Russians, they love Trinity church. Here we

190

can sing our hymns and pray our prayers and hear our sermons in German. And that's why I'm excited that you will be our Mission Fest preacher. You're one of us."

'One of us.' Those words struck a bell in Rudy's heart and reverberated long after they'd disappeared into the late summer air. He'd been 'Roosky' in Treysa. Back in Germany he'd been the man without a country. Now here, after only days in America, he was 'one of us.'

Katherine called them in for dinner. As they walked into the house, Pastor Affelt cheerfully added, "One more thing Rudolph, you'll be paid for the sermon and the collection for the day will go to your Center in Germany". As Rudy followed the pastor into the house he reflected, *after only a few days here, we are already talking money. This too is America.* The missionary to Africa dream still shimmered but its colors were less vibrant.

SEPTEMBER 16, 1923 TRINITY CHURCH

Rudy's knees bounced nervously on the floor of the wagon. In less than an hour he would be standing before a real congregation and preaching an actual sermon. Back in Germany he'd led small groups of people in worship and delivered messages. But speaking at a Mission Fest, in a new country to a church full of people… He kept swallowing, trying to summon saliva to his parched mouth. Even though he'd had a month to prepare, and he'd practiced his delivery pacing back and forth under the Russian olive trees behind the Shock's house, he feared he'd appear unpolished or amateurish.

As they rolled northward along the dirt road, they startled up flocks of long-legged killdeers that cartwheeled into the morning air trilling out their name: killdee, killdee, killdee. The road was full of wagons and Model T's driving out from farmsteads also on their way to church. Rudy hoped they would not return home disappointed.

When they pulled in to the church yard, Rudy was stunned to see how many rigs and autos already stood on the hard-packed sod behind the church. Next to the church, tarps held up by poles and tied down with ropes shielded tables made of rough boards set on saw horses. Baskets tied up with dish towels and dark blue roaster pans were already set out. Clearly the crowd planned on consuming more than the Holy Word today.

Rudy sat in the front pew while Pastor Affelt welcomed the members and visitors to the Mission Fest, then led the gathering in the hymns and liturgy. The familiar melodies and words managed to assuage Rudy's fears enough so that he was able to stand, breathe and swallow when the pastor introduced him.

"Brothers and sisters in Christ, today at our Mission Fest, we are privileged to have with us Herr Rudolph Heupel." He smiled at Rudy, "Or should I say 'Deacon' Rudolph Heupel. He studied at a deacon training center in Germany and will be telling us about that ministry today. His brother Jacob is the president of the North Church and his sister Katherine and her husband Fred and family are members at Hope Church. He has come to us from Germany with his wife Ida and their daughter Ida Maria. But he was born in Freidorf in what is now called the Ukraine. He is a true German Russian like so many of you. We are grateful to God that Herr Heupel can bring us God's word today."

The pastor shook Rudy's hand and directed him to the pulpit. Rudy took the two steps up into the dark wooden octagonal pulpit, unfolded his sermon manuscript with trembling hands and at last looked out over the congregation.

His first words quavered but as he spoke, they grew stronger. "Four years ago, I heard a Mission Fest speaker preach about his ministry in Africa, and I felt called by God to become a missionary to that continent. I do not know how God's Spirit will use my words today, but I doubt many of you will feel called to leave your fields and flocks and head to a far-off land."

Here and there in the congregation, on the usually serious faces, smiles broke through. Rudy was encouraged. He banged his fist on the pulpit. Everyone snapped to attention.

"Bam! Have you ever had a door slammed in your face? Not a good experience. It might mean, 'Go away' or 'I hate you' or 'no job for you' or 'you are not one of us'. Ten years ago, when I was 20, I traveled to Treysa, Germany, to a place called Hephata. Hephata means 'Be opened!' It is the opposite of a slammed door. Hephata is the word Jesus used when he met a man who could neither hear nor speak. Jesus took him aside, put his fingers in the man's ears, touched the man's tongue and said, 'Hephata.' Immediately, the man's ears were opened and he could hear, his tongue was unlocked and he could speak. The Deacon Training Center is called Hephata because it opens doors to people who have had all sorts of doors slammed in their faces. Let me tell you about Hephata Deacon Training Center."

Rudy used his words to create a vision for the congregation. He began with the people. With vivid words he brought to life the men and women with deformed limbs and damaged brains; the orphaned and abandoned children with affection starved eyes. Then he described the deacons, the nurses and the aides who lovingly labored to open the doors of love and care and value for the Hephata residents.

He helped the congregation see the hushed cemetery, where every headstone was the same, just as all people are equally God's children. He helped them envision the garden where staff and residents weeded, watered and harvested together.

He told of the toys and baskets made by those confined to wheelchairs. Finally, he related the stories of his own work leading Christmas worship services and Bible studies. He humbly admitted how the residents had challenged his own prejudices. He finished with these words.

"Our Lord Jesus looked at a man who'd been excluded from full life, shut out from community. Jesus saw him, ached for him, said 'be opened' and changed his life.

"I have only been here for month. I do not know much about your life. But I do know that we all are sinners and live in a world marked by sin. In such a world, doors get slammed in people's faces. Who are those people in your family? In your neighborhood, in your town? Do you see them? Do you admit they are in your midst?

"Today Jesus invites all of us to go closer to them, to look at them, really look at them, and find ways to say 'hephata', 'be opened'. Brothers and sisters in Christ, that is your mission. Amen."

Silence held Rudy and the congregation for two heartbeats. Then Rudy took a deep breath, a soft sigh swept through the room, and Rudy stepped down from the pulpit. Pastor Affelt stood and embraced Rudy, then went into the chancel to lead the rest of the service. Rudy sunk exhaustedly onto the pew.

After the service, Rudy stood alongside the pastor shaking the hands of the exiting worshippers. Nearly everyone murmured as they squeezed his hand, "Guten morgen, danke." Katherine gave him a brisk hug and Jacob grabbed both of his arms, "Sehr gut little brother, very good." Rudy's heart was so light he felt as though he could float above the families sitting down to eat the pot luck feast.

An hour later he was sitting with baby Ida on his lap, feeding her bits of kuchen. He'd eaten more than his share of fleischkuechle,(meat pasties) wurst,(sausage) and potato salad. Sitting in the warm shade of the tarp, a languorous wave of drowsiness washed over him. He longingly eyed the dark shadows under the wagons standing behind the church. *Ahhh, wouldn't a nice nap be--.*

"Ahh, Herr Heupel, here you are." The pastor had removed his black gown and white bib collar. His white shirt blazoned in the noon sunshine. "May I snatch you away from your family for a second?"

Rudy handed the baby to Ida and walked with the pastor to a quiet spot near the rear of the church.

"Rudolph, after hearing you today, it is clear. You should go to the seminary."

Rudy shrugged and sadly grinned. "Thanks, Herr Pastor. But I have a wife, a child and another baby coming in two months. I have to think about their well-being. I have no money for seminary."

"You should go to the seminary, and we've decided to pay for it."

A jolt of electricity pierced Rudy's heart. He was stunned, now fully awake. "But how…I mean… who is 'we'?"

Pastor Affelt laughed at Rudy's befuddled look. "Do you remember growing up in the church in Freidorf?" Rudy nodded and the pastor continued.

"If the pastor raised an idea and the council president agreed, was there ever any dissent?"

Rudy shook his head as his puzzlement grew.

The pastor continued, "Since today is mission fest, the other two congregations in our parish worshipped with us here at Trinity. That means that all three congregational presidents are in attendance. After they'd eaten their fill and had a glass of beer, or two, I called them together."

He grinned and then went on. "I reminded them that though crops were poor in much of the state, our harvest here was bountiful so prices would be better than last year. Then I suggested that our parish could sponsor you at the seminary as our commitment to mission. They all thought it was a great idea."

Stunned, Rudy leaned back against the church. "You mean you'd pay me to go to school?"

"We would pay your tuition at the seminary and give you money for food and lodging."

A cloud crept over Rudy's face. "But my family, my wife and—"

The pastor raised his palm to interrupt. "I've already talked with Mr. Schock and your sister. Your wife and children are more than welcome to stay with them during the first year as you get started."

"I...this is like a dream...I don't know what to say..." Rudy reached out to shake the pastor's hand. "What do I do now?"

"The first semester has already started, but you can register for the second semester. I know some of the professors and I'll write to them tomorrow. Maybe they can help us find a place for you to live. I'll stop by this week and we can talk more." He clapped Rudy's back and walked away.

The shrieks of children and bellowing laughs of the farmers filled the church yard. The afternoon races and games had begun. Rudy would have run back to Ida had his legs not felt so wobbly. He slid onto the bench beside her, wrapped his arm around her and the baby, and with a joyful tear slowly sliding down his cheek, told her the news that would shape the rest of their lives.

NOVEMBER 15, 1923 ELGIN, NORTH DAKOTA

The waiting room of the Elgin Community Hospital smelled of stale cigarette smoke mingled with disinfectant. It was 4 a.m. and other than Rudy's heel nervously tapping on the scuffed linoleum floor, all was quiet. Ida's water had broken the night before at 8 p.m. and they'd arrived at 9 p.m. The nurses had whisked Ida into one of the hospital's dozen rooms and Rudy had sat alongside her bed, squeezing her hand whenever the contractions pulsed through her body. An hour ago, Dr. Lorenzen had arrived, Ida was wheeled into the delivery room and Rudy was shooed out into the waiting room.

Now weariness battled with nervousness and Rudy rubbed his red rimmed eyes just as the doctor stepped in to the waiting room. He pulled down his cotton mask, smiled and extended his hand. "Congratulations, Herr Heupel. You have a sturdy baby boy."

Rudy sprung to his feet and enveloped the doctor's hand with both his hands. "Danke, thank you, thank you. And Ida? How is she?"

"She's worn out, but she is fine. You can see her, but only for a few minutes."

Rudy shook the doctor's hand once more then hurried down the hall. A nurse stood at the doorway to Ida's room. Ida was propped up by two pillows. Her light brown hair haloed her weary face.

"Look what we've done, Herr Rudolph," she smiled as she pulled back the swaddling blanket. At the sight of the tiny red face of his first-born son, Rudy choked on his tears. Unable to speak, he gently stroked the tiny forehead with his hand.

Ida covered her husband's hand with her own. "We now have another Rudolph in the family."

Rudy bent and kissed her cheek. "Ja. We will let him have Rudy and I will reclaim Rudolph. You are so wunderbar."[wonderful] Ida smiled and closed her eyes.

From the doorway the nurse said, "Herr Heupel, we need to let her rest now. If you'd like, you can lie down on a cot we have in the back room until morning."

Rudy thought to himself, *its already morning even though the sun won't be up for a few more hours.* But he just nodded and followed her direction. He sighed as he stretched out on the thin mattress spread over squeaking springs. His limbs and eyes whimpered for sleep, but his mind, fueled by emotion, whirred and clattered like a threshing machine. *A father again, another generation, new responsibility...We make beautiful babies. Will I be able to care for them? Do I dare go away from them? How will they manage if I am far away? Thank you, good Lord, such a wonderful wife...* His thoughts whirred incessantly even as he at last sunk into an exhausted sleep.

JANUARY 2, 1924 NORTHERN PACIFIC RAILWAY

There is no kindness in a North Dakota winter. Rudolph's tears froze on his cheeks as he left the Schock house and hurried across the yard and jumped in to the neighbor's Model T for a ride to the train depot. The interior of Herr Schmidt's small car was just as frigid as the brittle air outside, but at least the passenger and the driver were out of the wind.

Rudolph buried his face in his scarf. He didn't want Herr Schmidt to see his red eyes. He'd just kissed his giggling thirteen-month-old daughter and tickled her with this moustache, held baby Rudy to his breast and felt the softness of his breath on his cheek, wrapped his arms around his wife and felt her struggling to swallow sobs.

Rudolph had many goodbyes in his past: leaving his family in Freidorf, bidding farewell to his fellow deacons at Treysa, departing from Germany last year. None of those partings had riven his soul as the moments in the stuffy Schock kitchen.

The car rattled over the rock-hard ruts on its way to town. The train heading east would be arriving in an hour. In another twelve hours Rudolph would be in St. Paul, Minnesota. Pastor Affelt had assured him that a pastor friend of his would meet him at the station and take him to the apartment they'd found near Lake Phalen and only blocks from Luther Seminary, College and Academy. He was already enrolled for the second semester scheduled to begin on Monday.

For the first hours of the journey, Rudolph forced himself to study the book of basic English given to him by John, Katherine's oldest son. John, like most children in the region, had only spoken German at home and was forced to learn English when he entered the public schools. Rudolph had been told that although some of his seminary classes would be in German, others would be in English. The specter of failure had haunted his sleep for months.

Steam from the locomotive's boiler was directed back into the passenger cars but the warmth fought a losing the battle with the arctic air clutching the countryside in its grip. Rudolph had to stamp his feet to fight the chill. As they moved eastward, the snow cover grew ever deeper. When he'd boarded the train in western North Dakota, snow was piled in drifts in ditches and against the sides of buildings, but many of the fields held only a dusting of white. Now, as they pulled out of Fargo, the train often moved through ten-foot cuts in the drifts and the entire landscape was an eye searing sheet of white. Neither in Freidorf nor in Treysa had Rudolph witnessed such snow or shivered from such cold. He trembled with apprehension and frantically struggled to ward off despair.

I've been deluding myself out there in western Dakota. I'm truly living in a foreign land. English is hard, classes will be hard, the wolves of loneliness and guilt will beleaguer me. Mein Gott, can I do this? Do you want me to do this? Am I following your plan for my life or is it my ego? Lord Jesus, I know you said your followers must deny themselves, take up their cross and follow you, but...this, this ...it's painful. My spirit is as bleak as this harsh winter. Is this truly the cross you are calling me to bear?

By the time they reached the St. Paul Union Depot the winter sun

197

had long died. Rudolph's vaporous breaths were swallowed up in the cloud of steam from the engine as he stepped off the train. He gripped his valise and walked into the waiting room.

He nervously scanned the crowd. There! —A tall man in a long overcoat held up a cardboard sign that simply read 'Heupel'. Rudolph allowed himself a relieved sigh and threaded his way through the crowd toward the man. He extended his hand, "Herr Pastor Braun?"

The man smiled and reached out his gloved hand. "Ja. Herr Heupel? Sehr gut. [very good] You made it. Such cold, ja? Come, my wife has some hot soup waiting for you at my home." Rudolph hurried to keep up. They stepped out between the white columns at the front of the building, down the steps and along the sidewalk.

Pastor Braun chattered the entire way, "After dinner, we'll get you to your apartment. It's on Forest Street, only four blocks from the seminary. We were lucky to find it. It's small but clean. Furniture is old but still solid."

Herr Braun kept up his monologue as they climbed into his car and drove through the dark streets. The pastor's warm welcome and eager words began to thaw Rudolph's gelid fearfulness. He closed his eyes and silently prayed. *Danke Herr Jesu for kind people. Help me to trust you more. Keep my little family safe and warm and healthy. Give me strength to carry my cross.*

MONDAY, MARCH 3, 1924 ST. PAUL

In his first weeks in Minnesota, Rudolph had tried to diagnose his malaise. He thought of "Heimweh". His German-English dictionary translated it as "homesickness." Initially he was caustic. *How can I be homesick when I have no home? Maybe I am sick because I have no home at all?*

Then he would pick up his photograph of Ida and the children. *No, I mustn't lie to myself. Here is my home...Here is my heart... I truly have heim weh: 'home hurt.'*

But as the snow kept falling during the short wintery days of January and the darkness fell like an icy cloak by four every afternoon, he identified another component of his melancholy. He missed the sunshine. During his few months in western North Dakota he'd savored the bright sunny skies. Even in December the few storms that had brought snow and driven temperatures below zero had blown through quickly. Within days the sun had returned. But here in Minnesota, days and weeks of gray glacial skies added another layer to his depression.

Early in February, the skies and Rudolph's spirit began to grow lighter. The lectures were challenging, the readings were demanding and the classroom atmosphere was more open than it had been in Germany. Because he was older than most of the other students and had recently come from war-ravaged Germany, he was initially treated with deference and distance. But those barriers gradually fell, dismantled by the curiosity of some students: "What was it like during the war? How did you survive? Did the flu kill many in Germany?" and by Rudolph's many questions: "What does 'hermeneutic' mean? What does Herr Professor want us to write? How do I catch the trolley? Where can I get good German wurst?"

Now, on the first day of classes in March, Rudolph was beginning to genuinely feel like a seminary student. He was walking out of the Main Hall mentally chewing on Professor Fischer's lecture on God's "Hidden Work". He felt a tug on his arm and a voice snagged his ruminations.

"Rudolph, hey, isn't that for you?" He looked up into the ruddy face of his classmate Adam who was pointing across the street at a blue-suited boy standing beside a bicycle. The young messenger was holding up a letter and shouting, "Heupel? Rudolph Heupel? Telegram for Rudolph Heupel."

Rudolph ran across the street with quivering legs. "Ja, ich bin…I am Rudolph Heupel."

The young man straightened up and formally extended his hand, "Western Union Telegram for you sir. It arrived only an hour ago." He rolled his bike off of the snowy berm, back onto the cleared road and pedaled away.

Rudolph's hands trembled as he removed the thin yellow single sheet from the envelope.

Baby Rudy died last night. Pneumonia. Funeral on Saturday.
God help us all. Bruder Jacob

Rudolph blindly stumbled to a bench and crunched down upon its snowy pillow. An immense wind reverberated in his ears. His open eyes saw nothing. He felt again his son's last breath on his own icy cheek. His chest, against which he'd once held that tiny warm body, was a hollow husk. He slowly rocked in silent grief, his feet buried in the snow.

"Rudolph, what is it?" Adam was sitting beside him repeating these words until finally Rudolph handed him the telegram.

"Ai, mein Gott." He threw his arm across Rudolph's overcoated shoulders. Rudolph stopped rocking but sat stiffly. Every few seconds shivers spasmed his body.

"You've got to get out of the cold. Come, I'll buy you a coffee." He tugged the silent, grief ravaged man up and walked with him to the café.

Despite the stuffy heat of the café, Rudolph sat with his overcoat tightly buttoned. His hands curled around the thick white porcelain coffee cup as if it were a life line thrown to a drowning man. Adam sat and patiently waited.

After ten minutes Rudolph murmured, "How far is it to the telegraph office?"

"Too far to walk."

Rudolph's voice cracked now. "Is there a trolley?"

Adam shook his head. "Forget that. I'll talk to Gustav. He has a car. We'll take you there."

Rudolph shrugged, then began shaking his head, "He was only three months old. So tiny, my son, my son." He lifted his hands to his eyes and let the tears stream through his fingers.

Two hours later Rudolph shuffled out of the Payne Avenue Western Union Telegraph Office to the car where Gustav and Adam sat waiting. He climbed silently into the back seat.

"Now where to?" Adam looked back at Rudolph who appeared to have aged twenty years since the morning.

"Could you take me to my apartment on Forest Street? I think…I need to sleep." Rudolph rasped.

"But don't you need to buy train tickets?"

"No…I.. I sent a telegram."

"We know that, but didn't you tell them when you'd be coming?"

Rudolph turned his head and looked out at the gritty snow banks and the pale sun in a yellowish sky. He didn't want to say anymore. He was weary beyond words. Yet he felt obliged to give them an answer.

"My wife...she knows, the family knows, there's no money for such a trip. I sent a telegram with Job's words, *'The Lord giveth and the Lord taketh away. Blessed be the name of the Lord.'* That's all...all I can afford." Rudolph swallowed a sob and dropped his head.

Adam turned back toward the front, then leaned forward to catch Gustav's eye. Silently they drove toward Forest Street.

*   *   *

Rudolph stood facing into the icy north wind. Brown, gritty haze skimmed over the fields. Tumbleweeds advanced toward him, rolling in spasms, bouncing in jerks over the furrows. Small watermelon-sized thistle balls, then huge boulder-sized prickly spheres tumbled and caromed across the field. They came at him like a ragged wall.

As they approached, he turned to run but his legs were frozen into the iron hard soil. A dark menacing weed, bristling with clawing thorns bore down upon him. He screamed as it bounced and flew onto his face, into his mouth. It began twisting its way down his throat. He tore at his chest, coughed, hacked and—

Rudolph's own coughing ripped him from the nightmare. The tiny apartment was desert hot and dry. His tongue was stuck to the roof of his mouth. He lay gasping on his bed and put both hands on the chest of his sweat soaked pajamas.

Deep inside he felt a myriad of guilty barbs piercing his soul. *I should have been there. I put myself before my son, before my family. What sort of father am I? What sort of husband am I? How can I ever face my Ida again? I left her alone. She had to watch our baby die. She—.*

Someone knocked on the door. Rudolph sat up, grabbed his robe, stepped across the room and slowly opened the door.

"Guten Morgen, Rudolph, good morning. Sorry to wake you. Can we come in?" Adam and Gustav stood in the dark hallway.

"Ja, of course." He ran his hand through his hair and rubbed his whiskery face. "What time is it?" He cleared clothes and books from the two kitchen chairs for his visitors, then slumped down on his bed.

"Seven. The sun has just come up." Adam answered. He glanced over at Gustav who tilted his head in a go-ahead gesture.

"It's early but we have to hurry....you...I guess I should explain first. Yesterday, after we dropped you off here, we went back to the seminary and told the school about...about your loss. And, well, we

201

wanted to help. We took up a collection for a train ticket, round trip." He held up a fat envelope.

Rudolph sat hunched over on the sagging bed, too stunned to speak.

Adam stood, then crouched down beside his classmate, "Rudolph, you need to go back for the funeral, your family needs you there. You need to be there for your own sake, too."

Rudolph moaned, "It's too late."

Adam tugged at him, "For the baby, yes. But not for your marriage, not for your daughter. Weren't you called by God to love them first?"

At this reminder of his duty, Rudolph's chin lifted and a flicker of life returned to his eyes, "Na sicher, [of course]. They are my first vocation. But this money...I can't—."

Gustav looked at his watch. "The Northern Pacific leaves in two hours. We should get down to the depot and buy tickets."

"Ja, ja, danke, danke." Rudolph nodded, dropped to his knees, pulled the travel worn valise from beneath the bed and began packing for the trip. He tossed in clothes, winter boots and an abundance of sorrow and tormenting guilt.

MARCH 8, 1924 NEW LEIPZIG

Rudolph lay on his side, his chest pressed to Ida's back and his arm wrapped around her. They both stared at the silvery slice of brittle moon that hung in the center of the little window on the opposite side of the small bedroom in the Schock home. Normally, two of the Schock children shared this room with Ida and her babies. Tonight, only fifteen-month old Ida Maria softly whistled in her sleep in the crib at the foot of their bed.

"Little Rudy...he is so cold out there in the ground." Ida murmured into the darkness.

Rudolph gave a tremulous sigh, "Cold, cold, ja. I think we're all cold, inside and out."

They'd lowered the tiny coffin into the reluctant earth a dozen hours ago. The cemetery soil had been frozen so hard the neighbors had built a fire to thaw out enough dirt to dig the small grave. The slate gray sky had spit out a scattering of snowflakes as Rudolph and Ida said goodbye to their first-born son. Ida's knees had given out when the coffin was lowered and if Rudolph and his sister Katherine had not been clinging to her, she'd have toppled in after the pine box.

The women had served a lunch after the funeral and though Rudolph and Ida were new to the community they had sat and received the quiet condolences of the neighbors and the many acquaintances of the Heupels and Schocks.

They lay now, too exhausted to sleep.

"And now...What'll we do?" Ida whispered.

"I don't think I can go back and leave you and Ida Maria." Rudolph pulled her closer.

Ida shivered in his arms, "And I don't think I can stay here."

Rudolph's muscles and voice tightened, "Why? Have they been mean?"

"Nein, they've been kind. But... Outside is always freezing, inside—so many people. The house is small and in every corner will I see the baby. Before, he took most of my attention but now...now if I stay here, I'm afraid of what'll happen to my mind."

The grieving parents lay in silence. A forlorn coyote howled far off in the hills. The yard dogs, too cold to get excited, gave only one perfunctory bark, then curled up once more in the arctic night.

"Could we make it together in St. Paul?" Rudolph whispered more to himself than to Ida. The question hung quivering in the night air.

Ida choked, "Liebe, we have to, we must...or else..." Her body trembled as she tried to control her sobs.

MAY 23, 1924 ST. PAUL

"Look baby, up there in the leaves, see the birdie." Ida set down her grocery bag and pointed up into the dancing leaves and red flowers of the maple tree.

"Birdie, birdie," the baby babbled from her perch on her mother's hip. Ida Maria's wispy white hair fluttered in the late morning breeze and she waved her chubby arms.

"We better get home before your daddy comes for lunch. It's a b-i-i-i-g day." Ida grabbed her bag and they hurried down Magnolia Street. The Minnesota spring had arrived not a moment too soon for the Heupel family.

The early March move to St. Paul had been made in a blizzard and they'd been stranded on the train in Fargo for nearly a day.

When the three of them arrived at the miniscule apartment on Forest Street, Ida frenetically swept and scrubbed, as though her life, their survival as a family, depended on a pristine environment. The next weeks brought gray days of rain, then ice, then soggy snow.

Rudolph spent his days in class or in the library trying to catch up on the lessons he'd missed. Ida spent hours staring out of the second-floor window at her bleary new world. If it hadn't been for her toddler, who needed feeding, changing, and attention, she might have considered…

Then April came. One day the sun bobbed up into a mostly clear sky. Ida bundled up the baby, descended the stairs, stepped out of the door and heard a robin say "good morning." Tufts of cloud skittered across the heavens, chased by a wind that, though still chill, seemed to hold the promise of warmer days.

Ida felt her lungs expand in a deep cleansing breath. She let Ida Maria walk wherever the sidewalk was dry but had to snatch her up whenever a puddle appeared. The girl seemed determined to soak her thin shoes in every bit of water. Rain, and even another snowstorm came the following week. But the sky and the air revealed that winter had lost its power struggle with the spring.

On April 13, Palm Sunday, as they were leaving the worship service at the nearby Lutheran Church, an elderly couple approached them on the patio. She was tall and finely dressed, he was even taller with grey hair and a moustache to match. He extended his hand to Rudolph.

"Herr Heupel, so, this is your family. How good to see you this morning. My wife and I've been talking about you."

"Herr Professor, good morning. I'm honored that… Ah excuse me. Professor Klein, this is my wife Ida and our daughter, Ida Maria."

"Guten tag, and this is my wife Rebekah." The professor and his wife shook hands with both of the Idas. "Come, let me tell you what we've been discussing." He led them to the edge of the patio, in the shade of a leafy ash and began. "Frau Klein and I live near the seminary."

"On Magnolia Street." Rebekah smiled.

The professor nodded, "Yes, on Magnolia Street and we have some rooms—."

"Actually, it's a small apartment," Rebekah interjected.

Her husband smiled. "Rebekah, and I too, would like to offer this apartment to your family. We understand your living quarters are very cramped."

Ida's eyes widened and she glanced up at her husband, who also looked stunned. Rudolph released a deep breath. "Herr Professor, what can I say? I, we…I'm afraid we can't afford much more than what we're paying now."

Ida half turned away, hoping to hide the tears that had sprung into her eyes. Rudolph was right and yet…

The professor waved his hand, "Ja, ja, we know this. We have an offer. Actually, it was Frau Klein's idea."

Frau Klein eagerly smiled, "There's a big laundry sink in the basement. You could do our weekly laundry and then your rent would be the same as what you are paying now."

Herr Klein chuckled. The young couple appeared dumbstruck. "Why not come over this afternoon and take a look. If it meets your approval, you could move in this week."

On Saturday, the day before Easter, the Heupel family moved into a tidy three-room apartment on Magnolia street only four blocks from the seminary. The brown lawns transformed into green carpets overnight. Buds thickened, birds arrived in flocks and the throbbing pain of loss in Ida and Rudy's souls eased into a deep ache, an ache that could be borne but would never disappear.

On this morning, May 23, Ida had waited until Rudolph left for class and then she'd hurried with her daughter to the nearby market. Though money was still extremely scarce, she had started doing laundry for other professors and even some students. She was delighted that today she had a few dollars to spend on her husband's thirty first birthday.

An hour later, just as she pulled the chocolate cake from the oven, she heard her husband ascending the stairs. His ponderous, heavy tread made her shudder. She picked up her daughter and opened the door.

"Papa, papa," the little one squealed and reached out for him. Rudolph reached out one arm and held her. In his other hand he clutched a letter. He shuffled to the kitchen table and thumped down. He lowered his daughter to the floor and sat wrapped in a mantle of melancholy.

Ida began to panic. "Lieber, what? What is it? Bad news?"

Rudolph sighed and waved his hand. "Nein, for you no. For me, well, I guess I shouldn't be so surprised." He held up the letter. "You know how deep our roots are in Hephata. Last November, I wrote to them. I told them about our new baby." He paused and swept his palm across his face.

"Then, I told them that I was going to the seminary to become a pastor and that I would like to continue to be a part of the Hephata brotherhood, maybe they could consider me as a missionary of the Center." In disgust he slapped the letter down on the table. "Today, almost six months later, I get their answer."

He picked up the crumpled sheets and read, "Lieber Bruder Heupel, It has taken an extremely long time before you receive my answer to your letter from 22 November. I'm sure you are very surprised about that, but I could not write to you until we had a Deacon council meeting again. Blah, blah blah…" Rudolph rolled his eyes then went on.

"Now Ida, listen to this: But now, dear brother Heupel, may I make an open statement: I got a bit scared when I read about your plan to train as a pastor in America. I believe, after many years of knowing you, your gifts lie in completely different areas. You are not created for theoretical lessons. You are absolutely suited to stand with your fellow man as a nurse and in other practical work. I'm afraid you will experience bitter disappointment when you enter the theological seminary. I am not writing this to make your heart heavy, but to save you from a thoughtless step and bitter disappointments later on. I kindly ask you to take a close look at your gifts and to make a living through your hands."

Rudolph tipped back his head and spoke to the ceiling. "He thinks he knows me. He watched me work, he saw my hands, but he never once asked what was in my heart or what God was calling me to do."

Ida nodded, lay her hand over her husband's, "Lieber, you're right. He's far away. It's different here. We don't need Hephata's approval."

Rudolph snorted, "And evidently Hephata doesn't need us. Here's the last paragraph of the letter: Now to your question, about further belonging to our Deacon house. We thoroughly discussed the question at Deacon's Day on 9 August 1923. After careful consideration, we are firmly convinced that your official membership in the Deacon house is worthless to you. So far, we have never done it, that a deacon who emigrated overseas continued to be a full member of our fraternity, and we think it right that we refrain from doing so. We cannot keep you on our list of active Deacons. Our decision may be painful for you at first, but it's meant for your own good as well as ours. I kindly ask you to continue to write to us. You can be sure that we too will do everything so that we do not lose touch with each other."[ii]

Rudolph threw the letter on the floor and Ida Maria gleefully began tearing it to shreds. He stood and began pacing the small apartment.

"Worthless, the Director says. My membership as a deacon is worthless to me…. I'm not German, I'm not Russian, I'm not American, I'm not a farmer, I'm not a wet behind the ears twenty-year-old student at this seminary. Now Hephata, the Brotherhood of Deacons, the one place where I once was somebody, has scratched me from their list too."

Ida watched her husband scuffling out into their tiny living room. She could hear him muttering. She considered snapping at him for his self-pity. She considered joining him. *If he feels rootless, what about me? At least he has a family here.* Instead she smiled to herself, walked out into the living room and embraced him in mid scuffle.

"Close your eyes. Keep them closed and let me lead you." She edged them both back into the kitchen. Ida Maria intrigued by this new game, clung to his legs.

Ida smiled, "Now, Herr Heupel, take a deep breath. Tell me what you smell."

"Mmm," he was grinning now. "I smell… a baby who needs a new diaper."

"Ja, and what else?"

He buried his nose in her hair. "I smell shampoo."

"And what else?" She giggled.

"Mmmm. I think I smell chocolate."

"Sehr gut, Herr Heupel. You may open your eyes." Ida released him and with pride held up her creation. "Frau Klein told me that chocolate cake is how Americans celebrate birthdays. And baby Ida and I spent all morning getting ready for you."

"Kuchen, kuchen, kuchen," the toddler clamored at her mother's knees.

"Lieber, pick up your daughter, sit at the table. I'll cut the cake. You don't need to be on any list, in any book, or on any roster. You belong to us and we belong to you. Happy birthday.

FEBRUARY 2, 1925 LUTHER ACADEMY AND SEMINARY CAMPUS, ST. PAUL

"Next preacher, Herr Heupel." Dr. Kramer, the professor of

homiletics, peered over the top of his glasses as Rudolph walked to the oaken podium. The room was hot and smelled: of the sweeping compound spread on the floor to absorb the slush from the men's boots, and of the nervous sweat from the dozen aspiring preachers.

Rudolph hoped his steps appeared confident. He placed his sermon notes on the podium surface and clutched its edges to stop the trembling of his hands. Two months ago, in this very room, he'd preached his first sermon in German and though he'd been tense, he'd also enjoyed the experience. Today he was to preach in English. He'd spent the night tormented by dreams that his tongue had become paralyzed. When two-year-old Ida Maria had cried at four a.m. he'd risen to change her and rock her back to sleep. Then, rather than return to the bedroom where his exhausted wife, entering her ninth month of pregnancy, was fitfully sleeping, he'd gone to the kitchen and practiced his sermon while pacing around the table.

Now he stood in his black suit and tie, silently begging God to keep him from sounding like an idiot. His voice broke and cracked as he began. "Brothers in Christ, the text for my message today is from Paul's second letter to the Corinthians, chapter four, beginning at verse seven." He cleared his throat and read the apostle's words with more confidence.

"But we have this treasure in clay jars, so that it may be made clear that this extraordinary power belongs to God and does not come from us. We are afflicted in every way, but not crushed; perplexed but not forsaken; struck down but not destroyed; always carrying in the body the death of Jesus, so that the life of Jesus may also be made visible in our bodies."

Rudolph closed his Bible and turned to his notes. Though his voice wavered, he managed to speak with fervor. "The great apostle compares the self to a clay jar, a simple everyday vessel. If he were with us today, he might compare himself to the glass milk bottle or jar of canning. Paul was a very big preacher and missionary but when compared himself to the message of God's love he was only a humble container. What is it then with us who today preach?"

As Rudolph spoke, his passion was clear. Yet it was painfully obvious that English was a foreign language to him. His accent was strong, his grammar was weak. But his sermon was sufficiently orthodox to satisfy Dr. Kramer. And perhaps undeservedly, Rudolph would eventually receive more than a passing grade in his homiletics course because on this day, when he'd read about being afflicted, struck down and perplexed, both the professor and his fellow students saw Rudolph as the embodiment of the apostle's words.

They knew about his plight in Germany during the Great War; they knew about the death of his son; they knew how close to poverty he and his family lived. Every student was taught not to use personal examples in their sermons, and Rudolph never once alluded to his own life. But those who sat in the stifling room and listened to this slim, mustached, world- weary German, were all caught up in pondering how God's power was still at work in the dire circumstances of life.

FEBRUARY 3, 1926 ST. PAUL

Thankfully baby Fred had his tiny fingers clamped tightly on the bottle and his lips securely fastened to the nipple. Rudolph's eyes had drifted shut and the hand holding his one-year old's bottle had relaxed. It was 3 a.m. and the weary father's head had drooped. His chin touched his chest and he snapped awake. The baby stared up at him and in the midst of his energetic sucking seemed to be smiling.

A year ago, when Ida's water broke, Rudolph had taken her to St. Paul's Ramsey Hospital. As they rode in the taxi through the icy streets her contractions began. After the first one had passed, she'd gripped his hand.

"If it's a boy, I'd like to name him Fred, after my father and brother."

Rudolph had murmured, "Ja, that would be nice." He'd tried to dispel the jab of sorrow as the image of his firstborn son's tiny coffin flickered across his mind.

One year later, this lively baby infant on his lap had claimed his place as the firstborn son. And though he was named after his father-in-law and brother-in-law, whenever Rudolph looked into this little one's twinkling eyes, he thought of another Fred: Fred, his Hephata bunk mate, his rambunctious and authority defying friend, his alter ego who'd tried to please his father and had been killed in the insanity of the Great War.

Their firstborn daughter Ida Maria was now three years old and slept in a tiny room meant to be the pantry. Their apartment's walls seemed to have contracted. There was no physical or mental space to read a book or write an essay. Guilt plagued Rudolph if he stayed at the library to work. Guilt assaulted him if he stayed home and tended his family. Final exams were only three months away. Every day gusts of panic rattled the windows of his mind. Beneath his fear of failure, a deeper dread brooded. Now as Fred emptied his bottle Rudolph's questions returned.

If I fail the exams, what happens next? And if I pass them, what happens next? Two babies now, one soon to arrive. What sort of father would take them to Africa? If not there, then where? Would anyone accept my faltering English? What if no one wants a man without a country? What if—

Ida weakly cried from the bedroom, "Rudolph, call Frau Klein to come watch the children. It is time. The baby is on its way."

Rudolph's dour ruminations faded. He cradled little Fred in one arm, struggled into his bathrobe and clomped down the stairs to fetch Mrs. Klein and ask her to call a taxi for yet another ride to Ramsey Hospital.

May 23, 1926 LAKE PHALEN, ST. PAUL

Miracles, like sneezes, must come in threes. Rudolph chuckled to himself as he stretched out on the blanket spread upon the sandy beach of Lake Phalen. Both Ida Maria and Fred were napping beside their mother who was dozing with a sleeping baby Betty in her arms.

Everyone sleeping at once. Surely the greatest of the three miracles.

An hour earlier in the Sunday sunshine the little family had walked the six blocks from home to the lake. The sprightly spring breeze hinted at warmer days ahead. Ida Maria had squealed with glee when the lake came into view and had begun trotting toward the water. Fifteen-month-old Fred who'd gone directly from crawling to running did his best to keep up with his sister.

"Halt, halt, Kinder." [Stop children] Rudolph had laughed and trotted after them. "Stop, kids, the water is still too cold." He'd snatched up Fred. Ida Maria had stopped at the edge of the lake.

Rudolph helped his wife spread out their blanket on the sand. The never-ending stress of coping with three little ones still showed on her pale face, but the sunshine and breeze brought a sparkle to her eyes. While she'd laid out the picnic lunch, Rudolph had taken his two oldest children back to the lake's edge. He'd held out a scrap of bread for them to see.

"Watch what happens when I throw this in." As the crumbs hit the surface, hundreds of silvery minnows darted and swirled, gulping down the tiny morsels. The children's eyes had widened, Ida Maria had clapped her pudgy hands in delight and baby Fred had murmured over and over again, "fssh, fssh."

The open air had activated everyone's appetite and they devoured the picnic Ida had prepared. And then that third miracle had happened: All three children and their mother, basking in the warm sunshine with full stomachs, had fallen asleep. Rudolph smiled and laid back on the blanket. *Another miracle in a week full of miracles.*

The first miracle had happened on Monday, only six days earlier. Rudolph had come to campus to see if any results of the final examinations had been posted. He was on his way to the library bulletin board, when someone shouted, "Herr Heupel, Herr Heupel."

In front of the administration building, a tall woman was waving to him.

"The president wants to speak to you."

Rudolph had met the president several times, a kindly former professor of church history. But he'd never been to his office. He now turned his steps toward whom he supposed was Dr. Bartz's secretary and tried to fight off the icy fingers of panic that threatened to squeeze his heart.

"Good morning, Herr Heupel. I'm glad I saw you. Dr. Bartz wanted me to contact you." She was smiling broadly. Rudolph hoped that was a good omen. He followed her down the hall. She tapped once and then opened the door. The president stood as Rudolph entered.

"Ah, Herr Heupel, you're here already." He came around his desk and held out his hand. "Or I should say, more correctly, Herr Pastor Heupel." He grinned as Rudolph's eyes swam and jaw fell open. "Here, you'd better sit down before you fall over."

Rudolph's knees trembled as he dropped into the padded chair in front of the president's desk.

"Did you not think you'd pass the examinations?" Dr. Bartz asked as he returned to his own chair.

Rudolph released a long sigh. "Herr Doctor, I hoped, yes. But the courses have not been easy, and with my English... And then my family...So, I really did pass?"

The president leaned forward and folded his hands on his desk. "Yes, Rudolph you did. Of course, we cannot call you 'pastor' until you are officially called by a congregation and ordained into the Lutheran ministry. That is why I wanted to see you. There are congregations seeking pastors and we hope to find one for you soon. However, as you are not a US citizen, we do not know how that factor will affect your placement."

Rudolph sat in silence. He was not surprised by the president's comments. He stared at the dust motes dancing in the sunlight and recalled the words of Jesus from the book of Luke: ***Foxes have holes, and birds of the air have nests, but the Son of Man has nowhere to lay his head***. He sighed. *But Jesus didn't have three children and a wife. How long must I wait?*

The president broke into his thoughts. "Rudolph, I know how hard these years have been for you. You've done good work under difficult circumstances. Don't agonize over what you can't control. Be thankful that you've made it this far." Then Dr. Bartz came come around the desk and threw his arm around Rudolph's shoulder. "Well done, good and faithful servant."

Lying on the blanket, six days after that day, Rudolph could still feel the warm strength and hear the warm words of the president. He closed his eyes and smiled. *A miracle, the first miracle of a miraculous week.*

Miracle number two had happened only two days ago. Ida and the girls were napping in the bedroom. He had just finished rocking Fred and easing him down into his crib for his afternoon nap when someone knocked on the door. He opened it and Frau Klein held out a letter.

"Rudolph, a letter for you." She held out the envelope and her face suggested she wanted to say more. Rudolph held his breath, dreading what he knew would come before long: a question about the rent. But she evidently changed her mind and silently turned and descended the stairs.

The letter was postmarked 'New Leipzig' but the handwriting wasn't that of his sister or brother. He grabbed a kitchen knife and carefully slit open the envelope.

> Dear Herr Heupel,
>
> I am Wilhelm Mueller. I am the president of the council for the three country churches north of New Leipzig and Elgin: North Church, Hope Church and Trinity Church. As you know, we have been supporting your study at the seminary. We have

now heard that you have completed your required classes.

Three weeks ago, Pastor Affelt announced that he had taken a call to Iowa, close to where his aged parents live. He will be leaving us at the end of June.

Last Sunday we had a congregational vote in the three churches and it was decided to invite you to be our pastor, beginning this July. We hope that you will prayerfully consider our invitation and respond as soon as possible.

Your brother in Christ,
Wilhelm Mueller

Rudolph sat on the stuffed chair as though paralyzed. He could hear the normal sounds of a Minnesota spring: Chirps and warbles from finches and jays, giggles and shouts from children coming home early from school. Outside it was an ordinary Friday on an ordinary day in May. But inside, a miracle had materialized. The man without a home had been offered a home. The man without a country was wanted, needed and invited to shepherd a flock.

Gentle tears slid down his cheeks. He would wait until Ida awoke so he could share the news.

*   *   *

All of this had happened this past week. One week, three miracles. How blessed could one man be? Rudolph lay on the blanket alongside his family and allowed the first tendrils of sleep to weave their net around him. He felt himself quietly drifting. Then contentment, a warm bath of serenity, surrounded him. He could still hear the gently splash of waves, still feel the blanket beneath him, but some part of him floated above it all. And though there was no voice, no sound, he heard or felt or sensed God speaking to him: all is well, be at peace, all is well.

AUGUST 15, 1926 TRINITY LUTHERAN, NEW LEIPZIG

"Ahooga, ahooga," The strangled-goose-honk of the Model A Ford burst the bubble of Ida's Sunday afternoon reverie. She'd just finished drying the dinner dishes when the car coasted into the church yard and stopped alongside the Trinity Church parsonage.

Rudolph, who'd conducted two worship services that morning, lay napping on the couch with his hands folded across his chest. The two youngest children were also asleep and little Ida was sitting on the kitchen floor drawing.

Ida opened the door just as the passenger emerged from the dusty old Ford.

"Sophia! Mein Gott!" She flew down the steps and into the arms of her friend. Between hugs and laughter, she said, "Such a wonderful surprise. You should've written. I could have baked something special."

Sophia giggled, "Ja, ja. I could've done that. But then I wouldn't have been able to see this look on your face."

A stocky man with a black brush moustache came around the car holding a squirming little girl.

"Ida, this is Marvin, my husband and our little Hilda. She just turned two."

He lowered the little girl who immediately clung to her mother's leg. He smiled, gave a small bow and extended a calloused hand.

"Frau Heupel, maybe you remember me from Hephata. I shared the dormitory with Rudy."

"Herr Becker, I can't say that I do, but Rudolph talked of you and I'm so glad you're here. Come on in." She winked at the couple. "Let's go wake up my lazy husband."

As they entered the kitchen, Rudolph, still rubbing sleepy eyes, shuffled in from the living room. He froze, gasped, then threw open his arms and shouted, "Marvin, how long has it been? And Sophia, as beautiful as ever."

The hugs and tears and loud voices awoke the sleeping babies. The next minutes were spent with mothers and fathers oohing and aahing over the children, giving a bottle to the baby and comparing parenting stories.

From Ida's letters, Sophia knew about the loss of little Rudy and about Ida's struggles with emotional and physical exhaustion. Today she saw some of Ida's old pluck.

"Ida, North Dakota must agree with you. You're still as thin as a cattail but you look strong."

"And you, my friend, you're as curvy as ever and, let me guess, maybe expecting another baby Becker?" Ida teased.

"I'm four months along. Doing well, I'd say. It's Marvin here who's dragging."

"What? Are you sick?" Rudolph asked.

"Nein, nein. Sophia makes such a big deal. I've had this pain in my hip for a few months and my left leg sometimes feels like its full of needles. I've sort of gotten used to it."

Sophia lowered her daughter to the floor beside little Ida and dismissingly waved at her husband. "Ach, you rock headed German Russians, you're all alike. If it's nothing, why do you groan in the morning when you get out of bed and groan at night when you crawl under the sheets?"

Marvin rolled his eyes and shrugged. Sophia put her hand upon his knee.

"Rudy--or should I call you Herr Pastor?" Before Rudolph could respond, she charged on. "I remember how you fixed my back when I fell in the Witch's Tower back in Treysa. You know it's the middle of harvest season. But I finally convinced Marvin to come here today so you could try to give him some relief. That is, if you still do that sort of thing..."

Rudolph gave a quick pregnant glance at his wife. Then he put down his squirming toddler who was eager to bother the little girls, and smiled at Marvin, "Na sicher, of course, for a friend I'll do what I can. Let's go to my office. I've got a bench in there." He stood and couldn't help but notice Marvin's jaw clenching as he rose from his chair and followed him out.

Ida stood and stirred the coals in the cook stove to heat water for coffee. Sophia waited until her friend sat again, then laid her hand on Ida's arm.

"So, tell me, how're you doing?"

For a long moment, Ida seemed to stare down at the children. She looked up with a wan smile. "Well, from my letters you know things weren't easy. After baby Rudy...after we moved to Minnesota, for the first months...if it hadn't been for my daughter, I wouldn't have gotten out of bed. Sweet girl, she saved me without knowing it. Then two more babies, mountains of laundry, no money Rudolph desperately studying day and night.... Sehr schwer, [very hard]..."

The door opened and Rudolph briskly entered.

"Get me some hot towels. I've been massaging but since his nerves have been pinched for so long, his muscles have been twisted and are so tight."

Ida went off to fetch towels and Sophia asked, "Do you think you can help him?"

"Ja, ja, don't worry. It'll just take some time for me to stretch out those muscles and then reset those nerves."

Ida returned, soaked the towels with the water she'd been heating, then wrung them out and handed them to her husband. He sped out the door and she sat down again.

Sophia said, "Very hard, I know, you wrote me of those days. I remember how tough you always were during our time at Hephata. To hear you so low…I cried when I read your letters."

Ida nodded then a gentle smile graced her face. "I'm sorry I made you cry, but writing those letters soothed my pain."

The kettle was boiling now and Ida arose, poured the coffee grounds into it, and then set it on the counter. She sat down and smiled.

"Sophia, I'm just guessing, but you and Marvin look like a happy couple. Has he lived up to the picture we painted for you back in Germany?"

Sophia filled the room with boisterous laughter. "Oh my, Ida. It's been a crazy and wonderful three years. I think I wrote you about how he didn't meet me at the train? He hadn't gotten our last letter. So, I asked around if anyone knew Marvin Becker and I was told, 'Well, that's the bachelor living a mile north of town.' I left my bags with the depot agent and hiked down the dusty road until I got to an unpainted shack. I marched up to the door, knocked a couple of times, the door opened and I said, 'Are you Marvin?' He gave me a once over, and then said, 'Ja. Are you Sophia?' I said, 'Ja.' And that was that."

She giggled with delight at her own story, then spoke seriously. "Ida, he's a good man, hard worker, doesn't drink and he's good with Hilda. Honestly, I've had more trouble getting used to this wide-open country than getting along with my Marvin."

Ida nodded. "This land makes me feel so tiny. I thought I'd miss my family, and of course I do. But what I miss even more are trees." She stood and took two coffee cups from the white wooden cupboard, filled them with coffee and brought them to the table.

She sighed, "I wake up every morning and my eyes beg for a tree, any kind of tree. But my poor German eyes are always disappointed. I guess the homesteaders had to plant some trees around their homes in order to claim their land, but here on the church property all we've got are a few scrawny lilac bushes and nothing more. Everywhere I look I feel like an ant."

Sophia blew on the steaming cup, took a sip then teased her friend. "Well Ida, you are now the wife of the Herr Pastor. Doesn't that give you some power? Can't you command the parish to plant trees?"

It was Ida's turn to laugh out loud. "After six weeks? Maybe if I'm still here in six years. But you know me, I'm not much of a commander."

Rudolph's office door opened and Marvin emerged. He was flushed and his shirt was untucked. His grin melded sheepishness with relief. Rudolph followed, carrying an armload of damp towels. He opened the door to the basement laundry room and tossed them down the stairs. He turned and shook his finger in mock anger at Sophia.

"Next time, don't let this pig-headed German Russian walk around for months with his bones all out of joint. Once they get out of place, they're as stubborn as he is. I finally got enough stretch in the muscles to reset things. I've told him he should take it easy for a few days, but he reminded me that its harvest time."

Rudolph rolled his eyes, then handed her a yellow tube. "I know what that means. So, at least you can rub this liniment on his lower back every night. That might keep the muscles loose."

Marvin lowered himself gingerly onto the kitchen chair as Ida took two more cups from the cupboard. He sipped his coffee, then asked, "So, tell me Rudy, or I guess I should say Reverend Rudolph, do you have enough work to keep you busy? I remember how you never liked to waste time."

"Ha, ha, Brother Marvin, what a joker you are. I've got three congregations to take care of, twenty-five youngsters in confirmation classes, babies to baptize, couples to marry, funerals to conduct and sermons to write."

Hilda and Ida began screeching. Little Freddie was trying to steal their pencils. Rudolph snatched up the rascal and continued.

"Besides all the other church work, we've got three little ones to feed. That means a garden. Thank God, Pastor Affelt and his family got a garden started before they left. We've got some potatoes, squash, beans and cabbage for winter. But next spring we'll have to double the garden. I'd like to get one or two milk cows and some chickens."

Marvin interrupted Rudolph's animated soliloquy. "Ja, ja. I was joking. Our pastor up in Golden Valley goes non-stop too." Marvin stopped and put both hands on the table. "About those chickens: next spring when I order my baby chicks, I'll order a couple dozen for you too. They come out of Bismarck, one day old, in a covered, flat cardboard box and the mailman delivers 'em right to your door."

Both Ida and Rudolph began to protest, but Marvin cut them off. "Nein, this isn't wohltatigkeit [charity]. All that you did for my Sophia over the years, and now for me…This is simply our way of saying danke schon." He gave a stiff nod as if the case was closed. "So please, accept those chicks as our thank you to the two of you."

The daylight in the parsonage slowly dimmed as the sun slipped behind the church. But as the four adults laughed and chattered, and from the safety of mother Ida's lap, the baby watched the three children play, the parsonage glowed with the brightness of good friends reconnecting.

Later, after the Model T had honked and rattled its way out of the church yard, after the three children were asleep and his wife was preparing for bed, Rudolph stood out on the balcony of the second story bedroom.

The night was velvet, the air soft and warm. Myriads of stars spangled the sable sky. In the hills to the north, a mile behind the parsonage, a solitary coyote mourned. Rudolph thoughts were pulled westward a mere three hundred yards to baby Rudy's tiny grave in the church cemetery. *Only two years ago and yet a lifetime seems to have passed.*

Earlier on this Sunday, one of his parishioners had proudly handed out cigars to announce the birth of a new son. Now, as he gazed out into the August night, Rudolph slowly puffed on the cigar and mentally chewed on a new insight, a seed that had sprouted that very afternoon when he'd glanced at Ida and ushered Marvin into his office.

Years ago I unpinched a nerve in Ida's neck, then she asked me to help Sophia. Now Sophia brings her husband to me. Will Marvin bring someone else some day? I fixed brother-in-law Fred's back, Will Fred send someone? If every person I help sends another person, or two…What will happen? Have I opened a door that I'll never be able to close?

FEBRUARY 7, 1927 TRINITY LUTHERAN

"Aren't you afraid?" Ida murmured weakly.

"Afraid of what?" Rudolph insisted and leaned closer to the bed.

"You know…" She sighed exhaustedly. Every February for three years she'd borne a baby. She had scarcely enough energy to speak, much less argue. But the tiny, red-faced boy lying in the crook of her arm needed a name and she was trying to resist her husband's choice.

"With all of the names in our families, why must we try 'Rudy' again? It seems dangerous..."

Rudolph stood and moved to the frost crusted window in their bedroom. "Dangerous? Aren't we all in God's hands? We don't believe in bad luck or hidden curses." He turned and looked at his pale, drained wife and the son he'd secretly hoped for. "A family needs a son with the father's name. When Fred was born, it was too soon, the future was too cloudy. But now...... His name will be Rudolph and we will call him Rudy."

Ida acquiesced. Once her husband invoked tradition on top of theology, even if she had been at full strength, her case was doomed. She did what she could. She closed her eyes and whispered, "Lieber Gott, give little Rudy health and hope. Bitte, please, give me the strength to be his mother."

Rudolph kissed them both then hurried out of their home into the harsh, frigid, winter wind. Although Monday was supposed to be his one day of rest, he'd promised the Mueller family that he'd come to their farm and visit their eighty-year-old mother who was drifting slowly toward death. As the Model T bounced along the frozen gravel road, this father's prayer of thanksgiving for his new son was repeatedly derailed by the clamoring demands of his neverending pastoral responsibilities.

OCTOBER 31, 1927, GRANT COUNTY COURT, CARSON, NORTH DAKOTA

"State your name," the court clerk intoned. His few strands of gray hair seemed to float above his pink scalp as he bent over the document in front of him.

Rudolph stood and spoke in his best declamatory voice, "Rudolph Heupel."

August Loock, Ida's brother who'd arrived from Germany in August, had accompanied Rudolph on the thirty-mile drive to the county seat. Now he sat wide-eyed, watching the proceedings. As soon as he learned enough English, he hoped to follow in his brother-in-law's footsteps.

The clerk continued with a speech clearly worn threadbare from countless repetition."Mr. Heupel, you are here today to declare your intention to become a citizen of the United States of America. You will have up to seven years from this day to petition the court for citizenship. At that time, you will have to bring two witnesses who can attest that you have lived in this country for at least five years and that you are a person of good moral character. Do you understand?"

"Ja, I mean, yes, sir."

The clerk read from the document before him. "Your occupation is minister of the Gospel and your age is thirty-four, correct?"

Rudolph replied, "Yes sir," and smiled to himself. *How fitting that today is Reformation Day. On this day, at age thirty four, Luther nailed a declaration of freedom to the church door in Wittenberg. Today at the same age I take my step toward freedom in this land of the free.*

The clerk droned on, verifying the data Rudolph had provided, then cleared his throat and adopted a solemn tone. "Mr. Heupel, now listen carefully: Is it your bona fide intention to renounce forever all allegiance and fidelity to any foreign potentate, state, or sovereignty, and particularly to the German Reich? If so answer, 'Yes, that is my intention.'"

Allegiance and fidelity...Have I ever given any such thing to any nation? To the Russia where I was born? To the Germany that nearly starved me?

Rudolph threw back his shoulders, "Yes, that is my intention."

The clerk smiled briefly at Rudolph's enthusiasm. "Now, one last question: Do you declare that you are not an anarchist, not a polygamist or a believer in the practice of polygamy, and that it is your intention in good faith to become a citizen of the United States of America and to permanently reside therein? If so, answer, 'Yes, so help me God.'"

Rudolph's affirmative answer nearly rattled the windows in the clerk's office. He signed all three copies of the document. Then the clerk, with a flourish of self-importance, opened a desk drawer and withdrew a heavy, black metal implement and with an exaggerated grunt, embossed each sheet with the county court's seal.

*   *   *

The envelope with Rudolph's copy of his declaration of intention lay on the cracked leather car seat between the two men. As they

220

bounced along the rutted road Rudolph lustily sang 'A Mighty Fortress is Our God.' August's thin tenor joined in.

When Rudolph paused for breath, August began to quiz him, "I understood most of what was said, but what does it mean when you declare you're not a believer in poly…poly-gamy?"

Rudolph's bellowing laughter rose louder than the Model T's clatter. "Ach, brother August, I wouldn't worry too much about that one. After you find yourself a wife, you'll see how easy it will be to declare you're a non-believer in polygamy."

MARCH 11, 1928 TRINITY CHURCH

The weary pump organ squeezed out the last notes of the closing hymn. The congregation put the hymn books in the pew racks in front of them and waited for the pastor's benediction. But instead, Pastor Heupel asked them to be seated. Whispers and murmured inquiries filled the church.

"Herr Huber has asked to read a letter before we are dismissed. Herr Huber, please." Rudolph sat down in the front pew and a tall, raw-boned blond man stood and moved to the front. He nervously tugged at his frayed shirt collar and then opened up a newspaper.

"I subscribe to Der Staats-Anzeiger [the State Gazette]. It comes out of Bismarck once a week. Most of you know they get letters from our old home country and they publish them for everyone to read. On Friday there was a letter from my cousin Horst in Klein Neudorf. I'd like to read it to you."
Reinhold Huber's voice was strong. Even though he stumbled over some words (or perhaps because he stumbled) the silence and the sorrow in the chilly church deepened as he read.

"To live in these times is sad. There is no end to the payments to the government. There is great poverty in the entire area. Many people have had to sell their last grain to pay the production quota assessment. The future does not look bright. If we have another crop failure this year (from which may God spare us) then it will be worse than in 1921. The reserves are totally exhausted. The granaries are swept clean and many families have no bread to eat and no seed for sowing.

"I used to be a well-off farmer. Now I've become a beggar. I still have two cows and one horse. Thank God, he still can pull the wagon. No one has any draw horses anymore. Six farmers together pull a plow. You can imagine how that goes. The farmers are all exhausted and we are all the same now, hungry and naked.

"Even so, we do not want to become discouraged; our God is still alive even though today many say, 'There is no God.' We will not be misled by such people but rather hold fast to our confession of faith. We will not abandon our trust but be comforted again by trust in Him. Hilda Zimmerman sends greetings to her children in America."

Reinhold looked up to the congregation. "Hilda is my wife's mother." He returned to his reading with a voice thickened by emotion. "Hilda mourns the fact that her children in America do not give a sign that they are still alive. She is laboring under intense need. I hope that her children will do their duty and send her some financial support from time to time, so that she doesn't need to live in poverty in her old age. Hunger hurts."[iii]

Reinhold's wife was crying. Other women were wiping their eyes with their handkerchiefs and some men were swiping at their eyes with the backs of their hands. Every person in the room had family members living in what was now part of the Union of Soviet Socialist Republic. Everyone felt the sharp knife of Hilda's mourning. Rudolph had spoken with Reinhold and the congregation's council president before the worship service and now stood alongside the nervous farmer.

"Remember in February when we began the Lenten journey toward Easter? We talked about the sacrifice made by God for our sake. I asked you what sacrifices we followers of Christ might be asked to make. I believe Brother Reinhold has opened a window onto a need that is close to all of us. We can respond if we are willing to sacrifice."

Rudolph nodded to Herr Mueller. "Your council president and I are inviting you to consider a special offering that we will receive on Easter Sunday. We will send it to the Lutheran Church in Klein-Neudorf for distribution. I know we can't help all of those in need, but let's not use that as an excuse to do nothing. Please stand now and receive the final blessing." The congregation filed out of the church, quieter than usual. The March wind still stung and the sun hadn't yet melted all of the snow. Some families did not linger. They went directly to the long horse barn that lay east of the parsonage, got their horses and buggies and hastened homeward. A few families stood in the lee of the church and quietly shared news and gossip.

All of the families who'd been in church entered the new week not only thankful to be in America and not in Russia, but also aware of the precarious nature of farming anywhere in the world. What would happen to their families if one day the rains stopped falling?

SEPTEMBER, 1929 TRINITY CHURCH

Rudolph looked up from the scribbled sermon notes on his desk. The afternoon sun was washing the church yard in burnished light. His office was now in the south end of the parish school house that stood on the northwest corner of the church lot. Rudy smiled to himself. *As usual, Ida was right.* Six months earlier, she had erupted in frustration. Or, as one of the farmers would say, 'she stood up on her hind legs and told him what needed telling.' He chuckled ruefully as he remembered her outburst.

She had confronted him as he came out of his office. "Rudolph, I am fed up. This has been going on too long. Today I washed the sheets but it was drizzling outside, so I hung them across the chairs by the cookstove. Then that family from Mott came in for treatment and since you already had someone in your office, they sat down to wait. They got my clean sheets all dirty. Yesterday I washed the kitchen floor and Herr Hodell came to see you and he tracked in mud and I had to do it all over. Stimmt. [Enough.]" Her eyes glinted with menace.

He'd been married long enough to know that he needed to find a solution, and soon. The number of people coming to him for pinched nerves and sore backs and twisted knees had grown every month. He did need more space.

During the lull after the haying season and before the harvest, a few men from the congregation had walled off one end of the parish school building and turned it into an office. Now during the week, the school building served as the waiting room for those who came to him for help. Since it was fifty yards away from the house, it was quieter and he could get more work done. But on some days, when the schoolhouse was empty and silent, he would look up from his study and wistfully sigh. He missed the cheerful chatter of a houseful of children.

On this Friday afternoon he was putting the final touches on his Sunday sermon when he heard a car pull into the church yard. From his window he could see a slight man scurrying toward his office. Rudolph stood and opened his office door as the man entered the

---

building.

"Are you Doctor Heupel?" The man bounced in with his hand outstretched and a jaunty grin on his thin face.

"I am Reverend Heupel, no doctor." Rudolph took the outstretched hand and the man shook it with fervor. Without releasing his grip, he began to chatter.

"Ja, ja, of course. So good to meet you. My name is Harvey Fruh. The Becker family from Ipswich in South Dakota told me all about what you did for their son Marvin. I think he lives north of here, ja?"

He released Rudolph's hand, took a breath and continued. "I'm a salesman and I was up in this area, and last night outside of Mandan I got a flat tire and when I was changing it, one of the bolts was so tight and I put all my weight on it and something popped in my shoulder and it hurt like hell, ah, sorry, I mean it hurt like the devil...I guess that's not much better, eh? Anyway, I remembered what the Beckers said about you and thought I'd stop by to see if you could help me."

Rudolph led the man into his office. *The man chirps nonstop like a sparrow on a fence post. He looks a little like one too.*

"Please take off your suit coat and sit here on the bench."

"Before you start, I suppose I should ask what you charge."

Rudolph waggled a finger, "Nichts, [nothing]. There's a basket by the door. Put something in if you'd like. I put it all into the church treasury. Now sit please"

He placed his hands on the man's shoulder. He traced the muscles, the tendons and ligaments with his fingertips. He could feel the tight muscles relax as he gently massaged with his warm hands. He sensed more than felt the place where the pain throbbed. A ligament seemed to be displaced. He rubbed the joint, all the while chatting with the salesman about weather, the crops, the condition of the roads. Then quickly, sharply, he twisted the shoulder. They both heard a small 'pop'.

"Ohhh. Ahhh." The salesman rolled his shoulder. "Amazing. Reverend Heupel you definitely have healing hands." He remained on the bench, in no hurry to leave. "Do you know Frau Hafner from Eureka?" Rudolph shook his head.

"Well, she's a braucher—"

Rudolph snapped, "I'm not a braucher. I'm a pastor. What I do has nothing to do with magic or special words or spells. I'm a simple servant of our Lord and anything I do is by His power."

Herr Fruh, in true salesman fashion, plunged ahead undaunted. "Of course, I know. And she does plenty of hocus pocus mumbling. Sometimes she has special salves and herbs and she does this action with string, and of course she says the Lord's Prayer, and I heard she even sometimes whispers a Hail Mary or two. Only for her Catholic patients, of course."

Rudolph walked to the office door. It had been a long day and the chirping was eroding his patience.

The salesman grabbed his coat, then stood, but rattled on. "What I wanted to say is that Frau Hafner gives some people pills made by the Luyties company? Have you heard of it?"

Before opening the door, Rudolph picked up a worn book and opened it. "Nein, I've not heard of it and I don't hand out pills. I can't hand out pills. I'm not a doctor. Please, Herr Fruh, sign here. I keep track of all the people who come to me for help."

The salesman took the pen offered to him, paged through the book and whistled softly. "Whew, how many hundreds have you treated?"

Rudolph shrugged, "Probably over two thousand by now."

The salesman pointed the pen at Rudolph, "Reverend, I bet some people come to you with more than muscle or joint problems, problems you can't fix with healing hands, ist das nicht wahr? "[isn't that true]

Rudolph shrugged and the intrepid salesman nodded, "Yes, I'm sure. And, you know some people feel better if you give them some medicine even if the medicine is only a fake pill."

Rudolph remembered his work with the wounded soldiers. There were days when they had no more aspirin to ease the men's pain. So, without telling the soldiers, they gave them pills that looked like the aspirin tablets but were mere salt tablets. Many of the men said their pain diminished. The chirping salesman was right. Rudolph reluctantly nodded in agreement.   "So, Reverend, these pills made by Luyties are not fake pills, but they are not so strong that only a doctor can hand them out. Herman Luyties, a German from Bremen I think, came to St. Louis and he'd learned all about homeopathic medicine from a doctor in Germany. He started a pharmacy company and now they send medicines all over the country. All of them have numbers. "199's" are for backache, "22s" are for sour stomach. I take them if I eat too much wurst and drink too much beer."

Rudolph gradually ushered the man out of his office. "Well, Herr Fruh, beer is still illegal so I'd think you can't find too much of it." The two men began walking across the churchyard toward the man's car.

"Ha, you're right about that, Reverend. Prohibition. What a cruel joke for us German Russians." They'd reach the salesman's car and Rudolph was eager to send him on his way.

But Herr Fruh wasn't finished. "Before I go, I want to give you something for your kindness to me. I didn't put anything in the basket because I wanted to give you this box. It's a sample box of Luyties pills. Try them out. If you want more, you can buy them from me when I'm in the area again, or if you choose, you can order them yourself." He handed Rudolph a sealed cardboard box, grabbed the pastor's hand and after a dozen 'dankes' finally hopped into his car and rolled out onto the gravel road to New Leipzig.

For a moment Rudolph simply stood and savored the sudden chirpless silence. He stared at the box. *Homeopathic pills…I suppose I could hand some of them out. There could be no harm in that. Could there?*

OCTOBER 27, 1929, TRINITY CHURCH PARSONAGE

Sunday dinner was over, the dishes were washed, and now lively, warm conversations between the six families filled the parsonage. In the living room, the women sipped coffee and swapped child-raising stories. All of the mothers had abundant tales to tell. Rudolph and Ida's brood had grown to five with the birth of son August last December. The youngest children were taking their afternoon naps in the upstairs bedrooms. The others were outside, laughing and squealing in the church yard.

The six men sat out on the south-facing front porch. They were protected from the brisk northwest breeze so the last vestiges of the sun's fall heat made the ambiance warm, but not nearly as warm as the conversation. Between puffs of cigars and cigarettes the men were asking questions and offering opinions on the week's events.

To Ida's great delight, earlier in the year, her brothers Fritz and Heinrich had joined their brother August who'd arrived two years earlier. Her joy was only slightly dampened by the fact that they'd left because of the creeping chaos in Germany where her parents, two brothers and four sisters still lived. The brothers were now worrying about the turmoil that might be stirring in their new home.

August, whip thin with icy blue eyes, leaned forward in his chair and asked, "On the radio, we hear about this great crash in New York. Everyone makes such a fuss. How can this crash in New York have anything to do with us? It's so far away."

Rudolph waved his cigar and rolled his eyes. Then, he spoke in Russian to his brother Jacob, and brother-in-law Frederick, "How can I even begin to explain to these newcomers?"

Switching to German, he began, "You need to remember, we're not a small country like those in Europe. Even though New York is thousands of miles away, and completely different from North Dakota, it's still part of our country. What happens there sends ripples here too."

Heinrich the oldest of the three newly arrived brothers, asked, "But isn't the stock market about investments and banks and huge companies?"

Of the entire group, Jacob had been in the U.S. the longest and experienced his share of financial difficulties. He snorted, "Where do you think we get the money to buy seed and fertilizer? We borrow it from the banks. And who do you think buys our wheat? The big companies in Minneapolis. If something happened to them, we'd be in trouble."

Fritz was a stocky, clean shaven young man and his vision of farming had been shaped by the some of the small subsistence farms of northern Germany. He wondered, "But wouldn't the farmers survive even if prices dropped?"

Rudolph, the only one of the men who'd lived in Germany, Russian and the US, said, "Here in America, everyone, even farmers, need money to survive. And especially here in North Dakota, we can't survive without coal to heat the house. Sugar, salt, coffee, mein Gott--what would we do without coffee? We have to buy it all. Last year wasn't so bad but sometimes the winters drag on forever and the cellars are bare before we have fresh things to eat."

Stolid, mustached Frederick Schock had quietly listened to the conversation. Now he blew a smoke ring into the air and declaimed in a low raspy voice, "This past June was the driest June ever. I harvested enough wheat to pay off my loans. But I barely had enough left to buy new school shoes for the kids." He took another deep draw on his cigarette. "If we don't get a snow cover this winter, and if the rains don't come next spring, it won't matter if the banks fail and Minneapolis mills shut down. Our situation will be sehr, sehr ernst." [very, very serious]

The men blew smoke into the air and silently ruminated on Frederick's baleful words. The air was growing chillier and the melodious laughter of the children was counterpointed by the raucous cawing of crows scavenging for the last few kernels from the cornfield next door.

New Leipzig, N. Dak.
October 15, 1931

Dear Dr. K. and Hephata brothers.

I received the Hephata newsletter and your note of August 13. Thank you for both of them. Though I am far away from you, I continue to believe I am part of the Brotherhood, at least in spirit.

I am grieved to hear that the Hephata mission is being slandered by the Communists in Germany. I am sure that hurts your financial support. Why must those who seek only to do good endure such suffering? Our Lord often said that his followers must carry their crosses. May all of us bear the burdens put upon us with patience.

I am including a picture of some of my children posing on top of our car. They are all lively, healthy and make me laugh when I take myself too seriously. Our daughter Helen was born in September so we now have three boys and three girls. They fill our house with joyful spirit. We have also taken in a young girl whose family could not support her. Viola Merz is thirteen and has been a tremendous help for Ida with the housework and with the children.

You will remember that when I was in Treysa, I

tried to become a German citizen but the Great War made that impossible. Then after their revolution, the Russians would not recognize me as their citizen either. Now, after eight years in America, I finally can claim to be a citizen of this land.

On October eighth I denounced allegiances to all foreign powers, and specifically to the German Reich. Then I took an oath of allegiance to the United States of America. I know what the book of Hebrews says, that on this earth "we have no lasting city", but doesn't every man yearn to have a place he can call home? By the hand of our Lord God I have found a home in North Dakota, U.S. of A.

I am sending you one dollar to help with Hephata's ministry. I had hoped that the congregation would take a special Mission Fest offering for you, but that was impossible. The spring rains which are needed to germinate the wheat were so sparse that in some fields the seeds did not even sprout. Then in July, we had withering heat and what grain there was shriveled on the stalk. With so little rain, the hay crop also was meager. Rather than see all of their cattle starve this winter, many farmers sold much of their stock, keeping only enough to rebuild their herds when the rains return.

All of us are anxious about the winter ahead. If there is no snow, then the farmers' fields will enter next spring even drier than this year. If there is much snow and a long winter, there might not be enough hay to keep the farmers' cattle alive.

Naturally, the fate of the farmer is also the fate of the farmer's pastor. I cannot demand that my congregation pay me with money it does not have. In fact, I've agreed with the church council that my salary will be reduced for the coming year. The men promised that if next year's harvest was better, they would repay me in the fall. I can only pray that it will be so.

Our family has two cows and seventy chickens so we do have eggs and milk. This summer we pumped many buckets of water from our well and were able to grow a very good garden, despite the horrific heat in July. Three women from the neighborhood came and helped Ida can fruits and vegetables, sausage and chicken. Some congregation members who cannot contribute to the church budget have pledged to supply us with bacon and ham. If God so wills it, we will have enough food to see us through to spring.

Before I close, I must tell you of a memorable event in my ministry. On September 17th, I was honored to be the liturgist for a worship service in the nearby town of Elgin celebrating the twentieth year of ministry for my colleague, Pastor George Landgrebe. George is eight years older than I and more experienced in ministry in this country. He is a mentor and a good friend. He has been at Zion Lutheran for twenty years. I cannot imagine what it would be like to stay that long in one place.

I will continue to pray for you and for Hephata, that Germany's political and economic storms will not keep you from caring for the little ones so dear to our Lord's heart.

Your brother in Christ, Rudolph Heupel

AUGUST 1, 1932 TRINITY CHURCH

The two pastors watched the dozens of rawboned children bursting from the parish schoolhouse.

"How many do you have this year, Rudolph?" George asked.

Rudolph couldn't keep the pride from his voice. "Fifty-one when we started five weeks ago. Now we're up to sixty-three. We might add a few more this last week."

George Landgrebe, pastor of the church in Elgin, fifteen miles away, couldn't resist teasing his younger colleague. "You must be the Rattenfänger von Hameln or should I say of New Leipzig?"[literally "ratcatcher" of Hamelin, ie Pied Piper]

Rudolph kicked a ball that had escaped the cluster of little boys

230

and laughed. "Some of these kids are as rowdy as calves on a spring day, and some of them are shy as baby rabbits, but so far, no rats."

George stepped back as a shrieking gaggle of little girls playing tag swept by. "But where do they all come from?"

"We have three congregations you know. All the way up north to the Heart River and east to the Hope church." Rudolph grinned and elbowed his friend. "Besides, we German Russians take God's word seriously. 'Be fruitful and multiply.' In January we added little Herold to our own tribe. We now have seven."

"Ja, I heard. You've almost doubled the size of my family. Hey, did you hand out cigars to celebrate? Or do you hoard them all?"

"I can find a panetela for you, George. I'll get one before you go. Right now, I've got to open the church doors. The kids are going in for singing in a few minutes. I've finally trained them to open their mouths and use their lungs." The two men walked around to the front of the church and stood on the front steps looking out over the golden wheat field across the street.

"Rudolph, where do you get your energy? Six weeks of Bible school, three congregations... and I suppose you still have people coming for treatments."

"Ja, by the hundreds, every week." He crossed his arms across his chest and shook his head. "It seems that the German Russians would rather come to me than go to the clinics. Some say they don't trust the doctors, some say the doctors don't understand them. For whatever reason, they come to me, and well...I can't turn them away."

George frowned at his younger colleague. "No, I suppose not. But how do you find time to prepare confirmation classes and your sermons?"

"Confirmation classes...ja, I need to make them better. And sermons..." Rudolph chuckled at his mentor. "I just keep telling them to stop sinning, love the Lord and love their neighbor. They all claim to love the Lord, and it's not too hard to love your neighbor when he lives at least a mile away. Now if I could just get them to stop sinning...."

George shared the laughter. "Sin, where would we preachers be without that? Out of a job I suppose. So, what counts as sin for you and your people? One of my colleagues in Elgin says drinking and dancing are sins."

Rudolph mused, "Prohibition is on the way out I hear, so then drinking will be legal. Sinful? Jesus turned water into wine for the Jewish wedding. I have no doubt if he'd been out here for one of our weddings, he'd have turned it into beer. As far as dancing …well, I stay away from that not because it's sinful but because at the seminary we were told that pastors needed to keep a distance from rowdy activities."

George blustered. "Ja, such things are petty. As far as I'm concerned, the biggest sin right now is the way the government treated the Bonus Army in D.C. Imagine, sending in tanks against our own Great War veterans, and burning their camps. Our own government."

Rudolph, who'd experienced first-hand what travesties governments could visit upon their citizens, sighed. "Some of my members have heard from their relatives what Stalin and his government has been doing in the Ukraine, and all over Russia. The people are starving by the millions. I don't know whether to pray for, or mourn for, my family in the USSR."

George nodded, "Schlimm, sehr schlimm. [bad, very bad]. I think maybe with all that goes on these days in our country and world, we need to preach most often about Christian hope. At least this summer, for our people, the rain has been decent. The harvest will be good. What do you think, Rudolph, does that mean our salaries will get raised next year?"

The children began streaming into the church past the two men. Rudolph rolled his eyes. "Mein Freund, [my friend] I wouldn't count on that miracle. Come in now, sit in the back pew and listen to these little ones. They sing like angels."

JULY 10, 1933 TRINITY LUTHERAN

"Here comes the mailman!" Ten-year-old Ida Maria shouted as Oscar Hintz's model T clackety-clacked up the hill. She stopped working the water pump and began running to the gray tin mailbox nailed to the top of a fence post at the entrance to the church yard. Eight-year-old Fred scampered after her, doing his best to grab onto her skirt.

Their weary pastor father brought his empty bucket back from the row of tomatoes and grabbed the pump handle. As he pumped, his gaze swept out over the oats field that stretched from the church yard north to the top of the slope. The vista was bleak. What should have been a solid, waist-high wall of oat stalks heavy with grain was a bleached white field with sparsely sprinkled feeble stems. Rudolph grimly mused. *The whole field reminds me of baby Herold's head, nearly bald with a few tufts of wispy hair. Herr Mueller won't feed many calves with the oats from that field.*

The land across most of the state had been relentlessly baked by an unforgiving sun since April. The spring had been one of the driest ever recorded. The harvest would be meager. The nationwide economic depression was battering North Dakota even harder than other states. Wheat prices had fallen to twenty-five cents a bushel. The latest report from the state agricultural commissioner stated that total farm income this year would drop by fifty percent.

The produce from this garden would be the pastoral family's main defense against hunger throughout the long winter. Rudy finished filling the bucket as the two children came back from the parsonage. Their seven-year old sister Elizabeth trailed after them.

"What came for mail?" Rudolph asked.

"Just the New Leipzig Sentinel and a letter," Ida Maria said. "Vater, let me carry the bucket."

"No, me, me," clamored Fred and grabbed for the handle.

"It's heavy. You can carry it together, one on each side." Rudolph watched as his two eldest children struggled and sloshed water down the path toward the tomatoes.

Stocky little Elizabeth stood beside her father and watched her siblings. "It made Mutti cry," she murmured.

"What did?" Rudolph asked.

"The letter, it made Mutti cry." She sighed. "It must be a sad letter."

Rudolph wiped his hands on his denim trousers and shouted. "Ida Maria and Fred, after you water the tomatoes, you can start on the cabbages. I'll be right back."

He slipped off his dirty boots as he entered the kitchen. Ida sat at the table, handkerchief in one hand, the letter in the other.

"Liebe, what is it? Has someone died?" He sat down and put his arm around her.

"Nein, nein. Nothing that terrible. Not yet..." She sniffled and handed him the letter.

The letter had been written by her brother Klaus who still lived in the family home in northern Germany. The first lines talked of family events and the local harvest. The following paragraph spoke of more ominous events.

Ever since Hitler became chancellor in January, our Germany has gotten more and more frightening. We now have something called the "Geheime Staatspolizei" or "Gestapo". No one knows what this new police force will do but if it is filled with Nazis, we fear the worst. Earlier this month the Nazis encouraged the German Students Union to burn all 'un-German' books. They even stooped to use Martin Luther's burning of the papal documents in the 1500's to justify their degenerate deed.

On May 10th 22,000 books were burned in Berlin. We don't know if any of the books we have are on the 'un-German' list, but we've packed most of ours in boxes under the bed.

Now comes the most frightening news. At the end of this month, the government passed something called the "Law for the Prevention of Hereditarily Diseased Offspring." Can you imagine that. Someone in the Nazi government is deciding who may or may not have children. I sit here in my kitchen and look at my club foot and wonder when they will come to sterilize me.

Rudolph lay his hand upon Ida's. "Poor Klaus, I can understand his worry. But surely no one in the German government would go out looking for a poor man living in a tiny village. I'm sure he'll be alright."

Ida wiped her eyes. "You're probably right. Klaus sometimes has too much time to think, and fret." She cocked her head. "But what about Hephata?"

Rudolph's eyes snapped to attention and whispered, "Ja, Hephata." He saw again the residents he'd cared for: the ones with twisted limbs, those with minds that wandered, or mouths that hung open. Were they in danger of being victimized by this new law? Would the government really send out doctors to traumatize these poor souls? He shook his head to dispel the sinister cloud that threatened to engulf his mind.

*　　　　*　　　　*

He set the battered buckets beside the pump. The vegetables had enough water for at least two days. He looked to the western sky. The sun was sinking down into a pale, flawless, liquid orange sky. The persistent North Dakota wind had become a gentle whisper. It was a beautiful evening. But the beauty simultaneously announced a bitter truth. Tomorrow would be another hot and dry day. The drought would continue. He would most likely need to repeat the watering by Thursday, maybe sooner if the temperature skyrocketed. As he walked toward the house, he stomped his feet trying to pound off the mud from his shoes. He was halfway home when a cart, pulled by a single horse clattered into the yard. Rudolph stopped as it rolled to a stop in front of him.

"Herr Roth, what brings you out as the sun is setting?"

"Es tut mir leid [I am sorry] Herr Pastor, but I need your help. My arm…"

"Wait, Herr Roth. Let's go into my office, then you can tell me what is going on."

Rudolph walked wearily to the office which was lit only by the afterglow of the sun. He bade Ernest Roth sit and pulled up a chair in front of him.

"Now, what is going on with your arm?"

"This morning, I was milking my only milk cow that hasn't gone dry. She's a calm old Jersey. But today, I think a horse fly must have bit her in the wrong place. Anyway, she jerked up her hind leg and caught me on the arm. I been kicked before so I didn't really pay much attention, thought the sting would go away. But it's gotten worse by the hour. Could you take a look, maybe give me some relief?" He held out his arm.

Rudolph put one hand beneath the arm and gently ran his fingers up and down the entire length.

"I'm afraid I can't help you. You have a broken bone. It's not displaced but it is broken. Tomorrow you should go to the clinic and have them put on a cast so it heals properly."

The farmer's mouth and shoulders drooped. "Ach, I'd hoped for better news."

"I'm sorry, my friend. I can only wrap your arm to keep it stable until you get a cast." After he'd wrapped the arm Rudolph opened a bottle of Luyties pain tablets and shook out a dozen pills into an envelope. "I can give you a few of these pills. Take three of them tonight. They will ease your pain and help you sleep."

Rudolph walked the aching farmer back to his wagon and helped

235

him climb up to the seat. "You go early to the clinic and get that cast. The sooner the better."

Herr Roth nodded and shook the reins with his good hand and the cart rattled back out onto the road. Rudolph walked slowly to the parsonage. The day had succeeded in draining all of his energy.

JULY 11, 1933 TRINITY LUTHERAN

The morning had been productive. Rudolph had managed to finish the lessons for next week's Bible School and also gotten a start on his sermon preparation. Now was walking across the church yard anticipating the meat loaf that Ida was preparing for dinner. The meadowlarks were cascading melody out of the periwinkle sky and his children were laughing and scampering around the front porch. Rudolph's smile spontaneously slipped into a whistle until...

Ernest Roth's horse drawn cart wheeled into the church and stopped beside Rudolph. He looked up at the farmer silhouetted against the sky.

"So, you've already been to the clinic?"

"Ja, and look." He held up his arm. "No cast."

Rudolph helped him descend the cart. "What happened?"

The man's face was drawn and weary with pain. "They said it was not broken. They used their new x-ray machine and said they saw no cracks."

"Come into the shade." Rudolph led Ernest to the side of the house. He felt the arm once more. He could not only feel the crack but he could sense the pain that permeated the arm.

"Herr Pastor, I told the doctor that you'd said it was broken. The doctor shook his head and said 'verfluchter Quacksalber' [cursed quack]."

Rudolph clenched his teeth, drew a deep breath and managed to swallow a curse of his own. He pulled his fountain pen from his shirt pocket. "Look, Herr Roth," Rudolph drew a line on the farmer's arm. "Here is where the break is. I'm certain. You must go back to the clinic and insist they take another x-ray."

Rudolph looked at the confusion and discouragement on Ernest's face. He drew a deep, decisive breath, "Come inside. Let's have some meat loaf. Then I'll drive you to the clinic myself."

Two hours later, Rudolph sat in the shade beside his car, waiting for Herr Roth to emerge from the clinic. They had agreed that it would be best for the pastor not to accompany the farmer. At last, the door opened and Ernest came out. He held up his arm which now was wrapped in a white cast from elbow to wrist.

As he climbed into the car, he chuckled. "Herr Pastor, I showed them my arm and said I would not leave until they did another x-ray. The doctor grumbled but went ahead and took it. When he looked at the results, he went 'huh' but he didn't say one word. He just went ahead and put on the cast. When he was done, he didn't even look me in the eye. He turned away and said, 'There. Now go home.'"

Rudolph put the car in gear and drove out of the clinic parking lot. He managed to quash the sinful desire to gloat, but he allowed himself a smile that lasted all the way back home.

SEPTEMBER 5, 1933 TRINITY CHURCH

"Whoa, whoa." Wilhelm Mueller tugged on the reins of his spirited red gelding. The hay wagon pulled to a stop in the church yard.

The Mueller boys began whistling and whooping. "Wake up you lazy Heupels. Time for school."

For the nine months of the school season, at seven thirty in the morning, every Monday through Friday, Willie Mueller loaded his children onto his hay wagon, headed east, stopped at the church, picked up the pastor's children, then headed a mile and a half north to the one room school house. At four in the afternoon, when school was dismissed, he was there to retrieve them.

In the fall and the spring, the children sat on the straw bales and sang, shouted and laughed into the vast Dakota sky. In the winter, Herr Mueller opened the bales and threw a tarp over the wagon. The children crawled into the dark cave and snuggled into the straw to keep warm. Herr Mueller sat on his seat, the icy wind blasting into his face. Some wintery days, despite hat and scarf, his face would be a fiery red and icicles would hang from his handlebar mustache.

But this was September, the first day of school. The morning was balmy and the sky was dotted with cottony clouds. The children's spirits were as high as those of the Mueller's horse.

Ten-year old Ida Maria, eight-year old Fred, and seven-year old Betty skipped out of the house swinging their lunch pails with the enthusiasm of experienced veterans. Frau Heupel walked slowly across the church yard, carrying Helen her three year old, and holding the hand of six-year old Rudy who was reluctantly beginning his school adventure. Five-year old August scampered around the wagon, infected by the high spirits of the morning.

Ida encouraged her shy son, "See, Rudy, all the others are ready to go. You'll be fine. Betty and Ida will help you get settled." When he resisted and clung to her wash dress, she teasingly threatened him, "You better climb up and take your spot or August will take it."

Before she knew it, little August was trying to clamber up the side of the wagon. Now Ida laughed, "Ach, du lieber [Oh, my God]." She grabbed for her rambunctious son, set him on the ground and boosted Rudy onto the wagon.

The ever-patient Herr Mueller grinned, shook the reins, clucked to his horse and the wagon spun out of the yard, turned north and so began another school year.

OCTOBER, 1934 TRINITY LUTHERAN

"M'r henn ka kreuts, m'r kenn ka soreje, M'r henn noch a bissel sauerkraut fa morje"

[We have no worry, we have no sorrow,   We have a little sauerkraut for tomorrow]

Dan Baesler, one of Rudolph's parishioners and friends, finished the ditty with a rueful chuckle. "My dad came over from Russia in the 1880's. He used to sing that song when the food was scarce. My Dakota buddies sang it in France during the Great War. They always teased, because I was the troop cook. Now it looks like we'll be singing that song a lot this winter."

Rudolph tried to grin. "We never sang that one in Freidorf, but we could have sung it for years on end in Treysa." They were sitting in Rudolph's office talking about the disastrous drought that kept tightening its knuckle-cracking grip on the state. The miserly skies had held back half of the state's normal yearly rainfall. Some pastures had not even sprouted green grass in the spring.

Many farmers, Dan included, were selling their cattle to the only buyer available, the federal government. Twenty dollars a cow and four dollars a calf was a pittance, but a dead animal was worth nothing.

Dan rubbed the stubble on his chin. "I've sold most of my herd but I'm trying to keep a dozen cows alive. Yesterday, my wife and I went out with the hay wagon and drove along the fence line. Mile after mile, the tumbleweeds were packed four feet high against the wires. Tumbleweeds aren't hay, but they might keep a critter alive. So, I forked those ugly balls up to the wagon and my Sophie stomped them down. I still can see the bloody scratches covering her legs. Es war kein schöner Anblick. [It was not a pretty sight.]

The family dog started barking out in the church yard. Rudolph swiveled his chair and gazed out the window.

"It looks like the sheriff's car. Wonder what he wants?"

The two men rose, left the office and walked out of the parish school house toward Elmer Rieger, the county sheriff. He was a tall, raw-boned, jocular man, but today he looked as though he'd eaten a meal of badly cooked fleischkuechle.

"Sheriff Rieger, what brings you up north here?" Rudolph said as he approached the grimacing sheriff."

"Pastor Heupel, I'm not here because I want to be. But we all have to obey orders, we all have to do our duty. I'm sure you understand that.

Rudolph shrugged, "Ja, I guess so."

The sheriff continued, "I mean, it's nothing personal, what I gotta do here. I don't want you to hold it against me."

Dan waved his hand, "Ach, Elmer, quit stomping around in the weeds. Say what you wanna say."

The sheriff reached into the car and grabbed a large envelope and pulled out a sheet of paper. He cleared his throat and read. "Mr. Rudolph Heupel, this is to inform you that the North Dakota Medical Association has opened an investigation to determine if you are practicing medicine without a license, which would be in violation of North Dakota law and could result in criminal penalty. You are invited to appear before the Association's board meeting in Bismarck at 10 a.m. on November 12 to answer questions in regard to this matter."

The blood pounded in Rudolph's ears. 'Investigation', 'violation', 'criminal'—the stony words thudded against his chest. *No, not true, not true. But...How does this American justice work? I'm a citizen, but my English is bad, I was born in Russia, and I've got German blood. Will there be justice for a man like me? What chance do I have?*

He stammered, "But, but Sheriff I—."

The sheriff shook his head, "I'm sorry, Pastor. I really am. But I can't discuss this with you. I'm just the messenger. Here's your

---

239

invitation."

He handed Rudolph the envelope, put one foot onto the running board of his car, then turned around. "You oughta go, Pastor, otherwise they could subpoena you."

He climbed in, made a tight circle in the church yard, got back onto the gravel road and sped southward toward town.

Rudolph and Dan stood immobile watching the dust cloud disappear.

After a moment, Dan muttered, "Gottverdammte Ärzte." [God damned doctors.]

"Nein, nein, my friend." Rudolph shook his head and sighed, "God does not damn doctors and we shouldn't either. I'm just afraid of what they will do to me. I've only been a citizen for one year...They couldn't put me in jail, could they? My family, what would they do without me? And my parish? Maybe if I promise to quit, they won't punish me. That's what I'll do. I'll--

Dan grabbed Rudolph's elbow. "Pastor, don't think that way. You've done nothing wrong. When you show up, they'll see that. And before that meeting, you'll have the whole town behind you, I guarantee it." He firmly turned the stunned pastor toward the parsonage. "Why don't you go into the house and lie down. You're as white as a sheet."

Dan watched his pastor walk stiffly toward the parsonage. Then he climbed up into his buggy, shook the reins and headed toward the neighbors. He had news that needed spreading.

NOVEMBER 12, 1934 BISMARCK, NORTH DAKOTA

Pastor George Landgrebe pulled his dark blue Plymouth into the parking lot of the Medical Association office building. His friend Rudolph nervously picked at his hands in the passenger seat.

"Rudolph, you need to relax. This'll be a conversation, not a trial."

Rudolph wearily rubbed his red rimmed eyes. "Easy enough for you to say. They aren't questioning you." He had asked George to drive, both because his own car was no longer reliable and because George had a quick and logical mind that might keep Rudolph from missteps.

He had resolved to answer questions with simple, honest answers and trust that the Lord would take care of the rest. Still, he felt better knowing he had a friend at his side.

They walked toward the red brick building. The lawn along the sidewalk was white with frost, each grass blade a silvery spear. Rudolph shivered in his wool suit as he entered the lobby.

"Guten tag, Herr Pastor." A half dozen people greeted him with grins and handshakes. Some were farmers from his congregations, some were residents of New Leipzig.

As he shook hands he asked, "Have you driven all the way here for my sake?"

"Na sicher" [of course] answered Theodore Hertz, owner of the town hardware store. He held up a manila envelope. "And we've got another fifty letters supporting you and your work...all of your work."

Rudolph shook his head and smiled, "What can I say? Danke, danke."

A door opened and a young woman stepped out. "Mr. Heupel? The board is ready for you." As Rudolph moved toward the door, the group stirred, intent on following him.

The woman held up a hand. "Wait a moment, please." She stepped back into the room. A minute later she returned, "the room is small and we don't have enough space for all of you. Mr. Heupel, you may bring only one person in with you."

Theodore responded for the group. "No problem. Here Pastor George, take the envelope. We'll be out here, waiting and praying."

Rudolph and George entered and were ushered to seats at the end of a long rectangular table. Five men sat on each side of the table and at the head sat a heavy jowled, bespectacled man with steely gray hair and pale blue eyes.

"Good morning, gentlemen. My name is Dr. Gordon Benson, chairman of the North Dakota Medical Association. Thank you for coming in this morning. Please introduce yourselves."

After the introductions, Dr. Benson opened up a folder on the table in front of him. "Reverend Heupel, it has come to our attention that great numbers of people are coming to you for health-related matters. Would you say that is true?"

"Ja...Yes that is true."

"How many people would you say come to you in a month?"

"Everyone who comes to me signs their name in a notebook. I counted last night. In October, two hundred and four came to my office."

A thin man in a rumpled suit sitting next to the chairman piped in. "Ah, so you have an office?"

George leaned over and whispered into Rudolph's ear. Rudolph nodded, "I am a pastor in the Lutheran Church. I serve three country congregations and the parish has made an office for me where I prepare my sermons, my lessons and do counseling for my members. When people come to me, I receive them in my church office."

Dr. Olson then asked, "Reverend Heupel, it has come to our attention that you sometimes prescribe medications. Is that correct?"

Rudolph was puzzled and turned to George. George murmured a few words, Rudolph nodded and turned back to the doctor. "I do not prescribe medications. Only a doctor can do that. I sometimes recommend some homeopathic pills, pills that can be ordered through the mail or bought in stores. Maybe you have heard of Luyties?"

The chairman shook his head in dismissal and went on, "I'd like you to tell us what is it exactly you do when people come to you."

Rudolph shrugged, "It depends on what their problem is. If they come with back problems I massage and try to realign their vertebrae. If they have headaches I will check to see if they have pinched nerves. If—"

A short man who sat next to George asked with a definite edge to his voice, "Sir, may I inquire, what training has prepared you to do such things?"

Rudolph knew enough not to speak about his God-given 'gift' to medical professionals. How could they understand his warm hands, his ability to sense pain? Instead he said, "I was trained in nursing practices and anatomy at the Hephata Deacon Academy. I served as a certified deacon and helped treat wounded soldiers."

"By your accent, I assume those would be German soldiers?" the short man continued. When Rudolph nodded, the man continued, "So were you a German citizen?"

Rudolph sighed. *Liebe Gott, not this again.* "Nein, I mean no, I was not a German citizen. I was born in what is now the Ukraine but after the Great War I was not a citizen there either." His voice now held an edge of its own. "I am an American citizen and have lived in this country for over a decade. I have pledged my allegiance to this country." George gently patted Rudolph's arm.

Dr. Benson interrupted, "Gentlemen, Reverend Heupel's citizenship is not our concern at this moment. Let's focus on the issue at hand. Now, tell me Reverend, what have you done to attract such a large number of patients to your office?"

Rudolph was puzzled, "What do you mean?"

"How have you advertised or promoted your services?"

Rudolph shook his head, "Nothing, I've done nothing."

All around the table the men shared skeptical glances. George cleared his throat and caught the attention of the chairman. "May I say a word?" Dr. Benson nodded his permission.

"Reverend Heupel is part of the German-Russian community which reaches many parts of eastern Montana, western and south-central North Dakota, central South Dakota, Nebraska, and even Kansas. These families spread out but they always stay connected. And if someone finds a good product, a good treatment, he tells his neighbors, who tell their neighbors, who tell their neighbors. Doctor, I have lived in such a community for over twenty years and I can tell you, it's all word of mouth. It's a remarkable network."

Another doctor, on Rudolph's side of the table, asked what others certainly were wondering. "Tell us Reverend, how much do you charge for your services?"

Rudolph smiled and shook his head. "Nichts, nothing."

"You mean you have no set fee?" The doctor was incredulous.

Rudolph shrugged, "I put out a basket and they can put something in it if they choose to."

"Ahh, so I suppose you strongly suggest a donation amount," the short, cynical doctor smirked.

Rudolph vigorously shook his head. "No, no I say nothing. Some people give, some don't. Whoever comes, I try to help."

The cynical one persisted, "Well, Reverend Heupel, can you tell us how much was 'donated' last week?"

"Ja, Doctor, I can." Rudolph pulled a sheet of paper from an inside pocket of his suit coat, slowly unfolded it and read, "one dime, two nickels, three pennies, two pounds of potatoes and a smoked duck."

Laughter rippled around the table. Dr. Benson smiled and closed his folder. "Reverend Heupel we thank you for your forthright answers. At this point we assume they are truthful answers. We will do some further investigation. If that investigation verifies what you have told us, then I can see no reason why you cannot continue with your work. Do you understand?"

Rudolph took a deep breath and answered, "Yes, doctor, I

understand."

George held up the manila envelope. "Doctors, I have more than four dozen letters from community people who support the work of Reverend Heupel. I am sure they will confirm what he has told you today." He handed the envelope to the now scowling small man beside him who passed it down the table to the chairman.

"Thank you, gentlemen for coming in this morning. Have a safe drive back to New Leipzig."

Rudolph stood on slightly wobbly legs and followed George out of the meeting room into the lobby. True to their word, his supporters were waiting for him to emerge. At the sight of the relieved grin on his face, they smiled and gathered around him with back slaps and handshakes.

After a lunch at Woolworth's with the entire group, they all returned home. George drove his Plymouth south out of Bismarck then westward on Highway 21. They were dissecting what George called a 'conversation' and Rudolph termed an 'interrogation', when George began giggling.

"What, George, what?" Rudolph asked.

"One dime, two nickels, three pennies, two pounds of potatoes and a smoked duck…what an answer!" Then he slowly shook his head. "I don't know why you do it, Rudolph. I don't know how you can keep at it."

Rudolph sat silently for several miles. Then he spoke quietly, as if to himself, "Why do I do it? When one of God's children comes to me and asks for help, how can I say no? I am a pastor, yes, that's my call and my profession. But this other, this gift that I've been given..if I deny it, I'm denying something that is rooted in my soul."

He fell silent for a few minutes, then added, "As for how I can keep at it.." he shrugged and smiled, "as long as God gives me the strength to get up in the morning I keep going. One of my old teachers used to say, "better to burn out than rust out.""

The two pastors, both inclined to burning rather than rusting, laughed and squinted into the setting sun as they headed down the highway toward home.

APRIL 14, 1935 TRINITY LUTHERAN

From the beginning the worship service was listless. Everyone, including the pastor, suffered a lack of enthusiasm. The joyful spirit

244

of God's people gathering to give praise was missing. Unquestionably, the weather was the leading factor. The entire spring had been desert-dry, and since Wednesday the blue seemed to have been sucked from the sky and replaced with a brownish haze suffused with foreboding.

Now Rudolph stood in the pulpit and surveyed his flock. A few men and women gazed back at him with attentive eyes. Most seemed to be staring into a fearsome future. A few sat with eyes drooping from weariness. Living in North Dakota had become a daily trial. No one carried an extra ounce of fat, no one displayed any ardor, and no one smiled.

These people were his neighbors, and like them he was a parent who worried about sustaining his family. Like them his heart quavered as each day dawned cloudless and parched.

But these people were more than his neighbors. They were his parishioners. As their pastor he was charged with speaking a message that touched their real lives in this very moment. He was expected to preach God's word into their reality.

He opened his Bible. "The sermon text for today is from Psalm 121. *I lift up my eyes to the hills—from where will my help come? My help comes from the Lord, who made heaven and earth. He will not let your foot be moved; he who keeps you will not slumber.He who keeps Israel will neither slumber nor sleep. The Lord is your keeper; the Lord is your shade at your right hand.The sun shall not strike you by day, nor the moon by night. The Lord will keep you from all evil; he will keep your life. The Lord will keep your going out and your coming in from this time on and forevermore.*"

He closed his Bible and swept his eyes across the room. He stopped and pointed over his shoulder.

"Behind me is that range of hills that runs for miles to the west. Up there are only a few coyotes. But in ancient days many religions used to build altars on hilltops like those. They figured the higher up they got, the closer they'd get to their gods. The people of Israel were often tempted to go up to these altars. They were tempted to lift their eyes to the hills. When things get bad, all of us are tempted to look for help in all sorts of places. From where does our real help come? Today we are reminded that our true and lasting help comes from the Lord. As the psalm writer says, *'The Lord will keep your going out and your coming in from this time on* and

---

245

forevermore.'"

He stopped and looked out at his congregation. *Can these men and women believe that promise? Their cattle die, their wheat seeds lie in scorched earth waiting to sprout. Can I believe it? My people suffer and my salary slides downward. Oh Lord, how can I call for faith when my own is flagging?*

"Many of us have families in the Ukraine who have suffered. Some of you experienced the horrors of the Great War. Has there been a time when God's people have been free of trouble? It's easy to have faith in God's goodness when the rains fall and the granaries are full. These days we are forced to confess that our faith is sometimes weak. We wonder if God has forgotten us out here on the plains."

A murmuring arose from the men's side of the church. Never had Rudolph heard anything above a whisper during one of his sermons. *Have my words so deeply offended?* Then he saw that the men were looking not at him, but stood with faces pressed against the glass of the west facing windows.

"My God, can it be?" the men muttered. Their wives rushed over to the windows and the children began crying. Rudolph stepped out of the pulpit and joined his flock.

From north to south, a swirling black line stretched across the entire western horizon. For a brief second Rudolph thought it was an approaching storm cloud. Then it struck him. Bearing down upon them was a black blizzard, a whirling dervish of dirt and dust. He stood transfixed as the line grew taller, became a ridgeline, then a churning mountain. One of the elders broke his spell.

"Herr Pastor, quick, bless us so we can go home. We've got to get our animals into shelter."

Rudolph hastened back to the chancel and raised his arm. "May the Lord keep your going out and your coming in now and forevermore. In the same of the Father, Son and Holy Spirit. Amen."

There was no lingering, no greeting at the door. Everyone hastened out into the eerie, electric air and sprinted to autos and buggies. In anticipation of what was coming, many were already wrapping scarves and handkerchiefs across their faces to protect themselves from the stinging, lung-burning dust. The line was now a massive wall, still maybe ten miles away but already they could see the roiling of the raging mass and hear the angry growl of the wind. Rudolph watched his people fleeing this apocalyptic cloud and prayed that all would safely reach their homes or find refuge with neighbors.

As he and Ida herded their frightened children across the church yard into the parsonage, he repeatedly shouted above the now howling wind, the words from the morning's psalm: "the Lord will keep you from all evil, the Lord will keep your life." As he chanted for the sake of his children, he prayed silently for himself, "O God, I believe, help my unbelief."

September 7th, 1936,
Trinity Lutheran Church
New Leipzig, North Dakota

Dear Hephata Friends,

I have not received any news from you for many months. I pray that this silence is only because your ministry takes up all of your time. How are the orphans, and the other 'little ones'? I hope they are all secure in the caring arms of the Hephata brothers.

Last week we received a letter from my wife's family with troubling news. Her brother Klaus was visited by government officials and, since he has a club foot, he was deemed unsuited to have children. He was sterilized immediately. We never thought this program would reach into Germany's tiny villages. Evidently the Nazi party is efficient in many ways. Has this law affected anyone at Hephata? I am hoping you have been spared this affliction.

I look forward to receiving news of how the Brotherhood is doing in Treysa and throughout Germany.

Our news from North Dakota is mostly bleak. In February we experienced the coldest temperature ever recorded in the state. In February it was -60 degrees. In July we experienced the hottest ever, 121 degrees. Our harvest was a disaster. On the radio we heard last night that one half of the population of our state is receiving relief from the government.

Our German-Russian farmers have not been spared

this calamity. Some of the families in my parish have sold their land, and gone to the cities, or to other states. Those who stay are stubbornly hanging on by their fingernails. They or their ancestors withstood hardship in Russia and have learned how to survive on very little. Even so, no one, including this pastor and his family, is looking forward to the winter which will soon pounce upon us.

I don't want you to think that all is bleakness. We continue to receive blessings from God's gracious hand. In March, Ida and I welcomed into this world another son, Herman Wilbert. Although I myself delivered five of our eight children, we felt it prudent to have the doctor from Elgin be present for this birth. Ida had experienced some unusual pains and I wanted to make sure all went well. Little Herman brings our family count to eight, five boys and three girls. By God's grace, all are healthy and full of life.

I'm writing this letter on what the USA calls 'Labor Day.' For you this comes on May 1, but here it's in the fall and marks the end of summer and the beginning of school. This year it is a very special day for our family. Tomorrow, our oldest child, our dear Ida Maria will begin high school. Since the high school is ten miles away in New Leipzig, she'll be living with a family that takes in farm children who want to study. Many of the farm children stop their education at the eighth grade because they need to stay home and help with the farm work. We've no fields to work or flocks to tend, and even if we did, both Ida and I want all our children to be well educated.

When the weather is nice, Ida Maria will come home on the weekends. But once winter comes, she'll have to stay in town. We must pay for her room and board. That won't be easy. Since so many of my parishioners have little money and are now paying me by bringing hams, bacons and chickens, I am planning to pay for Ida Maria's costs with some of those items. We are hoping this will be acceptable.

I have one more piece of good news to share. As I have written before, a great many people continue to seek me out for help with pinched nerves, aching muscles, and displaced joints. Almost two years ago I was questioned by the North Dakota Medical Association about my work with those who come to me for physical help. I answered all of their questions and they said they were going to investigate to see if I was illegally practicing medicine.

In February I received a letter stating that their investigation was complete and I was free to receive people who come to me for help. What a great relief! I have taped the letter to the inside of my desk drawer, both as a proof to anyone who might question my work and as a reminder of how God's mercy and grace never abandon me.

I am including in this letter one dollar for your ministry. I give it as a thank offering for what God has done for me and my family. I look forward to hearing from you soon.

Your brother in Christ, Rudolph Heupel

SATURDAY, MAY 25, 1940 TRINITY LUTHERAN

Sophia and Ida stood together in the spring sunshine. Today, North Dakota's perpetual northwest wind was only a teasing breeze that gently ruffled their cotton wash dresses. They were watching a busy crew of men working all along the northern and western fence lines of the church property. Sophia put her arm around Ida's waist and squeezed.

"Well, Mrs. Wife-of-the-Pastor, at last you're getting your trees. You must have finally put your foot down."

Ida's laugh was as bright as the sky, "And, just think, it only took fourteen years."

"Has it been that long? Where does the time go?"

Ida mused, "For quite a few years in the thirties it seemed like time had gotten stuck and we'd all dry up and get blown away."

Sophia nodded, "Ja, in Golden Valley quite a few people did get blown away. Some were driven all the way out to the west coast. Marvin and I hung on, just barely. The last few years we at least broke even."

Ida watched as the men began on the third row, digging holes and setting in the small leafy sticks. "I couldn't even bring up the idea of planting trees around here with everyone's crops dying. But decent rains last year, and plenty of snow in winter… I finally pushed Rudolph to bring it up to the council."

"You pushed Rudolph? I'd like to have seen that." Sophia laughed.

"After eighteen years together, I've learned a few tricks," Ida chuckled.

"I remember your wedding like it was yesterday. And now, my god-daughter is already through high school. Time does fly."

"Ida Maria, we're so proud of her. I'm so glad you came down for her graduation. This fall she's going to Dickinson Teacher's College on a scholarship. These days, I think it's the young people that give wings to time. All the rest of us just try to keep up. Imagine…in a couple of years we'll have four of our kids in high school at the same time."

The two turned and began walking back toward the parsonage just as a car pulled up to Rudolph's office. The young man who'd been driving went around the front of the car, opened the passenger door, then helped an older man out of the passenger seat. The two slowly made their way toward the parish school house door.

"Do you know who they are?" Sophia asked.

"No, no. Every day, from all over, people come to see him. Some days, more than thirty. He comes home exhausted. He doesn't take care of himself like he should. I tell him he should maybe cut back. He snorts and says, 'How? Should I tell 'em to go away?'" She sighs, "He can't say no. It's just who he is."

"Ja, you're right. When God gives you a gift, you have to use it. Besides, doesn't that work bring in extra money?"

Now Ida's laugh was full. "Extra money? Ha. A few dollars here and there, a ham, or a pound of bacon sometimes. You said it yourself, he has a gift. Rudolph says, 'How can I charge anyone when I'm just sharing a gift?'"

Now it was Ida's turn to put her arm around her friend's waist. "Come inside, have some coffee. Someone gave him a ham last week and I'll make you a sandwich.

FRIDAY, MARCH 14, 1941 TRINITY CHURCH

Ida hummed to herself as she prepared supper. Herold and Herman were playing in the living room, Rudy, Helen and August and just hopped off of Herr Mueller's hay wagon and were laughing upstairs. It was only 3:30 in the afternoon but her three oldest children would be coming home for the weekend and she wanted the meal to be special. She'd spent the morning making kuchens laden with custard and heavy with the peaches she'd canned last fall. Now she was peeling potatoes and slowly heating up the ham.

She'd been taught that humility was a virtue. The community in which she lived had little tolerance for anyone who was boastful. And her very Lutheran husband often preached that pride was a sin. So it was that Ida carried her pride carefully wrapped in humble gestures. On this day she smiled as she pondered how well her first born, Ida Maria was doing. She was now in her second year at the teacher's college. Fred was a sophomore in high school and Betty was a freshman. They both got excellent grades and had adapted well to living away from home. The only tarnish on the gold was Fred's occasional hijinks which prompted notes from teachers and letters from the family where they both were living.

She poked a fork into the ham, then stirred the coals in the cookstove. She wanted to make sure it would be done when they arrived. Just as she straightened up, she heard a bang. She ran to the window just in time to see the door to the horse barn slam against its frame. It needed to be closed. She opened the porch door and stepped out onto the steps.

"Mein Gott," she gasped. Fifteen minutes earlier there'd been no breeze, the sky had been a wintery pale blue, and the temperature had been thirty-five degrees. Now, it felt as though somewhere to the northwest an icy monster had opened its mouth and was emptying its snow laden lungs. The snowflakes came at her horizontally, pelting her face like icy bullets.

She dashed back inside, ran down into the basement and threw three large shovelfuls of coal into the furnace. The two-story parsonage would lose warmth quickly in a storm such as this. Gasping from the exertion, she ran back upstairs and peered out of the window toward Rudolph's office. It was only fifty yards away but now it was invisible in this sudden, unforeseen blizzard. She felt

---

panic clutching at her as she stared out into the swirling maelstrom of whiteness.

Then before her eyes a figure emerged, as if pushed by a giant hand and thudded against the side of the house. She screamed and the children came thundering down the stairs.

They all asked at once, "What Mutti? What happened?" Then they saw what was happening outside and fell silent. A moment later the porch door swung open and Rudolph came in stomping snow off his boots. He was white from head to toe.

He laughed, "Did you hear me bang against the wall? I stepped out of the office, the wind grabbed me, I started running and couldn't stop." He waved his arms and flung drops of melting snow like a dog shaking after a bath. "I couldn't see a thing. Good thing the house was in the way or I'd be halfway to Elgin by now."

The children joined in his laughter, but Ida moaned "Oh no," and slumped onto a kitchen chair.

Rudolph threw off his coat and moved toward her, "What, Liebe, what is it?"

"Don't you remember? Ida Maria was taking the bus to New Leipzig, then she, Fred and Betty were going to come home this evening with one of the Zimmerman boys. What if they are out on the road?" She chewed on her knuckle and her eyes welled with tears.

Ida's distress silenced the children. The wailing of the wind filled the quiet kitchen and sent shivers through them all. The two youngest ones snuggled close to their mother.

Rudolph spoke soothingly, calmly, "We don't know if they are out on the road. They might still have been in town when the storm came. Or when it hit maybe they stopped at a farm along the way. And who knows, this storm might blow out as quickly as it came. Have you checked the radio report?"

Minutes later they were all gathered around the old cherry wood Zenith radio in the living room. The single light bulb in the room flickered when Rudolph turned it on.

"I just hope the storm doesn't wreck the wind generator," he murmured as he adjusted the dials. The reception faded then grew stronger.

Finally, they heard orchestra music but it was abruptly interrupted by a beep, followed by the deep voice of an announcer, "The National Weather Bureau in Bismarck has issued a severe winter storm warning for all of North Dakota. Temperatures will drop well below zero in the next hours, snow will be heavy and winds over fifty miles an hour will cause whiteout conditions. Do not attempt to travel. Seek shelter and stay in place until the storm passes which will be sometime tomorrow morning. Stay tuned to KFYR for all weather updates."

Rudolph snapped off the radio and grumbled, "What a warning..like closing the barn door after the cows have escaped."

Ida shivered and wrapped her arms around Herold and Herman. "Let's pray for all of those trapped on the roads."

All of them folded their hands and bowed their heads as Rudolph prayed for every person in harm's way on this fearsome night. He finished with the words everyone was silently whispering. "And God, we beg you to watch over our Ida Maria, Fred and Betty, wherever they are tonight. Keep them safe, keep them warm. We ask this in the name of our Lord, Amen."

The rest of the family murmured, "Amen," just as the light dimmed and then flickered off. They stood uneasily in the darkness.

Rudolph sighed, "Ach, so now the wind generator has quit working." The banshee wailing of the wind rose to a shiver-inducing shriek. Rudolph clapped his hands. "What? We're not afraid of the dark, are we? Get out the lanterns, and let's eat. I'll bet your mutti has cooked up quite a Friday evening feast."

Rudolph hugged Ida who then led Helen into the kitchen to prepare the meal. Rudolph trailed after the boys who were scrambling to carry the kerosene lanterns into the dining room.

That night everyone went to bed early with full stomachs and extra blankets. At three in the morning Rudolph was awakened by a tapping on his arm.

"Rudolph, listen," Ida said.

He was instantly alert, "What? What is it?"

"The wind. It's stopped."

Rudolph slid out of bed, wrapped himself in his robe, and stepped across the icy floor to the window. The entire world was bathed in the pale light of the full moon. Drifts were piled up to the windows of the church and in every direction all he could see was an ocean of blue white crystal.

"Ja, the storm has passed. Tomorrow will be a cold and clear day... and we will know more..." He crawled back into bed and wrapped his arms around Ida and each of them silently prayed again for their children.

*   *   *

Rudolph was right. The day had dawned brittle and clear. Their thermometer registered minus ten degrees. But because the wind had completely died and the sun had set the new snow ablaze with light, the family's spirits had been rekindled.

All morning long the children took turns gazing out of the second story south-facing windows. They could see the road stretching southward for three miles. In some places thick fingers of snow drifts lay across the gravel track, but the fierce wind had swept other parts of the road bare of snow.

"A truck, look, a truck!" five-year-old Herman screamed as a black dot appeared on the horizon and slowly inched down the road. The other children raced back to the windows and their shouts drew their parents scrambling up the stairs.

"It looks like Melvin Buhler's truck with the snow plow," Rudolph said They watched as the truck reached a drift, plowed into the hard-packed snow, backed up and ran again into the bank, finally broke through and then charged ahead to the next obstruction. For the anxious family it was an achingly slow process. After fifteen minutes, the vehicle crossed the bridge a mile away and began its gradual climb up to the parsonage.

Exuberant twelve-year-old August, hopped up and down, "Can we run down and see if—.""

"No," Ida snapped, "Its below zero, way too cold. You will wait, like the rest of us." She would have added 'be patient' but she was just as desperately impatient and apprehensive as her children.

Rudolph not only had not heard her command, he had already descended the stairs and donned his boots and parka. The children heard the door slam, then saw him marching across the brittle banks to the road. The truck was now halfway up the hill, had rammed a stubborn drift and before the driver could back up, a figure hopped out of the passenger door.

Helen gasped, "It's Freddy!" The children cheered and Ida laughed and sobbed, "Danke, mein Gott, danke."

Rudolph crunched through the snow to meet his son. As they drew near one another, they might have run into each other's arms. But with Fred, Rudolph was not that sort of father, and with Rudolph, Fred was not that sort of son. They stopped a yard apart. Fred's face was red, his nose was running but he was grinning and

254

his eyes were filled with the sparkle of the icy blue sky.

"Have you ever seen such a storm, Vater? Wow!" He threw his arms into the air. "The wind slammed into us like we'd hit a wall. We had to--"

"The girls, Freddy, how are the girls?" Rudolph interrupted.

"They're OK, Vater. They're in the truck, they're more patient than I. am."

Rudolph's chuckle was muffled by his scarf, "Ja, no doubt about that. Come, let's get going."

While the truck slowly plowed up the hill behind them, Rudolph and Fred hurried toward the parsonage. As they marched up the hill, Rudolph did his best to keep up with his sixteen-year-old son. The cold air burned in this chest and he abruptly could feel every one of his forty-eight years.

Fred chattered as they walked, "We took off from New Leipzig and didn't even notice the weather. When we left the highway and turned north on the gravel road, the snow started falling. We drove another few minutes then the wind smacked the car so hard it started shaking. Wilbur was driving and he told us, he was going to turn around in the Mertz's farm yard and go back to town."

Between gasps, Rudolph managed a question, "You mean, you drove all the way back to town?"

"No, no. That was the plan. But the snow was so bad we couldn't see past the front of the car. Wilbur opened his door and looked down for the shoulder on the left side of the road to guide his driving. I told him, 'you better hope there's no idiot coming from the front.' He just grunted and said, 'that idiot would be looking for the shoulder on the other side.'

"Anyway, we drove another few minutes until he saw the entrance into the Mertz's farm and we convinced him not to go any farther."

By now they'd reached the church yard and the snow plow truck was right behind them. They could see Ida and the children with faces pressed against the kitchen windows. Fred finished his story

"This morning, when Mr. Buehler came out plowing the road, we asked him to give us a ride. We figured you might be worrying about us."

Rudolph puffed, "Ja, your mother was worried. I myself put it all in the Lord's hands."

Fred pulled open the door, turned around and grinned

sardonically at his father, "Of course, Vater, of course. You're convinced the Lord would never let us die." He stomped the snow off his boots and prepared to regale his family with his story.

Rudolph waited for his heart to stop thundering under his parka, then embraced his two daughters and led them into the warm parsonage.

*   *   *

The next day was Sunday. Some roads were still blocked and the temperature hovered near zero. And yet, as Pastor Rudolph climbed into the Trinity Church pulpit, the pews were full. He was not surprised. These were truly his people. Like he himself, they were tenacious. For fifteen years he'd seen them stubbornly persist through drought, dust storms, locust plagues, and blizzards. Their faith too was defined by stubbornness. They continued to worship their Lord, they persevered in prayer and praise, even in the bleakest of times.

He looked out at his flock, bundled up against the insidious cold that crept through every crack and crevice.

"Brothers and sisters, yes, it's cold, but to see you all here today warms my heart. These last few days have been full of tragedy for many. Three of my children, along with Wilbur Zimmerman were caught out on the road but they all were able to reach shelter. But forty families in North Dakota are grieving today because their loved ones were struck down by this devastating blizzard. Some are saved and others die. Who can make any sense of this? Where is God in all of this?"

He dropped his serious eyes down to the first pews below the pulpit, where his own children sat with the other young people. "Were those people allowed to die because they were sinners? Were my own children spared because they were so saintly?" Ida Maria and Betty allowed themselves small smiles. Fred rolled his eyes and grimaced.

"Our Lord Jesus wrestled with the same sort of question. A tower that was being built collapsed and eighteen people were killed. Jesus asked his friends, 'do you think these eighteen were bigger sinners than anyone else in Jerusalem?' Then Jesus answered his own question. 'No, but unless you turn your life around, you will die like they did.'"

He paused and looked again at his children, then gazed out over the congregation. On the night of the blizzard, after he and his family

256

had gone to bed, he had huddled under the quilts and listened to the lunatic wind. He'd thought of his parents and siblings, some now dead, others in misery in the Ukraine or in exile in Siberia, he'd thought of his Hephata brothers, some, like his confidant Fred, slaughtered in the Great War, others now facing unimaginable perils at the hands of the Nazis. And of course, interwoven throughout these memories was the throbbing angst for his children. Then, as the window panes rattled and his heart quaked, he'd thought of Jesus' tower story and what it might mean for his people. Now, he concluded his message with those thoughts.

"My friends, what Jesus teaches us, and what we were reminded of again this week is this: Life is a precious, fragile gift. It's not something we earn or deserve. We're given this gift and God calls us to use it well, to love and serve God, and one another. When an accident happens, when a life is cut short, when a loved one dies, we shouldn't look to God and ask, 'Why did you allow this?' or 'Why do you punish these people?' Instead we should look in the mirror and ask ourselves, 'What am I doing today with this gift of life? Am I living in a God pleasing way?'

I don't need to tell you that we live in a broken world, broken by sin and sorrow. None of us knows how many days we will have. Let us celebrate and savor each day, let us see each day as a gift and as an opportunity to serve. Amen."

The greetings at the door were warm and brief. Most people were eager to get home and thaw out in front of their coal stoves. But a cluster of men remained chatting in the aisle. Rudolph assumed they were talking about the blizzard. But as he drew near to them, he discovered they were talking about a different sort of storm.

Daniel Baesler turned to him, "So Herr Pastor, what do you think? Should we enter the war in Europe?"

Rudolph sighed and gave a crestfallen grin, "Ach, Dan, I just finished telling you all to celebrate each day... Now you come with such a hard, down to earth question..." He stopped, but no one spoke, waiting for him to respond.

Rudolph shook his head, "Dan, you were in the trenches in France. I can imagine what you saw. At Hephata, I tended so many young men with mangled bodies and damaged minds. War, all war, is hell on earth." He sighed more deeply, "And yet, Hitler and these Nazis..."

The men all nodded and Dan responded, "Ja...Hitler. If war is hell

257

then Hitler is the devil. Raymond, my oldest, is enlisting. He expects we'll be going to war."

Burly John Achtenberg growled, "My Arnold is doing the same. He says he can hardly wait to cut down a few Nazis."

Rudolph wore a heavy jacket beneath his long black robe. Nevertheless, he felt a chill run through his body, and his spirit. He murmured loud enough for the men to hear, "As I said this morning, we live in a broken world. And it is true, in einer zerbrochenen Welt wird es Scheiße geben [In a broken world, there will be shit.]"

They all returned to their warm homes, mulling over the cold truth of their pastor's grim conclusion.

JUNE, 1942, TRINITY LUTHERAN

"Why don't you come along?" Rudolph was finishing his breakfast and Ida was getting ready to fry more bacon for the children. It was Sunday morning and one of North Dakota's perfect spring days. The sky was robin's egg blue, and a few clouds, as airy as dandelion puffballs, floated lazily above. Because of abundant spring rains, the fields were emerald green and the ditches were lush with grass. The morning air still held a delicious chill.

"Come along with me to the early service at Hope Church. For once you can worship without worrying about the kids misbehaving."

"But, what about breakfast?" Ida asked.

"Ach, let Ida Maria and Betty take care of it. It's only a twenty-minute ride. When's the last time the two of us have gone out alone?" Rudolph grinned.

Ida untied her apron and chuckled. "I suppose a Sunday morning ride to church with the preacher is the best outing a pastor's wife can expect. Give me five minutes."

The road-weary Chevy clattered eastward with its passengers singing hymns loud enough to be heard above the rattling of the gravel against the bottom of the car.

Just as the squat walls of Hope Church came into view, Rudolph slowed the vehicle.

"Oh-oh. Looks like they had some rain here last night." The road between the car and the church was a soupy, muddy mess.

"Was jetzt?" [What now?] Ida wondered.

Rudolph ground the gears and finally got the car in reverse and backed up. Then putting the car into first gear, he grinned as he hunched over the steering wheel and floored the accelerator, "We'll just get up enough speed and plow through it."

The engine whined as they hit the mudhole, the mud and water sluiced away on either side of the car but when they reached the midpoint of the morass, the wheels started spinning and the car stalled.

Rudolph started the car, tried backing up, then going forward but the only result was the car settled deeper into the mud.

"Und was jetzt?" [And now what?] Ida couldn't help laughing as Rudolph looked increasingly frustrated.

"Ja, in ten minutes the service is supposed to start. We've got to start on time. After the service the men can push me out and we can make it back for the 10:30 service at Trinity." He looked over at Ida with a rakish grin. "But right now, we've got to walk."

"Walk? I've got my new shoes on and my dress will get full of mud," Ida was appalled at the idea. "I'll just stay in the car until after the service."

"Nein, nein, what would the members think if I left you stranded out here?" Rudolph was already climbing out of the Chevy and sloshing around to the passenger side. He opened her door, then turned around. "Come on, put your arms around my neck. I'll carry you."

Ida giggled, "Rudolph, bist du verrückt? [are you crazy]"

"Hurry up, we don't have all day." He grinned over his shoulder. "The longer we wait the more people there will be watching us."

Ida looked up toward the church and in dismay saw a cluster of people watching this spectacle. She quickly threw her arms around her husband's neck and allowed him to carry her piggy-back across the soupy mess. He grunted with every step and she could imagine them both toppling over into the muck. When they reached the dry ground, he carefully leaned backwards and set her down. Applause broke out from the watchers.

Rudolph's face was flushed and he was puffing. He looked down into her eyes with a tenderness she'd not seen in a long time. "After all the times you've carried me through the years, it was my chance to return the favor."

She would have kissed him, but the entire congregation was watching.

FEBRUARY 11, 1943, TRINITY CHURCH

Rudolph had walked out to the cemetery an hour before the memorial service was to begin. He came to clear his mind and bolster his own heart for the difficult hours ahead. He stood now before the tiny grave where his first-born son had been buried twenty years earlier. *If he'd lived, who's to say where he might be now. Would he have gone to the war? Would I have let him go to war? Could I have stopped him? Gott, mein Gott, help me to speak words of comfort today to these grieving families.*

He paced back and forth among the grave markers, rehearsing his message, then began walking back toward the church. Only the roof and steeple showed above the trees planted three years earlier. They now hid the cemetery from those sitting next to the west facing windows. He found this comforting. *We don't need more reminders of death. Better to see trees, even if they're bare, than this bleak cemetery.*

The weather was the best that could be expected for a February: twenty-five degrees with light breeze, and a ghostly sun peering through a thin gray sheet of clouds. Even so, Rudolph knew everyone would be glad they'd installed a furnace in the church the year before.

The memorial service for Raymond Baesler and Arnold Achtenberg was scheduled for 11a.m. By 10:45, the pews were full. There were no coffins. No one knew when, or even if, the bodies would ever return from the place they'd never heard of: the Solomon Islands. The front two pews on either side of the aisle had been reserved for the families of the two soldiers. After everyone else was seated, the families filed in and the service began. Amid occasional sniffles and quiet tears, hymns were sung, and scripture verses were read. Rudolph read he obituaries for both young men. Then he climbed into the pulpit and after taking several deep breaths, he spoke.

He began by telling of his own work with Raymond and Arnold in confirmation classes, how he'd come to know and appreciate the young men and their faith. He went on to talk about their devotion to their families and their commitment to their country. He spoke of war, how it was at some times in history a necessary evil. Then he moved to the heart of his message.

"What can give us the strength to move forward in the dark

260

times? Two weeks ago, the Baeslers received a letter from their son Raymond. They have given me permission to share it with you today. From Guadalcanal in the Solomon Islands, Raymond wrote this: *Don't worry folks. I am ready for whatever I have to face. I can truly say I haven't been afraid, and if God doesn't forsake me, I never will be. Without faith and hope it would be tough going, but not this way. I am happy to say that some days when going was tough and a lot of the boys were broken hearted, I cheered them up. My little Testament is about the most read book in the company.*"[iv]

Rudolph glanced at Dan Baesler whose head was bowed and his wife Sophie who had a handkerchief pressed to her eyes.

"After Raymond sent that letter, and before his parents received it, he was killed in a bombing raid. Arnold died four days later. How can these families, how can any of us move forward, through grief and sorrow?

"Are we afraid to face the pain that we know we will endure because of our loss? Raymond declared that he was not afraid. Why? Because he trusted that God would not forsake him.

"God did not forsake his own Son, but lifted him out of death into everlasting life. God did not forsake Raymond and Arnold. And God promises that He will not forsake you in your pain. Let me close my message with these strong words of Paul the apostle in his letter to the Romans: ***Who will separate us from the love of Christ? Will hardship, or distress, or persecution, or famine, or nakedness, or peril, or sword? No, in all these things we are more than conquerors through him who loved us. For I am convinced that neither death, nor life, nor angels, nor rulers, nor things present, nor things to come, nor powers, nor height, nor depth, nor anything else in all creation, will be able to separate us from the love of God in Christ Jesus our Lord.***

"To all of you gathered here today, and especially to the Baesler and Achtenberg families: May these words embrace and sustain you in the days ahead. Amen."

*   *   *

Why do I have such hard time talking to my oldest son? Rudolph needed to speak to Fred and had been sitting in the kitchen mulling how best to do it.

The day after the memorial service, Fred and Betty had come home from high school for the weekend. Now it was Sunday afternoon. Soon they would be riding back to New Leipzig and their rooms at the Groshanz family home.

Rudolph hollered up the stairs, "Fred, come down. I want to talk to you." When Fred appeared on the staircase, his father said, "Let's go to my office."

Fred scowled and reluctantly trailed his father across the church yard. They sat down in the chilly room and Fred emitted a disgruntled sigh.

"What now, Vater? Did you get another nasty letter from Mrs. G.?"

Rudolph waved his finger and smiled. "No. Should I be expecting one?"

Fred gave a lopsided grin and shrugged, "Well, who's to say with her?"

Rudolph leaned forward in his chair, "No, Fred, we need to talk about your future."

"Oh, that." Fred turned to look out of the window. "I've already told you, I'll get my grade up in history and I'll graduate in the spring. One 'F' isn't the end of the world."

"No, I'm not talking about that 'F', though I'm sure you got it for smarting off and not studying. No, we need to talk about after graduation."

Fred looked back at his father with a mock sincere face, "Well, I hear the blacksmith in town is looking for help."

Rudolph smacked his lips in disgust. "Fred, please, let's be serious. You've got a sharp mind and a way with words. You know we've talked about college."

"What about the war? Some of the guys in my class are signing up right after graduation." Fred's eyes flashed, "Don't you want me to do my duty?"

The father fixed sad eyes on his son and slowly shook his head. "No, Fred, your mother and I, we…. We've seen what war does do young men. We can't let you go."

Fred pursed his lips. "In two weeks I'll be eighteen. I can enlist without your permission."

"I know, I know," Rudolph was exasperated. "You could do that and prove to everyone that I have no power over you. But, Fred, think about your mother. She's buried one son already."

At the mention of his mother and her grief, Fred dropped his eyes, lowered his chin and said nothing. The distant cawing of the crows filled the edges of the painful silence. At last Rudolph spoke.

"Fred, you're my oldest son. In my tradition the oldest son follows in this father's profession."

Fred snapped his head up. "But——."

"Don't interrupt. Let me finish." Rudolph plowed ahead. "I've learned that those entering the ministry are exempt from the draft. The seminary I attended closed and merged with Wartburg College and Seminary in Iowa. I've contacted them and learned that they offer scholarships to the sons of former graduates. Fred, this fall, your mother and I want you to enroll in the college's pre-ministry program."

Fred now stared at the wall behind his father. Rudolph couldn't read his son's look. They sat in stony silence until a car horn honked.

Fred jumped up. "That's our ride into town. I better get going."

He reached the door, paused for a heartbeat, turned and opened his lips, closed them, and fled the room. Rudolph sat in his office and let his thoughts drift into the past. Thirty years ago, he'd known another Fred, another high-spirited young man who'd had a conflicted relationship with his father. He tried to forget how that story ended.

MAY, 1944 TRINITY LUTHERAN

In order to savor what I enjoy, I've got to tolerate this. Rudolph opened the door to the parish hall and the men filed in.

After eighteen years of ministry in this three-congregation parish, Rudolph still savored the preaching, the teaching, the healing and the daily contact with members and visitors. He tolerated the record keeping, budget planning and bickering that was a part of every religious institution. And tonight, as a dozen men gathered around the long table in the parish hall, he had to deal with another aspect of ministry that he tolerated, though with less and less patience: the church council meeting.

The evening air was warm and all of the men had worked in the fields since sunrise. No one was eager to prolong the gathering. The minutes were read, the treasurer's report was given, and the details of the fall mission festival plans were accepted without any discussion. The administrative wheels were smoothly spinning and Rudolph was already anticipating an early return to the parsonage. Then Victor Geissler threw a wrench into the gears.

"I was looking at the Bible School materials for this summer. My wife volunteered to be one of the teachers. I'm wondering…Isn't it about time that our kids learned to sing hymns in English?"

Victor was one of the more prosperous farmers in the region. His broad shoulders and chest strained against the dress shirt he was wearing. Unlike most of the other men, his face was fresh-shaven and his air neatly trimmed. He was one of those people who always smiled, a smile Rudolph had come to distrust. Victor now sat smiling at the pastor.

Some of the men had dropped their eyes, a few looked at Rudolph expectantly. *I wonder how many of them are thinking the same thing?*

Rudolph tried to smile back at his questioner, "Herr Geissler, your wife will be working with the lessons. Those are mostly in English, so she'll be comfortable with them. I'm in charge of the music and I'm more comfortable with the German hymns. Besides, we don't want our children to lose that part of their heritage, do we?"

Herr Geissler's smile grew icier, "My wife is comfortable speaking German and speaking English. Our boys speak German too but they prefer English. I'd like them to learn some of the English hymns because by the time they are men with families of their own, I'm sure all worship will be in English."

Murmurs rippled around the table. Rudolph couldn't determine if they expressed agreement or dissent. No one seemed willing to voice an opinion. Rudolph was disturbed by that troubling omen. Yet, like most of the other men this evening, he was weary and unwilling to prolong the meeting. He slowly nodded.

"Well, Herr Geissler, it's always hard to predict the future. But, I will take a look at the music plans and see what I can do."

Victor Geissler simply smiled and said nothing. The time for the next meeting was set, the motion to adjourn was made, the vote was unanimous, and everyone left for home.

Rudolph locked the parish hall and slowly walked across the church yard to the parsonage. He stopped and tipped back his head. The Milky Way's pale ribbon of light stretched across the black velvet sky. *In my heart and soul, that will always be the Milchstraße. Will it be so for my grandchildren, if I ever have any? Will they even speak to an old German grandfather? How much longer will anyone care to listen to this old German preacher?*

JUNE 8, 1945 TRINITY CHURCH

How is happiness measured? Is there a scale? A gauge?
Rudolph stood in his clerical garb in front of the altar waiting for the procession to begin. *Two months ago, when the county linesmen came and installed electricity in the parsonage and here in church, I was delighted. One month ago, when the insane Nazi forces finally surrendered in Germany, I was glad and relieved. But tonight...ahh, tonight my heart is exultant.*

The groomsmen appeared in the doorway and the organist began playing an entrance song as they walked down the aisle. One of them was Rudolph's son August who was trying to look older than a seventeen-year old. He was a stand-in for both of his older brothers. Fred was away at Wartburg College and Rudy, immediately after graduating from high school, left for his assignment in the US Navy. Rudy not only carried his father's name but also a good dose of his father's German Russian stubbornness. He had been determined to enter the war and no one's arguments could dissuade him.

Following August, came the groom's friend, Elmer Baesler. At last, behind the groomsmen, came the groom. Otto Stern, dark haired and soft-spoken, looked impressive in his army uniform. He came down the aisle, limping from his war injury and took his place in front of the pastor.

Now, the two bridesmaids entered. One of them was Hildah, the groom's sister and the other was Rudolph's daughter, Betty. Both young women were aglow with joy and emotion. As they took their positions, the organist paused, the congregation stood, and Ida Maria appeared in the doorway. The organist pulled out every stop on the little pump organ and began playing the Wedding March.

Rudolph's heart swelled and his eyes overflowed. As Ida Maria regally walked down the aisle, the proud father recalled her waving tiny hands in the crib in Marburg, toddling around their apartment in St. Paul, lifting her brothers and sisters down from Herr Mueller's hay wagon at the end of a school day. Now, here she was, their strong, vibrant, educated daughter, their first born, ready to become a married woman.

Rudolph read the scriptures and the prayers, then before leading the couple in the vows, he spoke more personally.

"Otto and Ida Maria, I would like to say a few words about love. There are times when a man and a woman will fall in love and then get married." He smiled and nodded to his wife Ida who sat smiling and teary eyed in the front pew.

"And then, there are times when a man and a woman will first get married and then learn to love." He smiled and nodded to Sophia and Marvin who sat beside Ida.

"Ida Maria and Otto, no matter how a marriage begins, it survives and deepens because of commitment. Each of you commits to give your best to each other. Each of you commits to do what you can to keep your marriage alive. Beneath all of your commitments is the Lord God's commitment to bless your union with His loving Spirit. Now, please turn toward each other and repeat after me your sacred vows."

First the nervous groom and then the radiant bride repeated the vows. Only the slightest tremble in the pastor's voice hinted at the jubilant emotions that washed over him.

After the ceremony, the wedding party and guests feasted in the parish hall. Marvin was seated beside Rudolph, and put his arm around his shoulder.

"Congratulations, brother. One wedding accomplished. Any more to come?"

Rudolph shrugged and smiled. "Who knows with young people these days? Our daughter Betty just finished her first year of nurse's training and we hope she finishes the course by next spring. But…" He rolled his eyes in mock exasperation, "She has a boyfriend who's aching to settle down with a wife."

Marvin swallowed a forkful of wedding cake and asked, "You don't approve of him?"

"Oh, no it's not that. You saw him. He was the other groomsman. He's a nice young man and comes from a good family. It's just…well, he's a farmer and we all know how hard it is to be a farmer in North Dakota. It's such an uncertain life. I don't want to see her suffer."

Marvin picked up his coffee cup, took a sip then turned in his chair toward his friend. "Rudolph, was denkst du? [What are you thinking?] Where will you find a life that is certain? A life without suffering? Brother, look at your own life—wars, hunger, drought. And look what you've accomplished in the midst of it all. As for your daughters and sons, they've got the spirit and blood of their parents. They'll be alright."

Now it was Rudolph's turn to throw his arm around his friend's shoulder. "Ach, Marvin, I guess I should practice what I preach, ja?

Maybe I'm just getting old and tired." He released the squeeze on Marvin's shoulder and sighed, "I think worry is just the burden that every parent is condemned to carry."

"Maybe you're right brother Rudolph, but tonight let's eat the cake and enjoy the party."

Rudolph picked up his fork and laughed with his friend. He did his best to submerge his worries about a reluctant Fred at college and a stubborn Rudy on a ship headed toward Guam. He refused to acknowledge the other worries that increasingly troubled his sleep.

SEPTEMBER, 1945 TRINITY CHURCH

"Since when do the parents get to choose the confirmation material?" Rudolph sputtered. "As the pastor I'm responsible for teaching the young people."

Victor Geissler's smile never altered but his eyes were black ice. Rudolph was sitting opposite him at the monthly council meeting. A minute earlier, without saying a word, Victor had brought out a stack of booklets and handed them to each member. When a copy reached Rudolph, his jaw clenched. Whatever the quality of the material, the fact that it was all in English sent a clear message to everyone in the room.

Still smiling, Herr Geissler spoke in an ingratiating tone, "Pastor, I simply called the church publishing house and asked them to send me copies of their best confirmation material. This is what they sent."

Rudolph looked over to the current council president for some support, but he, like the other council members, was busy studying the booklet he'd received. Rudolph's neck reddened and he growled across the table. "I suppose you're going to ask the treasurer to reimburse you for this stuff."

Geissler widened his eyes and smiled, "Oh no. I wouldn't dream of it. This is my donation to the congregation for the advancement of our education program."

Rudolph tried to bridle his tongue, but he lost his grip on the reins. "So, Herr Geissler, are you daring to suggest that the material I've been using is inferior? Or maybe you're telling us that you don't want your boys to study the catechism in German? Which is it?"

Victor's smile turned to a smirk, he shrugged his shoulders and said nothing.

Rudolph simmered and turned his gaze to the president who finally looked up and stammered, "Well, I guess..um.. Victor, ah, thank you for bringing this in. Ahh, um, Pastor, I'm thinking it wouldn't hurt to look these booklets over. Would it? I mean, I'm not saying… but you know, the kids and even the younger adults, they don't do German so much. I mean, maybe some parts of the classes could be in English. Your English isn't bad, Pastor."

Nods of agreement and comments like "Your English is better than mine, pastor" and "You could do this easy, Pastor," fluttered around the table.

Victor sat silently and smiled.

Rudolph fought the urge to stomp out of the room. His ire burned against Geissler's tactics, but his fear was focused upon the acquiescence of the rest of the council. *Don't they realize the game Geissler's playing? Or worse yet, maybe they're fully aware of what he is doing.*

The blood throbbed in his head. His fury rapidly ebbed only to be replaced by a lassitude that left him longing for his bed. He looked wearily around the table. "Was kann ich sagen? Mein Englisch ist schlampig.[What can I say? My English is sloppy] But I will look over the materials and see what I can do."

Herr Geissler dropped his head and smiled into his lap. The other men looked relieved, as though the issue had been resolved. The remainder of the meeting generated little discussion. Everyone, including Rudolph, was loathe to say anything that would delay their escape from the tendrils of tension that still lingered in the room.

*   *   *

After the meeting, Rudolph had trudged up the stairs to the bedroom, fearing he would not be able to sleep. But he'd slid under the blankets next to Ida and immediately plunged into the dark abyss of sleep.

Now, shortly after two a.m. his eyes flew open and he was wide awake. He didn't need to check the time. For many months now, sometimes two or three times a week, he'd been jolted out of slumber, always between two and two thirty a.m.

He eased out of bed and quietly opened the door to the upstairs balcony. He'd come to appreciate the night-time chill of North Dakota summer evenings. A shiver rippled down his back.

He stared out into the purple darkness and allowed the oft-submerged thoughts to surface. *Time is relative…Wasn't that what the little man on the train said so many years ago? Time has been flying, even out here in my little corner of North Dakota. Maybe I've been like an ostrich, burying my head in parish work and ignoring the stampede of time.*

Once a month, when I preach at the German service in the New Leipzig Lutheran Church, its only people my age and older sitting in the pews. I know Fred and Catherine's sons and daughters are going to the English services there. Mine would too, if I weren't the preacher out here…

But these are my people…I've baptized and confirmed and married them. I've cried with them at their loved ones' funerals, counseled them in their despair, massaged their aching backs, and relieved their pinched nerves. Ja, das sind meine Leute. [Yes, these are my people].

A breeze rustled the leaves of the elm tree alongside the balcony. Rudolph shivered, gently submerged his unsettling thoughts, crawled back into bed and sought the path to sleep.

APRIL 22, 1946 EASTER MONDAY, TRINITY CHURCH

Rudolph had just finished a treatment on Chris Zimmerman's back, sent the old farmer on his way, and now was examining the sermon texts for the coming Sunday. His office door flew open and ten-year-old Herman announced between gasps, "Mama said to tell you that George is coming for supper."

Rudolph grinned at his youngest's enthusiasm. "Thank-you. But you should call him Pastor George, or even President George. He's now the western district president of the of our Lutheran Synod."

Herman was ready to race back out into the yard to play but the word 'president' snagged his attention. "'District President'? What does he do?"

Rudolph laughed, "He travels a lot. Makes sure the pastors and the congregations are getting along. Why don't you ask him tonight? I'd love to hear what he says."

It was five o'clock when District President George Landgrebe drove into the church yard. He stepped out of his battered, dust-covered Dodge, put his hands into the small of his back and groaned. Rudolph went out to greet him.

"George, it looks like you could use a massage."

"Rudolph, I've just about driven this Dodge into the ground. The tires are smooth as glass. The springs are shot. Thank God the companies have gotten back to making cars again. Maybe next year the Synod will help me buy something decent."

He shook Rudolph's hand and laughed as they began walking to the parsonage. "I left Williston this morning. Imagine where I'd be if we were still under that patriotic speed limit of thirty-five miles per hour. I wouldn't be here to taste Frau Heupel's delicious supper, that's for sure."

During the entire meal, George entertained the Heupel family with stories and jokes, all the while demonstrating his appreciation for Ida's culinary skills. Little Herman had tried more than once to ask his question. Finally, after downing his second piece of rhubarb pie, Pastor Landgrebe pushed back his chair. Herman deemed the time was right. He was licking his lips and about to speak, when George stood up.

"Frau Heupel and children, I need to talk to your father alone for a few minutes. If you'll excuse us, we're going outside to walk and help settle this amazing meal."

Ida sent a quizzical glance to Rudolph. He shrugged, gave a slight shake of his head, then followed the president outside.

The sun had set, though the sky still clung to bits of fading light. The nighthawks were hunting for the first spring mosquitoes.

The two men stood with heads tipped back, watching the birds. The insect hunters circled, then dramatically plunged straight down. At the bottom of their dive, when they caught an insect, they would emit a 'woooop' and soar back up into the heights.

George began walking, "So, Rudolph, how long have you been here at Trinity?"

"It will be twenty years in June. I remember when we celebrated your twenty years at Elgin. I couldn't imagine staying anywhere that long."

"The years pile up don't they." They walked in silence along the west side of the church and George quietly asked, "Rudolph, have you thought about leaving Trinity?"

A subtle note in George's voice struck Rudolph's heart and he froze. "Why are you asking?"

George turned toward him, "Rudolph, I'm the district president. If you are thinking of a transfer, you should talk to me first."

"I...yes of course, I'd come to you. I haven't talked to anyone about anything. What's going on George?"

George shook his head and sucked his lower lip. "Ai, Rudolph. I believe you. I'm sorry. Yesterday the pastor out in Rhame told me he got a phone call asking if he'd be interested in coming to be the pastor at Trinity."

Rudolph's heart did a nighthawk dive and his voice rose, "Who was it? Did he say? I know who'd do something like that."

"Not so loud. You don't want your family to hear this." He took Rudolph's arm and they walked toward the tree windbreak. "Evidently there are two or three families that want more English in the worship and in the other programs. They've put pressure on other members to support them."

"But, how do they dare…?" Rudolph sputtered to a stop.

"Ja, Sie sind schamlos [Yes, they are shameless]. What they've done is in total violation of church policies. And, in the process, they've created a big problem for us."

"For us? For us? I'm the one that's got the problem." Rudolph snorted in disgust.

George gripped his friend's shoulder, "Brother, I know you're angry and hurt and you've got every right. But step back from all of that for a minute."

Rudolph took a deep breath and nodded.

George continued, "You have two choices. You can challenge the discontented ones to come out into the open and then fight to stay here. You might win and you might not. Or, you can simply leave, maybe go to another parish. The discontented ones will consider that a victory and this parish will look for a new pastor. Either way, your district president will be dealing for a long time with disgruntled members, a hurting pastor, and a parish that now has a shaky reputation."

Rudolph slowly chewed on George's words. He swallowed them and could feel them settle in his belly--icy, leaden lumps. "Even if I fight and win the battle, I'll still lose this war, won't I, George?"

George shrugged, "I know you Rudolph. You're a pastor who needs to be close to his people. You can't minister to people if you're always worrying about their feelings for you."

Rudolph nodded and sadly sighed, "Let's go back, I've gotten very cold." They walked side by side back around the church toward the parsonage.

"George, thanks for coming all the way out here. I don't envy your job. Will you stay with us tonight?"

"No, I've got some friends in Elgin who're expecting me. It's getting late. Please say good-bye to Ida for me." He paused a moment, then added, "I'll be in my office all week, if you want to contact me."

Rudolph's voice was as disconsolate as his heart. "Ja, George, I'm sure I will. But first things first. Tonight, I'll have to talk with my Ida."

He watched the Dodge's tail lights disappear in the dust. *I have no words that can spare her from the sorrow that is coming.*

*   *   *

Silence thundered in his ears and emotions seared his soul. He stared up into the empty darkness of their bedroom ceiling. Ida had just asked the question she'd been suppressing ever since Rudolph had entered the parsonage looking as though he'd buried another of his children.

Rudolph sighed raggedly. "George's news? Liebe, it was not good." He repeated the story the district president had told him and then shared with her what he and George had discussed."

Ida listened to it all quietly. When she spoke, there was a dull edge of anger in her voice, "But if we leave here, won't we be allowing the troublemakers to win?"

Rudolph nodded into the darkness, "Ja, but if I stay, make a big fuss, the whole parish might lose. The other two congregations aren't part of this affair. People will take sides, families will stop talking to other families. The parish might even split up."

Ida rarely argued with her husband, but she was already envisaging the pain she'd be forced to bear. "This isn't right. It's not your fault. Why should we all have to suffer?"

Rudolph reached for her hand. "That hurts me the most, knowing that no matter what I decide I'll be bringing pain to you and the children." He fell silent, then mused aloud, "I suppose in one way it is my fault… I'm still too much of a German Russian…and not enough of an American for this new generation. Was kann Ich tun?" [What can I do?]

"What can WE do?" Ida corrected him. "Where will WE go?"

"Ja, ja. You're right. We need to work all of that out." Rudolph's voice gained strength as he began strategizing for the future. "We'll want to leave with dignity. Not like scared rabbits. We'll want to leave without tearing apart all that I've built—that we've built—in the last twenty years."

He spelled out possibilities, talking far into the night. As he'd done so many times in his past, Rudolph was quashing his anguish beneath the road he hoped to build to the future.

Ida was mostly silent, awash in grief. She cringed at the thought of all the goodbyes: to so many dear friends, to the trees she'd come to love, to her fruitful garden, to this house—so shaped and rounded by her family's living, so infused with their tears, their laughter, their spirit. Already she sensed that whatever their next destination, she would be immensely lonely.

SUNDAY, MAY 12, 1946 TRINITY LUTHERAN

Like many married couples, Rudolph and Ida, were comfortable being together in silence. But on this chilly, sunny afternoon, as they rattled home in their battered Chevy, their silence was the product of exhaustion.

They'd both attended the 8:30 a.m. service at Hope Lutheran where Rudy had led worship and then made his dramatic announcement. Then they'd done the same at the 10:30 a.m. service at Trinity Lutheran. After a quick lunch they'd driven to small St. John's Lutheran for the 3:00 p.m. worship service, again ending with the news of their departure. Now, they both felt like the gray, threadbare dish rags that snapped in the wind on the clothesline next to the parsonage.

They drove into the church yard and pulled into the horse barn that now served as the car garage. They sat in the semi-darkness, not yet willing to face their children. August, Helen, and Herold, the three teenagers, were still sulking. They were being yanked from the only home they'd ever known and they had not been consulted. Ten-year-old Herman alternated between confusion and excitement.

The engine clicked as it cooled and Rudolph broke the silence. "Did you notice how the congregations reacted differently to our announcement?"

Ida slowly shook her head and wearily said, "I was sitting in the front at every church. I couldn't tell."

"At Hope and St. John's everyone sat back in shock and there were lots of tears. At Trinity, there were quite a few that reacted that way, but some others just sat stone-faced." Rudolph paused and ruefully added, "At least they didn't smile."

"Quite a few of the women asked me why we'd chosen to move

to Hebron. I told them what I could, that both my brother and his wife and your brother and his wife were retired there. I didn't say anything about their help with the house…"

"They don't need to know our business," Rudolph snapped. The fact that he'd had to borrow money from both August and Jacob to make the down payment had pricked his ego. Even though he'd insisted to the men that the money was a loan and not a gift and that as soon as he could straighten out issues with his church pension, he'd repay them, his own neediness still rankled. For the past month he'd repeatedly prayed for patience and humility but the Lord was unusually slow in answering his petitions.

Neither of them made a move to leave the car, overcome by emotional exhaustion. At last Ida said, "Marianne and Virginia asked what we were going to do with the chickens. I told them I planned to butcher and can as many as I could. They offered to help. They've been so kind." She wistfully whispered, "Oh, how I'll miss them."

Rudolph nodded, "Ja, so many good people here. At least a dozen men said they planned to give me retirement gifts. We sure will be able to use the money."

"I don't think everyone believed you when you said you were retiring."

"Well, what was I supposed to say without getting into all the messy business? Besides, I'm leaving here without a call to another parish, so technically, I am retiring. George says up in the Hebron area I could be a supply pastor for a while, fill in for pastors who are sick, or vacationing and for congregations that can't afford a full-time pastor."

Ida lifted the door handle and began to climb out of the car. She could have said more. The idea of her own retirement never entered her thoughts.

August would graduate next week, but she would still have three other children to get ready for school every day. There'd be meals to make and a house to clean. But she doubted there'd be space for much of a garden, and she would miss the fussy hens and the cantankerous cows.

What she could have said, but didn't was this: Dear husband, I will do all that I can to move our family and make a new home. But, please, please, don't forget, I may be smiling, but my heart is weeping.

CHRISTMAS EVE, 1946 RURAL HEBRON, NORTH DAKOTA

Stille Nacht, Heilige Nacht. [Silent night, holy night] Rudolph stepped out of his car and heard Frau Sprecher, the congregation's organist, playing the notes of his favorite carol inside the humble country church. The night sky was sprinkled with icy stars, the temperature hovered near zero and the customary North Dakota wind had surrendered for this holy night. Rudolph stood in the crisp calmness and reflected on his own serenity.

He, Ida and the three children still living at home had settled into new routines in Hebron. Though he still had no full-time call, he was filling in for this congregation as it worked on its future plans. He was pleased to be preaching every Sunday.

Six months ago, when he'd left Trinity, he'd thought the healing ministry he'd conducted there was at an end. He was stunned when the opposite had occurred. He was seeing more people than ever. The word of mouth network was ever-growing and now that he lived in a town and had an address, he was always busy. The community's support of his work astounded him. Only months after his arrival, the town's Lions Club bought a small three room building with imitation brick siding and gave it to him for a clinic. He was spending hours every day tending to those who sought his healing touch. With the help of his visitor's donations and his pension he'd begun to repay the loan he'd received from his relatives.

Rudolph pondered how different his own mental attitude was this year. Every December for two decades he'd had at least two Christmas Eve services and two Christmas Day services. The children's programs, the extra choir rehearsals, the competing demands from the three congregations, not to mention the pressure of preparing two different messages—these all took their toll on his usual good spirit. As much as he cherished the traditions, he'd come to mentally cringe as the holiday drew near.

But this evening he savored his own inner stillness. Since he was the temporary pastor for this tiny Lutheran congregation north of Hebron, tonight was his only Christmas responsibility. Ida was at home preparing for tomorrow's feast. On Christmas day, he could sleep late and enjoy the day with his children, most of whom would be present to fill the house with laughter. His daughter, Betty and her new husband Elmer would be there. They had gotten married a week ago and their delighted faces as he'd led them through their vows still brought a smile to his face.

Several sets of car lights slowly moved down the road toward the church. A half a foot of snow lay like a white shroud over the prairie. The snow was so cold that it squeaked as Rudolph strode toward the door.

He stepped inside just as Frau Sprecher started practicing Von Himmel Hoch [From Heaven Above]. She was a short, stout, round-shouldered lady and wore a crimson coat as she vigorously worked the pedals and concentrated on the notes. Rudolph glanced at her, chuckled and silently mused at how much she reminded him of a Rhode Island red hen.

Without warning, Rudolph was transported back to the parsonage and church yard of Trinity, surrounded by the red hens, the cows and his own flock of children and parishioners. Just as his ribs, long ago broken and now healed, still ached when the weather changed, so Rudolph's heart was struck by a pang of sorrow as he was reminded of the vibrant ministry he'd left behind.

Twenty minutes later, after singing many favorite Christmas carols and reading again the birth story, Rudolph stepped into the small pulpit and looked out over this congregation. Only a handful of younger adults and very few children were in the pews. Most of the members were gray haired. They were glad to have a German-Russian pastor whose words still carried the flavor of their left-behind homeland. Rudolph had reflected on their mutual heritage as he'd prepared his Christmas eve message. He'd contemplated his own quarter century in America. As he prepared to speak, he recalled the words of his seminary professor: 'The first audience for every sermon is the preacher himself.' That advice had never been truer for him than it was tonight. He cleared his throat and began.

"Many of you, or your parents and grandparents, pulled up roots in South Russian and came to this country looking to replant your lives, hoping to make a home for yourselves and for your children. My brother and sister did that as well. Thanks to them I was able to come to America. But in order to do that, I first pulled up roots in South Russia and moved to Germany. Then I pulled up roots in Germany, though I will admit my roots were not too deeply established in that troubled country.

"People in every land want to put down roots. If they are uprooted or if they uproot themselves, they work mightily to find a

276

new place, a safe place where they can again put down roots. Everyone longs for a home, for a place to belong.

"Tonight, we heard again the story of Mary and Joseph. They are forced by the government to travel away from their home. They are uprooted and sent to Bethlehem. After the baby Jesus is born, they cannot go home to Nazareth but are uprooted once again and must run away from the murderous King Herod. They flee to Egypt.

"Tonight, we are reminded that when God decides to come into our world, he comes as one whose roots keep getting pulled up. He goes from Bethlehem to Egypt to Nazareth. Then, when he begins his ministry, Jesus leaves his family and roams the countryside. And by his own words, *'Foxes have dens and birds have nests, but the Son of Man has no place to lay his head.'*

"Tonight, we celebrate the wonder of our God who is willing to enter our world and love us in a way that we humans can understand. And this love surely works in our lives when we are rooted and settled. But Christmas helps us to see that when our roots are pulled up, when our lives are confused, when we wonder what tomorrow will bring—in all of those troubling times, God also is at work

"The Christmas story shows us that we dare not love our roots so much that we are unable to follow where our Lord is leading us. It may be in the times of uprooting that God is leading us to where we need to go.

Tonight, let us give thanks for our God who is willing to enter our confusing, troubled world and embrace us with his powerful love. Amen."

*   *   *

If noise were heat, the inside of Rudolph's old Ford would have been fireplace warm. But though the car heater rattled and whirred it was no match for the brittle night air. Rudolph wrapped and unwrapped his fingers around the icy steering wheel as he left the church yard and drove home.

Greetings at the church door had been brief. Like Rudolph himself, everyone was eager to return to the warm refuge of home. His thoughts clattered like the gravel striking the bottom of his old Ford.

I'm not sure if the good folks in the pews tonight understood what I was trying to say. All of them are far more settled, more rooted than I am. These months have been daunting, but I think we're finding home here. God willing, next year will be less traumatic than this one. And surely God is willing. Isn't He?

APRIL, 1947 HEBRON, NORTH DAKOTA

"You hold the syringe like this, insert under the skin like so, and then press firmly on the plunger," the young physician's assistant gave Rudolph an injection into the flesh of his belly.

"Ja, ja, I know how to give injections," Rudolph snapped. "I spent years doing it. I've administered more injections in my life than you have," he grumbled. He still was digesting the news he'd received an hour earlier from the clinic's doctor.

The doctor had entered the exam room, pulled up a chair and looked directly into Rudolph's face.

"Herr Heupel, you have high blood pressure and need to begin taking medication immediately. You need to lose twenty pounds, and," the doctor paused and took a deep breath, "you have sugar diabetes."

For months, Rudolph had been desperately submerging dark suspicions of this diagnosis in his subconscious. These dire fears now bobbed like corks to the surface of his mind and a wave of nausea swept over him. He closed his eyes and saw his mother's diabetes-wracked skeletal body propped up in bed. He saw his younger self standing helplessly beside her as she died. He tried unsuccessfully to suppress a moan.

The doctor's voice pulled him back to the present, "Please, Herr Heupel, listen. Diabetes is no longer a death sentence. We now have treatment. A daily insulin injection will replace what your pancreas has stopped doing."

Rudolph opened his eyes and forced himself to focus on the doctor's words.

"Of course, you'll have to modify your diet. Stay away from white bread, sweets, fatty meat, fried food and beer." He handed his patient a sheet of paper. "Here is list of what to avoid."

Rudolph glanced at the list and managed an anemic smile. "Doctor, this isn't a diet modification, it's a diet death sentence."

The doctor chuckled. "Ja, well, you're not the first German-Russian to deal with the consequences of your food preferences. But believe me, what you eat can make a big difference in your health." He shook Rudolph's hand then stood. "Stay here and my nurse will come in and demonstrate how the injections must be done."

After the nurse's lesson, Rudolph stopped at the drug store and picked up his first box of insulin bottles and his high blood pressure medicine. He stepped out into the April sunshine and began walking home.

I'm fifty-four, about the age when Mutti died. Yesterday I didn't feel old, but today…When I show Ida this diet list, she'll say, 'I told you so.' She might become a zealous enforcer. Ach, one more Dorn im Fleisch [thorn in the flesh], Mein Gott, give me strength to endure.

NOVEMBER 11, 1947 BISMARCK, NORTH DAKOTA

"If they have a boy, I think they should name it after me," Rudolph declared as he and Ida walked toward Bismarck's JC Penney store. The church convention had ended at noon and Ida wanted to do some shopping before driving back to Hebron.

Ida laughed, "Ach, 'Rudolph' is such an old name. You keep forgetting that here in America people aren't stuck with the same ten names over and over again. We'll let Betty and Elmer choose the name. Besides, the baby isn't due until the middle of January and they'll probably change their minds a dozen times before it's born. We should just be glad that we'll finally have a grandchild to hold."

"Pastor Heupel, wait," someone behind them shouted. They turned to see Gottfried Buchholz, a former neighbor and parishioner trotting toward them.

"Guten Tag, Gottfried. Slow down before you have a heart attack," Rudolph laughed as the old farmer approached. But the look on the man's face erased Rudolph's humor. His own heart turned to ice. "What is it?"

Gottfried spoke between gasps, "Have you heard about your daughter?"

Ida clutched Rudolph's arm. "Our daughter? What about her?"

The old man shook his head, "You better go up to St. Alexius Hospital, right now." He turned away from the couple and began walking back down the sidewalk.

"Gottfried, wait. What—?" Rudolph cried.

But Herr Buchholz kept walking, turned his head and shouted over his shoulder. "Just go to the hospital."

The frantic couple hurried to their car and within minutes dashed up to the information desk at St. Alexius.

Rudolph gripped the counter "Excuse me. We're looking for our daughter. We were told she was here."

A large woman with dark hair slowly raised tired eyes and looked at the agitated man and the distraught woman clinging to his arm. "And what would be your daughter's name?"

"Ach, ja." Rudolph and Ida exchanged glances, then Rudolph said, "Probably Betty, Betty Baesler, she's seven months pregnant."

The receptionist slowly ran her finger down a list of names on a clipboard. "Baesler, no, no I don't see anyone with that name."

Rudolph was baffled. He looked down at his trembling wife. He swallowed, "Well, then what about Stern, Ida Maria Stern."

Again, the woman ran her finger down the list when she reached the bottom, her finger stopped and in a toneless voice said, "Stern, Ida Maria, Oh, she died."

For an instant those words hung in the air like an upraised knife. Then, like a puppet whose strings are suddenly slashed, Ida collapsed in a faint. Rudolph caught her before she struck the floor. He sat her down and leaned her against the desk.

Evidently suddenly aware of her insensitivity, the receptionist rose from her chair and scurried down the hall to find a nurse. After Ida was revived the couple was led into a tiny office.

A doctor entered and took a stool opposite them. "I'm so sorry for your loss. Your daughter died last night from an especially vicious form of poliomyelitis."

Rudolph shook his head, "But we saw her three days ago. She was fine."

"The virus directly attacked her respiratory system, and within hours paralyzed her lungs. Basically she…" the doctor paused, "she suffocated."

Rudolph had his arms wrapped around Ida who wept quietly. "Can we see her?"

"I'm sorry Mr. Heupel. She's no longer here in the hospital. Mr. Stern arranged for her body to be taken this morning."

'The body'—those leaden, stiff words jabbed at his heart and he groaned. He saw little Ida Maria's chubby cheeks on the deck of the Resolute, her first steps in the miniscule apartment in St. Paul, her hair steaming as she raced across the Trinity church yard, her beaming smile as she received her high school diploma, her wedding…All of this, all of her, reduced to 'the body'? *God in heaven why her? Why not me?*

The doctor stood, "I need to go, but I can call our chaplain, Father Groth, to come and spend some time with you."

"Nein, no thank you, doctor. I...we need to drive back to New Leipzig. Get ready for...for the funeral." Rudolph shook the doctor's hand then helped Ida stand. They leaned on each other and shambled outside, two broken reeds wavering in the cold, gray November breeze.

DECEMBER 9, 1947 TRINITY LUTHERAN CEMETERY

God will not let you be tested beyond your strength...so promised the apostle Paul. But Mein Gott, we are at our limit. Rudolph's bitter thoughts matched the fierce icy northwest wind blowing against his, and all of the mourners' backs, at the Trinity cemetery.

A month ago, everyone could see how distraught Betty was at her sister's death. Her eyes held sorrow but also a fluttering, like a frantic caged bird. She could not sit still and insisted on organizing the luncheon following Ida Maria's funeral and burial. The family pleaded with her to allow others to do this work. They begged her to rest for the safety of her soon to be born baby. But grief deafened her to their pleas. For days she moved non-stop. She organized the food donations and the placement of tables and chairs. Then on the day of the funeral she hauled out pitchers of water, carried trays of sandwiches and filled and refilled the coffee pots. Her feet swelled and her back spasmed so that in the days following the funeral she could barely walk.

Then, a week ago, seven weeks ahead of time, Betty's water had broken and she'd gone into labor. The Elgin Hospital doctors delivered the tiny boy, small enough to fit in his father's hand. The chief nurse, fearful for the infant's survival, baptized him as he lay in his mother's arms. The young parents named him Mitchell and watched him fight his doomed battle. He lived three days. Then he died.

Now Betty sat on an icy metal chair, wrapped in blankets. Her face was a white mask. Elmer, the bereaved father, knelt on the hard ground and lowered the tiny white coffin into the merciless earth. The tears froze on his cheeks. Rudolph and Ida and the rest of their family stood behind Betty, doing what they could to protect her from the raw wind.

When the burial ceremony was over, everyone hurried to their cars. But Rudolph and Ida lingered for a moment at the tiny plot where their own first-born son was buried.

"First son, first daughter, now our first grandson. Has God cursed us?" Ida's teeth chattered out her lament.

These words, coming from one who for so many decades seldom complained, sliced into Rudolph's heart. He wrapped his arms around her as her moans accompanied the wind. "Ida, my Ida, you've been so strong for so long. Today we can only ask that question. Tomorrow, or maybe next week we'll see things clearer. Come now, out of the cold. Betty and Elmer need us."

*   *   *

The reception luncheon was over. The embraces had been long and teary. Rudolph and Ida knew that Elmer's parents would support the grieving couple. Daniel and Sophie also knew what it was to lose a child. They'd been reminded of their sorrow out in that cemetery as they stood beside the tomb of their son killed at Guadalcanal.

Now Rudolph and Ida were on the highway heading north toward Hebron. Rudolph drove into the darkness and as the pavement unrolled before him, a parade of faces crossed his mind: Ida Maria's husband, Betty and Elmer, the family he'd left behind and lost in the Ukraine, his German Russian parishioners past and present.

We are a people well acquainted with grief. Sorrow and suffering have carved their names into our family trees. But the trees do not die. We are a stubborn people. We clutch our faith with sturdy, weathered hands. And we thrive. Beneath our grief runs fierce joy, beyond the suffering lies rejoicing. By God, we live, for decades and centuries, we live and flourish. Betty and Elmer, one day they will---

"Stop the car," Ida's sharp command startled Rudolph. He pulled his foot off the accelerator and let the car coast to a stop.

"Mein Gott, Ida, what's wrong? You scared me." He turned to her but she was not looking at him. She was leaning forward, head nearly touching the windshield.

"Turn off the headlights and look."

Rudolph turned off the lights and gradually his eyes adjusted to the profound darkness of the Dakota night. He gasped. "Northern lights. I've never seen them so bright."

Pale green curtains of light fluttered and flared across the entire northern sky. Purple spikes flickered and danced, one second brilliant, then disappearing, only to flash to life in a new location. Then in the northwest, a column of red light began to pulse. It throbbed against the sable sky and thrust ever higher.

Rudolph turned off the ignition, opened his door and stepped out into the brittle air. He folded his hands and gazed in awe at the heavenly artistry. Ida came and stood beside him.

Rudolph threw back his head following the rising red column of light. He spoke with reverence. "A pillar of fire. In the desert, in the deepest darkness, God gave his chosen people a pillar of fire to guide them to safety."

"Listen," Ida said, "the colors are singing."

They both held their breath and for a few seconds could hear what sounded like a distant wind whistling through trees. For the next ten minutes the couple huddled together in the arctic air, stunned by the beautiful display.

Gradually, the colors paled, the flickering slowed and disappeared. Rudolph and Ida sighed and reentered the car. They sat in silence while the motor warmed up. At last Rudolph pulled back out onto the highway and headed north. He reached out for Ida's hand and held it at the drove toward home.

JUNE 1, 1948, HEBRON, NORTH DAKOTA

Ein morgen für Dichter! [A morning for poets] Rudolph thought as he whistled in accompaniment to the sparrows chirping in the trees. He was walking the three blocks from his home to the small office that served as his clinic. The early morning chill was gracefully ceding to a delicious warmth. The cloudless sky was a breathtaking blue and the ever-present North Dakota breeze danced gently in the verdant canopy above him.

He expected there might be people waiting outside the door. Daily he treated dozens of people from all across the region: farmers who'd wrenched their backs, truck drivers with pinched nerves in their necks, high school athletes with assorted leg problems. As he approached his office, he saw something unexpected: parked in front of his modest office was a sleek, polished black car sporting a chrome grille and bumper that sparkled in the sunlight, all supported by spotless whitewall tires.

Whom has the Lord brought to me this morning? No one around here could afford a car like that.

Before he reached the car, a tall man in an elegant black suit and starched white shirt emerged from the back seat and extended his hand.

"Good morning. Are you Doctor Heupel?"

Rudolph noted the brown of the man's skin and his black moustache. He looked into the man's dark eyes, shook hands and smiled. "Good morning to you. I'm Rudolph Heupel. A reverend, and not a doctor."

A puzzled frown crossed the man's face. "But we were told you treated patients with nerve and muscle problems."

"Ja, ja. Every day I do those things for people who come to me. What is your name?"

The man bowed and answered, "My name is Omar Hamdan."

"Glad to meet you Mr. Hamdan. Now, how can I help you?"

"It's not me who needs help." The tall man opened the back door and pointed into the darkened interior. "Young Abdullah is the one we're concerned about."

Rudolph peered into the luxurious car. A thin boy's large frightened eyes stared back at him. Omar began to explain. "We've been traveling for three days. We've come from Saudi Arabia."

Rudolph raised his palm. "Please, just wait a moment." He slid into the car and sat beside the boy. "Good morning, Abdullah. My name is Rudolph. Do you speak English?" The boy nodded.

Rudolph chuckled. "You probably speak better than I do. How old are you Abdullah?"

The boy murmured, "Twelve. But I'll be thirteen in a month."

"Good for you! I'm fifty-five, an old man already. Is Omar your father?"

"No, no. He works for my father."

"Ah, so your father is an important man in Saudi Arabia?"

"I suppose so. He has many businesses and people call him 'sayyidi'. But I call him 'baba'."

Rudolph chuckled. "I'm not sure what those words mean, but 'baba' sounds like a good word for a boy to call his father."

Abdullah grinned up at Rudolph.

"So, my young man, would you like to come into my office? It's getting warm out here in the car and I have a fan inside. You can tell me all about your trip and what I can do for you."

The boy nodded. Rudolph slid out of the car and unlocked the door to his office.

He turned to find that Omar had reached into the car for Abdullah and was now carrying him in his arms. Rudolph held the door open as they entered the tiny waiting room. He pointed to a couple of chairs for his guests, then turned on the fan and opened the windows to the fresh morning air. He sat down opposite them and smiled.

"Well, I've never had anyone from Saudi Arabia in my office. I'm honored and curious. How in the world did you find your way here?"

Omar glanced down at the boy, then turned to Rudolph. "Abdullah's father, Mr. Khan, my boss, has a sister named Alya. Some ten years ago, at a banquet, she met an American engineer working in our oil fields. This man, Mr. Bauer, after years of conversations with the family, was given permission to marry Alya. Last year, Mr. Bauer, Alya and their two children moved out near Watford City where his company is drilling for oil."

Rudolph nodded, "Watford City, ja, I've treated some folks from there."

Omar continued, "Evidently one of your patients spoke to Alya. When she found out about Abdullah's problems, she sent a message to Abdullah's father. So, we have flown on many planes and finally this morning we have come."

Rudolph turned to the boy, "So, Abdullah, Omar says you have problems. Can you tell me about them?"

The boy dropped his head. When he raised it, teardrops trembled on his eye lids. "I...I can't feel my legs."

Rudolph leaned forward with his elbows on his knees. "Both legs or just one?"

Abdullah sniffled, "First it was just this one." He tapped his right leg then his left. "Then this one started to go numb too. Now when I try to walk..." He dropped his head and fell silent."

Omar spoke, "He was seen by our Saudi doctors who were baffled. A doctor was flown in from Europe. He insisted surgery was the only solution. But Abdullah's family was afraid of this. So when Alya spoke of a man with healing hands, it was decided I would come with the boy to see what you might be able to do."

Rudolph sat back in his chair and spoke to the serious Omar and the teary-eyed Abdullah. "I'm humbled that you've come so far to see me. Please understand, I'm no miracle man. Anything I do is by God's power. I'll do my best, and if it's God's will, we can fix your legs."

He stood up. "Now, Abdullah, can you try and stand up for me?" The boy pushed himself up with his thin arms. He wavered for a second on stiff legs then collapsed back on the chair.

285

"Ja, I see. Mr. Hadad, please bring the boy into this room." He led the pair into a tiny room that held only a firm couch and a folding chair. "Abdullah, I'm going to have you lie down on the couch facing up."

Omar lay the boy down and stepped back. Rudolph sat in the chair and pulled it close to Abdullah.

"Do the boys in Saudi Arabia like to play outside games?"

"Sure. Little kids play tag, we have races. My friends and I, we play soccer, or at least I used to play." Abdullah's voice fell.

"Ach, ja. It's hard not to play outside. So, is soccer a rough game?"

"Sometimes, a little. If you're a goalie you can get banged up."

"I see. And do you, did you, ever play goalie?"

"Sure, we all take turns. And I got whacked once pretty hard." The boy grinned.

Rudolph leaned forward in his chair, "You did? What happened?"

Abdullah propped himself upon his elbows, "My friend Ibrahim had the ball and was coming right at me. He faked to the left and when I dived that way, he kicked the ball and, pow! He smashed right into my hip with his whole body."

Rudolph grinned and cringed, "Ouch, I bet that hurt."

The boy smiled and nodded, "Yeah, I was aching, but I'm tough. I didn't let the other team know."

Rudolph put his hand on the boy's shoulder. "Ja, my young friend. I can see that you're tough. So, we're going to see if we can help those legs get better. And it might hurt a little but you're a brave boy, aren't you? Can you roll over now onto your stomach and I'll have a look at your back."

Rudolph helped the boy roll over. Then he slowly moved his hand down Abdullah's spine, vertebrae by vertebrae. When he reached the tailbone, he slid his hands out to the youngster's hipbones. "Does it hurt anywhere?"

The boy spoke softly, "No, not really. You have nice hands."

"Danke, thank you, son." Rudolph turned to Omar. "I'm going to do some massage for about fifteen minutes. You're welcome to stay or you can wait out in the office."

Omar nodded and watched as Rudolph began to gently knead the muscles in the boy's back. He soon left and Rudolph continued pressing with ever increasing pressure. He could feel the boy's body relaxing under his hands. Gradually Abdullah's breathing slowed and he fell asleep. Rudolph stepped out of the room and found Omar out front on the sidewalk, smoking a cigarette.

"Mr. Hamad, how long can you stay in Hebron?"

Omar threw down his cigarette and crushed it with his shoe. "What do you mean? Why--?

Rudolph interrupted, "Excuse me. I should ask, 'can you stay here at least two more days'? I think I can help the boy, but it'll take some time. Several of his vertebrae are misaligned and are pinching the nerves running to his legs. Unfortunately, his muscles and ligaments have adjusted to this misalignment and are now very tight. I need to first stretch and loosen them before I can release the nerves. This will be painful so I must go slowly. I'll need time."

"Of course, doctor. We will stay as long as needed."

*   *   *

Friday's sun rose into a brassy, hazy sky. By midafternoon purple clouds began piling up on the western horizon. The air grew so heavy that the birds stopped singing and the flies buzzed slower and lower. Omar stood outside Rudolph's office watching the storm approach.

In the small treatment room, Rudolph and Abdullah were sharing grins. Over the last three days, Rudolph had spent two hours every morning and two hours every afternoon, massaging and stretching the boy's muscles and ligaments. Yesterday Abdullah had yelped when Rudolph massaged his leg.

Rudolph smiled, "Ah, finally you feel something, ja?"

Abdullah's pained face slowly relaxed into a startled grin, "Yes, yes. It hurts. That's good isn't it?"

Rudolph kept working the muscles, "Ja, this means your nerves are coming back to life. They've been sleeping for so long."

Now, on Friday, in the humid heat of the afternoon, Abdullah was standing on the floor, slowly shifting his weight from one leg to the other. He grinned up at Rudolph.

"I can feel my toes, my knees, and all the way up. Look." He extended one leg, then another.

"Shall we show Mr. Hamad?" Rudolph opened the treatment room door.

They stepped out into the office as the first boom of thunder rolled out of the clouds. Abdullah moved stiffly to the outside door and yanked it open.

"Omar, Omar. Look at me!" Before Omar could turn, Abdullah

stepped out in front of him. The boy walked slowly in a small circle on the sidewalk.

"Allah be praised," the tall man murmured as he watched the boy's steps grow ever steadier.

Another rumble of thunder crashed overhead and huge raindrops began to splash.

"Come, Abdullah, let's get out of the rain," Omar reached out to grab his young charge.

"No," the boy giggled, "you can't catch me." He stiffly trotted down the sidewalk.

Omar could have easily grabbed Abdullah but he was disarmed by the boy's ecstatic delight. The youngster threw back his head and shouted joyously, his thin face and black hair glittered with raindrops, his once paralyzed legs danced with delight.

The two men watched him skip to the end of the block then return, soaked to the skin and still exuberantly laughing. All of them reentered the office as the cleansing rain continued to fall.

Omar began, "Doctor Heupel, you—"

"Reverend Heupel," Rudolph interrupted.

"Yes, yes, Reverend Heupel, you've worked a miracle."

"Nein, nein. I massaged muscles and moved bones. The one whom you call Allah and I call the Lord, He's the only one who works miracles."

"That may be, but the hands were yours. Abdullah's father authorized me to pay you."

Rudolph shook his head, "Since I do not charge, you cannot pay."

"But we must—"

Rudolph held up his hand, "The only thing you must do, is sign my register. You may give a gift for my congregation if you'd like." Suddenly he grinned and tapped his cheek with a finger, "And in Germany there's a training center that could use your support. I'll give you the address."

*　　*　　*

Thirty minutes later the thunder storm had swept past the town and rumbled eastward, and the black limousine had pulled away from the office and began its journey to the Bismarck airport. Before leaving, Little Abdullah had hugged Rudolph and called him jid [grandfather]. Omar had carefully folded and pocketed the slip of paper with Hephata's address, then bowed and clasped Rudolph's outstretched hand solemnly repeating, 'thank you, thank you,

Reverend Heupel.'

Rudolph filled his lungs with the rain-washed air as he walked home. Tattered cloud rags dotted the western sky. In the east, a luminous rainbow arced across the purple backside of the retreating storm. Rudolph whistled softly and smiled at the memory of Abdullah cavorting in the rain.

Who'd have guessed that the first child to call me grandfather would be from Saudi Arabia.

SEPTEMBER 11, 1949 HEBRON, NORTH DAKOTA

"Don't rush me. I'm fifty-three years old and finally getting to hold a grandchild of my own," Ida protested when one of her adult children suggested they stand and prepare for the big event.

She and Rudolph were sitting on their old tan, brocade couch, cooing at the dark-haired bundle in her arms. The living room was crowded. Rudy, back from his naval assignment was there with his bride Violet whom he'd married in February. Helen and her husband Don, married only four months, were comparing newlywed notes with August and Verda who'd been married only twelve days ago and had just returned from their honeymoon. Herold and Herman, the two teenagers wove through the crowd, eagerly soaking up the stories and jokes shared by the couples.

The baby in Ida's arms was the reason for the gathering. On August 13, Betty had given birth to a healthy little boy. This Sunday afternoon she and Elmer had driven up to Hebron to have him baptized. Normally the baptism would have been done at Trinity. The couple lived on a farm only three miles south of the church and regularly worshipped there. But not only was Rudolph Betty's father, he'd been her and Elmer's pastor for nearly two decades. Everyone, including Rudolph (especially Rudolph) believed it appropriate and proper that the first grandchild be baptized by the family's patriarch and pastor.

Rudolph stood at last and took the baby from Ida's arms. First, he looked out at the family surrounding him. *What a spirited, joyful company! So much life and laughter.*

Ida Maria's absence was a sad aching, assuaged only by his conviction that one day he'd see her again in heaven. Fred's absence—now that was a different, more disturbing matter. No one knew where he was. He'd not appeared for the beginning of the fall classes at the seminary. They'd gotten a post card with a quick scrawl, stating that he needed time to 'sort things out'. Where he was doing that sorting, and how long it would take, no one knew.

In an effort to set aside the disquiet his oldest son always seemed to produce, Rudolph looked down at the child in his arms. *Kleine Mensch [Little person] You'll grow with your momma and papa, surrounded by fields and animals, just as I did. Will you stay there? Will your roots plunge deep into the rich soil, the rolling hills and the banks of the Antelope Creek? Will you farm the land and tend the cattle? Or, will you look up, take the road out of that valley and seek your life in a bigger world, as I did? Either way, little one, you'll find God close at hand. And though I'm only your grandpa, and no prophet, I have an inkling that the Lord will lovingly disturb you.*

"Zeit anzufangen,"[time to start] Rudolph declared, then looked up into the eyes of his grinning family. They had all been waiting for him to finish his silent musing. He handed the child to Helen. She and her new husband had been invited to be the godparents. Rudolph decided to put on his black clergy gown and white collar. He stood now facing the parents and godparents with the rest of the Heupel clan gathered around them.

"Wir sind alle Kinder einer gefallenen Menschheit" [We are all children of a fallen humanity] Rudolph began intoning the formal and somber words of the baptismal liturgy. In the privacy of his own home, in the casual gathering in his living room, he could have adopted a more personal tone. But Rudolph believed in the power of these robust words and could not imagine depriving his first grandson of their majesty. He finished the readings and prayers.

"Jetzt das Wasser" [Now the water]. Ida handed Elmer a half-full crystal bowl. The new father grinned and stepped forward. Helen held the sleeping baby over the water.

The preacherly tone in Rudolph's voice melted away. As he poured handfuls of water over the child's dark head of hair, he tenderly said "Ronald Dennis Baesler, I baptize you in the name of the Father, and the Son, and the Holy Ghost."

The baby's eyes did not open but he trembled with each splash of water. The trembling may have merely been the infant's natural response to cold water. But it could have been a fearful tremor, a soul deep awareness that he'd been claimed by the supreme God. Or, it may have been a shiver of anticipation, a prescient delight in the new life that God had opened before him. Rudolph believed it was all three.

SEPTEMBER 9, 1951 RURAL HEBRON

"If you're retired, why are you preaching every Sunday?" Sixteen-year-old Herman asked from the back seat. He and his mother were joining Rudolph on the way out to a morning worship service at another of the many small congregations without a full-time pastor.

"Ach, retired, unretired, this makes no difference to your father," Ida laughed as they bounced over the rutted road.

Rudolph had been going over the morning's sermon in his mind as he drove, but his son's question derailed his thoughts. He spoke over his shoulder. "When you're a pastor, you never really retire. And even when you're a part-time pastor you're on full-time call. You'll find that out someday." To Rudolph's deepest gratification his youngest son had already declared his intention to follow his brothers Herold and Fred into the Lutheran ministry.

"But Fred said he was going to make sure and do plenty of hunting and fishing on his days off," Herman reminded his father.

Ida turned her head and shot a warning glance back at her son. That spring, Fred had graduated from Wartburg Seminary, and with his wife Alice and newborn daughter had moved to Penticton, British Columbia to be the pastor at their Lutheran church.

Like so many of the men who shared his German-Russian heritage, Rudolph believed that effusive praise led to the sin of arrogance. Nonetheless he was, in equal measure, proud and relieved that Fred had finally gotten his diploma and been installed as a pastor.

All of the Heupels knew that Fred's view of ministry and family did not exactly match that of his father's. Ida was irritated that on this beautiful day Herman had risked stirring the coals of Rudolph's frustration.

Rudolph swerved around a pot hole and shook his head, "Ja, well, Fred. Fred is… He's still a young man. He'll see. And, besides, who knows what they teach at the seminary these days? Fred's very smart. I'm sure he'll do fine. What I don't understand is why he had to go way out to British Columbia. Mein Gott, It's in Canada. About as far away from the rest of us as he could go."

291

Ida turned again to Herman with an 'I told you so' look in her eyes. She turned back to her husband, "Ja, Rudolph, ja. But the world seems smaller now, don't you think. Rudy is back on the Navy ship heading toward Korea, Herold is down in Iowa at the seminary. Everyone is busy, everyone is more scattered. Our three new grandkids…how often will we see them I wonder?" She'd spoken to mollify her husband, but as she reflected on her own life, could not resist adding, "Besides, Penticton is not too far from Alice's parents."

Rudolph heard the words, and the wistfulness behind them. He'd not forgotten the promise he'd made to Ida's father thirty years earlier, a promise he'd never kept. *Where has the time gone? Ida has never complained, still, I know…I wonder what a trip to Germany would cost? Her parents are gone, but her sisters…Wouldn't she love to see them?*

He didn't dare share these thoughts, not this morning, not without some research. Instead he did what pastors do on Sundays. He silently returned to rehearsing the morning's sermon.

JUNE 1ST, 1953 OVER THE ATLANTIC

"Sehen sie, es war alles in deinem kopf." [You see, it was all in your head] Rudolph grinned and nudged Ida in the seat next to him.

"I was worried about what was in my stomach, not what was in my head," Ida smiled.

"Maybe so. But here we are, two hours in the air, you haven't gotten sick and we're one sixth of the way to Frankfurt. Isn't it astonishing?" He gazed out of the window into the darkening sky. "Better than those long days on the SS Resolute."

Ida leaned back in her seat and chuckled at Rudolph's boyish delight. Ever since he'd begun planning this trip a year and a half ago, he'd been invigorated and enthusiastic. At first, she'd worried about the money. Five hundred dollars for one round trip ticket from New York to Frankfurt? But Rudolph had persisted.

"In 1953 I will be sixty years old. Who knows how many years we'll have left to travel? We'll spend some of my pension money. Don't you want to see your family?"

Needless to say, Ida yearned to see them all, especially her dear sisters. But, ever cautious, she'd fretted about the other costs.

Rudolph had cajoled her, "Liebe, we'll take the cheapest train to New York. In Germany your family will feed us. And the trains are cheap there."

Stripped of all her excuses, she finally was forced to admit, "I'm afraid of flying."

Naturally Rudolph, who himself had never flown, had mustered dozens of arguments, none of which completely convinced her. Eventually his arguments, combined with her longing to see her family, managed to propel her up the stairway and into this TWA plane. The sudden decision by her brother Henry to join them only made the trip more appealing.

Ida smiled to herself as she recalled the unrestrained expressions of delight that her sisters had sent her when they learned she would soon be arriving for a visit. She looked at Rudolph who was dozing with his head against the plane window. In their more than three decades together, he'd always been the one willing to venture into unknown territory. He'd always taken the lead and no matter her personal feelings, she'd always followed. Tonight at least, she was grateful for that arrangement.

JUNE 5, 1953 TREYSA, GERMANY

Since Adam and Eve were expelled from Eden, every garment of joy is sewn with threads of sorrow.

Rudolph stood with Ida beneath the leafy green shadows in the Hephata cemetery and pondered this truth; a truth he'd not only learned in his theology classes but had felt in his very flesh and bones. Today he was experiencing this reality once more.

After landing in Frankfurt and spending one night there, they'd taken the train north to Treysa. Rudolph had planned to walk from the train station through the winding streets and up the hill to Hephata just as he'd done when he'd first arrived forty years earlier. But his blood pressure was still high, and neither his legs nor his heart were what they once had been, so they'd taken a taxi instead.

Although the Hephata Deacon Training Center had officially removed Rudolph from their brotherhood, Rudolph had never removed Hephata from his heart. From the time he left Germany, Rudolph had never stopped writing to the people of the Deacon Training Center and they had never stopped replying and sending him the Center newsletter. During the drought and depression of the 1930's Rudolph had continued to send small monetary donations and boxes of clothing. During World War II communication had been cut off, but once the war ended, Rudolph renewed, and increased his donations.

The grateful administration feted Rudolph and Ida with dinners and tours of the Center's many new buildings. The couple spent hours learning how the staff had begun working with small groups of men and women in home-like settings. A few of Rudolph's former Hephata classmates now worked at the institution and invited the couple to their homes. The days had been full of laughter, memories, celebration and joy.

Today the mood was somber. Rudolph and Ida walked among the orderly white headstones in the Hephata cemetery. All the headstones were alike, a visible symbol of the Christian belief that before God, all people are alike, all equally dependent on God's grace. They stopped before headstones marking the graves of teachers, administrators, classmates and friends they'd known during their time at Hephata. Then they saw it.

"Ach, mein Gott," Rudolph sighed and held Ida's hand. They gazed down at the rectangular stone lying flat upon the ground. Engraved on the cold gray granite were words from Psalm 88 *My eye grows dim through sorrow. Every day I call upon thee, O LORD; I spread out my hands to thee.* Beneath those words was carved '385 Lämmer' [lambs].

The night before, the Hephata chaplain had told them the story. They'd been at a party hosted by the director. Everyone was sitting out on the patio, enjoying the warm evening when someone spoke of the 'dark days.' A sad silence fell over the group. Seeing Rudolph and Ida's quizzical looks, the director said, "Ja, this too is part of our history. Pastor Steurnagel, why don't you tell it."

The chaplain was tall and thin. His black beard was streaked with gray, his smile was kindly and his eyes seemed accustomed to sorrow. The entire company could hear the sadness in his rich baritone voice as recalled the events.

"The first time was in 1939. We had no inkling of what was happening. A jeep rolled up the hill, followed by a truck. They stopped outside the office. An officer emerged from the jeep and told the director he wanted to tour our facilities. The director asked him what was the purpose of the tour, the officer retorted, 'We do this for the sake of the Fatherland. That is enough.'

"So, the officer and his aide followed the director through the buildings. When they came to the wing where the physically handicapped lived, the officer ordered the aide to write down bed numbers. After the tour, they walked back to the vehicles and the officer shouted to two men who descended from the truck and followed the aide back into the building.

Then he turned to the director, 'We'll be taking fifteen of your residents for further examinations.'

'But sir, they need special care.'

The officer snapped, 'Don't you think your government knows how to care for creatures like this?'

The director paled and could only stammer, 'When...when will they be returned?'

The officer smiled, 'When the examinations are completed of course.'

The soldiers were already carrying out the boys and men and shoving them into the truck. By this time, the Center's aides and teachers had gathered and stood silently as the soldiers did their work. Some of the handicapped residents were crying loudly, others were so stunned they uttered no sound. When the truck pulled away, many of us cried. But none of us spoke."

The chaplain stopped, looked around and added, "I myself didn't speak because my sorrow was so great, but also because I was afraid that someone, anyone, might repeat my words to the wrong people. We were all living in a fog of fear."

The director nodded and continued the tragic story. "When a week passed and those fifteen did not come back, our fears became nightmares. What were the Nazis doing with our poor residents? Would they come again with trucks looking for more of what they called 'creatures'?" He shook his head as he recalled those years of horror.

"We tried to find places to hide some of our residents, homes that could take them in, but we were a nation at war..." With a hollow voice, husky with tears he finished the harrowing memory, "They came again and again, sometimes with a dozen trucks and soldiers with guns. They seized our precious little ones...three hundred and eightyfive...they took them, experimented on them, and killed them all."

Only the crickets broke the silence on the patio. After a few minutes, the chaplain spoke, "What our nation did to our Jewish brothers and sisters is now being called the Holocaust. We will all have to bear that burden. Here at Hephata, we carry another millstone: three hundred eighty-five lambs that we could not save. Someday we hope to have a suitable memorial. For now, we have only a simple stone in our cemetery."

Today, Rudolph and Ida stood before the cold granite marker, chilled by last night's grim account. Thought they did not speak it, they both were remembering their own precious lambs buried beneath the Dakota prairie.

"I'm cold. Let's find some sunshine." Ida tugged Rudolph's arm and they slowly walked across the green lawns toward the Hephata church.

"How can so much evil come upon this place that means to do only good?" Ida murmured.

Rudolph held her hand. "The hard questions, Liebe, you've never been afraid to ask them, but nobody on this earth has the answers."

They stopped before a gray statue standing in the center of the lawn next to the church. It depicted a tall woman holding a baby in the crook of her left arm. Three small children sheltered in the folds of her long cloak. The face was the face of a mother, a face full of love.

Ida's soft voice began humming a familiar melody. Rudolph nodded. "Ja, she reminds me of that hymn too. They quietly sang the song that had been sung at Ida Maria's funeral:
Neither life nor death shall ever From the Lord His children sever;
Unto them His grace He showeth, And their sorrows all He knoweth.

JULY 1953 CADENBERGE, GERMANY

"Nicht mehr!" [No more!] Rudolph held both his hands over his plate and laughed.

Alma, his sister-in-law, with a devilish grin, threatened to dump another plump sausage onto his plate. "How often will I be able to treat you to our homemade wurst?" she teased.

"I've already eaten more than I should," Rudolph groaned. "That's all we've done for the past three weeks. My doctor keeps saying I should lose some weight. His face will turn purple when I see him next month."

"Ach, doctors," Alma sniffed and playfully cuffed Rudolph's shoulder as she walked around the table looking for someone with an emptier stomach.

The time in Ida's hometown had glided smoothly from one day to another. Warm sunshine, friendly breezes from the North Sea and cheerful clouds in a pale blue sky had marked the days. Soft amiable evenings for outdoor visiting gave way to chilly nights for comfortable sleeping. The stories, teasing, and feasting went on non-stop.

Ida's three sisters and one brother, along with their spouses and children, still lived in the small town where they'd been born. The families moved easily from one home to another for meals, kaffee klatches, picnics and parties.

Rudolph leaned back in his chair, sated and relaxed, and reflected upon the family chatter surrounding him and filling Alma's spacious dining room. He was reminded of his old slippers.

Back in his bedroom closet in Hebron, lay a pair of slippers he'd worn for fifteen years. Ida had given them to him for Christmas. How she'd found the money during the worst of the Depression he never knew. Those slippers, leather and lined with fur, were broken in so well that his feet sighed with relief when he slipped them on. He stepped into those slippers without any forethought, never thought of them as precious, but he blustered and fretted when he could not find them.

Ida's siblings and their families lived and moved so easily and comfortably in and through their town and its surroundings. To Rudy it appeared as though their entire environment was like a pair of old slippers. *They're so unconsciously at one with their world. They live in this place and the place lives in them. They are so completely at home. Just imagine—generations in one place. One patch of ground, one horizon for an entire lifetime. How different my life has been, how different is my sense of 'home' from theirs. I wonder how many more homes I will have before I die?*

On one of the last days of Rudolph and Ida's stay, the entire Loock clan made the pilgrimage to the Cadenberge cemetery. Ida's brother Klaus had died during the war and was buried next to his parents. Ida's oldest sister, Katie had died shortly after her marriage. Her marker was next to her brother's.

Rudolph stood before the tombstone marking the resting place of Ida's parents. The scene on the day of their departure from Germany was vivid in his memory: Ida wrapped in the embrace of her sobbing father. *Herr Frederick, I'm sorry for making a promise I didn't keep.*

———

297

That day on the pier, you didn't believe me and you were right. I was foolish. I thought my saying it could make it so. Five years? Ten years? Nein. Thirty years it has taken for us to return. Please forgive me. Herr Frederick, maybe you have seen my daughter, your granddaughter, Ida Maria? Tell her I miss her; her mother and I miss her every day.

*   *   *

Ida wiped away her tears and settled into her seat. Minutes earlier, at the base of the steep stairway to the plane, she and Rudolph had been overwhelmed with vigorous embraces, laughter and weeping. Over and over again the sisters had declared, "Soon, maybe next year, we'll come to your home and visit, we promise."

Rudolph tightened his seat belt and wondered if the fulfillment of their promise would take as long as his had taken. He could never have imagined all of the disruptions that he and Ida would endure before Ida saw her sisters again.

JUNE 1954, RURAL ASHLEY, NORTH DAKOTA

Rudolph leaned back in his chair and put his feet up on his old desk. It was too large for this tiny office but its presence was like an old friend; it comforted him. He'd spent twenty years working on its solid oaken surface at Trinity Lutheran. For the next eight years it had served as a reception desk in his clinic office in Hebron. And now, to the surprise of desk and owner alike, it was in the church office of a small rural congregation outside of Ashley, North Dakota.

Three months earlier in Hebron, he'd received a letter from the president of this congregation. They had voted to extend to him an official invitation to serve as their pastor. Over the past eight years, Rudolph had received and rejected invitations from other congregations, but this one was different. He brought the letter into the kitchen and showed it to Ida.

She sat down, read it, then looked up, eyes wide with consternation, "You're not thinking...? Ai, you are. Why else show it to me?"

Rudolph took the letter, glanced at it again, then looked up, "Liebe, who do you think gave them my name, gave them the idea to call me?"

Ida reluctantly answered, "Fred, I suppose it was Fred."

Months earlier, their eldest son had brought his wife Alice, and their two children to Ashley and Fred had taken the position as pastor at Zion Lutheran Church.

Rudolph drummed the table with his fingers, stared at the window behind Ida and spoke, half to himself. "Fred actually gave them my name. He's opening a door, extending his hand to me."

Ida nodded in agreement, but then paused and added, "Ja, but you two are fire and ice. When you're fire, he's ice. When he's fire you're ice."

Rudolph shrugged, "Das ist wahr, [that is true], but maybe this is a chance for us to really get to know each other. Maybe the Spirit is moving to bring us together."

Skepticism was still written on Ida's face. Rudolph added, "Besides, you'd have a chance to get to know their two little ones. You always mention how you wish you could see those grandchildren more often."

Ida could have retorted that moving would take her away from the grandchildren who lived in Hebron. But she held her tongue. Rudolph would decide, as he always did, and she would follow, as she always did. She knew she would not have to wait long.

Unsurprisingly, the uprooting was quick and total. Within days Rudolph accepted the invitation, contacted a realtor and a moving company. The house sold almost immediately and three weeks later, they'd moved into the small parsonage next to the church ten miles from Ashley.

Now that the boxes had all been unpacked, Rudolph sat in his office, puffed on his cigar and wondered how difficult it would be to be a full-time pastor after eight years of semi-retirement. The congregation was small, all of the members held German as their first language. They had called Rudolph because they wanted a preacher who spoke in the cadences of their heritage. He looked forward to being their pastor.

Rudolph had already prepared a space in the parsonage to receive those people who would come to him for treatment of their muscle and nerve pains. In years past, Rudolph had treated people from Ashley. And, since Ashley was the county seat of McIntosh County, a center of German-Russian settlement, he had no doubt that his healing ministry would flourish here.

In the parsonage kitchen, Ida was preparing supper. They'd invited Fred and his family for a housewarming meal. Normally, she enjoyed cooking and baking. The rhythms soothed her; but this afternoon her spirits were ruffled. All her utensils, pots and pans were in new drawers or stored on new shelves. She was muttering to herself as she hunted for the flour sifter.

The woman of the congregation had brought hot dishes and fresh vegetables on those first few days as they unloaded the truck. They'd offered to help with the unpacking and given her advice about grocery and clothes shopping. They were kind and seemed genuinely pleased to have the new pastor and his wife in their midst.

As she rolled out the dough for kuchen, Ida hoped tonight's meal would be the first of many pleasant evenings. *God willing, we can begin to cool the fire and warm the ice.*

JULY 1956, ZION LUTHERAN PARSONAGE, ASHLEY

"What stinks?" Rudolph wrinkled his nose as he and Ida entered Fred and Alice's home.

"Ahh, that's the smell of money," Fred grinned. "Follow me, I'll show you."

Rudolph trailed Fred down the stairway leading into the basement. As he carefully picked his way down into the semi-darkness the odor grew stronger.

"Here we are," Fred chuckled, "fur-bearing money makers." He pointed to ten cages set against the far wall of the basement.

"What are they?" Rudolph asked as he approached the cages and saw beady black eyes staring back at him.

"Chinchillas. I bought twenty of them last week."

Rudolph's eyes adjusted to the darkness and he stooped to examine them. "They look like fat, furry mice."

"That's what they might look like, but they are expensive little critters. The fur from one hundred full grown chinchillas can make a coat worth up to five thousand dollars."

Rudolph's curiosity drew him closer, "But they're so small. How long does it take until—?"

Fred interrupted, "Vater, back up. They spray piss when they're scared."

Rudolph retreated out of range and sniffed, "Smells like they've been scared a lot. Whew."

"Ja, well, they're still getting used to their new home. In about nine months they'll be full grown. Then I can sell them and buy another batch of babies." Fred clapped his hands together with satisfaction.

Rudolph asked, "Is this your new hobby?"

Fred's eyes flared, "Hobby? It's about the money. I've got three kids, and another on the way. I don't know about your salary, but my pay check barely reaches to the end of the month. I've got to find ways to feed the family."

Rudolph shrugged in commiseration, "Ja, we pastors, we'll never get rich."

Fred tipped back his head and gazed at the open beams in the ceiling of the unfinished basement. He quietly said, "I guess I knew that even before you pushed me in that direction."

"Pushed you? I didn't push you," Rudolph protested.

"Oh Vater, come on. More than once you hammered at me, 'Fred, the oldest follows the father's profession.' Don't tell me you've forgotten that." Fred glared.

"Ja, ja, I did say that, but only because you seemed to have no direction on your own."

"Ha, I had ideas, directions but you never gave me a chance…Too bad Herold and Herman didn't come along first, then I would have been off the hook." Fred swallowed the bitterness in his mouth.

Rudolph tried to calm his own breathing, "And what would you have done?"

Fred extended his hands with palms up, "I don't know, lawyer maybe, or teacher."

Rudolph quietly said, "Well, I suppose it's not too late…"

Fred's laugh was acidic, "Vater, you're not serious. I've got a big family to feed, a car to pay for. It's too late, very much too late."

"But Fred, you're a good preacher, I've heard good things from your members. You're doing well as their pastor."

Fred shook his head, "Ach, this conversation is going nowhere. It's simple: For you, the ministry is a calling, for me it's a job." He turned away from Rudolph and spoke as he climbed the stairs, "Let's have supper."

APRIL 1957, RURAL ASHLEY, NORTH DAKOTA

This North Dakota spring was as fickle as Rudolph's worn-out Chevrolet. The tired car would rattle blithely along for days at a time and then suddenly chug to a complete halt half way into town.

March and April weather had been just as capricious. Yesterday had been balmy with golden sunshine. Today slushy snowflakes driven by a northeasterly wind splatted against the window of Rudolph's office.

Rudolph sat with his elbows on his old desk, head buried in his hands. Ida glanced in as she passed by the open door.

"Lieber, if you have a headache you should lie down. Should I get you some ice?" She worried about her husband's recurring headaches. He claimed they were caused by his wrestling with congregational budgets and cantankerous councils and by the tensions between his congregation and the one his son served in town. Ida feared that they were related to his struggles with diabetes and high blood pressure.

Rudolph looked up with weary eyes. "Why don't you bring me some coffee. I need to tell you something."

Ida hurried to the kitchen. This was so out of character. Her hand shook as she filled two mugs. She slowed her steps as she entered his office, set down his mug, then lowered herself into the chair in front of the desk.

He took a sip of his coffee and stared out at the gray wet sky. Ida knew he would speak when he was ready. The soft plops of the wet snow against the window was the only sound. Rudolph turned toward Ida, set down his cup, and sighed. "Fred just phoned. He's taken a call to a different parish."

Ida gasped, "But what about Herold's ordination on June 9th? You and Fred were going to do the ordination service at Zion. Father and son ordaining another son into the Lutheran ministry—a big day."

"He's not leaving until the end of June," Rudolph sighed.

"Did you know any of this was coming?"

Rudolph shook his head, "No, no. That's not Fred's way. He decides something, bang, without discussing it with a soul. I'd be surprised if he even talked it over with Alice."

"That's not fair, Rudolph, you don't know that. You're just upset that he didn't talk it over with you."

Rudolph reached back and began massaging his own neck, "No, that's not it. I'm upset because of where he's going."

"But that's none of our business either, he's a grown—"

Rudolph groaned, "He's going to Trinity in New Leipzig."

302

Now it was Ida's turn to sit in stunned silence. The wind had picked up and the temperature must have dropped for now the flakes had become pellets of sleet smacking into the window. She took a swallow of coffee and gave a slight shrug of her shoulders, "Well, that parsonage is bigger, enough room for his family."

Rudolph waved his hand, "Ach, that's not why he's going there."

"Since when can you read Fred's mind?" Ida wrapped her hands around her mug and took another swallow of the weak coffee. "Maybe he sees it as going home."

"Home? Since when do pastors ever have a real home?" Rudolph snorted. "Besides..." his voice trailed off.

The seconds passed and the silence grew ever louder. Finally, Ida asked, "Besides what?"

Rudolph's voice was pensive. "He wasn't always so happy at Trinity, or should we say, happy with me...I don't know...he is so often angry and frustrated...I just wonder if my old parish is the best place for him...too many ghosts around there, mostly of me. I was there for twenty years..."

The sleet had turned to tiny snowflakes and the wind had switched to the northwest. It looked like another April blizzard was sweeping across the state. The tired, brooding couple stared out at the storm and sipped their coffee. Ida broke the spell.

"I think you and I should go home." Before Rudolph could open his mouth in protest, she continued. "Pastors may not have homes, but retired pastors can have them. I think we should move back to Hebron. Two of our children live there, our brothers too; and now with Fred and his family, and Betty and her family living north of New Leipzig...It just makes sense. I'm tired, aren't you, Lieber? Aren't you tired?"

Rudolph was taken aback. For Ida this was a torrent of words. Not only were her words passionate, they were weighty with truth. He nodded. "Ja, ja, I'm tired." He rubbed his eyes and then looked out into the whiteness. "Thank God, it looks like the council meeting for tonight is going to be cancelled. I think I'm going to lie down. Could you get me some ice?"

FEBRUARY 26, 1960 HEBRON

A blast of icy air greeted Rudolph when he opened his front door. A bundled-up figure stood on the steps.

"Good morning, Mr. Heupel. My name is Jack Mercer. I called you last week, remember?" The young man's scarf was wrapped twice around his face. Rudolph could only see his watery eyes.

"Ja, ja. You're from the Minneapolis newspaper, aren't you?" Rudolph ushered the shivering man into living room. As the man removed his gloves and unwrapped his scarf, Rudolph chuckled, "I don't really know what a feature article is or why you'd want me in one, but, here I am."

The red-cheeked young man rubbed his hands together, trying to bring feeling back into his fingers. He shook Rudolph's hand, "We were told that you're quite a celebrity out here so I came to hear your story."

He began to open his briefcase, but was interrupted by Rudolph. "Celebrity? Not really. But if you want to hear any stories, you'll have to hear them in my office. I open at 8 a.m. So, put your scarf and gloves back on and let's walk. Its only three blocks."

The young reporter cringed but quickly wrapped up his scarf and followed the already bundled up Rudolph out of the door. They walked north, into a breeze that sliced its way through coats, sweaters and scarves. They approached a little building with no sign in the window or nameplate on the door, but with three cars idling at the curb.

"Some mornings there are a dozen cars waiting. Today the cold is keeping them at home." Rudolph said as he unlocked the door. The car doors opened and a half dozen people emerged and followed him and the reporter into the office. They took seats on the old church pews setting against the walls and looked expectantly at Rudolph.

Rudolph smiled at them, "Guten morgen, my friends. Before we get started, I want to introduce you to this young man. This is Jack and he comes from the newspaper in Minneapolis. If you don't mind, I told him he could watch us today."

Jack was still rubbing his fingers but nodded a greeting to the people seated on the benches, then added, "And, if it's all right, I'd also like to take a few pictures."

Rudolph caught the perturbed look on some of the faces and held up his hand. "Mr. Jack, I'll let you take pictures of me, but no faces of the others."

"Sure, sure," Jack hastily answered, "No faces and no names. I just want to get an idea of Mr. Heupel's work.

"It's not work he does," a short, stocky lady interrupted. "It's a healing ministry. I keep wanting to call him 'doctor' but he always sets me straight, isn't that right Herr Pastor?"

Rudolph shook his head and grinned, "Ja, Frau Lindemann, just a pastor and no healer either. God is the healer, remember? Come on in."

Rudolph led her into the treatment room, sat her down on a chair, and waved Jack in as well. Jack stood against the wall and Rudolph sat down facing his first patient of the day. She'd twisted her knee yesterday. He massaged the aching joint, flexed it, then had her straighten out her leg. He continued talking to her, and then gave a sharp, tiny jerk. Frau Lindemann grunted then sat back and sighed in relief.

Rudolph helped her up, "You'd best go easy on that knee for a few days. You strained some ligaments. Rub it down with some liniment and stay out of the cold." The whole operation hadn't lasted more than fifteen minutes.

Jack wanted to begin asking Rudolph questions but before he had a chance, Rudolph was ushering in a burly man dressed in bib overalls.

"Pastor, last night was our bowling night and, like a dumb klutz, I got my feet tangled up and slammed down on my shoulder right there on the alley. All night long my fingers tingled and my shoulder ached like a son of a ...." He caught himself, "It's really hurting this morning."

Rudolph began massaging the sore shoulder. Jack got out his camera and caught an image of Rudolph chatting with the bruised bowler. Rudolph smiled, "Just a sore nerve, I can feel the pain running right through here."

Jack cocked his head, "You can feel the pain?"

Rudolph shrugged, "I don't know how else to say it. It's just...Well, it's a gift God gave me I guess."

The morning slipped by: A young boy from the Fort Yates Reservation who'd fallen off a horse, a high school basketball player who'd twisted his ankle, a lady from Montana who'd hurt her hip when she fell on the ice.

Jack listened to their stories, watched the simple treatments and kind words that Rudolph gave each person. When they left the treatment room, he watched as one by one they wrote their names in a tattered spiral notebook. They all shook Rudolph's hand and profusely thanked him. Before leaving, some of them dropped a bill or two in an offering basket on his desk, some did not. Rudolph paid scant attention to the basket.

It was nearly 11 a.m. and the office was empty. At last Jack had a chance to ask the questions that had arisen as he'd watched Rudolph's activities. He pointed to the weathered notebook

"Mr. Heupel, how many people have signed your book?"

Rudolph picked up the notebook and replied, "I started this one last April. Let's see, almost 6,000. Maybe there would be more, but I had a little set-back in early December. The doctors said I had a minor stroke. My office was closed for seven weeks."

"So, I assume you've got other notebooks. How many people all together have you treated?"

Rudolph shrugged, "Well, I started my ministry in 1926..." He thought for a moment, "I'd guess around 100,000."

Jack whistled softly. "That's a lot of people. Don't the doctors around here complain?"

Rudolph smiled and told him of the 1930's investigation conducted by the North Dakota Medical Association, then of Abdullah from Saudi Arabia, then of other interesting patients.

Jack continued asking questions and Rudolph opened up. He regaled the young reporter with the stories of his life in South Russia, his harrowing times in Germany during World War I, and his years of ministry in New Leipzig.

Jack was still writing notes when Rudolph looked at this watch. "Ach, Herr Jack, it is almost noon. My wife will have dinner ready. If I am not on time, she'll scowl at me. Would you like to join us for dinner? I'm sure there'll be plenty."

The young reporter laughed and nodded. His stomach had begun growling at the mention of food. They walked southward to Rudolph's home. Now the wind was at their backs. The conversation and the entire experience in Rudolph's office had warmed the reporter.

"So, now what, Mr. Reporter?" Rudolph teased as they approached his door. "Is there enough to this Rudolph Heupel to write a story?"

Jack laughed, "Ha, I think there is enough here to write a book. On the first Sunday in March, make sure and buy a newspaper. Then you'll see."[v]

APRIL 1960, HEBRON AND NEW LEIPZIG

Rudolph picked up the ringing phone and heard his daughter Betty's voice.

"Father, you and Mom better come down to Trinity. It's Fred."

"What? What about Fred?" Rudolph's intensity brought Ida from the kitchen and she gripped Rudolph's arm.

Betty's voice cut through the static and crackling. "He's OK…No, not OK…Just come please. We can talk when you get here. You'll come, won't you?"

"Na sicher [Of course]. But can't you…Hello? Hello?

He lay the phone in its cradle. Ida was softly moaning and he hugged her. "Stay calm, Liebe. We won't know a thing until we get there. Come, let's go."

An hour later, they drove into the Trinity Church yard. A couple of pickups and another car were parked next to the house. As they climbed out of the car, they heard crying from inside the house. Ida gave a small cry and scurried toward the door. Rudolph hurried as fast as his legs allowed.

When he entered the kitchen, he was struck by an eerie heaviness hovering in the air. The room was crowded. Betty's husband and nearby neighbors had unusually somber looks of embarrassment on their faces, as if they'd seen some forbidden sight. Ida was wrapped in Betty's embrace.

Rudolph nodded to the others and moved toward Ida and Betty. When he reached them, he heard the sounds in the living room: Alice's soft weeping and a voice that was at one moment crying, then moaning, then nearly shouting. It was Fred's voice.

Betty whispered to her parents, "Fred went out with his gun. We don't know…maybe it was an accident. For weeks, months, he's been so agitated, on edge, angry… Let's go in."

Rudolph followed Betty and Ida into the darkened living room. The couple was sitting on the sagging couch. Alice had her arm around her husband's shoulder. Her face was wet with tears. Fred's mouth moved, no words emerged, but his eyes were one moment aflame, then the next dull and lifeless. He sat perfectly still but radiated latent energy, like a compressed spring. A wide white bandage covered his shoulder and ran under his armpit.

Ida gave a tiny shriek and flew across the room, dropped to the floor in front of her oldest son, and hugged his knees,

"Oh Freddy, my Freddy, don't hurt yourself, I love you, we love you. Oh, my son…" She broke into sobs. Fred's entire being relaxed, and he began stroking her head, adding his tears to hers.

Rudolph stood frozen in his tracks. For decades he had counseled, preached, lectured and consoled. Now he could not utter a solitary word. A welter of emotions paralyzed his tongue. *Oh Fred, what have you done to yourself? What have I done to you that brought you to this? I've failed you, hurt you, I know. So much pain, I can almost feel your agony. But…A gun? Oh God, you must see, dear God, that Fred knows guns. He's hunted, he's handled guns. Had he wanted to…had he intended to… No God, no, don't think for a minute that he wanted to die. He was crying for help, for rescue.*

Rudolph moved as in a dream to the couch and sat down beside Fred, careful not to touch the wounded shoulder of his grieving son. He lay his hand on Fred's leg and silent tears trickled down his age-worn face.

MAY 1960, TRINITY CHURCH

"Geh mit Gott, mein Sohn [Go with God, my son]." That was all Rudolph could manage to say. Now he stood with his hands folded beside Fred's sagging station wagon as Alice entered the car, checked on the four children in the back, and sat down beside Fred.

Fred replied to his father with a nod and a tight smile. He put the car in gear and began rolling out of the church yard. The children waved and threw kisses to their grandparents as they began their long journey.

The past month had been an exhausting parade of meetings with doctors, psychologists, church executives, congregational councils. Intense discussions, emotional conversations, difficult decisions— the weeks dragged on endlessly. But ultimately, resolutions were reached. For the sake of his health, Fred was leaving the Lutheran ministry. The Trinity congregation, whose attendance had been declining for years prior to Fred's arrival, would close and merge with the Lutheran Church in New Leipzig. Fred and his family would move to Oregon, closer to Alice's parents, and restart life.

Rudolph shielded his eyes and watched the dust plume from Fred's car disappear over the southern horizon. He couldn't speak aloud what he was feeling. He couldn't even name the hollowness expanding within his soul.

Now Fred is gone too. Our three oldest children…lost to us. Ida

---

*and baby Rudy under the prairie sod, and Fred looking for a future
on the other side of the mountains.*

The late morning sunshine dazzled Rudolph's eyes and for an instant he was nineteen again, standing in the cemetery in Freidorf. He remembered his father's demand that he never leave Freidorf. Now, standing in the Trinity church yard he recalled how he'd felt on that long-ago day: how visceral panic had gripped him when he'd felt trapped by traditions and religion.

Paul the Apostle must have been thinking about me when wrote, **I do not understand my own actions. For I do not do what I want, but I do the very thing I hate.** *God forgive me I I've forced Fred to flee from me and from the ministry. O God, give him the joy and freedom he could never find here.*

The dust from the departing car was gone, frisked away by the spring breeze. Rudolph turned around and allowed his eyes to slowly climb up the steeple to the cross stabbing the cerulean sky. He lay his against the wall of the church building.

Ja, Herr Gott, I know, there is no life without death. Children die, old people die, pastors die. And congregations die too. If there are no people, there is no church. I know that. And yet...I gave twenty years of my heart here, I nurtured and watered the spiritual lives of these good people, poured out so much of my precious time, much of which rightfully belonged to my family. Now the pews are empty, the pulpit is vacant, and the doors are closed. Herr Gott, I understand, I do. But still, I grieve.

Before they returned to Hebron, Ida and Rudolph walked two hundred yards westward to the cemetery. They tidied up the graves of Ida Maria and Baby Rudy. Memorial Day was only weeks away and many would come to visit the tombs of their loved ones. People would notice and comment if someone's grave was covered with weeds or dead flowers.

After they'd finished pulled the weeds, they slowly and painfully stood. The vast prairie stillness captured them and they lingered to enjoy the surrounding beauty. The short prairie grass on the hills to the north was pale green, the wheat fields on two sides of the cemetery were emerald carpets. To the east, dancing merrily in the breeze, stood the row of trees for which Ida had so long yearned. Rolling hills rose and fell to the south as far as the eye could see. A meadowlark landed on the cemetery fence post and began singing his joyful melody into the sky. Cloud shadows slipped majestically across the entire scene.

Rudolph filled his lungs with the pure air and released it in a cleansing sigh. He reached for held Ida's hand as they began walking to the car "They're all good parents, hard workers. Betty and Elmer's kids, they'll do well in the town church. Fred and Alice's kids will be fine on the West Coast too. It'll all work out, don't you think?"

Ida nodded and squeezed his hand, "Ja, Lieber, I'm sure it will."

JUNE 1960 RURAL HEBRON

Rudolph sat in the back of the little church while his youngest son led the singing for the Bible school children. Herman, home from Wartburg Seminary for the summer, had the small group of students singing in full voice.

"Genau wie Engel!" [Just like angels] Rudolph applauded when their song ended.

Herman laughed and ordered the children to bow to their one-man audience. Then he dismissed them, "You get thirty minutes to play, then we'll come back in for story time."

Herman followed the little mob down the aisle, then sat down next to his father. "They're nice kids. Too bad they're not here year around."

"Ja, well, half of them are grandkids, staying on their grandparents' farms for a few weeks. By the end of the month they'll be back in Bismarck or Dickinson or even Minneapolis. That's how it goes these days for these German Russian rural congregations." He reached for his Bible and eagerly asked, "What story are we teaching today?"

*   *   *

Three years ago, when they had returned to Hebron, Rudolph had promised Ida he would really and truly retire. But when a little congregation north of Hebron could no longer afford a full-time pastor and had begged him to conduct Sunday services, he looked at Ida and shrugged, "What can I do? When people are in need, we have to help."

He still enjoyed the weekly rhythm and though the small stroke he'd had in December had slowed down his walking, his tongue and voice continued to function so he could still do what he loved best, preach the Sunday sermon.

310

Since Herman had returned from the seminary in the middle of May, Rudolph had been relishing a new experience. He and his youngest son were working as a ministry team. The relationship had evolved naturally, without any planning or forethought.

One morning, early in June, he and Herman had been sitting in the kitchen nook, drinking coffee and discussing the sermon texts and choosing appropriate hymns for the worship service. Ida walked in and smiled, "What are my two pastors up to this morning?"

Herman toasted her with his coffee cup, "We're doing what pastors do—planning for Sunday's service."

Rudolph smiled in delight. *What a blessing. I can be a partner with my son in that which has given my life meaning. And he has found his calling in this same ministry. I've always been a solo worker. How would my work have been different if I'd had a teammate? Would I have been a better pastor? Would I have been humble enough to be a good partner? God knows how stubborn I can be.*

He chuckled to himself, then asked God a question. *Did you make all German Russians so sturkopfich[stubborn headed] or just the Heupels?*

JULY 17, 1960 RURAL HEBRON

The little congregation was struggling to sing the opening hymn. The organist, a woman in her eighties was doing her best. Since she was going deaf, she could not hear her own mistakes. The elderly men and women were also giving the most praise they could muster. Rudolph, sitting in the front pew, could not help smiling and thinking, *When the psalm writer said, 'make a joyful noise unto the Lord,' he must have been referring to us. Good thing Herman is here to cover our mistakes.*

Herman was singing the old hymn with his strong tenor voice and with obvious delight. Today was the celebration of the end of Vacation Bible School and, not only were the children going to be making small presentations, but Herman was going to give the sermon. Rudolph relished preaching but he'd never heard his youngest son preach, so he'd relinquished the pulpit for this special day.

As the congregation labored through the closing lines of the hymn, Rudolph stood with a small groan. His legs were aching. He wondered if his diabetes was causing the pains he'd been experiencing lately. He turned and smiled. The pews were fuller than usual. The parents of the children were all present, along with the usual aged members.

"Good morning brothers and sisters in Christ. This morning is a special day for us all. Our children will be reading today's scripture lessons and making a presentation of what they've learned in Bible School. Also, my son Herman will be delivering today's sermon. Even though all of his classes at the seminary are in English, he will be preaching in German, which I know will please most of you. Please stand as we begin our service."

The service went smoothly. The children's presentation was simple but well-rehearsed. The readers, two young girls, read slowly but never stumbled. Rudolph sighed expectantly as Herman stepped into the pulpit. As his son read the gospel text, Rudolph was struck by how much Herman resembled Ida. *Why haven't I noticed this before? Ah well, as usual, I'm so wrapped up in myself... He has his mother's face and her kind heart too. I think he'll be a gentler pastor than I've been.* Rudolph looked up and nodded as Herman began his message.

"I'm glad to be here this morning and thankful to my father for allowing me to preach." Herman looked down at Rudolph and grinned, "I know what a sacrifice he's making." Then with an even wider grin he pointed to Ida, sitting several pews behind Rudolph. "I would also like to say congratulations to my mother whose birthday is tomorrow." On cue the organist began playing 'Happy Birthday' and everyone joined in the singing. Ida's face reddened with embarrassment but her eyes gleamed with pleasure.

"I've chosen as the text for my sermon these words of Paul from his second letter to the congregation in Corinth. *'Therefore, since it is by God's mercy that we are engaged in this ministry, we do not lose heart.'*"

Rudolph looked up into the earnest face of this preacher, this man, his son. He felt his own heart swell in gratitude to God. *Your mercy has flooded my life, Herr Gott. How many years and miles have we traveled together? How many times have I fallen, and always you've lifted me up. How often have I been tempted to lose heart, but you've given me Ida who's never let me go. You've always surrounded me with people whose love lifted me, always lifted me.*

Herman's strong voice and clear words filled the small church.

Rudolph tried to absorb the message but his reverie continued to overwhelm him. *At this very moment, in Iowa, Herold is preaching to his congregation. Two sons in the Lutheran ministry. And Fred writes he and his famiy are doing well in Oregon. Gott, your mercy is never ending. Our children are healthy and have given us sixteen grandchildren. Dear Ida, our name and spirit will go forth into this world! Wie groß ist unsere Gott! [How great is our God.]*

Rudolph's joyful musing stopped when Herman ended his message with a ringing 'Amen'. If his religious and ethnic background had been different, Rudolph might have shouted, 'Amen, Alleluia.'

But he was a Lutheran and a German Russian. He simply stood and smiled, shook his son's hand when he descended from the pulpit, and called forward the ushers to take the Sunday offering.

FRIDAY, JULY 22, 1960 DETROIT LAKES, MINNESOTA

Rudolph stepped out of the little cabin into the humid morning air. The sunlight flashed and twinkled off the glassy surface of the lake. Far out on the water fishermen in aluminum boats were trying their luck. Rudolph was no fisherman and didn't particularly like swimming. At the speed he usually drove, it took nearly six hours to drive from Hebron to Detroit Lakes. But Ida always enjoyed the combination of pine trees and water that this summer resort town offered. He, Ida and Herman had arrived on Tuesday and would be leaving early Saturday morning so they'd be back in time for the Sunday service.

While waiting for Ida and Herman to get ready, Rudolph walked down to the water. He heard a strange buzzing. His first thought was horseflies but then realized the noise was inside his own head. *I need to get my morning coffee.*

Rudolph was waiting on the porch when Ida and Herman emerged from the little wooden motel cottage. He reached for Ida's hand and together they crunched across the gravel lot to the little restaurant half a block away. This was the third morning in a row they'd come here for breakfast, so when they entered, the smiling waitress led them to 'their' booth, the one with a view of the lake.

She returned shortly with menus under her arm and a steaming pot. "Three coffees coming up," she said as she filled their mugs. "I'll be back in a minute to take your orders."

Rudolph was reaching for his cup when his right eye began to itch. He lifted his hand and began to rub it, then jerked back his head. He felt as though his eye had been stabbed from the inside. Herman and Ida across the table from him seemed to swirl, then the entire world began revolving, and nausea surged throughout his body. His face grew red and, fearing he would vomit, he pulled out his false teeth and threw them onto the table.

"Lieber, lieber," Ida's panicked voice came to him across an ocean of internal noise. He tried to speak but could not find his tongue. He felt himself toppling over as the explosion in his head reverberated.

Herman managed to break his father's fall and lay him on the linoleum floor of the restaurant. Rudolph looked up and saw Herman's mouth move but no words penetrated the thunder in his own ears.

He stared at his youngest son whose face seemed to shift and pulse. Now the face was Fred's with his sideways grin, now Betty's with her kind eyes, then serious Rudy, now came the dimpled smiles of August and Helen, and then Herold's wide grin.

For an instant all was a blur, white streaks, then red. Then appearing over him was his Ida, his Ida before babies and troubles and heartbreaks. It was his Ida of the teasing blue eyes, Ida of the warm eyes under the trees at Treysa. He yearned, ached to say 'I love you' and even more whisper, 'thank you Liebe, thank you,' but not only was his tongue mute, his thoughts were dissolving.

The noise was fading now, he felt himself growing lighter, and then once again he saw blue eyes. Ida Maria, his beautiful Ida Maria, was smiling and beckoning to him. Without effort he was moving toward her, toward her lovely blue eyes, closer and closer he came, until all he could see was blue. Blue water, Blue Danube, the bridges arching over the great blue river. Now he was fifteen, dancing in Freidorf with Mutti, dancing, dancing, laughing and dancing toward a great light. He felt himself being lifted, then he gasped. And he was gone.

EPILOGUE

JULY 23, 1960 RURAL NEW LEIPZIG

The dogs started barking before the three children heard the car roaring down the dirt road that ran past their farmstead. The three eagerly ran to the front of their house to see who would hurtle past at such break neck speed. Instead of passing, the car careened into their farmyard.

When it finally slowed and stopped, they squealed with delight. Uncle Don, Aunt Helen and their two children had come for a visit. If they had been a few years older, these farm children might have questioned why this city family was racing into their yard on a Saturday afternoon. But they were young. Little Judy had just turned six on July 9. Larry had had celebrated his ninth birthday three days earlier. The oldest boy, Ron, was ten, only three weeks away from his eleventh birthday.

As the car skidded to a stop, the children giggled and whooped: cousins to play with on this endless summer day. Judy and Larry ran to Dwight and Annette. But Ron took one look at Don and Helen's faces as they burst from the car and sped up the sidewalk. His chest tightened. Something terrible must have happened.

Ron tried to follow his godparents into the house. Helen, kindly but firmly closed the door in his face and spoke through the screen. "All you kids stay outside and play for a while." Within a minute he heard wailing from inside the house. Don burst out, went back to his car and drove out to the field where Elmer, the children's father, was plowing.

Ron sat on the picnic table and anxious tears filled his eyes. Within minutes Don returned, Elmer threw open the car door, and ran into the house. Ron could see that he was crying. His strong, stolid dad was crying. The ten-year old's secure world had just suffered a fracture and he feared he would tumble into an unseen crevice.

The wailing inside the house swelled. Now all five children began crying, standing in a forlorn little clump under the feeble elm trees in the backyard.

At last Helen came out and called the children to the back steps. Her voice was husky from crying but she spoke calmly, "Kids, we have some bad news. Yesterday, your Grandpa Heupel died. He was on vacation in Detroit Lakes and a big blood vein broke in his head and the doctors couldn't fix it."

The children all started crying in earnest and Helen reached out to hug the little ones but Ron tried to escape. He hurried to the back of the yard, jumped over the low fence and crawled into a little nook under the lilac bush. He wrapped his arms around his knees and shuddered.

Though he'd not known anyone close to him who'd died, the very thought of death had long terrified him. Now Grandpa Heupel was dead. He had not been especially attached to his grandfather, but he knew how important he was for his mother and father, his aunts and uncles and for so many people in the community. Though he could not explain it, he realized with the intuition of a ten-year old that his grandfather, Rudolph Heupel, was an extraordinary man.

JULY 27, 1960 TRINITY CHURCH, RURAL NEW LEIPZIG

The sun was baking, the air was parched. It was a perfect harvest day. But throughout the region, tractors, trucks and harvesters stood idle. Today was the funeral.

For decades the tall white church nine miles north of New Leipzig had been known informally as "the Heupel church." Months ago, the congregation had joined the church in town and the building had sat locked and empty, a lonely sentinel on the prairie. But today on the funeral day of its namesake, the church had been reopened, and it was overflowing.

The funeral was to begin at 10 a.m. By 9 a.m. the pews were filled and, though the windows had all been propped open, the interior of the church was stifling. The open casket had been sitting at the front of the aisle, before the altar. But as vehicles kept arriving, the casket was wheeled back down the aisle into the doorway. People wanting to pay their respects now needed only to climb the two cement steps to view the body of the one they had called 'doctor' and 'pastor'.

The cars continued to pour in to the church yard. Crowds gathered outside, three and four people deep in a circle around the church, hundreds and hundreds of people, many from the German Russian communities all across the state, but also many others who had been touched by Rudolph Heupel's ministry.

They all came to honor the memory of the man who had made a

difference in their lives. More than any sermon, these grateful people were a living witness to the truth that God's love and mercy comes through the work of humble servants.

Unnoticed among the grieving adults was ten-year-old Ron, Rudolph's grandson, the only one of the grandchildren deemed by the family old enough to attend the funeral. On that day, the bewildered boy had not thought to ask how old was 'old enough.' Did his family mean he was old enough to share in the community's grief? Old enough to see his grandfather's body, embalmed and lying in a satin lined box? Old enough to see his parents cry and realize that the world, though deeply wounded, was not coming to an end? Old enough to understand death? Are any of us ever 'old enough' for that?

The boy stood alongside the coffin, beside his mother Betty and her sister Helen, and gazed with them at the body of the man who both figuratively and literally had touched tens of thousands of lives; the body of a man who had crossed continents and oceans, suffered privations and persecutions, and had clung fiercely to his faith, graciously shared his gifts, and poured himself out for the sake of others.

The boy's mother said, "Look at Dad's hands folded across his chest. That's just how he always slept Sunday afternoons on the couch." The boy had no way of knowing that within two decades he would sleep the same way after a Sunday morning of preaching.

That blistering hot day in July the boy had no way of knowing that one day he would follow his uncles and his grandfather and become a pastor. He couldn't have imagined that he would realize a dream that had once captured Rudolph. He would become a Lutheran missionary, not to Africa but South America.

Half a century later, this ten-year old boy would be captured by his grandfather's dramatic life and ministry. He would visit the places where Rudolph was born and studied, he would see Rudolph in his dreams. He would venture to inhabit the soul of his grandfather, the preacher and healer. And he would come to write a story about Rudolph. Not exactly Rudolph's story for only Rudolph could do justice to that, but Rudolph's story as lovingly imagined by his first grandson, a boy born on the prairies as was Rudolph, a boy who by the prodding of God's restless Spirit, also moved out to find his place, his ministry, and his home.

*   *   *

The grieving community buried Rudolph Heupel, son of George and Elizabeth Heupel, in the Trinity Lutheran Cemetery. His daughter Ida Maria, his infant son Rudy, and many people laid to rest by Pastor Rudolph himself, now shared with him the soil under the prairie sod. The crowds finally left and the sounds of the North Dakota summer reclaimed the little cemetery: the wind sighing in the ripening grain fields, the birds trilling in the ever-blue sky, and the ceaseless silence of eternity.

Trinity Lutheran Cemetery, New Leipzig, North Dakota

319

FACES AND PLACES IN RUDOLPH HEUPEL'S LIFE

The ruins of the Lutheran Church in Kassel in the Ukraine where Rudolph's parents were married. (current name of Kassel: Velykokomarivka).

House and garden in Kassel in the Ukraine

The open country north of Odessa in what is now the Ukraine

A cemetery in Freidorf (now called Balkove)[vi]

The current village of Freidorf (Balcove) in the Ukraine, north of Odessa

A family home in Freidorf (Balcove)

The Witch's Tower in the Treysa District
of Schwalmstadt, Germany

The city of Treysa, with the campus of Hephata Center at the top

Emmaus House at Hephata Deacon Center (Rudolph's dormitory)

Hephata students and staff; Rudolph is in the center of the back row

Hephata Students and Staff (Rudolph is seated on the far right)

German soldiers at Hephata (Rudolph is 5th face from right in the very back)

The Church on the Hephata Campus

Statue of comforting mother
near the church on the Hephata Campus

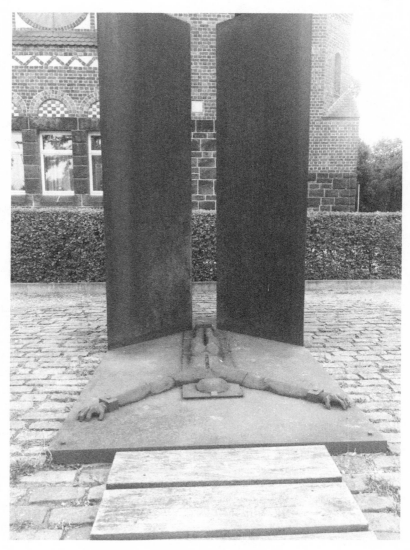

New Memorial to the 385 Hephata residents
killed by the Nazis

Passport Picture: Rudolph, baby Ida Maria, Ida (1922)

Rudolph Heupel, Seminary Graduation, 1926

North Dakota Threshing Scene, 1920's

Trinity Evangelical Lutheran Congregation
Church building and Parsonage

Pastor Rudolph, Ida, Betty, Fred and
Ida Maria on the steps of Trinity (1926)

Back Row, left to right: Ida Maria, Viola Mertz, Rudolph, Ida,
Herold
Second Row, left to right: Fred, Betty, Rudy, August; Helen in front.
(approx. 1933)

Back row, left to right: Helen, August, Betty, Rudy, Ida Maria, Fred
Front row, left to right: Herman, Ida, Rudolph, Herold
(approximately 1941)

Rudolph and Ida, 1947, twenty fifth wedding anniversary

Jacob Heupel (Rudy's brother) and his wife Katherine

Katherine Schock (Rudolph's sister) with husband Frederick and son
August

August Loock (Ida's brother) with wife Katie

FOOTNOTES

i Adapted from a book of 'war sermons' preached by a pastor in Liegnitz Germany during WWI

ii Extracted from an actual letter from Hephata to Rudolph

iii Adapted from several actual letters sent to the State Gazette and available on the German from Russia Heritage Society website. (grhs.org) Used with permission

iv From an actual letter from Raymond Baesler excerpted in the New Leipzig Sentinel, January 1943

v A full-page article about Rudolph was written by Mercer Cross and entitled, "A Pair of Hands—and N.D. Pastor is 'Doctor' to Many" and was printed in the Sunday, March 6, 1960 edition of the Minneapolis Tribune. See article below

vi This photo and the next two were taken by Melvin Bender and appear on the Germans from Russian Heritage Society website (ghrs.org) and are used with permission.

A Pair of Hands—and N.D. Pastor Is 'Doctor' to Many

By MERCER CROSS
Minneapolis Tribune
Staff Writer

HEBRON, N. D. — They drove through miles of below-zero cold to sit in a drab, drafty building and wait to see a little man with a pushbroom mustache and a thick German accent.

When they finally did see him, it was for a few minutes only—15 at most.

WHEN THEY entered the drab building they had two things in common: aches and pains.

When they left they felt better.

But the man they had driven so far to see isn't a physician — although many persons call him "Doctor" — but a minister.

More than 30 years ago the Rev. Rudolph Heupel learned his hands seemed to have the ability to quench the fire in throbbing nerves and bones.

If he weren't a minister he probably would be known as a chiropractor.

HE DIDN'T want it that way. His duty to the Lutheran church has always come first. Now 66, he serves a small country parish 20 miles north of Hebron.

Monday through Friday, from 8 to 11 a.m., he holds forth in the imitation brick shack on the north edge of town.

THE REV. RUDOLPH HEUPEL TREATS A 'PATIENT'
The Lutheran minister says church interests come first

Business was slow one bitter morning last week. Only three cars were parked in the lot outside the building when Mr. Heupel opened up.

In less than an hour he had treated a woman with a sore knee, a woman with a stiff back, an Indian boy who had fallen off a horse, a youth who had turned his ankle playing basketball and a Glendive, Mont., woman with an aching hip.

LATER in the morning a man from nearby Beulah, N. D., came in, complaining he had slipped and fallen in a bowling alley the night before.

"Just a nerve," Mr. Heupel said, massaging the man's shoulder and arm muscles.

More often than not the cast-off church pews and green plush-covered theater seats in the waiting room are occupied.

Although Mr. Heupel shies away from any kind of publicity, word of mouth has carried his reputation far beyond the borders of North Dakota.

In his lifetime, he estimates, he has treated more than 100,000 persons. His latest registration book, dating from last April 1, contains nearly 6,000 names.

IT WOULD contain more, but Mr. Heupel suffered a mild stroke last December

Mr. Heupel
Continued on Page Five

MR. HEUPEL: 'The Good Lord Helps Me'

Continued from Page One

and didn't see any "patients" for seven weeks.

How does the Russian-born preacher go over with the medical profession?

They've been getting along fine for years. Relations between Mr. Heupel and Hebron's one physician are friendly.

Back in the 1930's the North Dakota Medical association investigated Mr. Heupel for quackery.

The town of New Leipzig, N. D., where he then lived, rose to his defense with a united voice. The investigation died, and Mr. Heupel has had no trouble with the doctors since.

HE DOESN'T charge anyone who comes to see him. All contributions are free-will offerings, and many persons give him nothing. Most donations go to the church.

When Mr. Heupel finds something seriously wrong, such as a broken bone, he refers the person to a physician.

He gives no medications, writes no prescriptions, makes no house calls. Persons remain dressed while he manipulates their limbs or kneads their muscles.

This probably sums up, in his own words, Mr. Heupel's fundamental reason for maintaining the informal "clinic"

in a building bought for him by the Hebron Lions club:

"THEY'RE ALL in need. If your neighbor is in need, you have to help him."

Persons of all faiths come to Mr. Heupel. One lad's parents, who had relatives in southwestern North Dakota, sent their crippled son all the way to Hebron from Saudi Arabia.

"The good Lord helps me," he said. "If I didn't pray a lot I couldn't do it."

Mr. Heupel left Russia for Germany in 1913. He acquired his medical knowledge while working in a German hospital during World War I.

IN 1923 he came to the United States, intending to become a Lutheran missionary. He graduated from St. Paul seminary in 1926 and was sent to a pastorate in New Leipzig.

During the early days of his ministry, Mr. Heupel said, he set many broken bones because there weren't enough doctors in his area. This he no longer has to do.

With the exception of 21 months in a pastorate at Ashley, N.D., Mr. Heupel and his wife, Ida, have lived in Hebron since 1946. They have raised eight children of their own and an adopted daughter.